Fodor's EXPLORING

ireland

FODOR'S TRAVEL PUBLICATIONS

NEW YORK • TORONTO • LONDON • SYDNEY • AUCKLAND

WWW.FODORS.COM

© Automobile Association Developments Limited, 2006
(registered office: Fanum House, Basing View, Basingstoke,
RG21 4EA, UK. Registered number 1878835).

Published in the United States by Fodor's Travel Publications,
a unit of Fodors LLC, a subsidiary of Random House, Inc.,
and simultaneously in Canada by Random House of Canada
Limited, Toronto.
Published in the United Kingdom by AA Publishing.

Fodor's and Fodor's Exploring are registered trademarks of
Random House, Inc.

ISBN: 1-4000-1623-1
ISBN-13: 978-1-4000-1623-5
Sixth Edition

Fodor's Exploring Ireland

Author: **Lindsay Hunt, with additional "Hotels and
Restaurants" material by Polly Phillimore and Dr. Peter
Harbison**
Updated by: **Anto Howard**
Original Copy Editor: **Hugh Chevallier**
Cartography: **The Automobile Association**
Cover Design: **Tigist Getachew, Fabrizio La Rocca**
Front Cover Silhouette: **Blaine Harrington III**
Front Cover Top Inset: **The Automobile Association**

Northern Ireland mapping reproduced by
permission of the Director and Chief
Executive, Ordnance Survey of Northern
Ireland, acting on behalf of the Controller
of Her Majesty's Stationery Office
© Crown copyright 2005 (Permit No. 50121).
Republic of Ireland mapping reproduced by permission of
the Director of Ordnance Survey Ireland © Ordnance Survey
Ireland and Government of Ireland (Permit No. 7954).
A02413

Printed and bound in Italy by Printer Trento Srl.
10 9 8 7 6 5 4 3 2 1

How to use this book

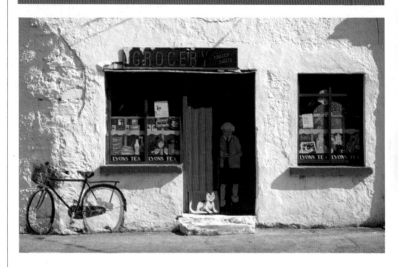

ORGANIZATION

Ireland Is, Ireland Was
Discusses aspects of life and culture in contemporary Ireland and explores significant periods in its history.

A–Z
Breaks down the country into regional chapters, and covers places to visit, including walks and drives. In addition, Focus On articles consider a variety of topics in greater detail.

Travel Facts
Contains the strictly practical information vital for a successful trip.

Hotels and Restaurants
Lists recommended establishments throughout Ireland, giving a brief summary of their attractions.

ADMISSION CHARGES
An indication of an establishment's admission charge is given by categorizing the standard, adult rate as:

Expensive (over €6.50), Moderate (€3.20–6.50) or Inexpensive (up to €3.20).

ABOUT THE RATINGS
Most of the places described in this book have been given a separate rating:

▶▶▶   Do not miss

▶▶   Highly recommended

▶   Worth seeing

MAP REFERENCES
To help you locate a particular place, every main entry has a map reference. This is made up of a number, followed by another number, followed by a letter, such as 542A. The first number (54) refers to the page on which the map can be found. The second number (2) and the letter (A) pinpoint the square in which the main entry is located. The maps on the inside front cover and inside back cover are referred to as IFC and IBC respectively.

Contents

5

HOTELS AND RESTAURANTS
269–283

Maps and Plans

Castletown House, County Kildare

My Ireland

Lindsay Hunt turned to travel journalism after a career in publishing. She has written, edited, and contributed to numerous hotel and travel guides, including books on Spain, France, Germany, Italy, Florida and, of course, Ireland.

Some years ago, I stayed at a country-house hotel so welcoming and convivial that I forgot to pay my bill before leaving. This was embarrassing for several reasons, the main one being that I was inspecting it anonymously for a well-known hotel guide. The amazing thing was the fact that my hosts also forgot to remind me about this trivial matter as they said goodbye. As I galloped back apologetically across three counties to redress my oversight, I wondered whether this could happen anywhere but Ireland. I'd never met the hotel owners before, but after a single night's stay they felt like old friends. Since then, the experience has been repeated many times in Ireland—feeling like old friends, that is, not neglecting to pay hotel bills. There are, of course, exceptions to the rule, but I guarantee that those who prove it will outnumber those who fall short.

I find the extraordinary kindness shown to me by many Irish people (north and south of the border) particularly touching because I am English—unmistakably so. While I feel neither personal nor collective responsibility for Ireland's history, I was slightly apprehensive about the welcome I would receive on my first trip to the Emerald Isle. However, this was entirely unfounded; the 'Hundred Thousand Welcomes' *(Cead Mile Failte)* slogan used by the Irish Tourist Board is more than mere blarney.

There is one memory from that first visit that is particularly vivid. It involves a party somewhere in Galway, full of Gaelic merriment and good *'craich'*, at which everyone joined in with a song, a story and a dance. The star turns were an Orangeman (a northern Protestant in favour of maintaining the union with the UK) and a committed Nationalist, who regaled the assembled company with a string of good humoured and hilarious jokes. One day...perhaps the trend will catch on.
Lindsay Hunt

Ireland Is

Many of Ireland's charms are straightforward. Visitors head there for the spectacular scenery and the warmth of the people. Ireland's real fascination, though, is its ability to confound people's preconceptions. The Irish can be as unpredictable as their country's fickle weather, changing in a moment from gregarious to taciturn, or from solemn to profane.

ONE ISLAND Is it one place or two? The South evokes all things green and Gaelic; the North is an outpost of the UK. To enjoy Ireland, you need barely be aware of this division. On both sides of the border are glorious landscapes, friendly people and plenty of good pubs. On one side the mailboxes are Irish green, on the other red, and for visitors (except in Belfast or at the border, perhaps) few other differences are apparent. There is certainly no need to feel anxious about visiting the North. Statistically, Northern Ireland is recognized as one of Europe's safest places.

On the edge of the island perches Dunluce Castle, in County Antrim

LANDSCAPES Ignoring the boundary, then, there are 32 counties of Ireland, each with its own distinctive character. Though at a glance Ireland may seem universally damp, mild and green, with no very high mountains and little variation of climate or landscape, it has more variety in its small confines than many larger countries. The scenery varies from rural pasturelands cut by many rivers, through wild boglands and low-lying hills, to the most spectacular mountain scenery (mostly in the west and north) sweeping down to the sea in high cliffs and craggy promontories. Offshore lie many islands, some of which are inhabited or contain ancient forts and ruined

10

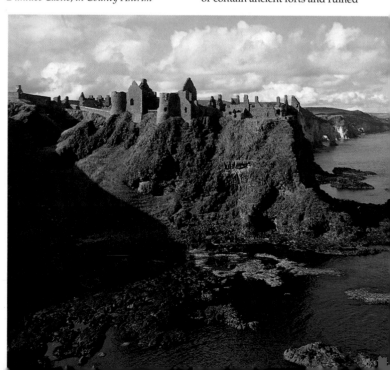

monastic settlements; several others are bird sanctuaries.

The commonest of Irish rocks, limestone, produces great systems of porous caves, some containing stalactites and stalagmites. Volcanic activity created the highlands of the North, and the extraordinary crystalline formations of the Giant's Causeway in County Antrim. The surface of the land was glaciated during the last Ice Age, leaving classic geological features such as U-shaped valleys, corries (circular hollows), tarns (small lakes) and eskers (long, winding ridges).

ECONOMY Ireland's continuing struggles since the 18th century was against economic depression and unemployment, and the resulting exodus of many of its most energetic and talented citizens abroad. The North continues to receive large amounts of investment directly from the UK to alleviate its chronic problems. However, since joining the European Union (EU), the whole of Ireland has benefited from vast sums in Regional Development Fund grants that are aimed at helping poorer EU member countries. Great improvements have been made to its road system, while funds have also been

The pace of life is noticeably slower to the west of the Shannon

11

allocated to develop tourism and manufacturing industries in the early 1990s. The tide turned, and from being one of the EU's poorest countries a few years ago, the Republic now enjoys a booming and rapidly growing economy, nicknamed 'the Celtic Tiger'. Many former emigrés have returned to seek work in their native island, particularly in the electronics and computer industries. Ireland now has about five million inhabitants, with a higher proportion of young people than virtually any other country in Western Europe.

PLANNING A TRIP For visitors, Ireland still seems pleasantly old-fashioned. The sociable, lively Irish are always ready to strike up a conversation, play some music or buy the next round of drinks.

If you have little time to spare, the best bet for a trip to Ireland is a short break in Dublin, combined with excursions to the Wicklow Mountains, or perhaps the Boyne Valley and the antiquities of Newgrange. If you have more time, head west for Connemara, Cork, Kerry or Donegal. Longer still, see the rest of the country, including its great monastic sites and grand houses. For extensive touring, you will definitely need a car, a bike, a horse-drawn caravan or even a boat on its huge inland waterways.

'If you think you understand Ireland,' some legendary wit once remarked, 'you've been sadly misinformed.' And, indeed, almost every aspect of Irish life is full of contradiction. That rule also applies to its politics, which are inextricably entwined with religion.

PARADOXES Certain elements of Irish political history may strike an outsider as somewhat contradictory:

• Anti-English feelings have long been associated with Ireland's Catholic majority, but some of Ireland's greatest nationalists (or at any rate critics of the English as Irish overlords) have been Protestants, some from English backgrounds. Examples of such men include Jonathan Swift, Henry Grattan, Wolfe Tone, Robert Emmet, Charles Stewart Parnell, W. B. Yeats and even William Gladstone. Two of the Republic's presidents have been Protestants.

• Both the Pope and the King of Spain supported Protestant William III's cause at the Battle of the Boyne, not the Catholic Jacobites (see page 36 for more details).

• Only about 2 per cent of the Republic's population are Protestants, yet many of its most

Ministerial buildings next to Leinster House, seat of the Irish Parliament

important churches are actually Church of Ireland (Protestant), including both of Dublin's cathedrals.

• Northern Irish Unionists, far from being in line with the UK, are often in bitter opposition to London. While British politicians have met, talked and reached amicable agreements with the Republic's leaders, the Unionists, until the 1998 Good Friday Agreement, had adamantly rejected all compromise.

IRELAND'S CONSTITUTION The Republic of Ireland's constitution operates under a prime minister (*Taoiseach*), two chambers (senate and assembly), and a president (who is largely a ceremonial figurehead). Its main political parties sprang up during or soon after the struggle for independence in the early 20th century. Since then, parliamentary power has been dominated by Fianna Fáil (Soldiers of Destiny), the party set up by Éamon de Valera in 1926. In 1933 its equally conservative rival,

12

Mary Robinson, Ireland's first woman president (1991–1997)

Fine Gael (Tribes of Gaels), appeared. Roughly speaking, these parties mirror the positions taken by pro- and anti-treatyites during the Civil War; in other words, they either accepted (Fine Gael) or rejected (Fianna Fáil) Ireland's partition in 1921. Both parties have found it difficult to achieve majority rule, and elections (based on proportional represent-ation) often result in an uneasy stale-mate followed by behind-the-scenes horse trading with minority parties to form a workable coalition.

The wild card is Sinn Fein, the political wing of the IRA. Originally founded in 1908 (making it older than any other party), it has achieved massive popular support at certain stages in its history, but now commands only a fraction of Southern Irish votes. In 1990, Sinn Fein and the IRA began the slow

move from the bullet to the ballot box, which culminated in an IRA cease-fire and the 1998 Good Friday Agreement on power sharing between Nationalist (including Republican) and Unionist parties. Today, both parties continue to do battle, but thankfully through purely political means.

A CONSERVATIVE MENTALITY The winds of change are blowing through Irish politics, a notable event being the election in 1991 of a woman president (a possibility absolutely discounted by social historians only a few years before). Mary Robinson was a liberal attorney with known sympathies for certain issues (such as the liberalization of divorce laws) that currently perplex Ireland. The position of women in the Republic is much affected by the power of the Catholic Church, and Pope John Paul II's reaffirmation of its doctrines on contraception, abortion and divorce. Ireland ranks last among the world's developed countries in access to birth control (though the impact of AIDS has had a sharper effect than decades of religious dogma), and until 1996 was alone in Europe in having no civil divorce. A booming economy and child abuse scandals in the Catholic Church have pushed the South further towards the liberalism of mainland Europe.

Catholics complain justifiably of their lack of civil rights in Northern Ireland, yet the Republic's Protestants would also have an interesting case in any international court of human rights. But on both sides of the border compromise seems a real possibility, with liberalization in the south and a tentative move towards power-sharing in the north.

13

Ireland's musical traditions date back over many centuries, but the current scene is exceptionally lively, with interest in popular folk music encouraged by tourism. Irish musicians are prominent in rock and country-and-western groups, and some virtuoso performers, such as James Galway, have become world famous.

A CELTIC TRADITION The poems and stories related by Gaelic bards at court were often accompanied by music, most typically played on the harp, Ireland's national emblem. The 12th-century historian, Gerald of Wales, praised the deftness of Irish fingerwork, and the expertise of Irish harpists was recognized as far afield as Renaissance Italy. After the Battle of Kinsale (1601), the great Gaelic clan houses declined, along with their patronage of the arts. Music was perceived by the ruling English as potentially dangerous, arousing nationalist sentiments, and it was suppressed along with other aspects of Irish culture. Musicians became itinerant, travelling from house to house to seek their fortunes at the hands of the new aristocrats; the

The tradition of live folk music lives on in countless Irish pubs

blind harpist, Turlough O'Carolan (1670–1738), was the most celebrated exponent of this tradition. The 18th century witnessed a new flourishing of musical talent in Dublin's Anglo-Irish circles, mostly influenced by European developments; Handel's *Messiah* was performed for the first time in the capital in 1742, conducted by the composer.

Meanwhile, traditional music continued to be played in Gaelic households. The ancient styles were either plaintive melodies with no distinct rhythms (possibly inherited from Spanish or North African cultures), or brisk, lively dance tunes. In 1792, a great harp festival held in Belfast aroused interest in more traditional Irish forms, and folk tunes increased in popularity. The lyric ballad, with words by such poets as Thomas Moore set to music, was sung in elegant drawing rooms

14

throughout Ireland. Many budding musicians left their native land, as did many writers, to seek fame in England. John McCormack, the famous lyric tenor, spent most of his life in the United States (see page 240).

IRISH INSTRUMENTS Most distinctive of the instruments used in Irish music, besides the harp, are the *uilleann* (elbow) pipes, a relative of the Scottish bagpipes but with a more elegiac tone particularly suited to reflective Irish tunes. The violin (simply called the fiddle in Ireland) is held casually on the shoulder and played with only a small section of the bow. Expert Irish fiddlers are technically highly skilled, however; Fritz Kreisler is said to have declared that if he practised for a thousand years he would never be able to play as well as the Sligo fiddler, Michael Coleman. The *bodhrán* is one of the most ancient Irish instruments, a goatskin drum played with a small stick. Wind instruments include the tin whistle (no mere toy to a skilled player) and the flute, whose capacities have astounded worldwide audiences in the hands of James Galway.

THE MODERN SCENE In the 20th century Irish music played an important role in the revival of nationalist sentiment, and has subsequently achieved enormous popularity. The most usual venues to hear it are *ceilis*, where whole communities gather to dance and make music, or pubs, where *seisuns* (sessions) are held all over Ireland. The popularity of Irish music is unquestionably affected by tourism, sometimes losing both its dignity and its authenticity in the process. In the summer, when an audience is guaranteed, every pub seems to offer musical happenings. Out of season, however, they may be quite difficult to find. Doolin in County Clare is a particularly well-known mecca for groups of musicians. Other forms of music are encouraged at major festivals—opera

In Ireland, as in the Celtic areas of Britain, dance continues to be an important facet of life

at Wexford (see panel page 144), light opera at Waterford, and jazz at Cork.

One of the most influential figures in Irish music in modern times was Seán O'Riada. Though classically trained, his main interest was folk music, which he greatly popularized. His group, Celtóirí Chualann, was a forerunner of the world-renowned Chieftains. The tradition continued through groups such as the Clancy Brothers and the Dubliners. The stage spectacular Riverdance has ignited a global interest in traditional Irish music and dance. Other groups have taken a different line, notably U2, The Corrs, Westlife and The Pogues, while individual performers include Van Morrison, Enya, Sinéad O'Connor and Ronan Keating.

no one pal
The daylight
Loitered bene
ith lips of
wild
Oscar

The Irish are famously articulate. From the loquacious Celts, alleged by the Greek traveller Strabo (writing around the time of the birth of Christ) to be fond of 'wordy disputes' and 'bombastic self-dramatization', through the Earl of Blarney, to today's stage Irishman, words have been a constant source of delight—sometimes at the expense of action. Oscar Wilde said, 'We are the greatest talkers since the Greeks—but we have done nothing'.

A PROLIFIC STREAK The Irish have written much; Ireland's contribution to English literature in all its forms— poetry, drama, novels, essays—is colossal, considering the size of its population. It seems as strong today as ever, with new talents bursting onto the stage and filling bookshops with new novels and poems.

Four writers have won Nobel prizes (W. B. Yeats, George Bernard Shaw, Samuel Beckett and Seamus Heaney). Both speech and writings take innumerable forms, but are characterized by a natural flamboyance, passion and wit, coupled with idiosyncrasy. Much of the inspiration

Jonathan Swift, satirist and cleric

comes from the tensions generated by persecution and oppression.

THE GAELIC HERITAGE Besides Ireland's outpourings in English, it has a rich Gaelic tradition. At various periods during the imposition of English rule, the Gaelic language (now mainly referred to as 'Irish') was suppressed. After independence, strenuous attempts were made to revive it; indeed, it was declared— and remains—an official language. Éamon de Valera wanted to use it for political reasons, to assert Ireland's separate identity from Britain. Ireland's first president, Douglas Hyde, was a distinguished Gaelic scholar who loved the native language for its own sake. Despite compulsory schooling in Gaelic, and

❏ Ogham script was used in Ireland from the 4th century and, though eventually superseded by the Roman alphabet (introduced by Christian missionaries), continued to be used into the 8th century. It was written as a series of scratched lines, and usually appears on commemorative standing stones or monuments. Its uses for practical purposes were very limited. The key to interpreting the characters is the *Book of Ballymote*, written in 1391 in Sligo. Examples of ogham stones can be found in several places; there is a good one in the church at Killaloe (Clare) and another two in the abbey ruins of Ardmore (Waterford). ❏

Samuel Beckett

regular radio and television broadcasts, the use of Gaelic as a first language has dwindled to a few areas largely in the West, and there is now little writing in Gaelic.

ANGLO-IRISH WRITERS The first flowering of Anglo-Irish literature occurred during the late 17th and early 18th centuries. Jonathan Swift (see page 62) was the giant of the age, publishing savage satires to expose the hypocrisy and injustice of life under English rule. In a lighter vein, Oliver Goldsmith, R. B. Sheridan, William Congreve and George Farquhar entertained English upper classes with their lively comedies of manners. Edmund Burke wrote philosophical and political essays in elegant prose, complex enough to win present-day admirers from the whole political spectrum. Irish writing in the 19th century came thick and fast, from George Moore and Maria Edgeworth's sharply observed novels about the Irish 'Big House', such as *Castle Rackrent*, to Shaw, Oscar Wilde and Yeats towards the end of the century, and even Bram Stoker, who introduced the world to Dracula. Anthony Trollope, though born in England, wrote many of his novels while working in Ireland; some, such as *Phineas Finn*, have Irish characters.

THE TRADITION LIVES ON In the 20th century, Irish writing reflected the turmoil of independence, and a long twilight of censorship. Modern Ireland out-pruded the English Victorians, sending many great writers into self-imposed exile (James Joyce and Beckett are the two outstanding examples); J. M. Synge's and Seán O'Casey's plays caused riots in Dublin. Novelists and poets have proliferated within and without Ireland, however. Patrick Kavanagh, Louis Macneice (now deceased), and Seamus Heaney are among its best-known modern poets; Maeve Binchy, Molly Keane, Edna O'Brien and Roddy Doyle are popular novelists, along with Brian O'Nolan (Flann O'Brien) and Christy Brown. Frank O'Connor, Seán O'Faoláin, Mary Lavin and Liam O'Flaherty perfected the art of the short story, and talented dramatists include Brian Friel, Hugh Leonard, Billy Roche and Frank McGuinness. The writer Christopher Nolan won great acclaim for his poems, *Damburst of Dreams*, and his novel, *Under the Eye of the Clock*, while author Frank McCourt won a Pulitzer Prize for his best-selling novel, *Angela's Ashes*.

The formidable George Bernard Shaw

In today's Ireland, it seems almost impossible to imagine the grim days of the 19th century when many poor people did not have any food to eat besides potatoes, and even those were frequently scarce. Nowadays, it is possible to eat both well and heartily all over the island.

18

CHANGING TASTES Tourism has made a vast difference to the standards of cuisine in Ireland. Until recently, there was hardly any tradition of eating out in many districts, except perhaps on very rare occasions at a local hotel. Patterns of diet were conservative, based firmly on 'meat and two veg' (somewhat over-cooked), potatoes (of course) and large quantities of dairy fat. Now things are very different. Tourist demands for predictable, inexpensive fast food are met, as everywhere, with hamburgers and pizzas—a better bet being fish and chips. But more sophisticated tastes have introduced organic foods and vegetarian restaurants (almost unheard of before), and a vast number of new eateries, often French in style, have

A traditional—and substantial—Irish breakfast

opened in the main visitor centres. Food 'events' such as Kinsale's Gourmet Festival or Galway's Oyster Festival arouse great interest. With VAT (sales tax) at its present high rate, eating out in the Republic of Ireland is expensive, particularly if you like a drink with a meal. Casual (but respectable) dress is the norm just about anywhere.

One of the best meals in Ireland (as in Britain) is breakfast. A 'traditional Irish breakfast' (or the 'Ulster fry' north of the border) is a brimming plateful of bacon and eggs with soda and potato breads. Accommodation rates are nearly always quoted with a full breakfast included, so you might as well fill up for the day and get your money's worth!

IRISH CUISINE Whatever Irish cuisine lacks in finesse, it nearly always makes up for in copiousness, and ingredients are of a high quality. Home-grown produce includes rich dairy foods, beef, lamb and pork, a fascinating range of Irish cheeses and a great variety of seafood. One of its great favourites is bread. Traditional Irish soda bread made with butter-milk, eaten fresh and warm, is a banquet in itself. At midday, a basket of Irish bread, a bowl of seafood chowder and a glass of Guinness makes a cheap and completely satisfying lunch.

There has been a welcome return to simple, hearty Irish food, and Irish stew and potato dishes feature on many menus. Try colcannon (potatoes with onions and white cabbage), champ (potatoes mashed with butter and chopped chives) or coddle (potatoes with boiled bacon and onions). Black puddings use up those bits of pig not usually found on the dinner table, including its blood. At teatime, try barm brack, a delicious sweet tea bread made with dried fruit and spices.

Fish can easily be found in most of Ireland, and you don't have to be rich or posh to enjoy oysters here. If you're adventurous, try dulse or carrageen (types of seaweed), used to make various desserts—a change from apple pie and ice cream.

WHISKEY AND STOUT All alcohol (especially in the South) is highly taxed and expensive, although measures of spirits are larger than in the US. Take advantage of your duty-free allowance if you like a

If you wish to order half a pint, ask for a 'glass'

drink. Pubs, though, are more than mere boozing sheds; they are the social heart of many communities and often full of life and atmosphere, especially if there is some music. Pub food is rarely very imaginative, but you can usually get snacks at lunchtime, and coffee all day. At some stage every visitor should try Ireland's 'nectar', Guinness (see panel on page 56). Some consider it tactless to request Scotch in an Irish pub—try the local Bushmills, Powers, or other Irish brands, either straight or with a splash of plain Irish water. It is also delicious in Irish coffee, or in one of those creamy liqueur concoctions. The local lager is Harp (brewed by Guinness). If you prefer something akin to English bitter or US dark beer, ask for Smithwicks ale.

19

Not for nothing is Ireland called the Emerald Isle. Its greenness is legendary, the stuff of postcards and purple prose—and the national colour. As you travel through the island, landscape after landscape seems to scorch the retina with shades of that vivid Kelly green.

In a few remote areas old farming methods are still employed

❏ 'Wearing of the green' takes place on St. Patrick's Day (17 March), when Irish people all over the world join in national celebrations to commemorate their country and their patron saint. The largest festivities and grand parades are held in Dublin. Traditionally, everyone on that day wears a shamrock, Ireland's national emblem. This cloverlike plant is alleged to have been used by St. Patrick to illustrate the nature of the Trinity to King Cormac at Cashel. ❏

THE COLOUR OF IRELAND In places Ireland is chocolate brown or almost black, the colour of stripped bogland, glinting with clear pools that mirror the sky. It is grey with mist or cloud, with the wan limestone of the Burren, and the lace of stone walls. It is splashed with yellow furze, scarlet fuchsia or purple heather. Most of all, though, it is green, a verdancy induced by frequent rain and the tempering effects of the Gulf Stream.

Ireland is still a predominantly rural country, with few mineral resources and little heavy industry. For centuries, the main changes to its landscapes were brought about by farmers who cleared the primeval oak woods and drained the peat bogs to make pastureland. Sheep, cattle, oats, and barley have been raised on its fertile soils since neolithic times. Later, crops such as potatoes and flax have waxed and waned according to the vagaries of economics, and recently the rate of change has accelerated, particularly since Ireland's membership of the European Union (EU). Agricultural grants flood into Irish farmers' pockets, enabling them to introduce more intensive methods of production. The use of artificial herbicides and fertilizers is growing, causing pollution to seep into waterways, threatening wildlife. Compared with some other EU countries, however, the problems are minor. Ireland has successfully attracted 'clean' industries, such as electronics and financial services, rather than the mills of more industrialized nations.

GREEN CONCERNS Nearly all of Ireland's original oak forests have long since been felled for fuel and building materials. New forestry is replacing some of these trees, but mainly (until recently) with non-native conifers. Many old Anglo-Irish estates are now in state hands and forest parks, and broad-leaved woodlands are being planted, sometimes on stripped peatlands. The exploitation of the bogs continued unchecked for many years, and large areas are virtually denuded. Boglands, however, are now recognized as a unique and irreplaceable habitat for many rare species.

Other threats to Ireland's wildlife are significant. Increased tourism means more disturbance of Ireland's wild places. The Office of Public Works has angered conservationists by proposing construction of visitor centres in sensitive areas such as the Burren, Boyne Valley and Wicklow Mountains (court cases have forestalled two of these so far). Unfortunately, more places for people mean fewer places for wildlife.

A GOLD PROBLEM Another threat to the environment is the discovery of gold in Mayo, Galway and the Sperrin Mountains of Northern Ireland. Gold has always been known in Ireland, of course—prehistoric peoples used it for their ornaments—but until recently it was thought to be uneconomic to extract it. The Croagh Patrick site in County Mayo is particularly sensitive, for it is both an area of scenic beauty and a site of great religious importance, where St. Patrick is said to have banished the snakes from Ireland and where thousands of pilgrims gather annually. Prospecting for minerals disturbs the landscape and can threaten the surrounding area with serious pollution by heavy metals and cyanide.

PINK TROUT In certain coastal areas, puzzling signs have sprung up by the roadsides, depicting a fish, with the legend 'Save the Sea Trout' emblazoned on it. This reflects a growing local concern about the effects of one of Ireland's fastest-burgeoning industries—fish-farming. The farming of salmon and trout in huge hatcheries in Galway and Donegal has affected wild populations in ways not yet fully understood. One theory is that vast numbers of parasitic sea lice among farmed fish are debilitating wild species. The fish on your plate is just as likely to have been reared artificially and fed pink-tinted hormones as to have swum the ocean and leapt waterfalls.

The greenness of Ireland, here seen on Mizen Head, County Cork

21

The passion for competitive sports of many kinds reaches unprecedented heights all over the Republic. Its specialist games such as hurling and Gaelic football draw capacity crowds and cause vast excitement. Soccer is also popular, and Irish hopes were raised by the national team's qualification for the 2002 World Cup in Japan and Korea.

22

THE BIG MATCH When there's a big match on, even the least enthusiastic sportsman or woman is condemned to know about it. Flags and banners of the colours of the competing county teams sprout all over the land, on telegraph poles and gateposts, from car windows and rooftops. Switch on the radio for the news, and you will find nothing of importance has happened in the world, except the match. Needless to say, huge crowds cause boisterous disruption to everyday life (especially on the roads), and plenty of noise in the pub afterwards, but they are rarely the occasions of hooliganism once seen at British soccer matches. Highlights of the year are the All-Ireland hurling and football finals, held at Croke Park, Dublin, in September, where

tickets are prized. In the past, however, Gaelic games were regarded as a focal point for nationalist sentiment, and were alternately discouraged or banned by English authorities, and fostered by Republicans. In 1884, the Gaelic Athletics Association (GAA) was formed in Tipperary to halt the spread of anglicized games and promote Irish ones. The organization, like the Gaelic League, was a fertile recruiting ground for political activists.

Rugby enjoys limited popularity, but is remarkable in that the national team represents *all* of Ireland, with southern nationalists playing alongside northern Unionists.

HURLING This fast and furious game has an ancient pedigree, dating back to before the Christian era. The Ulster champion Cuchulainn was

The distinctly Irish sport of hurling

renowned for his prowess at hurling, and teams of warriors are supposed to have played it for days on end. It is something like no-holds-barred lacrosse, played with an ash stick or 'hurley' and a small leather ball—'sliotar'. Players (15 a side) may strike the ball any distance and at any height, or carry it on the hurley. It's most popular in Cork and the southeast and west of Ireland, but also played in Antrim, almost exclusively by Catholics.

GAELIC FOOTBALL

There are two types of football in Ireland (Gaelic and soccer), with

minimal support for the Gaelic game among Protestants. The ball is smaller than a soccer ball, and teams score one point by hitching the ball over the crossbar, or three by putting it into the goal below the crossbar. The game requires great strength and stamina.

VISITOR ACTIVITIES As a visitor, you are unlikely to do more than watch these exciting pastimes, but there are splendid opportunities for exercise in many forms, especially golf, equestrian sports, cycling and fishing. There are more than 300 golf courses throughout Ireland (this number continues to rise), some of international class or in wildly beautiful settings, especially in the North. Green fees vary considerably. Many claim Ireland is an unparalleled fishing destination, both for the quality of the sport and its low costs. Sea fishing for shark is popular in some areas (such as Achill Island). Permits are necessary on privately owned waters (and on public waters in the

North), and you need a national licence for rod fishing for salmon or sea trout.

That other Irish passion shared by the British is racing (horses and greyhounds), and many towns have dog-tracks or racecourses. Sailing centres are mostly in the southwest, between Youghal and Dingle, with lake and river or canal cruising focused on Lough Derg, the Shannon River, the two Loughs Erne and the Grand Canal. In May 1994 the restored Shannon–Erne waterway opened, enabling boaters to cruise all the way from Upper

Gaelic football it may be, but handling of the ball is allowed

Lough Erne to the mouth of the Shannon. Hiking is increasingly popular in Ireland. Many long-distance footpaths are now in place, and more accessible open spaces are planned. In the meantime, take sensible precautions before setting out. Prepare for bad weather, take the best map you can find, and let someone know where you are heading.

Both Bord Fáilte and the Northern Ireland Tourist Board produce plenty of literature on specialist sports.

The bogs of Ireland once covered immense tracts of the central lowlands. To former generations, it would have been inconceivable that they could ever disappear, or perhaps that it would matter much if they did. However, conservationists now recognize them as unique ecosystems, and are racing to ensure that what little is left is preserved before they all vanish.

24

THE FORMATION OF THE BOGS After the Ice Age, the saucerlike bowl that forms the centre of Ireland lay awash with lakes. These gradually filled up with compost from lakeside vegetation and, eventually, peat accumulated because the micro-organisms that cause decay cannot survive in these wet conditions. There are two main types of bog in Ireland. Blanket bog, composed of dead sedge and grass, develops to a depth of 6m (20ft) in the wettest areas and is found mostly in mountainous parts of the west, or in the Slieve Bloom Mountains. Raised bog, consisting mostly of sphagnum moss, covers wider areas of the central plain, where rainfall is lower. This gradually builds up into a dome above the ground water and can reach depths of 12m (40ft).

Roundstone Bog, Galway, one of the last untouched bogs in Ireland

A VANISHING LANDSCAPE As a result of massive exploitation, the boglands have shrunk to a fraction of their original size. Ireland has almost no coal or oil reserves, so peat has always been used as fuel. In the past, turf (the Irish term for peat) was cut by hand, using a spade or *sleán*, and many people still have 'turbary rights' to cut turf on local bogs. The top layers of living plants are removed and replaced on the cut surface to encourage regeneration; as a result, the effects of cutting peat by hand were minimal.

In 1946, Bord na Móna (the Peat Development Authority) began mechanical digging, and now great tracts can be seen laid waste in black, sodden wildernesses, later replanted with coniferous timber. Peat moss from the surface layers is bagged up and distributed to garden centres, while peat from the lower levels is used for fuel—about a quarter of Ireland's electricity comes from peat. It has become obvious that if the present rate of extraction continues there will soon be none left, so some of the best bogs are now protected as nature reserves. About 10 per cent of Ireland's land surface is peat bog, but bogland is still disappearing at an alarming rate.

A UNIQUE ECOSYSTEM Bogland flora is fascinating and very varied indeed. The only plants that can survive are highly specialized—some have roots reaching deep down through water-retentive mosses into a compost of half-rotted vegetation; other, fly-trapping plants supplement their diet with animal protein. Few mammals can survive true boglands, but rare insects, flowers and birds can be seen. The bogs are also of great interest to archaeologists. Their virtually sterile environment preserves animal and vegetable matter—tree stumps, bog butter (see panel on page 239), even corpses have been pulled from the bog, virtually intact, after centuries.

SAFETY ON BOGS Walking on peat bogs can be dangerous. Some deep pools may be disguised by soft mats of vegetation. It is easy to get lost as there are few paths or visible land-marks. An insect repellent is useful at some times of year, and rubber boots are essential.

BEST BOGLAND ATTRACTIONS:
• **Bog of Allen Nature Centre** Lullymore,County Kildare (tel: 045 860133).
• **Peatlands Park** near Dungannon, Lough Neagh, County Armagh

Re-creation of a bog village at Glenbeigh, County Kerry

(tel: 028 3885 1102).
• **Céide Fields** Ballycastle, County Mayo (tel: 096 43325)—neolithic settlements preserved in bog.
• **Corlea Trackway Exhibition Centre** Kenagh, County Longford (tel: 043 22386)—pre-Christian timber track found beneath bog.
• **Clonmacnoise and West Offaly Railway** Shannonbridge, County Offaly (tel: 0905 74114)—9km (5.5 miles) tour over bog.
• **Raised bogs:** Mongan and Clara (both County Offaly).
• **Blanket bogs:** Roundstone (County Galway), Owenduff (County Mayo), Slieve Bloom Mountains (County Laois).

For more information, contact the Irish Peatland Conservation Council, Lullymore, County Kildare (tel: 045 860133); the National Parks and Wildlife Service, Office of Public Works, 51 St. Stephen's Green, Dublin 2 (tel: 01 661 3111) or in Northern Ireland, Peatlands Park (see above).

25

The tradition of Irish storytelling can be traced back to the Celts, whose sagas of epic battles and great champions, gods and supernatural events were passed down orally at firelit feasts, then transcribed by early monks in manuscripts such as The Book of Leinster.

INTERWOVEN TRADITIONS Irish mythology is incredibly complex; different accounts of similar stories are often interwoven with other traditions, and echoes of other Indo-European legends can often be found—epic tales of Greeks and Romans, for instance, or biblical stories. At first the stories were not written down, but related orally as evening entertainment, which meant embroiderings in every telling. A trained *file* (bard) was expected to be able to relate about 350 full-length

The Children of Lir

tales in poetry by heart, and would spend years learning his art. The early Christian fathers were the first to record these legends, sometimes interspersing them with their own material and turning Celtic gods into Christian saints (such as St. Brigid).

THE CELTIC REVIVAL Although bardic traditions declined under English rule, interest in Celtic legends revived sharply towards the end of the 19th century under the influence of writers such as W. B. Yeats and the rise of Irish nationalism. The leaders of the Easter Rising of 1916 were imbued with ancient myths, seeing themselves as heroes battling against dark forces of evil. Even today, paramilitary groups sometimes use mythological rhetoric to justify their violence.

Celtic mythology remained alive in rural Ireland until the age of television, with a storyteller in every parish; superstitions and tales of fairy folk and monsters still abound. Ireland's leprechaun is the best-known figure of popular lore—the little man in green who mends shoes and guards his crock of gold—while the banshee is a more sinister creature, a female spirit whose wailings are believed to portend a death. Places associated with ancient magic are often treated with great respect by country people, for fear of disturbing whatever spirits or fairies inhabit them.

GROUPS OF SAGAS Irish sagas are classified in four main groups. The Mythological Cycle deals with pre-Celtic gods and heroes and their long-running and complicated struggles for supremacy; the Children of

A romanticized depiction of Cuchulainn by E. Wallcousins

Lir is one of the best-known stories. The Ulster Cycle contains the epic adventures of the Red Branch Knights of Navan Fort and their champion Cuchulainn, one of the most famous being the Cattle Raid of Cooley. The later Ossianic (or Fenian) Cycle revolves around another hero, Finn MacCool (Fionn mac Cumhaill), builder of the Giant's Causeway and Gráinne's betrothed (see page 28). The Historical Cycle (or Cycle of Kings) recounts tales from various early Irish kings, and is similar to Malory's tales of Arthur. The Celtic 'otherworld', *Tír na n'Og* (the Land of Eternal Youth, believed to lie somewhere on an island in the far west), figures in these sagas—the paradise every culture dreams of for its afterlife, where pain and suffering are no more.

THE CATTLE RAID OF COOLEY This was one of the first stories to be written down. Queen Maeve of Connaught became jealous of her husband's possessions, in particular his magnificent white bull. She tried to obtain the mighty brown bull of

The Flemish cartographer Ortelius chose an east–west orientation for his 16th-century map of Ireland

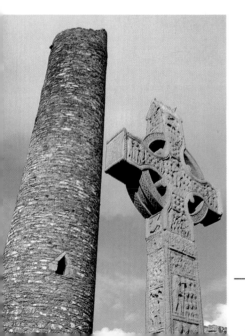

Cooley to match it, at first peacefully, then by force. The hero of Ulster, Cuchulainn, defended the province alone, and defeated Maeve's army. But he was mortally wounded, and died strapped to a stone pillar, facing his enemies.

GRÁINNE AND DIARMUID The very beautiful Gráinne was betrothed to the ageing hero, Finn MacCool, but fell in love instead with the handsome Diarmuid. They eloped, taking refuge under dolmens. Eventually, Diarmuid was killed by a boar on the slopes of Benbulbin Mountain in Sligo. The story has clear parallels with Tristan and Isolde.

CUCHULAINN, HOUND OF ULSTER
At the age of five, Setanta, nephew of King Conor, set out to join his uncle's court, taking his hurling stick and ball with him to play on the way. At a banquet held in the house of Culainn, he was attacked by a great mastiff guard dog. Setanta hurled the ball down the beast's throat and killed it. Culainn was glad he was safe, but distressed at the death of his dog, asking 'Who will guard my house now?' Setanta promised that he would take over the role of protector, and so found his new name—Cuchulainn, the Hound of Culainn, and champion of Ulster.

See panel on page 238.

Biblical stories are carved onto 10th-century Muireadach's Cross at Monasterboice, County Louth

Ireland was

Remnants of Ireland's prehistoric and early Christian past lie scattered throughout the island, although many are shrouded in mystery and still a puzzle to archaeologists. The megalithic tombs of the Boyne Valley or the ornamental jewellery of early populations are evidence of highly sophisticated peoples.

PREHISTORIC IRELAND The earliest inhabitants to have left traces of their existence probably arrived from Scotland in about 6000BC or 7000BC. These were hunter-gatherer peoples who slowly adopted more settled lifestyles and advanced methods of farming as the Stone Age progressed. They wove cloth, made pottery, fished from coracles (simple boats), raised stock and cleared trees to plant a few grains. One of the earliest settlements is Glenaan, in the Glens of Antrim, where flint axe heads have been found.

The clearest legacy of the Neolithic Age is burial places. Between 4000BC and 2000BC, many megalithic tombs (using large blocks of stone) were built. Most impressive are the passage tombs at Newgrange, but important sites can be found in Sligo and eastern Ireland (the court tombs of Creevykeel; dolmens, like those at Proleek; and wedge tombs, as at Labbacallee in County Cork). From the Bronze Age (1750BC onwards) came stone circles or mysterious single standing stones, such as those at Drombeg in Cork or Lough Gur in

Limerick. Little is known of the people, but ancient lore terms them the *Fir Bolg* (Bag Men, because they carried fertile soil to rocky fields in large leather bags), a short, dark race who lived to no more than 30 or so.

THE CELTS In about 700BC a new wave of invaders began to arrive on Irish shores: the Celts, a disparate group of tribes whose cousins can be found all over Europe. Driven west by the Romans, who called them *Galli*, they were known as *keltoi* by the Greeks, and became Gaels in Ireland. Their loose clan structures revolved around a leader or chieftain (*Taoiseach*—the word still used for Ireland's prime minister) who was elected rather than dynastic. As time progressed, leadership became more centralized under a single high king, though the idea of 'nationhood' never developed fully in Celtic times; clans continued to live in isolated settlements of round huts, protected by sturdy defences or by lake moats.

CELTIC LEGACIES Some aspects of Celtic culture seem to have filtered into the Irish character. The Celts were hospitable folk who enjoyed feasting, music and storytelling. Their love of adornment is evident in the gorgeous jewellery they made—bands of decorated gold and other metals, of great artistry. Most of all they loved fighting—no mere internecine squabbles, but epic battles between warrior champions epitomized by the legendary heroes, Cuchulainn and Finn MacCool. Elevated to semi-divinities, the myths (perhaps the Celts' greatest legacy) tell of their great deeds, ringing with the clash of sword on

Drombeg Stone Circle, County Cork

30

shield, dripping with gore. They worshipped many gods, often adopting the sacred sites of past inhabitants for their rituals and royal residences (Tara is one of the most celebrated). Efforts to propitiate these gods were unsparing—vast quantities of treasure were heaped on the altars of the dead, and grisly sacrifices took place. One of the most chilling rituals was the 'wicker man', a huge effigy of straw and wood filled with living creatures—men, women, children, animals—and set alight.

BEYOND ROMAN RULE Ireland is unusual in western Europe in having no significant Roman history. The Romans gazed across at the Emerald Isle, and Tacitus wrote, somewhat airily, 'I have often heard Agricola declare that a single legion, with a moderate band of auxiliaries, would be enough to finish the conquest of Ireland', but they never colonized it. (Cynics say that, if they had, the roads might have been better!) As it was, the Celts held sway in their piecemeal fashion through several Christian centuries. Some re-colonized west Britain in the first centuries AD, joining with the native Picts to plague the Romans along Hadrian's Wall. These Irish Celts were known as Scots, some of whose descendants are the Protestant occupants of Ulster, now regarded by some extreme Nationalists as aliens.

PREHISTORIC AND CELTIC SITES

After the arrival of Christianity in the 4th century, Ireland enjoyed a golden age while the rest of Europe languished in the dark aftermath of the fall of the Roman Empire. Monasteries flourished as great cultural centres, and Irish missionaries travelled back to mainland Europe to spread the Good Word.

VIKING INVADERS The good times were not to last. From AD795, pirate raiding parties began to attack Ireland's shores, envious of the riches of the Celtic monasteries. By AD837 a wholesale Norse invasion was taking place, and this time the interlopers stayed. The native Gaels and monks built Round Towers as lookouts and refuges, and reinforced their simple wood or wattle dwellings and churches with hard stone. The Vikings caused immeasurable destruction and bloodshed as they arrived, but later settled into more peaceable habits, often intermarrying and becoming assimilated with the local population. Though illiterate, they had many skills, and founded sophisticated walled cities to defend the estuaries by which they had entered Ireland (Waterford, Wexford, Cork, Dublin, Limerick). They passed on their great knowledge of seafaring and boat building, established

Fearsome Strongbow now lies peacefully in Dublin's Christ Church Cathedral

important foreign trade links, and introduced coinage. Some converted to Christianity. The Vikings were eventually routed at the Battle of Clontarf (near Dublin) in 1014 by the famous High King, BrianBorú. Unfortunately, a retreating Viking treacherously dispatchedBorú after the battle, and Ireland's chances of becoming united under a strong leader receded again.

MACMURROUGH AND STRONGBOW In one of the subsequent feuds, Dermot MacMurrough abducted the wife of a rival chieftain, Tiernan O'Rourke. The other clans turned on him. In retreat, with many of his lands and his Leinster throne lost, MacMurrough sought help from abroad. Henry II of England, already considering the conquest of Ireland, and with the support of the Pope (himself an Englishman), allowed MacMurrough to recruit from among his barons. Richard FitzGilbert de Clare, Earl of Pembroke, better known as Strongbow, was rewarded for his

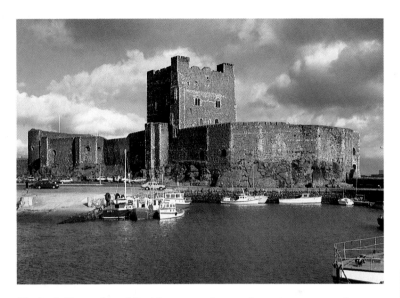

The Anglo-Norman keep of Carrick-fergus Castle has walls 2.5m (8ft) thick

timely aid with the hand of MacMurrough's daughter and great parcels of land. The Normans had arrived, and they stayed. In England, Henry II looked anxiously over his shoulder at these powerful adventurers and decided to assert his authority. He came to Ireland with his army and demanded allegiance from Irish leaders who, also fearful of MacMurrough and Strongbow, gave it. From then on, England was Ireland's overlord. Henry granted the province of Meath to his follower, Hugh de Lacy, and empowered him to act as deputy governor. English control radiated from the Dublin area, which later contracted to a small region about 48km (30 miles) north, south and west of the capital, defended by an earth rampart, known as the Pale.

NORMAN RULE Irish subkingdoms were established farther afield ('beyond the Pale'), enabling Gaelic rulers to hold sway as long as appropriate tributes were paid to England and loyal support given in times of war. Needless to say, not all Ireland's inhabitants were content with such meek subjection, and many rebelled. Land was confiscated as punishment, leaving an enduring legacy of resentment among the Gaelic chieftains, and great English estates began to develop, based on the feudal manorial system. All the colonizers remained free; the Irish peasantry were serfs, tied to the land. Nonetheless, their lot in a productive estate under strong leadership may well have been happier than before. In 1177, John de Courcy invaded Ulster and conquered it swiftly. On Strongbow's death without heirs, Henry's son, Prince (later King) John, took over as Lord of Ireland. Anglo-Norman administrative structures of government and law were set up within Ireland, great castles were built and city walls strengthened. Outside the towns, clan chiefs and Norman lords protected themselves with tower houses, sometimes enclosed by a 'bawn', a high wall with turreted corners.

Henry and his heirs consolidated their claim on Ireland by invoking heavenly allies and strengthening the position of the Church. The monasteries flourished anew, and many great churches and abbeys were built, emerging gradually from modest Romanesque to lofty Gothic as architecture progressed. The Irish Church was reorganized along Roman lines and Continental monastic orders appeared—Augustinians, Cistercians and Franciscans.

The Normans, like the Vikings, invaded with ferocity, but integrated surprisingly quickly. English rulers perceived a dilution of their influence as the distinctions between Anglo-Norman and native Gael blurred.

CATHOLIC REPRESSION In 1366, one of the most repressive of attempts to subdue Ireland took place. The Statutes of Kilkenny aimed to quell the Anglo-Norman tendency to 'go native'. Irish citizens were prohibited from intermarrying with Normans, forbidden to enter walled cities, and their dress, language, names and customs were outlawed. Like all such measures, they were doomed to fail, and Gaelic influence continued to grow until the Pale had dwindled to a small area immediately around Dublin, despite the construction of many more castles across Ireland.

While England was enmeshed in the Wars of the Roses (1455–1485), a powerful Anglo-Norman family, the Fitzgeralds, extended their influence over much of east and southeast Ireland. The Tudor kings, who gained the English throne after the war, saw the Fitzgeralds (warily) as allies. But when Henry VIII renounced the Catholic Church, handing out its land to his Protestant supporters, Lord Offaly of the Fitzgerald house of Kildare (Silken Thomas) staged an insurrection. Thomas was defeated and executed (see panel on page 70), but the precedent was set for future stands against the English Crown. Henry tried to assert his overlordship, demanding that the mutinous lords surrender their property and assume vassal status. When they refused, he took their lands and gave them to the first Protestant 'planters' from England and Scotland.

THE FLIGHT OF THE EARLS In the latter half of the 16th century, the

Fourteenth-century English settlers are brought provisions

34

Cromwell in Ireland

process of plantation continued under Mary I, a Catholic, and then Elizabeth I, who fought four wars in Ireland in defence of the Reformation. Her aims were to assert the Protestant religion and to prevent any intrigues against England hatched by Ireland and Spain. The first plantation attempts were failures—more rebellions took place, led by the Desmonds of Munster, and more seriously, by Hugh O'Neill, Earl of Tyrone, a formerly compliant court protégé who had hoped to become Lord of Ulster.

When he realized how little autonomy he would have under Elizabeth he joined forces with Red Hugh O'Donnell, Earl of Tyrconnell, and resisted. The final showdown came at the Battle of Kinsale (1601). Spanish reinforcements caved in under siege, O'Donnell fled to Spain where he met his death, and O'Neill was forced to sign the Treaty of Mellifont, unaware that Elizabeth I had died six days earlier. All the lands of the defeated chieftains were handed to planters from Scotland, encouraged to emigrate by James I. The proud O'Neill and Red Hugh's brother and successor left Donegal forever in 1607, in the sad exile known as the Flight of the Earls.

PLANTATION This cleared the way for further plantation, this time more successful. Ulster's new settlers were hard-working Calvinists, chalk to the Catholic cheese, and they have never integrated. They quickly made great improvements to the land they acquired, introducing advanced methods of agriculture. Many of the settlers were skilled craftsmen, bringing new talents to its workforce.

In 1641 at Portadown, the dispossessed Irish made another attempt to regain their lands, violently and killing many Protestants. Gaelic leaders allied with the 'Old English' Catholics to defend their faith, property and political rights in the Confederation of Kilkenny. Meanwhile, in England, the Civil War began. Rumours of atrocities towards Ulster planters circulated, so Cromwell brought over 20,000 Ironsides, storming Drogheda and Wexford, slaughtering thousands, and sending many into slavery. Most Catholic landowners were dispossessed and banished west of the Shannon River ('to Hell or to Connaught', in Cromwell's phrase). When he had finished, much of Ireland was devastated and its Catholic population had dwindled to half a million, bitter beyond belief at English injustice.

THE Right Honorable and vndaunted Warrior OLIVER CROMWELL Lo: Governour of IRELAND

35

The agony of Cromwellian times was briefly dispelled by the restoration of Charles II in 1660, although he was never in a strong enough position to help Irish Catholics significantly. The dangerously pro-Catholic leanings of his successor, James II, precipitated the Glorious Revolution and William of Orange's accession. James II fled to France, from where he invaded Ireland for a last stand.

THE BATTLE OF THE BOYNE James II was initially successful at drumming up support in Ireland, but his ambitions were thwarted when he reached Derry. There the young trade apprentices slammed the gates of the city, and (London) Derry endured the longest siege in British history. The Protestant cause prevailed, but only after much suffering, which further polarized Anglo-Irish attitudes. In 1690, William III won his decisive victory over Jacobite (Catholic) forces at the Battle of the Boyne. Further conflicts took place at Athlone, Aughrim and finally Limerick, where the Jacobite army eventually surrendered with honour. The Treaty of Limerick granted civil rights to Catholics, but the English reneged on it, to Ireland's everlasting disgust. Measures were taken to consolidate Protestant ownership of land and Catholic subservience.

William III senses victory at the Battle of the Boyne…

PENAL LAWS A series of repressive laws were passed, collectively known as the Penal Code. This forbade Catholics to practice their religion publicly, or educate their children in the Catholic faith. They could not enlist for military service, buy land or inherit it other than by equal division among all sons. Viable estates became useless divided parcels of land. If one child converted to Protestantism, he (or she, as daughters were allowed to inherit in this case) would get everything! Land ownership by Catholics tumbled to about 14 per cent by 1700, and Irish language, music and literature were suppressed. Once again, opposition fanned the flames. 'Hedge schools' (where teachers and pupils could hide) were run for Catholic children, and Mass was said in secret, with members of the congregation acting as lookouts for English spies.

GEORGIAN IRELAND The 18th century in Ireland was peaceful and full of achievements—literary, artistic and economic. Many of the great country houses of Ireland date from this time (naturally, these were for the Protestant settlers, not the native Irish). Greatest of all the architects of this period was Richard Cassels (anglicized as Castle or Cassel), from a Protestant family who had settled in Germany (see panel on page 250).

Whole villages and towns were planned, with wide streets, tree-lined malls and grand civic buildings. Domestic architecture excelled in Dublin, with dignified terraces and squares satisfying the new aspirations of the city-dwelling middle classes. Comparatively few churches survive from Georgian times (in particular Catholic ones), but they generally followed neoclassical patterns inspired by Greek temples. Michael Stapleton and the Swiss-Italian Francini brothers were masters of stucco work, a popular medium in Ireland in the mid-18th century. Literature and music flourished (see pages 58–59 and 62–63), as did many applied arts, such as silverware and furniture-making.

AN ATTEMPT AT REFORM The surface prosperity and success of the Anglo-Irish Protestant Ascendancy hid tensions seething among the underprivileged peasantry, many of whom lived in appalling conditions. The Catholics were not the only ones to suffer; Presbyterians were also disadvantaged, and during the 18th century many Ulster settlers

…while the vanquished James II flees from Irish shores

emigrated to seek their fortunes across the Atlantic. Protestants were irked by Westminster rule, and gradually a spirit arose in favour of more autonomy. The American Revolutionary War appealed to both Catholic and Protestant sentiment, and prosperous merchants ceased to equate their interests with those of England.

Henry Grattan, a Protestant lawyer, was at the forefront of this movement. He entered Parliament in the same year as the American Revolution began, declaring 'the Irish Protestant could never be free until the Irish Catholic had ceased to be a slave'. Westminster sat up and listened. In 1782, Grattan's Parliament was formed, an assertion of Irish constitutional independence. Some minor measures to alleviate the lot of Catholics were passed. Before any major achievements could be seen, the spectre of the French Revolution intervened in 1789, and once again, England battened down the hatches of reform.

37

Ireland caught the prevailing revolutionary mood from France and, for a while, Dublin's inhabitants went around calling each other 'citizen'. In the countryside, violence grew as secret societies dedicated to overthrowing their oppressive landlords maimed horses, burned barns and drove cattle over cliffs.

38

RELIGIOUS TENSIONS During the days of the Penal Code, Irish Catholics had learned that dissimulation and evasion were necessities for survival. To follow their faith, they had to attend secret meetings and, as they had no redress in law, they took the law into their own hands. As Cecil Woodham-Smith says in *The Great Hunger*, 'These were dangerous lessons for any government to compel its subjects to learn, and a dangerous habit of mind for any nation to acquire'. After relaxation of the laws that had prevented them from owning land, many Catholics moved to Ulster, forcing up prices. The Ulster planters began to feel threatened and formed their own ruthless organizations. A vigilante group called the Peep o' Day Boys attacked Catholics, burning them out in dawn raids and, in 1795, the Orange Order was formed to defend Protestant interests.

Emmet prepares for the insurrection that was to cost him his life…

WOLFE TONE AND ROBERT EMMET
In 1796, the radical Protestant attorney Wolfe Tone (see page 42) set up the Society of United Irishmen in Belfast. Initially it existed as a middle-class debating society, but after its suppression by Prime Minister William Pitt, it became seditious. Tone rallied support from France and attempted a naval attack on Bantry Bay (see page 151). After its failure, Pitt imposed martial law. United Irishmen were rounded up and publicly tortured to inform on their comrades, but fury at this led to open revolt, and in 1798 thousands took up pikes and rusty swords against the English soldiers. Over 30,000 died and Tone was captured, later committing suicide in his cell.

All concessions to Catholics were withdrawn, and, on 1 January 1801, the Act of Union was passed, centralizing government in London. Initially the mood was buoyant; triumphant proclamations of equality were made for England, Ireland,

...and the life of the unfortunate Lord Kilwarden, caught up in the chaos caused by Emmet's uprising

Scotland and Wales within the new legislative structure, but the high hopes were unfounded. English imports swamped the Irish economy and its industries collapsed. Ireland was now hopelessly divided between the impoverished Protestant ruling class and the dispossessed and powerless Catholics. Robert Emmet, a middle-class Protestant, staged yet another abortive uprising of United Irishmen, and was hanged. His speech from the dock inspired future generations of freedom fighters.

DANIEL O'CONNELL Twenty years later, a new inspirational force arose in the form of Daniel O'Connell (see page 42), known as the Liberator, who championed the cause of Catholic emancipation and the repeal of the Act of Union. Voting rights were granted to Catholics in 1829, but O'Connell's attempts to change Ireland's fate peacefully failed.

In the mid-century Ireland was struck down by the complete failure of the potato crop in 1845, 1846 and 1848. Terrible famine ensued, but the British did little to help; while Ireland starved for lack of potatoes, vast quantities of beef and grain were being exported to Britain. A million died, and a million emigrated.

CHARLES STEWART PARNELL The next great figure on the political stage was Parnell (see pages 42–43), who campaigned for Home Rule and reform of the oppressive land tenancy laws. The English Prime Minister Gladstone's attempts to introduce a Home Rule Bill were rejected by the House of Lords, despite a groundswell of support for it. More violence took place, and in 1882 the British chief secretary and the undersecretary for Ireland were stabbed to death. British opinion turned against Home Rule and, by the turn of the 20th century, the scene was set for the breakup of Ireland. The Sinn Fein party (meaning roughly 'Ourselves Alone') was formed by Arthur Griffith in 1908, advocating secession from Britain. On the brink of war, Britain finally acceded to demands for Home Rule in 1914, but postponed it until hostilities had ceased. The Irish Republican Brotherhood (precursors of the IRA and with financial support from emigrants in the US) staged the Easter Rising in Dublin (see pages 54–55) in 1916; meanwhile in Ulster, the Orangemen prepared for battle.

Ireland's history since partition has been tragic, at least in the North. The IRA's ceasefire in 1994, followed by a wary resumption of negotiations, gave the war-weary province a fragile respite from its exhausting Troubles. Although the peace process has been agonizingly slow, the 1998 Good Friday Agreement and a decade without politcal violence has given the people of Ireland, and Britain, new hope that it will return for good on both sides of the Irish Sea.

40

THE CIVIL WAR In 1918, Sinn Fein, led by the Easter Rising veteran Éamon de Valera, won a massive 73 seats at the general election, and independence was declared at a meeting of the first Dáil Éireann (Irish Parliament). The Irish Republicans (now the IRA) attempted to undermine British control using guerrilla tactics, and British soldiers (the Black and Tans) were brought over to maintain order. Under the 1920 Government of

British Prime Minister Lloyd George, left, meets de Valera in 1921

Ireland Act, separate parliaments were created for Northern Ireland (the Six Counties, which remained within the UK), and Southern Ireland, which was granted dominion status under Crown authority. The Anglo-Irish Treaty was signed in December 1921 by Michael Collins and Arthur Griffith. De Valera refused to accept its terms, and Ireland was plunged into a disastrous and bloody civil war. Many politicians, British and Irish, hoped that partition would be temporary, and that eventually the two sectors would unite peacefully when emotions ran less high. They failed to take account of Loyalist feelings in the North. Under Sir Edward Carson (see page 43), Protestant Unionists resolved to fight to the death to prevent being absorbed into the new Irish Free State.

EIRE IS BORN A victory by the pro-treaty forces in the south was followed by 15 years of inward looking, parochial government. In 1932 de Valera's new party, Finna Fáil, took over power and held it for 16 years.

The new Ireland suffered badly in interwar depression, made worse by de Valera's poor relations with Britain. In 1937, political links with Britain were reduced, and the name of Eire was introduced. During World War II Ireland remained officially neutral. Over 50,000 citizens of the Republic enlisted voluntarily in the British armed services, but anti-British feelings were sufficiently strong to encourage some collaboration with Germany, too. De Valera was the only world leader to offer condolences to the Reichstag on the death of Hitler.

After the war, many people emigrated from Ireland; ironically many chose Britain for their new home. Many also headed to the US where Irish/Americans were rapidly becoming a political force with an interest in the Troubles. The election of the forward-looking Sean Lemass in 1959 signalled a welcome break from the politics of Kilmainham Gaol, which de Valera had symbolized. Gradually, economic prosperity increased and Ireland's stifling doldrum of artistic censorship and priest-ridden Victorian morality began to lift. Ireland joined the European Community (EC) in 1972. Soon after this, immediate benefits were felt in agriculture, tourism and the construction industry.

THE TROUBLES CONTINUE The upswing did not improve the situation in the North. In 1968, the civil rights movement began, demanding equality for Catholics. Demonstrations and marches provoked rioting on both sides; Derry was a particular flashpoint. In 1969, British troops were sent to protect the Catholics, who were now barricaded in ghettos, but soon their protective role was perceived as an aggressive one. Just eight days after Ireland joined the

The Irish delegation to the Anglo-Irish Treaty of 1921

EC, 13 unarmed civil rights demonstrators were shot by British paratroopers (the event became known as 'Bloody Sunday'). An angry crowd burned down the British embassy in Dublin, Stormont (the Northern Irish parliament) was suspended, and the province came under direct rule from Westminster. The IRA made a resurgence in a new 'Provisional' guise.

Since 1972, persistent attempts have been made to bring the two sides together. 'Power-sharing executives' came and went, at Sunningdale in 1973 and at Hillsborough (the Anglo-Irish Agreement) in 1985. The latest initiatives, begun in 1994, offer renewed hope. A series of meetings between constitutional nationalists and Sinn Fein led to an IRA cease-fire and direct talks with the British government. The election of a Labour government in 1997 reignited the movement for peace, and on Good Friday 1998 all the major parties in the North signed an agreement that would see an end to violence, the establishment of a power-sharing executive and direct rule, plus guarantees of civil rights for the Catholic minority. Large majorities of voters on both sides of the border approved the agreement. Disagreements over disarmament, the role of the Protestant police force and the British Army have stalled progress, however, and the search for a lasting peace in Northern Ireland remains elusive.

It is impossible to ignore Irish history as you tour the country. Its central figures (heroes or villains, depending on your point of view) keep cropping up. What follows puts just a few of them in context, and pin-points one or two places closely associated with them.

42

PATRICK SARSFIELD, 1st Earl of Lucan (died 1693). Hero of the 1691 Siege of Limerick, with 500 troops, he made a daring raid on William III's supply train at Ballyneety, destroying all his munitions. After the Treaty of Limerick was signed, he sailed to France (Flight of the Wild Geese) and died, fighting again, in Belgium. He was married in Portumna Castle (Galway).

WOLFE TONE (1763–1798) The father of Irish republicanism, this middle-class Protestant lawyer founded the United Irishmen in

Sir Edward Carson, as depicted in 1912

Belfast in 1791. After a period in America, he instigated two unsuccessful attacks using French naval support, at Bantry Bay in 1796 (see the Armada Exhibition at Bantry House, page 151), and in Donegal during the Great Rebellion of 1798. After capture at Letterkenny he was sentenced in Dublin to be hanged, drawn and quartered, but cut his throat before it could be carried out, lingering in agony for seven days.

ROBERT EMMET (1778–1803) A disciple of Tone, Emmet staged an abortive revolt in 1803, planning to seize Dublin Castle. Emmet was sentenced to the same grisly death as Tone, whereupon he said, 'When my country takes her place among the nations of the earth, then and not till then let my epitaph be written'. Padraic Pearse, leader of the Easter Rising of 1916, paid tribute to his sacrifice.

DANIEL O'CONNELL (1775–1847) Known as the Liberator, O'Connell was a witty, eloquent and brilliant lawyer who gave up his career at the bar to fight for Catholic emancipation and the repeal of the Act of Union. Elected MP for Clare (1828), he won popular support, greatly alarming British authorities, although he always renounced violence. His house at Derrynane (Kerry) is a museum to his memory.

CHARLES STEWART PARNELL (1846–1891) A political giant, Parnell (a Protestant) was born at Avondale House in Wicklow (see page 92). Elected MP for Meath in 1875, he campaigned tirelessly for Home Rule and agrarian reform. In 1877, he founded the Irish Land League with

Charles Stewart Parnell

Michael Davitt. He used peaceful tactics, favouring 'filibustering' (disruption of parliamentary debates by long speeches) and 'boycotting' (ostracizing oppressive landlords). His career ended in a scandal involving the wife of a fellow MP.

SIR EDWARD CARSON (1854–1935) Champion of the Ulster Unionists and the architect of partition in 1921, Carson was a Dubliner, knowing little of Ulster or its people. A brilliant lawyer (defending Lord Queensbury at Oscar Wilde's trial), he organized resistance to Home Rule and Irish independence, founding the Ulster Volunteers, an armed band of Loyalists. He is buried at St. Anne's Cathedral, Belfast.

Dublin celebrates the release of Daniel O'Connell, September 1844

MICHAEL COLLINS (1890–1922) Born near Clonakilty in County Cork, Collins was an imposing Republican hero who took part in the Easter Rising. His tactics were ruthless and he was responsible for some brutal killings. He signed the Anglo-Irish Treaty, intended to partition Ireland peacefully. A British signatory, F. E. Smith, said, 'I may have signed my political death warrant'. Collins replied, "I have signed my death warrant." Anti-treatyites ambushed and killed him near Macroom (Cork) a few months later.

ROGER CASEMENT (1864–1916) Born at Ballymena, County Antrim, this career diplomat was knighted by the British in 1911. He was arrested as he landed at Banna Strand near Tralee in 1916 in a German submarine containing arms for the Easter Rising. His case was not helped in those days by the knowledge that he was a practising homosexual, and he was hanged for treason. His grave is in Glasnevin Cemetery, Dublin.

ÉAMON DE VALERA (1882–1975) 'Dev', the 'Long Fellow', was born in New York, but grew up at Bruree, Limerick (where there is a small museum). A veteran of the Easter Rising (pardoned because of his dual nationality), he, more than any politician, determined Ireland's course after the formation of the Free State, and was the founder of Fianna Fáil (Soldiers of Destiny). Three times premier, he was president from 1959 to 1973, but did little to heal the divisions between North and South.

43

Above: Ha'penny Bridge over the Liffey
Right: looking north up O'Connell Street, named after Daniel O'Connell, "the Liberator"

DUBLIN The capital's very size and city-like qualities in what is still a largely rural country make it atypical, yet it encapsulates so much that is endearing and exasperating about Ireland that it represents the Emerald Isle better than any other town. Not that the rest of Ireland necessarily thinks so: Dublin is regarded with the same mix of wistful envy and resentment by its provinces as most capital cities, and its inhabitants as a race apart. Some locals feel the recent tide of economic prosperity has washed away some of the grimy character that lent the city its charm. But the old Dublin lives on behind the facades of new apartment complexes and the faces of bustling professional types. It's a city of pubs, churches, grand buildings and fine museums, boozers and talkers, down-to-earth commerce and airy pipe dreams—above all, an intimate place whose pulse must be taken over some time, possibly through a glass of Guinness.

THE FAIR CITY? It is indeed a beautiful place, set on a broad river basin fringed by the majestic sweep of Dublin Bay and the tantalizingly close Wicklow Mountains. Yet the 'fair city' of song was better described by James Joyce, one of its most famous citizens, as 'dear, dirty Dublin'. The best of its Georgian architecture rivals anything that can be seen in Bath or Edinburgh, but much has been destroyed by development or sheer neglect. Some of the demolition is forgivable; those pretty Georgian facades often disguise impossibly friable brickwork and tottering

Dublin

*St. Patrick's Cathedral,
Dublin*

*Right: A beautiful
stained-glass window
greets visitors to the
Writers Museum in
Dublin*

DUBH LINN

The *dubh linn* (dark pool)
that gave its name to the
city was the confluence of
the Poddle and the peat-
coloured waters of the
Liffey. From the 9th
century it was the harbour,
where the original Norse
settlers moored their long-
ships on the low-lying
banks below their fortress.
A grilled opening in the
south wall of the quay by
Grattan (or Capel Street)
Bridge shows the last
remains of the Poddle
River, which now runs
underground for the final
5km (3 miles) of its
course. This site was the
port of Dublin until the
18th century, when a new
one was built to the east
by the Custom House. The
original Gaelic name for
Dublin (still its official
name in Gaelic) was Baile
Átha Cliath (town of the
hurdles). This name is visible on the front of some
buses, on road signs and
on postmarks.

The motto means 'happy the city whose citizens are obedient'

foundations that only total reconstruction would cure. What has replaced those seemly proportions sometimes defies belief, however, especially around gap-toothed St. Stephen's Green or mutilated Fitzwilliam Street. The main thoroughfare on the north bank, O'Connell Street, is disappointing, its monumental dimensions and few remaining dignified buildings interspersed with seedy fast-food outlets and dull office buildings. But the area is gradually being improved with the Luas tram system now linking O'Connell Street with Smithfield, with its cobbled plaza and new apartments being built. Fortunately, though, Dublin has avoided the high-rises that have ruined the skylines of other cities, and north of the river, the unsightliness is really due to dereliction. Now, thankfully, the process is being reversed, and Dublin's fanlit doorways glow amid newly restored surroundings.

THE SOCIAL DIVIDE To some extent, as in London, the great divide is the river. The Liffey neatly bisects Dublin from east to west, meeting the Poddle near the Grattan Bridge and forming the *dubh linn* or dark pool, that gives the city its name (see panel on page 46). The respectable classes enjoy elegant architecture, chic restaurants and fashionable shops now based mostly in the south around St. Stephen's Green and Trinity College. Street crime, some drug-related, some intensified by stubborn inner-city unemployment, is more of a problem here than in Belfast, though less than in many other capital cities. But in its salubrious quarters Dublin is a distinctly enjoyable and friendly place. A conversation struck up with strangers is not regarded as a sign of impertinence or lunacy, but a simple acknowledgment of fellow humanity. There is a natural and wholesome friendliness about both its citizens and the very atmosphere of the city.

Laid out by Sir Arthur Guinness in 1880, St. Stephen's Green is one of the city's most popular meeting places

THE CAPITAL Although the central areas feel compact and can be explored on foot, the capital is by far the largest city in Ireland. Currently the Greater Dublin area contains about a million people, almost a third of the Republic's population, many of whom have drifted in from country

The magnificent coffered dome of the City Hall; this building, on Lord Edward Street near Dublin Castle, was designed between 1769 and 1779 by Thomas Cooley

BILLY-IN-THE-BOWL
This extraordinary character terrorized the neighbourhood of Stoneybatter, near Arbour Hill in northwest Dublin, in the mid-18th century. Billy was born without legs, but learned to get about by propelling himself in an iron bowl with his arms. Naturally his upper limbs developed great strength, which he turned to criminal use. He lured passersby to his side by appealing to their sympathy, then seized them and strangled them for their purses. When he was eventually convicted for his multiple felonies, he was sentenced to 'as much hard labour as his condition would allow' for the rest of his days.

areas in search of work. A large proportion of Dublin's inhabitants are under 25. It is a cosmopolitan city with many nationalities and social groupings drawn by the booming economy, but there is by no means the same racial mix as in, say, London or Paris. Dublin has declined somewhat since its 18th-century heyday, when great architecture sprang up all over the city, when the first performance of Handel's *Messiah* was held here, and when it was considered one of the foremost cities of Europe. Things have improved in recent years, however, with Ireland's entry into the EU and a vast influx of funds for redevelopment making great changes to the city.

A newfound prosperity and confidence inspires the Dublin scene: Georgian buildings and their contents are cherished and conserved, restaurants buzz with patrons and many fashionable celebrities have made the city their second home.

Traditional music in Dublin's Brazen Head pub

CHIEF O'NEILL

The new Chief O'Neill complex in the Smithfield market area of Dublin contains a snazzy hotel and restaurant. The eponymous Chief wasn't the head of any ancient clan, but rather of Chicago's police force at the beginning of the 19th century. Francis O'Neill left Bantry, Co. Cork, for America in 1865 when he was just 17 years old. After adventures in the New World as a sailor, school teacher and shepherd, he joined Chicago's police force and rose to power. However, O'Neill is remembered and loved in Ireland not because of his career, but because of his hobby. He was one of the most important collectors and publishers of traditional music, his books preserving hundreds of tunes and melodies that would otherwise have been lost forever.

From the oriental collection at the Chester Beatty Library

▶▶▶ Bank of Ireland 463C

College Green, tel: 01 677 6801
Open: Mon–Wed and Fri 10–4, Thu 10–5
Admission: inexpensive

Straight across from Trinity College, this striking neoclassical building was created in 1729 to seat the Irish Parliament. After the shameful self-dissolution of that body in 1801, the building was sold to the Bank with instructions that its interior be changed so that it might never again be used as a debating chamber. Much of the original structure was maintained, including the pedimented portico fronted by six great Corinthian columns. Inside the main banking hall has a coffered ceiling adorned with delicate stucco rosettes. Just down the hall, in the original House of Lords, tapestries still hang celebrating the Battle of the Boyne under the 1,240-piece Waterford crystal chandelier. Guided tours are given every Thursday at 10.30, 11.30, and 1.45.

▶▶▶ Chester Beatty Library 462B

Castle Street, tel: 01 407 0750, www.cbl.ie
Open: May–end Sep Mon–Fri 10–5, Sat 11–5, Sun 1–5;
Oct–end Apr Tue–Fri 10–5, Sat 11–5, Sun 1–5. Admission free

Sir Alfred Chester Beatty (1875–1968) was an American mining engineer of Irish ancestry. By the age of 40 he had acquired a vast fortune, but had also developed incipient silicosis, so turned his prodigious energies to the more sedentary occupation of collecting exotic fine art. He made many trips to the Middle and Far East to add to his hoard and improve his health. He settled in Dublin in 1950, and gave his astonishing collection to the nation in 1956, living on to attain the grand age of 93. Occupying Dublin Castle's elegant clock tower, the collection contains outstanding examples of mostly oriental and Middle Eastern art, including gorgeously decorated Chinese silk robes, Japanese *netsuki* and lacquer boxes, illuminated manuscripts and scrolled Korans, books of jade or ancient papyrus, snuff bottles and rhinoceros-horn cups, woodblock prints and miniature paintings. Apart from its academic importance, the collection is simply beautiful to look at and should not be missed.

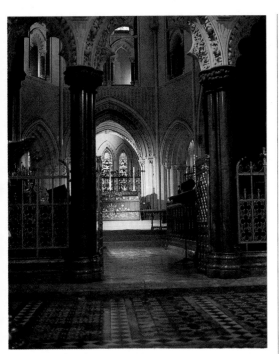

DVBLINIA
This entertaining, multi-media presentation of life in medieval Dublin can be seen in the old Synod Hall over the bridge from Christ Church. It features a model of Dublin c1500, a display of items unearthed from Wood Quay and a medieval maze, along with an exciting audio-visual show.

51

▶▶▶ **Christ Church Cathedral**   *462B*
Christ Church Place, tel: 01 677 8099, www.cccdub.ie
Open: Mon–Fri 9.45–5, Sat–Sun 10–5. Admission: moderate
Oddly for a staunchly Catholic city, both of Dublin's cathedrals are Protestant. Christ Church is the seat of the Anglican Bishop of Dublin and Glendalough. It has been a Protestant church since 1551 and is inevitably closely linked with English rule of the city, though it has some rebellious streaks in its history: In 1487, the Yorkist Pretender, Lambert Simnel, was crowned here by his supporters in a counterclaim to Henry VII's throne. The cathedral stands within the original city walls, and until 1871 it was the official state church. Its long history stretches back before the Anglo-Norman invasion to 1038, when Sitric Silkenbeard, the first Christian Viking King of Dublin, founded a wooden church on this site. This was replaced by a stone edifice in Norman times. Part of this, the south wall, collapsed in 1562, and the north wall is still about 45cm (18ins) out of line. Today, the buttressed, grey, early Gothic buildings show evidence of a ruthless 19th-century restoration that time has not yet softened. Inside, are the tomb of 'Strongbow' (Richard de Clare, Earl of Pembroke, who commanded the Anglo-Norman invasion in 1169) and the heart of St. Laurence O'Toole, arch-bishop and patron saint of Dublin, in the chapel of St. Laud. Some of the original 13th-century tiles are incorporated into the floor, and the eagle lectern is also medieval. The crypt contains an odd jumble of quaint broken statues and the city stocks. Other curiosities include the bodies of a cat and a mouse, which apparently died in full flight when they both got stuck in an organ pipe, and the 1689 tabernacle and candlesticks of James II.

THE FENIAN SOCIETY
This secret, militant group was formed in a Dublin timberyard on St. Patrick's Day 1858, financed by $400 donated by expatriate Irish who had emigrated to the United States during the Famine years. Its members were bound by oath to loyalty to the aim of establishing an Irish Republic. From it the Irish Republican Brotherhood, and later the IRA, developed, and it was suspected of many terrorist activities in its efforts to get the British out of Ireland. Parnell's Land League had links with the Fenians, which damaged an otherwise sympathetic hearing in Britain. Its anticlerical, Republican stance put it at odds with the Catholic Church, and known members faced excommunication. Today, Republican paramilitary groups are allegedly still partially financed by expatriate funds.

The Throne Room of Dublin Castle also contains a brass chandelier weighing more than a ton

▶▶ Dublin Castle 462B

Dame Street, tel: 01 677 7129, www.dublincastle.ie
Open: Mon–Fri 10–5, Sat–Sun 2–5. Admission: moderate

This is no longer so much a castle as an assembly of courts, offices and ceremonial accommodation dating from many different periods. Although it stands on high ground that was originally a strategic site at the junction of the Liffey and the Poddle, it is now hemmed in by the surrounding buildings and offers little in the way of a city landmark. Nor does it command significant views; in fact, Queen Victoria is said to have been so disappointed by the rear outlook onto slum tenement buildings that she insisted a wall be built so that she shouldn't be reminded of such indigent neighbours next time she visited. The castle has been a fortress, prison, viceregent's residence and function rooms for important state occasions. It also serves as a useful hotel for high-risk VIPs whenever they visit to discuss Ireland's tangled affairs. Dublin Castle has also been a venue for peace talks and a headquarters during Ireland's 1996 presidency of the EU.

The most castlelike part of the building still standing is the round Record Tower, dating from the 13th century. It stood on the site of an earlier Viking fortress, sections of which have been excavated and can be seen in the undercroft (vault), along with the old moat and bits of city wall. After 1684, a lot of the structure had to be replaced because of fire, and much of what you see now dates from the 18th century. The church next to the Powder Tower is the Church of the Most Holy Trinity, modelled in neo-Gothic and consecrated in 1814 on the site of the earlier Chapel Royal. The arms of all the viceroys from 1172 to 1922 can be seen inside. Modern buildings around the courtyard house the tax office and conference facilities. One of the most charming parts of the older buildings is the inner courtyard with its clocktower.

Visits are by guided tour only, which, though informative, are somewhat impersonal. If you have time to wait, it is a good idea to see the photographic exhibition in the reception building (where they serve good refreshments) to get a clear idea of the layout of the complex. Inside, you see the main state apartments (provided no functions are going on there), which are sumptuously furnished to provide a suitably opulent setting for the many dignitaries who have made use of the castle. Vast Waterford chandeliers, tapestries, hand-tufted Donegal carpets mirroring the ceiling plasterwork and Adam fireplaces abound, revealing the palatial lifestyle led by the viceroys acting on behalf of the Crown. St. Patrick's Hall is one of the most impressive rooms, all cluttered with banners and coats of arms, beneath an ornately painted ceiling. It is now used for the inauguration of Ireland's presidents. The throne room contains a massive throne believed to have been brought to Dublin by William of Orange after his victory at the Boyne. During the Easter Rising the castle was briefly threatened by an assault from the roof of the nearby City Hall. After the suppression of the rebellion, the captured rebel, James Connolly, was held (wounded) in one of the state rooms before being taken to Kilmainham to face execution.

LIMITED RESOURCES
As the centre of English power in Ireland, Dublin Castle was for centuries probably the most heavily guarded fortress in the country. Yet, during the Easter Rising in 1916, insurgents abandoned a scheme to take the castle —without knowing that, at the time, it was manned only by a corporal's guard.

53

Dublin Civic Museum has a section devoted to fire-fighting. In this is a collection of fire-insurance plaques, such as the one below. They were once placed on houses to guide the insurance companies' own firemen to houses insured by them

▶ Dublin Civic Museum 473B

58 South William Street, tel: 01 679 4260
Open: Tue–Sat 10–6, Sun 11–2
Admission free

Housed in what was once the City Assembly House, the Dublin Civic Museum traces the history of the city from Viking times with items from excavation sites, old maps, photographs and prints. The city's mercantile past is portrayed in sections devoted to various aspects of Dublin's trade and industry, and there is an interesting section on transportation, including a model of the Howth tram. One curiosity is a sculpted head of Lord Nelson, placed here after his column in O'Connell Street was blown up in 1966, on the 50th anniversary of the Easter Rising.

The Easter Rising was a curious event, tiny in comparison with the rebellion of 1798, for instance, with only about 2,000 people actively taking part in it. It was disastrously badly organized and commanded very little public support, but its martyred heroes still glow in the imagination of Republican Ireland as icons in the struggle against British rule.

PEARSE MUSEUM
This little museum can be found in the house once run by Padraic Pearse and his brother William as a boys' school. Their curriculum placed a strong emphasis on Gaelic studies and Irish culture. The United Irishman Robert Emmet courted his bride in the grounds. The house is devoted to memorabilia connected with Pearse's life and the events that led to his death. It stands in St. Enda's Park in Rathfarnham, a southern Dublin suburb.

The General Post Office soon after the Easter Rising

Irish heroes The leaders were Padraic Pearse and James Connolly. Pearse, a shy schoolmaster, was an unlikely commander, but he was inspired by a kind of mystical belief that bloodshed was necessary to cleanse Ireland. He was an Irish Volunteer, a group pledged to establish Home Rule at all costs. James Connolly was a more practical man, a socialist, born into a poor Irish family in Scotland, and in the British army at 14. He founded the Irish Citizens Army, closely allied to the Irish Volunteers.

The Rising On Easter Monday, 24 April 1916, Pearse, at the head of 150 men armed with ancient rifles and farm tools, took over the General Post Office, where he solemnly read out a stirring document proclaiming the new Irish Republic. Meanwhile, volunteers took over other buildings—a brewery, lunatic asylum, factory and bakery. Many Dubliners were as bemused as the British forces by the collapse of the city into chaos, and, instead of joining the rebels, they made tea for the British. The fighting lasted for six days, and on the Saturday Pearse surrendered, by which time over 400 people had died. Twice as many police were killed as rebels and four times as many civilians. Much of central Dublin lay in ruins and the leaders of the Rising were even less popular than they had been at the start.

54

Fighting lasted for six days, after which much of central Dublin lay in ruins

The tragic aftermath Then the tide turned. Instead of listening to the advice of moderate Home Rule supporter John Redmond not to execute any of the rebels, the British shot 14 of them, including Pearse and Connolly. From then on, they were heroes in the classic Republican tradition. The release of hundreds of Irish internees later that year (among them Arthur Griffith, founder of Sinn Fein, Éamon de Valera and Michael Collins) did nothing to assuage the bitterness that surrounded the aftermath of the Easter Rising. The fact that thousands of Irishmen died just a few months later on the battlefields of the Somme, fighting in the British Army, was all but eclipsed. A bronze statue in the rebuilt General Post Office, depicting the mythical hero, Cuchulainn, at the moment of death, symbolizes the glorified leaders.

Kilmainham Gaol This prison (*Inchicore Road, Kilmainham, tel: 01 453 5984. Open: Apr–end Sep daily 9.30–5; Oct–end Mar Mon–Sat 9.30–4, Sun 10–5. Admission: moderate*), last used as such in 1924, is an excellent museum documenting the Irish struggle for independence. Many political prisoners were held here—United Irishmen, Fenians, Land Leaguers. It is a gripping and memorable place and a fascinating, if partisan, insight into political and prison history. The main body of the prison, a classic barnlike shell of metal stairways and chicken-wired galleries, contains numerous display cases of items and documents. The guided tour begins at the scaffold where just one prisoner was hanged, and continues to the west wing where political internees were held in tiny, separate, dark cells. Passing the much more comfortable room where Parnell was imprisoned for seven months, it leads, finally, to the stonebreakers' yard where 14 leaders of the Easter Rising were executed by firing squad. James Connolly had a gangrenous leg and was shot strapped to a chair. Joseph Plunkett was married to Grace Gifford by candlelight in the prison chapel, two hours before he was shot. They were allowed ten minutes together.

The monument in the General Post Office

The children's corner at Dublin Zoo...

GUINNESS
Arthur Guinness established his brewery in Dublin in 1759 and soon began experimenting with a London-brewed beverage made with roasted barley, known as 'porter' (after its popularity with the porters of Covent Garden). By 1799, he concentrated all his production efforts on this distinctive drink, a rich black liquid topped with that 'foamous' creamy head (as James Joyce called it). After the Napoleonic Wars of the early 19th century, an even stronger ('extra stout') beer was produced, and it rapidly reached most parts of the globe, even the South Pole (freezing is not generally recommended!). Though technology is now greatly advanced, the basic recipe of Guinness remains the same—Irish-grown barley, soft water, hops and the strain of yeast Arthur Guinness used in 1759. A highly successful marketing policy has employed many talented artists in poster campaigns. The profits from Guinness have funded worthy enterprises such as the Wexford Opera Festival and the Georgian Society.

▶ **Dublin Zoo** 461C
Phoenix Park, tel: 01 677 1425, www.dublinzoo.ie
Open: Mar–end Sep Mon–Sat 9.30–6, Sun 10.30–6; Oct–end Feb Mon–Fri 9.30–5, Sat 9.30–5, Sun 10.30–5
Admission: expensive
Established in 1830, Dublin's zoo is the third oldest in the world. It is attractive, set in 11.7ha (29 acres) of gardens with fauna roaming in pleasant surroundings. Its most celebrated inhabitants are the lions, one of whom achieved undying fame as the beast roaring above the MGM film studios' logo before every cinematic presentation.

▶▶ **Guinness Brewery and Storehouse** 461E
St. James's Gate, tel: 01 408 4800, www.guinness.com
Open: Jun–end Jul daily 9.30–9; Sep–end May daily 9.30–5
Admission: expensive
Way upstream of most central sights is a Lowryesque skyline of smoking factory chimneys and giant metallic storage vats. This is the largest brewery in Europe, producing what can only be described as Ireland's *vin du pays*, though in fact it was first invented in London. Arthur Guinness's famous 'porter' is shrouded in a sort of misty-eyed Celtic mythology that declares it can never be the same drunk outside Dublin, or from a can, or that the art of pulling a pint takes years to learn. This may be nonsense, but the production process is certainly a complex one and conditions of storage are important. You can't visit the brewery itself, but Guinness have converted the nearby 1904, six-floor, brick warehouse into 'The Storehouse', a high-tech museum that borders on a temple dedicated to 'the black stuff'. Every floor has exhibits taking you through the brewing process, from grist and malt to a hundred years of Guinness advertising. Highlights include the top-floor, circular Gravity Bar with 360-degree glass walls and an unrivalled view of Dublin.

▶▶ **Hugh Lane Gallery** 462D
Parnell Square, tel: 01 874 1903, www.hughlane.ie
Open: Tue–Thu 9.30–6, Fri–Sat 9.30–5, Sun 11–5
Admission free (Bacon Studio: expensive)
The pictures are displayed in an elegant house designed by Sir William Chambers for the Earl of Charlemont in 1762. This north Dublin area is no longer very fashionable, but the house is a fine example of early Georgian architecture and its contents are even more splendid, and in some ways it is more enjoyable and intimate than the National Gallery. Corots, Courbets and Monets glow on the plain walls, along with some good Jack Yeats. Francis Bacon, arguably Britain's premier 20th-century artist, bequeathed his studio to the gallery, where it has been reconstructed.

▶▶ **Irish Museum of Modern Art** 461B
Royal Hospital, Military Road, Kilmainham, tel: 01 612 9900, www.modernart.ie
Open: Tue–Sat 10–5.30, Sun noon–5.30. (Royal Hospital tour every 30 minutes; Museum of Modern Art tours Wed and Fri 2.30, Sat 11.30). Admission free
This museum deserves a visit, more for its glorious setting than its contents. Based on the style of Les Invalides in Paris, the Royal Hospital is one of the finest 17th-century buildings in Ireland, constructed in 1684 as a home for

...and the children's corner at the Municipal Gallery

retired soldiers. Restored in 1986, it now houses ultra-modern works of variable quality. There are lively temporary exhibitions, as well as educational and community theatre and visual arts events.

► Old Jameson Distillery 461C

Bow Street, tel: 01 807 2355, www.irish-whiskey-trail.com
Open: daily 9.30–5.30; tours every 30 minutes
Admission: expensive

The original Dublin distillery of Jameson Whiskey has been converted by Irish Distillers into a museum showing the production process of the 'water of life'. An audio-visual show and a model of an old distillery illuminate visitors, who are treated to a tasting If you are touring, there are larger and better whiskey distilling attractions in Northern Ireland (Bushmills) or County Cork (Midleton).

►►► Kilmainham Gaol 461B

See Focus On the Easter Rising, page 55.

HUGH LANE
When Hugh Lane went down with the *Lusitania* in 1915, he bequeathed a problem as well as a magnificent art collection. He had left his estate "to the nation." The difficulty was (in the light of contemporary political events) to decide which nation he meant. Britain naturally claimed he intended the collection to be British, whereas Dublin said it should stay in his native land. Eventually the dispute was settled with a classic British compromise. The collection was simply split in two parts. Half the pictures stayed in Dublin, half in the National Gallery in London and every five years they changed over. Would that all Anglo-Irish problems could be solved so amicably! (Under a new agreement, most of the bequest is now actually on view in Dublin.)

57

A re-creation of a cooper's workshop at the Guinness Brewery

The period from about 1714 to 1830 was Dublin's apogee, a great flowering of architecture, literature, philosophy and art. The quality of Irish craftsmanship in silverwork, glassware and furniture, and in Dublin's superb Georgian buildings, epitomizes the 'age of elegance'.

Dublin's heyday After the depredations of Cromwell's visits and the turmoil of Williamite battles, the 18th century was a time of comparative peace and prosperity in the English Pale. For the upper classes, life was highly civilized. Aesthetes and businessmen, wealthy gentry and talented artists merged resources to make Dublin one of the foremost cities of Europe. Terraces, parks, squares, imposing monuments and dignified town houses burgeoned throughout the central parts of the city, bounded by the Grand and Royal canals. In 1757, the Wide Streets Commission, Europe's first planning authority, established new guidelines for building development, and in 1773, the Paving Board set up sensible regulations on lighting, cleaning and drainage, making densely populated residential areas much more

58

The figure of Hope rests upon her anchor atop the magnificent Custom House

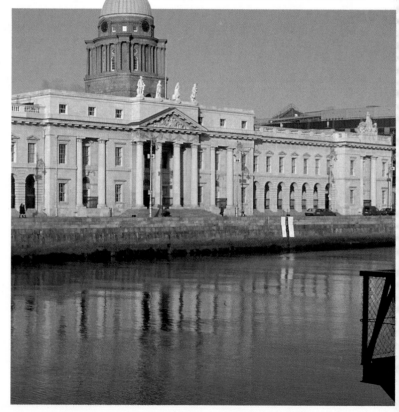

salubrious. This confident assertion of the good life for the Anglo-Irish Ascendancy disguised the wretched lot of the poor; in 1770, even the English viceroy was forced to admit that the Irish peasantry were 'amongst the most wretched people on earth'.

North of the Liffey In the earlier years of the 18th century, Dublin's fashionable centre of gravity lay north of the river, and the first typically Georgian housing appeared around Mountjoy and Parnell (formerly Rutland) squares and Henrietta Street. These did not fare well after conversion to tenement buildings when the Act of Union caused a dramatic fall in property values, and the buildings long presented a sad picture of neglect and decay. But a sharp rise in the housing market has led to a spate of restoration and development in areas such as **North Great George's Street**. Other quality examples can be found in **Parnell Square▶▶**. The **Hugh Lane Gallery▶▶** (see page 56), is in a splendid town house of the period; **Belvedere House▶** on Great Denmark Street, now a Jesuit college, is another. Two grand set pieces north of the river, monumental buildings designed by James Gandon, can be seen to advantage from the opposite bank of the Liffey. The weighty **Custom House▶▶** of 1791 (tel: 01 679 3377, see panel) floats on a fragile platform of pine planks on swampy riverside land. Farther west is the **Four Courts▶** of 1785 (tel: 01 872 5555), the seat of the High Court of Justice for Ireland. The Courts of King's Bench, Exchequer, Common Pleas and Chancery radiate from a circular central hall, liveliest at lunchtimes when bewigged lawyers hob-nob with their clients. Another Gandon building stands away from the river, in Henrietta Street: The **King's Inns▶** (1795–1827) were Dublin's Inns of Court (tel: 01 874 4840). The **Rotunda Maternity Hospital▶▶**, the first specially built maternity hospital in Europe, has superb stucco work in its chapel (tel: 01 873 0700).

South of the Liffey The best preserved and the most enjoyable examples of Dublin's Georgian heritage can be seen south of the river. The shift in popularity occurred around the year 1750, after the construction of the opulent **Leinster House▶▶** (now Ireland's parliament building, tel: 01 618 3000) for the Duke of Leinster in 1745. At the time, he was ridiculed for his choice of a green-field site away from the hub of fashionable Dublin, but as he rightly predicted, 'Wherever I go, they will follow.'

Dublin's Georgian heritage was largely spared aerial bombing during the World Wars, but it has fared ill at the hands of 20th-century developers and politicians. After the creation of the Free State in 1922, renovation of buildings reminiscent of English rule was not exactly a high priority. Much thoughtless and irreparable destruction took place. But there is still much to enjoy among the fanlit doorways of its 18th-century squares. A new generation of conservation-minded citizens who do not blame bricks and mortar for Ireland's disastrous history now seem bent on preserving what is left.

See the following two pages for a walk around Dublin's finest Georgian buildings.

TAILOR'S HALL
Not far from Christ Church (on Back Lane) stands Dublin's only surviving guild hall, quite different architecturally from anything else you will see in the city. It is now the headquarters of *An Taisce* (broadly speaking, the Irish equivalent of the British National Trust, see pages 230–231), which is dedicated to the conservation of historic buildings and scenic landscapes. Tailor's Hall (*Admission: donation*) dates from 1706 and has a fine 18th-century interior with tall Queen Anne windows and a minstrel's balcony.

North Great George's Street: The lantern above the door was lit when the mistress of the house was 'at home to visitors'

INSPECTING GEORGIAN DUBLIN
The Custom House, Four Courts, Bank of Ireland and Leinster House (while Parliament is in session) are not officially open to the public. Nevertheless, it is occasionally possible to visit these buildings. If you are genuinely interested in the interiors you may be able to persuade a friendly official to let you in, or ask at the tourist office, as guided tours are sometimes available.

Walk

A walk around Georgian Dublin

See map on pages 46–47.

Within the bounds of 18th-century taste, Irish craftsmen found great scope for personal expression, and the details of buildings are hugely varied and imaginative. Little touches, such as door-knockers, coal-hole covers and boot-scrapers, are the rewards of a wander around Georgian Dublin.

College Green is a good starting point for exploring Dublin. This was the centre of power during the 18th century until the Act of Union centralized government in Westminster. What is now the **Bank of Ireland▶▶** (see page 50) was built by Edward

St. Stephen's Green

Lovett Pearce between 1729 and 1739 to house the Irish Parliament. During banking hours, visitors may see the former House of Lords, sumptuously furnished with a Waterford chandelier, 18th-century tapestries and coffered ceiling. **Trinity College▶▶▶**, on the other side of the Green (see page 72), dates mainly from the 18th century. Its 90m (300ft) facade, attributed to Theodore Jacobsen, was built between 1752 and 1759 and the **Provost's House▶▶** on the corner of Grafton Street is one of Dublin's grandest Georgian mansions.

Turning down Kildare Street, you find Georgian **Leinster House▶▶▶**, the most imposing of several monumental public buildings (see pages 58–59), while nearby Molesworth Street contains three early Georgian houses built for Huguenot families between 1736 and 1755. Known as **Dutch Billies▶**, they are a revival of a style popular after William of Orange's conquest, featuring curvy gables and huge chimneys. On Dawson Street, 18th-century buildings include: **St. Ann's▶▶** of 1720 (see page 70); the **Royal Irish Academy▶** (tel: 01 676 2570) of 1785, housing a splendid library of Irish manuscripts; and the balustraded facade of the Lord Mayor's residence, **The Mansion House▶** (tel: 01 676 1845), a Queen Anne building that dates from 1705, is sometimes open for exhibitions. **St. Stephen's Green** is one of the landmarks of the Georgian city, although its buildings date from many periods and its park was not laid out until Victorian times (see page 68). The best of the Georgian buildings are: the 1806 **Royal College of Surgeons▶▶** (tel: 01 402 2100), scarred by the Easter Rising; **Newman House▶** (tel: 01 475 7255), Nos. 85 and 86 on the south side, original home of the Catholic university (one of these houses, ironically, was built for a vehement anti-Catholic, Thomas "Burnchapel" Whaley, by the great 18th-century architect Richard Castle); and **Iveagh House▶▶** (1736), now the Department of Foreign Affairs (not open). Off St. Stephen's Green are **Harcourt Street**, **Ely Place** and **Leeson Street**, with many attractive and well-preserved domestic town houses.

Leinster House, designed by Castle

Fitzwilliam Street▶ contained the longest stretch of Georgian buildings in Europe until an astonishing piece of civic vandalism in the 1960s permitted a hideous office building to tear a hole in it. The Electricity Supply Board (whose administrative headquarters it is) has now sheepishly rebuilt one of the houses it tore down. **Number 29▶** (tel: 01 702 6165. *Admission free*) is open as a little museum, and its elegant rooms re-create something of the atmosphere of late Georgian times. **Fitzwilliam Square▶▶**, although not the largest or most famous Georgian example, is actually one of the best preserved. Many fanlit doorways retain original features such as glass recesses for lamps and antiburglar spikes set in the walls. A glance down Mount Street reveals the attractive late-Georgian church of **St. Stephen's▶▶**, known as the Pepperpot from its unusual dome. In the mid-18th century, the **Grand Canal** beside the church would have been a bustling highway of commerce and passenger traffic.

Merrion Square▶▶▶ is the final great "set piece" on this walking tour. The blue plaques on many

houses commemorate famous former occupants, suggesting how fashionable it once was. Planned in 1762 for Lord Fitzwilliam, it is one of the finest of all Dublin's squares. Oscar Wilde's parents lived here, as well as statesman Daniel O'Connell, W. B. Yeats and many other respected figures.

Georgian elegance in every detail

Dublin is an emphatically literary city. Most great Irish writers gravitated there at some stage so, to some extent, the literary history of Dublin is the literary history of Ireland. The ghosts of Yeats, Shaw, Synge, Beckett, O'Casey, Wilde, Swift and others haunt its streets and bookshops. The National Library, near Leinster House, contains a splendid collection of first editions and works of 17th-century Irish authors, as well as later writers, including Swift, Goldsmith, Yeats, Shaw and Joyce.

Top: Oscar Wilde

JAMES JOYCE TOWER
The 22-year-old Joyce spent only a week or so there in the August of 1904, though he later immortalized it in the first chapter of his masterpiece *Ulysses*. The Martello Tower belonged to Oliver St. John Gogarty, an ebullient surgeon and poet, who invited Joyce to stay with him there. For more details of his eventful stay in the tower, see page 97.

STELLA AND VANESSA
Jonathan Swift's women friends are immortalized in his letters and other writings under pseudonyms. 'Vanessa' was Esther Vanhomrigh, who lived in Celbridge, County Kildare (at Barberstown Castle, see Hotels and Restaurants, page 280). Swift met her in London in 1708 and may even have fathered her child. She followed Swift to Ireland but broke off her friendship with him when he became involved with 'Stella'. The second great attachment of his life was another Esther (Johnson), with whom he had a deep but apparently platonic relationship. Memorials to Swift and Stella can be seen in St. Patrick's Cathedral (see page 71).

Georgian flowering Along with its architecture, Dublin's literary scene blossomed during the 18th century, a time of great intellectual ferment and scientific discovery. One of the giants of the era was the Dean of St. Patrick's Cathedral, Jonathan Swift. Probably the greatest satirist in the English language, he is most famous for *Gulliver's Travels*. He was a Protestant and obviously part of the Anglo-Irish Ascendancy, but some of his bitterest invective was directed against the cruel and unequal conditions of the Irish poor. In *A Modest Proposal* he attempted to stir up the complacent attitudes of the time by suggesting, deliberately outrageously, that Irish children should be fattened up for English tables.

Swift's contemporaries included William Congreve and George Farquhar, both of whom were educated at Trinity College, Dublin. Like many other Irish writers, however, they soon left for London, as did the later authors, Oliver Goldsmith and Richard Brinsley Sheridan. During the 19th century, dramatists who achieved greatest fame were Oscar Wilde and George Bernard Shaw (who lived on until 1950), both of whom, following the usual pattern, left their native land to dazzle London society.

The Gaelic Revival Meanwhile, however, another strand of writers began to receive attention in Dublin. At the end of the 19th century a renewed interest in all things Irish (the Gaelic Revival) was inspiring artists such as W. B. Yeats and his friend George Russell; Celtic myths interweave their work. The turn of the 20th century saw a great flourishing of theatrical talent, this time a home-grown version using Irish, specifically Gaelic, themes. John Millington Synge's works for the Abbey Theatre were among these, followed by the pacifist works of Sean O'Casey. Both these writers were controversial and aroused much furore when they broke away from the norms of light social comedy.

James Joyce The literary giant most closely associated with Dublin, James Joyce (1882–1941), is surprisingly not among Ireland's four Nobel Prize-winners (Beckett, Shaw, Yeats and Heaney), three of whom have strong links with the capital, too. Joyce, however, lived and breathed the place, although he always had a love–hate relationship with it and spent most of his adult life abroad. He referred to his native city as the 'centre of paralysis': 'How sick, sick, sick I am of Dublin. It is a city of failure, of rancour and unhappiness. I long to be out of it,' he wrote. The works in which Dublin appears, almost as the central character, are *A Portrait of the Artist as a Young Man*, *Ulysses*, *Dubliners* and *Finnegan's Wake*. Ironically, Joyce, spurned and hounded into exile while he lived, is now fêted by the tourist authorities as one of the city's greatest ambassadors—every step of his Dublin-set masterpiece *Ulysses* is carefully documented in self-guided walks and wall plaques. Keen followers of his work can buy a map and follow the route taken by Leopold Bloom on that famous 16th of June. The trail leads well out of the city centre to the southeast suburbs of Dalkey and Sandycove, with its James Joyce Tower that features in the opening chapter of *Ulysses*. Inside is a museum set up in 1962 by Sylvia Beach, original publisher of his great novel, containing Joycean memorabilia and some letters. Next to the tower is the Forty Foot Pool, where Buck Mulligan (based on Gogarty, see panel) swims at the start of *Ulysses*. Nearby Dalkey was the setting for Flann O'Brien's novel, *The Dalkey Archive*.

The prolific George Bernard Shaw

BRENDAN BEHAN
Of all the characters who trod Dublin's literary stage during the course of this century, few were more rambunctious than Brendan Behan—variously remembered as a lovable rogue or an arrogant sot— whose over-indulgence of Guinness contributed to his untimely death in 1964 at the ripe young age of 41. During his creative years, the pubs in Dublin were officially closed on St. Patrick's Day, and one of the few places where one could openly get a drink was at the annual dog show in the Royal Dublin Society's premises in Ballsbridge. On repairing there one St. Patrick's Day, Behan is said to have howled 'Who the hell brought a ****ing dog into a place like this, anyway?'—or words to that effect.

William Butler Yeats (1865–1939) from a drawing by his brother Jack B. Yeats, November 1896

Walk

A walk around literary Dublin

See map on pages 46–47.

Most of Ireland's great writers spent time in Dublin, and this walk explores some of their haunts.

Start off in Parnell Square, at the **Dublin Writers Museum**. Housed in a restored 18th-century mansion, this contains a fascinating collection of first editions, portraits, manuscripts and memorabilia. A couple of doors away is the **Hugh Lane Gallery▶▶** (see pages 56–57), where you can see works by Jack Yeats and a portrait of Maud Gonne, who drove his brother, W. B. Yeats, to heights of romantic distraction.
On the corner of Granby Row, the **National Wax Museum** displays effigies of the writers Joyce, Yeats,

It's worth looking up when visiting the Dublin Writers Museum

Shaw and O'Casey in a suitably bookish setting. In the centre of the square lies the Garden of Remembrance, a park commemorating all who have fallen for Irish freedom. Plans for the Easter Rising were made in a house nearby, and the captured rebels were held prisoner in this square overnight. The fountain pool and its swan sculptures by Oisín Kelly evoke the myth of the Children of Lir, turned into birds for 900 years (see page 236). The rest of Parnell Square is taken up by the **Rotunda Maternity Hospital▶▶** (see page 59). Founded in 1745, it has excellent plasterwork and woodcarving. Part of it is now the Gate Theatre, where many Irish and foreign playwrights staged productions from 1929 onwards.

Leaving Parnell Square at the southeast corner, head for North Great George's Street, where heartening restoration work of the fine Georgian houses has taken place. One of them (No. 35) contains the **James Joyce Centre**: library, bookshop, Joycean walks, lectures and more (tel: 01 873 1984). Belvedere House in Great Denmark Street is another well-preserved Georgian mansion, now a

On the Ulysses *trail along the streets of Dublin*

Jesuit college (Joyce was a former student). A detour up Temple Street North leads to Eccles Street, site of Leopold Bloom's fictional home in *Ulysses* (No. 7 no longer exists, though you can see the front door in the Bailey pub on Duke Street). Heading northeast, you reach St. Francis Xavier's Church, an ornate Jesuit building. Mountjoy Square was once home to several writers, this side of town having cheaper rents for impecunious writers than the classier, and more expensive, south bank. Sean O'Casey lived at No. 35 and later at 422 North Circular Road, using the area as the setting for *Shadow of a Gunman* and his other plays for the Abbey Theatre. Brendan Behan grew up in 14 Russell Street.

Continuing down Gardiner Street, you follow the same route as Leopold Bloom on that famous day in June 1904. Up Railway Street stood Bella Cohen's Brothel, immortalized in *Ulysses*, typical of many houses of ill repute in this area. Cutting down Waterford Street and Marlborough Street, note the Pro-Cathedral, Dublin's most important Catholic church. On Abbey Street is the **Abbey Theatre**, where many significant dramatic productions are staged. The theatre was first opened in 1904 under the auspices of Lady Gregory and W. B. Yeats. One of its most memorable productions was the first staging of John Millington Synge's *Playboy of the Western World*, which caused riots among the Dublin audience because of its depiction of a parricide and its mention of an item of female underwear ('shift'). Sean O'Casey's play, *The Plough and the Stars*, also caused a furore because it bravely refused to idolize the leaders of the Easter Rising. The Abbey was burned down in 1951, and rebuilt in a modern, blockish style. Once back on O'Connell Street there are more Joycean sites—Prince's Street, by the General Post Office, where Leopold Bloom worked at the *Freeman's Journal* and Graham Lemon's sweetshop.

Finish the walk over the bridge at Trinity College, in the Long Room, where the ghosts of many graduate *literati* stalk, from Swift and Goldsmith to Shaw and Wilde, connecting Ireland's current lively writing scene with those unknown monks who illuminated the Gospels of the *Book of Kells* in the 8th century.

One of many memorials to Joyce

The intricate beauty of the Tara Brooch, housed in the Treasury of the National Museum. Despite its name, it has no known connection with Tara in County Meath

▶▶ National Gallery *474B*

Merrion Square West, tel: 01 661 5133,
www.nationalgallery.ie
Open: Mon–Wed and Fri–Sat
10–5.30, Thu 10–8.30, Sun
12–5.30 Admission free

The National Gallery has about 2,000 works are on show at any one time, representing Irish, US and all other major European schools of art up to the 19th century. More recent works are on display at the Irish Museum of Modern Art, housed in the Royal Hospital, Kilmainham and the Hugh Lane Gallery (see page 56).

The National Gallery first opened in 1864, with only a tiny fraction of the paintings it now possesses. Much of it's growth was due to the energies of William Dargan, a railway magnate largely responsible for building Ireland's rail network. He was the moving spirit behind the Dublin Exhibition of 1853, using the profits to found the gallery, and his statue stands on the lawns near the entrance gate. The building was designed by Francis Fowke, who also designed the Victoria and Albert Museum in London.

The collection contains a number of works by Jack B. Yeats, brother of the poet, W. B. Yeats, which make a gritty contrast to the sentimental productions of other members of the Irish School. Other highlights include Degas's *Ballet Girls* and Caravaggio's *The Taking of Christ*. The Impressionists are well represented, as are Italian and Dutch schools and earlier French artists from the 17th century onwards. A fascinating collection of Irish portraits lines the grand staircase, culminating in the fiery Countess Markiewicz, who was furious at being pardoned for her part in the Easter Rising (see pages 54–55). There is also a coffee shop and restaurant. A new, ultra-modern wing has been added to house travelling exhibitions.

▶▶▶ National Museum of Archaeology and History *473B*

Kildare Street, tel: 01 677 7444, www.museum.ie
Open: Tue–Sat 10–5, Sun 2–5. Admission free

This museum houses many of the finest masterpieces of Irish Celtic art from the Bronze Age to the Middle Ages. Its greatest treasures (appropriately housed in the Treasury) include the Tara Brooch, the Ardagh Chalice, the Cross of Cong, the Shrine of St. Patrick's Bell and many other exquisite pieces of gold jewellery and croziers. The Tara Brooch is perhaps the most important, and most copied, of all Celtic jewels. It dates from the 8th century AD and is made of white bronze, silver gilt, amber

VIKING FOUNDATIONS
One of the first additions to the National Museum's collections was a Viking sword that came to light when the builders were digging the foundations for the museum just over a century ago.

and glass, and although it measures only about 5cm (2in) across, it is intricately decorated with scrolls, spirals and strange beasts on both sides. The Ardagh Chalice, from about the same period, is inspired by Byzantine art—a shapely wide goblet of gilded bronze, chased with gold filigree and studded with coloured glass.

A department called *Ar Thoir na Saoirse* (The Road to Independence) has mementoes of the Easter Rising and the Civil War, including a fragment of the flag flown over the General Post Office in 1916. Other sections contain superb porcelain of Irish, English, European and Asian origins, many items from Japan, rare textiles, glass, ceramics, silver and old musical instruments such as Irish harps and uilleann pipes. A particularly interesting section called 'Viking Age Ireland' shows what life was like for those fierce Norsemen, using exhibits from settlements in and around Dublin. Temporary exhibitions are regularly mounted. Collins Barracks (*Open* as all National Museums) in Phoenix Park has been taken over by the museum and now houses a growing collection of glass, silver, furniture and other decorative arts.

►► National Museum of Natural History   473B

Merrion Street, tel: 01 677 7444, www.museum.ie
Open: Tue–Sat 10–5, Sun 2–5. Admission free
This is part of the National Museum but is housed in a separate building. In a large hall, a crowded display of taxidermy can be seen, including a comprehensive collection of Irish mammals, birds, fish and insects, together with various mineral exhibits. Upstairs are animals from other parts of the world, while whales once stranded on the Irish coast now hang from the roof.

The gallery of Dublin's Natural History Museum

Weather permitting, it is never difficult to find a place to get away from the traffic noise in Dublin. The Georgian layout of the city naturally produced a system of spacious squares and landscaped gardens around its principal monuments, and Dublin is full of green open spaces, neat and municipal, or wilder and more natural.

Town squares The most famous of the Georgian squares is **St. Stephen's Green**, which was formerly common land. In 1880, Lord Ardilaun (heir to the Guinness fortunes) paid for the present gardens to be laid out, and they now encompass 8.5ha (21 acres) of lawns, flower beds, paved walks, shrubberies and an ornamental lake with wildfowl. Bandstands, statues and pergolas dot it at intervals; its various monuments include Henry Moore's memorial to Yeats and a statue of Wolfe Tone amid stone slabs ('Tonehenge'). The gardens are open during daylight hours, when they become one of Dublin's most popular spots for strolling or having a lunchtime sandwich.

   Merrion Square is another attractive open space dating from Georgian times. The restored Rutland Fountain is inset in its railings. During the Famine years (1845–1848) a soup kitchen was set up in this well-heeled residential square to feed starving refugees who poured in from the devastated country areas. Today you are more likely to find artists selling their wares on weekends.

Phoenix Park At the west end of the city lies the huge open space called **Phoenix Park**. It stretches along the Liffey for about 5km (3 miles) and covers 688ha (1,700 acres), about five times the size of London's Hyde Park. The park's name comes from the Gaelic *fionn uisce*, meaning 'clear water', referring to the spring in the Furry Glen. In it are lakes, woods, fields, a racecourse and sports grounds. It also contains Dublin Zoo (see page 56) and the headquarters of the *Garda Siochána*, or Irish police force. Its most striking monuments are the 60m (200ft) obelisk to Wellington and the Phoenix Column, erected in 1747 by Lord Chesterfield, a former lord lieutenant. The parklands once belonged to Kilmainham Priory, until they were seized during the Reformation, and later became a deer park owned by the Duke of Ormonde (deer still roam the park, descended from the original herd). During the 18th and 19th centuries, it was a fashionable place with desirable residences, one of which now houses the Irish president. The so-called 15 acres (now playing fields) were well known as a duelling place in the 18th century. Violence of a different type erupted in 1882 when Lord Cavendish, the chief secretary, and Burke, the undersecretary, were stabbed here by obscure malcontents called the Invincibles. The assassination caused a great furore at Westminster, where the question of Home Rule for Ireland was at last being seriously debated. The park's main entrance is at the southeast corner, off Parkgate Street.

The Three Fates quietly watch life pass by from their vantage point in St. Stephen's Green

68

Other green spaces A little way east lies **Arbour Hill Cemetery**, a quiet memorial garden where the leaders of the Easter Rising are buried, their names carved in stone beside a copy of the stirring proclamation of independence. Dublin's other interesting cemetery is in **Glasnevin**, in the north of the city, where lie the graves of Éamon de Valera, Gerard Manley Hopkins and Roger Casement (see page 43). Close by are Dublin's **National Botanic Gardens►►**, set up in 1795, and containing about 20,000 species of plants and trees, including specialist rose and vegetable gardens. The ornate glass-houses known as the Curvilinear Range were constructed by Richard Turner, a famous 19th-century iron founder also responsible for producing the Palm House in Belfast. Riverside walks lead through bog and peat gardens and the arboretum (tel: 01 837 4388).

One of Dublin's wilder spaces is **North Bull Island**, a strip of dunes and beaches off the coast, reached from the road to Howth. It is now a nature conservancy area, but visitors can walk out along the causeway to the lighthouse. You can see many species of birds there, and further information can be gleaned either from the guided tours or at the interpretative centre.

The Curvilinear Range of greenhouses at the Botanical Gardens

Poet James Mangan, St. Stephen's Green

▶▶ St. Ann's Church 473B

Dawson Street
Open: Mon–Fri 10–4 and Sun for
services. Admission free

This church's Italianate facade of 1868 in neo-Romanesque granite disguises an 18th-century interior including polished wood balconies and ornate plasterwork. Wooden shelves beside the altar were constructed to hold loaves of bread for the poor, a bequest left by Lord Theophilus Newtown.

▶ St. Mary's Abbey 462C

Meetinghouse Lane, tel: 01 872 1490
Open: Jun–end Sep Wed 10–5
Admission: inexpensive

Remnants of the Pale's most prominent Cistercian monastery, founded by the Benedictines in 1139, lie here. Much of the stone was removed to build Essex Bridge nearby, and only the chapter house still stands.

St. Ann's is built from pale granite interspersed with single courses of red brick

▶▶ St. Michan's Church 461C

Lower Church Street, tel: 01 872 4154
Open: Apr–end Oct Mon–Fri 10–12.45 and 2–4.45, Sat 10–12.45, Sun service at 10am; Nov–end Mar Mon–Fri 12.30–3.30, Sat 10–12.45, Sun service at 10am
Admission: inexpensive

In a run-down area at the back of the Four Courts, this church (begun in 1095) arouses a certain ghoulish excitement for the mummified corpses in its vaults. Visitors can only see them as part of a guided tour as access is via locked hatches outside the church walls. Their preservation is due to the hygroscopic action of the surrounding

SILKEN THOMAS
In 1534, the 10th Earl of Kildare, known as Silken Thomas for his love of fine clothing, mutinied against Henry VIII. He declared vengeance on the Henry at St. Mary's Abbey for his apostacy against the Catholic Church and the supposed beheading of his father (a false rumour). Thomas was captured and executed in 1537.

Some believe that one of the mummified bodies in St. Michan's Church is that of a medieval Crusader

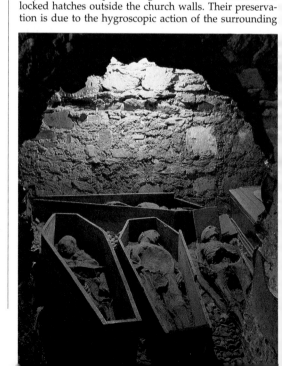

magnesian limestone, plus a few whiffs of methane gas from some subterranean disposal site. Handel is supposed to have played the organ here, and at the 'penitent's pew' malefactors knelt to make their offenses public.

▶▶ St. Patrick's Cathedral 462B

Patrick's Close, tel: 01 475 4817, www.stpatrickscathedral.ie Open: May, Sep–end Oct Mon–Fri 9–6, Sat 9–5, Sun 10–11 and 12.45–3; Jun–end Aug Mon–Fri 9–6, Sat 9–4, Sun 9.30–3 and 4.15–5.15; Nov–end Apr Mon–Fri 9–6, Sat 9–4, Sun 10–11 and 12.45–3. Admission: moderate

The precise status of this cathedral is a puzzle. Just a short distance down the road stands another Church of Ireland cathedral, Christ Church. The two have always been great rivals. St. Patrick's is the national cathedral, the home of the first university in Ireland (1320–1520), and is Ireland's largest church. It is legendarily associated with St. Patrick because of a neighbouring well, where the saint was believed to have baptized many converts. From 1191 onwards, the original church was replaced by the present building, much restored in the 1860s on the proceeds of Guinness. The cathedral stands in a desolate wasteland of tenement housing, outside the city walls. By far its most celebrated incumbent was Jonathan Swift, author of *Gulliver's Travels*, who was Dean here from 1713 to 1745 and is buried in the cathedral beside his beloved 'Stella', Esther Johnson. A plaque is inscribed with Swift's self-penned epitaph which, translated from the Latin, reads: 'Where fierce indignation can no longer rend the heart,/ Go traveller, and imitate, if you can, this earnest and dedicated champion of liberty'. Nearby is a memorial verse from Alexander Pope dedicated to Swift, and Swift's death mask, chair and writing table can be seen in the north pulpit. At the west end of the church is a 17th-century monument to the Boyle family. The young Robert (later to formulate Boyle's Law) is on the lowest tier. Mattins (9.45am) and evensong (5.35pm) are sung on most days.

Next to St. Patrick's is **Archbishop Marsh's Library▶▶** (tel: 01 454 3511), similar to (but smaller than) the Old Library of Trinity College. The barrel-vaulted upper room houses a wonderful collection of ancient leather-bound tomes in dark floor-to-ceiling cases. Several fascinating manuscripts, such as old herbals with beautiful plant illustrations, are separately displayed. Swift's annotated copy of Clarendon's *History of the Great Rebellion* is here, among 25,000 other volumes. Cages where readers could be locked in to consult valuable books can also be seen.

▶▶ Temple Bar 462C

The epicentre of Dublin's revival in the last decade has to be ultra-trendy Temple Bar. Renowned for its restaurants and nightlife, the narrow-streeted, cobblestoned area south of the Ha'penny Bridge also has some notable sights. **Meeting House Square▶▶**, named for a nearby Quaker house, is *the* gathering place for young Dubliners; in summer, a stage is erected in the open area for free performances. **Gallery of Photography** (tel: 01 671 4654; *open:* Tue–Sat 11–6, Sun 1–6. *Admission free*) has a permanent collection early 20th-century Irish photography. **The Ark** (tel: 01 670 7788; *open:* Mon–Sat 9.30–4. *Admission free*) is a children's cultural centre including an outdoor theatre.

CHANCING YOUR ARM
A curious feature in the nave of St. Patrick's Cathedral is a freestanding wooden door with a hole in it. This was formerly the chapter door of the south transept and is the subject of an intriguing tale. The warring earls of Kildare and Ormonde confronted each other at the cathedral in 1492, where Ormonde had barricaded himself inside the church for protection. The Earl of Kildare offered to make peace, and cut a hole in the door through which he thrust his arm to shake hands with Ormonde. The phrase 'chancing your arm' was born.

71

St. Patrick's has no crypt because the Poddle River flows directly beneath the cathedral

Dublin

AN ANCIENT THEFT

The *Book of Kells* was stolen one night from the western sacristy of the great stone church of Kells (Meath) in 1007. The *Annals of Ulster* tell that it was recovered after two months and twenty nights, 'its gold having been taken off it and with a sod over it'.

Above: The Old Library of Trinity College
Below: TCD's frontage extends for over 90m (300ft)

▶▶▶ Trinity College 473C

College Green, tel: 01 608 2308, www.tcd.ie
Open: daily 7am–10pm. Admission free

This single-college university was founded by Elizabeth I in 1592 on confiscated monastery land, ostensibly 'to civilize Ireland with both learning and the Protestant religion'. Small wonder, then, that it became a source of division in the city. Catholics were always allowed entry to the college, and free education—provided, of course, they converted; up until 1966, Catholics had to obtain a special dispensation to attend on pain of excommunication. Now, however, the proportion of Catholic students at TCD, as it is known, is about 70 per cent. The 'honour roll' is impressive: Edmund Burke, Jonathan Swift, Oliver Goldsmith, Bram Stoker, Wolfe Tone, William Congreve, Oscar Wilde, J. M. Synge and Samuel Beckett have all passed through these hallowed portals.

Today TCD occupies a prime location at the heart of Dublin, in an oasis of gardens and parks. Little remains of the original buildings; the imposing, classical facade and Corinthian columns give it an unmistakably 18th-century feel. Inside, like ancient English universities, its buildings are arranged around quadrangles of lawns and cobbles. The theatre, examination hall, chapel, dining hall and the old brick student accommodation known as the Rubrics can be seen as you pass from the Front Court to the Library Court. The campanile, by Charles Lanyon, marks the site of the original priory. To the right is the Old Library, where the *Book of Kells* is housed.

Since 1801, Trinity College has had the right under copyright law to claim a free copy of all British and Irish publications, and it now houses nearly 3 million volumes in eight buildings. About a kilometre (half a mile) of new shelving is needed every year to keep up with all the new publications.

Bus tours roll up to visit Trinity's concession to the tourist industry, a 40-minute video called *The Dublin Experience* that gives a brief history of the city in the Arts Building behind the library, from late May to October.

The intricate decoration and bright colours of this Latin text of the Gospels gives clear proof of the inventive skill and dedication shown by early Irish scholars. The glowing patterns illuminated not merely the pages of the text, but the whole of the Christian world.

The **Old Library of Trinity College**▶▶▶ houses about 2 million volumes, stacked in a double-decker layer of huge floor-to-ceiling shelving in 20 bays of a splendid cathedral-like hall accurately called the Long Room, measuring 64m by 12m (210ft by 39ft). The building was designed by Thomas Burgh in 1712; its barrel-vaulted ceiling was added in the 19th century in order to provide more much-needed shelf space. At the far end of the library are two harps, one of them traditionally associated with the great Irish king Brian Ború (926–1014), though actually from the 15th century. By far the most famous and precious of all the treasures in the Old Library of Trinity College is the 8th-century illuminated manuscript of the four Gospels, known as the *Book of Kells*. Inscribed in Latin on vellum parchment, its pages are magnificently ornamented with patterns and fantastic animals. The designs closely resemble the interlacing patterns found on Celtic metalwork and are obviously influenced by those traditions. Although the manuscript was certainly kept at the monastery of Kells in County Meath, there exists some doubt whether it was actually produced there, some authorities believing it may have been copied in Iona or Lindisfarne. The book's 680 pages were rebound during the 1950s into four separate volumes. Two of these are generally on display in the Old Library, with the pages being turned every so often to give a different view. Conservation of such a priceless document is of the utmost importance and a constant battle; you may have to be content with a facsimile version. The Colonnades is an exhibition area featuring annually changing displays and a well-stocked shop. Besides the *Book of Kells*, there are several similar manuscripts kept at Trinity—the *Book of Durrow*, the *Book of Dimma* and the less colourful *Book of Armagh*.

The startlingly beautiful and complex Book of Kells

73

THE OLD LIBRARY OF TRINITY COLLEGE
Tel: 01 608 2308. *Open:* May–end Sep Mon–Sat 9.30–5, Sun 9.30–4.30; Oct–end Apr Mon–Sat 9.30–5, Sun noon–4.30. *Admission: expensive.*

Genealogy is now big business in Ireland, and hundreds of visitors annually attempt to find their roots. Around 60 million people, mostly in North America and the Antipodes, are estimated to be of Irish descent. Of these, by far the largest number live in the US (40 million), 5 million live in Canada and another 5 million in Australia and New Zealand. The rest are somewhere in Britain or scattered around the globe.

74

Before it became the Heraldic Museum, No. 2 Kildare Street was the home of a gentlemen's club. On one of its columns (and visible from the road) are two monkeys playing the gentlemanly sport of billiards

An exhibit at Dublin's Heraldic Museum, showing the Irish harp

Finding your roots Ancestor-tracing is particularly popular in Dublin, where most of the records are held, and in the west of Ireland, which saw vast emigration during the Famine years. Ulster also has strong links with the New World; many 'Scotch-Irish' Protestant settlers have made their homes in Canada or the United States. In September 1992, Ireland staged a large cross-border Homecoming Festival. Along with the *ceilis* (evenings of folk music and dancing) and the *craich* (fun) went many more earnest events such as clan rallies and history seminars, and lots of hints on the tracing of forebears.

The great interest in origins is fostered by recent research overseas. Canada, for example, has carried out a detailed survey on Irish settlement of its Atlantic seaboard. For many people, a visit to Ireland is a chance to see the Old Country, to track down the family town or homestead, and perhaps look up a few living relatives.

Irish archives A burgeoning number of organizations and centres throughout Ireland will now help you draw your family tree. Increasingly, family records and databases are being computerized and interlinked, making it much quicker and easier to track down records that would have taken hours of patient poring over documents in the past. Inevitably, there's a cost involved, but unless your roots are particularly elusive, the charges are generally quite modest. You could just pay a small fee for a five-year search through the births, marriages and deaths certificates, or considerably more for a detailed survey of several generations, neatly documented. Research concentrates mainly on civil and parish records, census forms, wills, papers dealing with land or property transactions, etc.

Emigration records Irish data is somewhat patchy. In 1922, at the start of the Civil War, the Public Record Office, then housed at the Four Courts in Dublin, was shelled and many documents were lost (fortunately some copies were kept elsewhere). During the Famine years, scant records were kept of those who emigrated or died on the way—such was the despair and chaos of those times. The best bet is to start at the other end, where detailed immigration papers were completed in most American and Australian ports of entry. Seven volumes of immigrant records list every arrival into New York from 1846 to 1851 (*The Famine Immigrants*, published by the Baltimore Genealogical Publishing Company). Australia's records are also good, particularly of those who left Ireland on 'assisted passage' schemes, or who were deported for a criminal offence (often a trivial misdemeanour or political involvement—the chances of unearthing some serial killer in the family archives are small). Contact the National Library in Canberra, or the Mitchell Library in Sydney.

If you want to track down your Irish roots, try to do as much research as you can before you arrive. Living relatives, family papers and records in your own country are the first sources to tackle. Build up as complete a picture as you can of the ancestors who emigrated—full name, trade, religion and which town or county they came from. (Many emigrants named their new homes after their former parish or town, which can be a clue). When you arrive, visit one of the organizations or genealogy centres in the county of origin. It is wise to make an appointment in advance, especially during the summer. The Republic's tourist office, Bord Fáilte, produces an information sheet on tracing your ancestors, which contains useful advice, lists of publications and addresses. (Please enclose international reply coupons or a self-addressed stamped envelope if you write for advice.)

NORTHERN IRELAND ADDRESSES
Public Record Office of Northern Ireland, 66 Balmoral Avenue, Belfast BT9 6NY (tel: 028 9025 1318; www.proni.gov.uk). Ulster Historical Foundation, 12 College Square East, Belfast BT1 6DD (tel: 028 9033 2288). Association of Ulster Genealogists and Record Agents, Glen Cottage, Glenamehan Road, Belfast BT4 2NP.

PROVINCIAL ADDRESSES
Clare Heritage Centre, Corofin, County Clare (tel: 065 6837955). Mayo North Research and Heritage Centre, Enniscoe, Castlehill, Ballina (tel: 096 31809). Roscommon Heritage and Genealogy Centre, Strokestown (*Open:* May–end Sep; tel: 078 33380). Irish Family History Foundation, 1 Clarinda Park North, Dun Laoghaire, County Dublin. Irish Family History Society, P.O. Box 36, Naas, County Kildare (www.irish-roots.net)

DUBLIN ADDRESSES
The Heraldic Museum—full of arms, banners, crests and such like, 2 Kildare Street, Dublin 2 (tel: 01 661 8811). National Library, Kildare Street, Dublin 2 (tel: 01 661 8811; www.nli.ie). National Archives, Bishop Street, Dublin 8 (tel: 01 478 3711; www.national archive.ie). Births, Deaths and Marriages, Joyce House, 8–11 Lombard Street East, Dublin 2 (tel: 01 671 1000). Registry of Deeds, Henrietta Street, Dublin 1 (tel: 01 670 7500). Genealogy Bookshop, 3 Nassau Street, Dublin 2.

Banners in the Heraldic Museum add a colourful touch to ancestral history

Hotels

THE SHELBOURNE Dublin's grandest hotel is no less than an institution. The 19th-century Shelbourne, on the most fashionable 'Beaux Walk' stretch of St. Stephen's Green, is part of the nation's heritage; in the movie of Brian Moore's novel, *The Lonely Passion of Judith Hearne*, it is the ultimate proof of wealth and status. The Irish Free State's constitution was drafted here in an upper room. Despite its lofty pedigree, the Shelbourne is pleasantly unstuffy. Everybody is welcome, at least for a coffee or a drink in the Horseshoe Bar. For the restaurant, you are advised to dress up a little and remember your wallet. A head-to-toe renovation means the hotel will be closed until late 2007.

CHEAPER ALTERNATIVES If you find the Shelbourne's tariffs are a bit steep, there are plenty of other options, though nothing is inexpensive in Dublin anymore. The best bet if you want somewhere within reach of most of the sights and stores is to stay south of the river, somewhere around the St. Stephen's Green area, or farther out in the pleasant residential suburb of Ballsbridge. Many attractive Georgian town houses have been stylishly converted into guesthouses and small hotels, where you can glimpse something of Dublin's former glory in an appropriate setting. The Georgian House is probably one of the best, and also best-located, of these, with a lively seafood restaurant. An excellent and refreshingly different style is provided at No. 31 Leeson Close, in an architect's former home (see panel).

Farther south, the tariffs will be lower and the buildings more recent, probably Victorian or Edwardian. Be prepared for a bus or taxi ride to the city centre. Some of the best are Butlers Town House, Raglan Lodge, Ariel House and Merrion Hall. Elsewhere in the city, pick your location with care: Some areas are not particularly pleasant for walking after dark. The seedier dives around Connolly Station and off upper O'Connell Street are best avoided, and are not even particularly cheap. The Gresham Hotel,

NUMBER 31

One of Dublin's most surprising guesthouses lies hidden behind a high stone wall in a quiet cul-de-sac off Leeson Street. The former home of a leading architect, Sam Stephenson, it is now a coveted, small B&B. The centre of these double town houses has been gutted to create a large, sunken sitting room with a small bar. Huge breakfasts are served in an upper dining room overlooking a roof garden billowing with exotic vegetation, while intriguing objects bestrew the house. The rooms are simple, but all have good bathrooms. The atmosphere is civilized, but relaxed.

The Shelbourne faces St. Stephen's Green

Hotels

The Gresham Hotel, O'Connell Street

ISAAC'S
This popular hostel, also known as the Dublin Tourist Hostel, can be found a block or two behind the Custom House on the north bank of the Liffey. It is an agreeable conversion of a wine warehouse dating back to the early 1700s, and as far as possible its architectural features have been kept intact. For simple accommodation at a low price it is hard to beat. The self-service restaurant (*Open:* daily from 7.30am, and to nonresidents) serves cheap, filling fare with an emphasis on organic and vegetarian dishes. There is music laid on in summer. A similar hostel (with the same name) exists in Cork.

one of Dublin's best and longest-established, once in a prime location on O'Connell Street, now suffers from tacky surroundings.

If you want a hotel with all the trimmings, try one of the modern business hotels such as the Conrad or the Westbury. Buswell's, a favourite haunt of politicians and journalists, has more character and a certain 18th-century cachet. Jury's, the Dublin flagship of a well-known Irish hotel chain, or the Burlington can provide all possible facilities, including lively nightlife, in modern boxlike premises south of the river.

FARTHER OUT If you have a car, consider staying even farther out in the more peaceful suburbs, or on the coast, say in Dalkey or Blackrock. Parking in the city centre is always difficult, and a car is a constant security risk. Fitzpatrick Castle in Killiney is a good out-of-town choice, complete with fairytale turrets. There are many cheaper B&Bs in the coastal areas. It will be difficult to enjoy Dublin's night scene (or pubs) staying this far out, however.

HOSTELS AND SELF-CATERING If you are on a tight budget and want to stay centrally, consider a hostel. You may have to share a room, but an increasing number of decent, privately run hostel-style rooms are now available. Isaac's (see panel) is a good bet for young travellers. For slightly more comfort, Avalon House in Aungier Street (near the Carmelite Church) offers simple but stylish accommodation and a pleasant coffee shop.

Apartments and houses can be rented at all price levels, and some even have maid service. A number are listed in Bord Fáilte's self-catering (rentals) guide. There are no central campsites in Dublin: The nearest you'll get is somewhere south of Dun Laoghaire or in Donabate to the north of the city. Unofficial camping is not recommended and may be risky.

BOOK AHEAD Accommodation in Dublin is plentiful, but the best is not inexpensive and can fill up rapidly during special events or conferences. Book ahead if you can. The tourist office provides a booking service and will telephone around (for a fee) if you turn up on the spot. (See also Hotels and Restaurants, pages 269–283.)

Outside the Shelbourne Hotel

DUBLIN CODDLE

4 slices of bacon
4 large sliced potatoes
4 large sausages
black pepper
2 onions, sliced
cornflour
Place the bacon, sausages, potatoes and onion in a pot and cover with cold water. Bring to a boil and simmer gently for 1–2 hours until the meat is cooked. Thicken with cornflour, season with black pepper, and serve immediately with fresh soda bread.

Food and drink

A WIDER CHOICE Although Ireland cannot claim to be the gastronomic capital of the universe, the eating scene in Dublin is immeasurably better now than it used to be, with a far wider choice of cuisine, and more emphasis on healthy, high-quality ingredients rather than filling, high-fat dishes. Needless to say, there is plenty of fast food available, especially in areas north of the river. Most outlets are predictably indifferent, with the exception of a couple of good fish and chip shops (such as Burdock's) and pizza joints (like the Bad Ass Café). For gourmets, the city has plenty of choices in the classy town-house restaurants around St. Stephen's Green, most of which produce classic French *cuisine moderne* dishes, but you can expect to pay handsomely for the privilege there. The best of these (Patrick Guilbaud, Chapter One, Thornton's) have earned their high reputation; others verge on pretension.

For several years now Dublin has been home to a number of very good ethnic restaurants—the Rajdoot and Shalimar produce interesting Indian food, the Imperial and the China-Sichuan are the best of the Chinese restaurants, while, for Italian food, Il Primo and Nico's are recommended. Besides foreign cuisine, though, Irish cooking is making a healthy comeback, so you may try a Dublin coddle (boiled sausages, bacon, onions and potatoes in a thickened sauce; see panel) or oysters and Guinness. One of the most unusual restaurants serving Irish food is Gallagher's Boxty House, in the lively Temple Bar quarter. (A 'boxty' is a sort of Irish potato pancake with all kinds of savoury fillings.) The ambience and decor are agreeable and the prices not at all expensive, hence its popularity, although the food could be more reliable.

PUBS Dublin pubs concentrate on drinking rather than food, but the demands of tourism have meant that more and more serve snacks at lunchtime, though the selection is rarely particularly imaginative. A civilized touch, however, is that most will serve coffee at any time of day, including, of course, an Irish coffee. The mystique surrounding the serving of Guinness is less overt here than you might

Stop for refreshment in a Dublin café, like this one in O'Connell Street

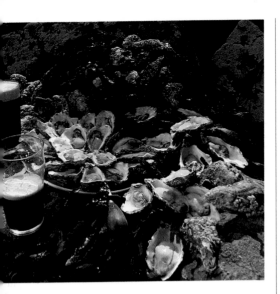

Two Irish favourites, oysters and Guinness

BROWN SODA BREAD
4½ cups wholewheat flour
1 cup white flour
1 teaspoon salt
1 teaspoon bread soda
⅓ cup oatmeal
2½ cups buttermilk
Sieve all the dry
ingredients together. Make
a well in the centre, pour
in the buttermilk, and stir
until the mixture forms a
soft dough. Turn on a
floured surface and knead
lightly to form a round disk
roughly 35cm (15in) in
diameter. Cut a deep
cross into the dough with
a sharp knife. Place on a
buttered baking dish and
bake in the middle of the
oven, 220°C (425°F), for
15 minutes, then reduce
the temperature to 180°C
(350°F) for a further 25
minutes until rich and
crusty. Cool on a wire rack.

79

expect, but if you look as though you would appreciate it, a shamrock might be etched deftly into the creamy head.

CAFÉS For lunchtime snacks some of the most attractive restaurants are in museums or shopping centres, such as the National Gallery, Hugh Lane Municipal Gallery, Kilmainham Hospital, Dublin Castle, Kilkenny Shop and the Powerscourt Townhouse. One place that cannot be ignored is that great institution known as Bewley's Café. A number of cafés were originally set up by a Quaker family of tea and coffee importers over a century ago to enable customers to sample their products. The most famous, Bewley's Oriental Café, survives on Grafton Street, a wonderful dark, mysterious emporium of stained glass and mahogany is now a pleasant café and pizza and pasta restaurant. Upstairs is a pricey fish eatery.

OTHER OPTIONS If you don't want to spend too much in the evenings, head for Temple Bar, which is young and upbeat. Restaurants here come and go with the wind, but some of the more long-lasting ones include the Elephant and Castle and the Bad Ass Café.

If you want an excursion, there are several excellent restaurants in some of the coastal resorts: Morel's in Dun Laoghaire, Ayumi-Ya in Blackrock or King Sitric in Howth are perhaps some of the best. Seafood is usually excellent. Check what days they close before you plan your excursion.

On Sundays, Dublin can be a desert as far as eating goes. Many of the good places are closed, and those that stay open are likely to be fully booked. If you are in the city on a weekend, plan your eating well ahead of time and make sure you have a table.

Cuisine more Italian than Irish is advertised on this wall in Cecilia Street

Shopping

MARKETS At the north end of Grafton Street is an eye-catching statue in bronze, affectionately known to Dubliners as 'the tart with the cart.' The subject, of course, is the famous Molly Malone (see panel), wheeling her wheelbarrow. To find today's Molly Malones, you will need to head for the old-fashioned street markets held in Moore Street (mostly selling fruit and vegetables, off Henry Street near the General Post Office), or alternatively the Liberties in Meath Street beyond Christ Church Cathedral, where dozens of stalls of inexpensive clothing and household goods are on sale. Georges Street Arcade is great for organic food and quirky clothing.

SHOPS FOR VISITORS Most visitor shopping is done in rather different surroundings, either in the safe, if highly priced, confines of a modern hotel, or in one of the city's specialist shops. The main shopping area in the centre of town lies between Grafton Street and O'Connell Street. The big department stores are there—Clery's and Eason's north of the river (along with Marks and Spencer and bargain basement shops such as Dunne's in the Ilac Centre or Arnotts), and more exclusive Brown Thomas in Grafton Street. Many international chain stores such as Benetton, Next and Principles can also be found around pedestrianized Grafton Street. Smaller side streets contain most specialist craft and fashion shops. Nassau Street is a good area to head for if you are looking for typical Irish craft products such as ceramics, knitwear, tweed, linen, crystal or Celtic jewellery. The outlets vary considerably in quality, one of the best being the excellent Kilkenny Shop, with a fine stock of traditional Irish crafts. Others worth checking out (also situated in Nassau Street) are the exclusive tweed and clothing store, Kevin and Howlin, the Sweater Shop for Aran knitwear, Blarney Woollen Mills and the House of Ireland. For traditional Irish music, Claddagh Records (2 Cecilia Street) and Celtic Note (Nassau Street) are among the best shops.

MOLLY MALONE
In Dublin's fair city where the girls are so pretty I first set my eyes on sweet Molly Malone. She wheeled a wheelbarrow through streets broad and narrow Crying 'Cockles and mussels, alive, alive-O!'

Nassau Street has a fine range of shops, from second-hand bookshops to retail outlets more geared to visitors

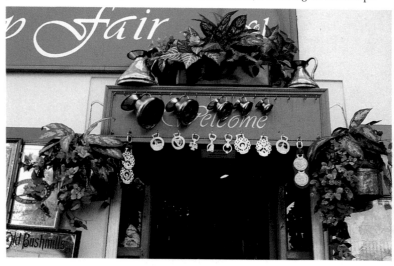

Dublin boasts a number of shopping malls. One of the best is in the imaginatively reconstructed shell of an 18th-century building, called the Powerscourt Townhouse, with splendid plasterwork ceilings and exterior facade (just off Grafton Street). Another central shopping mall is on St. Stephen's Green, an unmissable, modern, greenhouse-like structure with yet more shops and cafés. Tierney's has one of the better craft displays here.

Bookshops are legion in this literary city, most of them around St. Stephen's or College Greens or the quaysides. Several of these sell collectable second-hand volumes. Fred Hanna's (27/29 Nassau Street), Greene's (Clare Street), Hodges Figgis (54 Dawson Street) and Stokes (Georges Street Arcade) are some of the best known, besides the larger and more general retailers, Waterstone's and Eason's. For antiques, head for Francis Street in the Liberties (beyond Christ Church Cathedral).

BEYOND THE CENTRE Out of the city centre, the suburbs of Blackrock and Dalkey have their own shopping complexes and markets, not necessarily worth a special trip. The malls at Tallaght, Dundrum and Blanchardstown, however, merit a visit. Closer into town on Pearse Street (take a bus two or three stops from Pearse Station) is the Tower Design Centre, a 19th-century sugar-refining tower now run by the Irish Development Authority and housing about 35 separate craft enterprises producing souvenirs in fashions, stained glass, painted silk, knitwear and jewellery.

PRACTICALITIES Shopping hours in Dublin are generally Monday to Saturday, 9am–6pm, with some of the smaller shops geared to visitors (as well as Marks and Spencer and Brown Thomas) also opening on Sundays. For non-EU residents, the VAT waiver scheme called Cashback makes high-taxed Irish goods more attractive, although there is a fair bit of red tape involved in claiming this back at Dublin or Shannon Airport. Collect a form as you shop, and have it stamped when you leave the country.

Shopping is an enduring pastime for these two Dubliners

81

A crowd-pulling display in Brown Thomas, Grafton Street, one of Dublin's most famous shops

JOYCEAN PUBS

In The Bailey (Duke Street) Joyce fans can find the door of No. 7 Eccles Street, the fictional home of Leopold Bloom in *Ulysses*, rescued by the pub's proprietor, John Ryan, from a builder's skip. At Davy Byrne's, you can be served a faithful version of the lunch Bloom enjoyed there on 16 June 1904 (Bloomsday)—a glass of burgundy and a Gorgonzola sandwich.

The capital has a thriving youth culture

Nightlife

DECISIONS, DECISIONS Dublin is famous for its pubs—over 900 of them if you care to count—and for its theatre. These form the core of the city's evening entertainments. Like most capital cities, however, it can offer much more—many kinds of music, from rock to classical, around two dozen cinema screens, and a whole host of nightclubs and wine bars. Some larger hotels offer well-advertised cabaret shows, Jury's being the most widely publicized.

Over the last decade a host of clubs has sprung up around the city centre, especially in the Temple Bar area. Youthful Spirit, and the dance hothouse known as PoD, are two of the most popular. They are at their liveliest on weekends (Thursday to Sunday) and get going after 10pm. Check out also Lillie's Bordello, off Grafton Street, and Rí-Rá off South Great George's Street.

PUBS Pubs and bars are scattered all over the city and take innumerable forms, some modern and plastic, others ancient and Victorian, most of them somewhere in between, suitably 'modernized' for visitors. The 'pub of the moment' is difficult to pin down, with fashions changing, although regulars may stick to one or two favourites all the time. Most of the well-known places are very busy at night despite the high cost of alcohol in Ireland. They seem generally good-tempered, but they can be very noisy and boisterous. Some have notable gay scenes; others may be popular with drug users, of which Dublin has many.

Some of the best-known and most 'characterful' bars on the south side are Doheny and Nesbitt (5 Lower Baggot Street), O'Donoghue's (Merrion Row), Toner's (139 Lower Baggot Street), Neary's (1 Chatham Street); farther west are the Stag's Head (1 Dame Court, off Dame Street) and Mother Redcap's (Back Lane, off High Street). Near the Liffey, upriver from O'Connell Street, the Brazen

In 1897, the Star of Erin music hall changed its name to the Empire Palace. A few years later it became the Olympia Theatre, as it remains to this day.

Head (20 Lower Bridge Street) and Ryan's (28 Parkgate Street) still have old-fashioned interiors. Ryan's is a confection of mahogany and brass unchanged since 1896. The Brazen Head claims to be Ireland's oldest, where Wolfe Tone and Robert Emmet dreamed of Irish independence. Davy Byrne's and the Bailey (both in Duke Street) have Joycean associations that keep them eternally popular.

MUSIC AND THEATRE Many of the pubs offer evening music sessions, Irish traditional, jazz, etc. Whelan's (and its sister Venue The Village next door) on Wexford Street is a top live-music venue for local and UK bands. Dublin, of course, has launched many a rock or pop star on the way to fame and fortune: U2, the Chieftains, the Dubliners, Sinéad O'Connor and Chris de Burgh have all performed in Dublin's nightspots on many occasions. For more classical music, head for the National Concert Hall in St. Stephen's Green; the Royal Hospital at Kilmainham also stages a number of concerts and evening events. One of the theatres offers music on weekends—Midnight at the Olympia on Fridays and Saturdays involves dancing between aisles of plush red seating. Earlier in the evening (and during the week) it usually offers an assorted range of lightentertainment. The Gaiety is similarly popular. For more heavyweight theatre, head for the Gate or the Abbey, where Dublin's great theatrical tradition started. The annex to the Abbey, called the Peacock, and the Project in Temple Bar, specialize in avant-garde or experimental work.

FILM There isn't much of an art film scene in Dublin, although some films may be released three to four months later in Dublin, than in New York. Most of the two dozen screens on or near O'Connell Street are fairly run-of-the-mill or downright seedy. For an alternative, head for the Irish Film Institute in Temple Bar. There are some cinemas in the suburbs (such as in Blanchardstown and Tallaght). To find out what's going on in Dublin, get the *Irish Times*, which has daily listings, or the magazine *Big Issue*, sold by street vendors all over the city.

THE ABBEY THEATRE
The Abbey is one of Dublin's most classic traditions, yet it has staged some controversial productions. The first performance of J. M. Synge's *The Playboy of the Western World* in 1907 caused riots because an Irishman used the word 'shift' (meaning petticoat) on stage. Police had to be called to protect Synge from the outraged audience for over a week. In 1926, O'Casey's play *The Plough and the Stars* caused a similar uproar when the national flag was shown in the presence of a prostitute. After a later production of this play in 1951, the theatre burned down (accidentally).

83

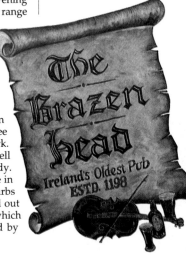

The Rubrics at TCD

SIGHTSEEING TOURS

Dublin Bus runs sightseeing bus tours of Dublin using open-top vehicles (covered in wet weather). The heritage tour visits 10 locations near city sights, and with an all-day ticket you can hop on or off at any point. Buses run hourly between 10AM and 4PM in high season.

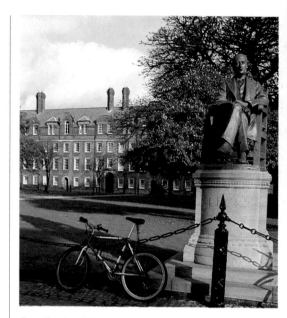

84

Dublin's coat of arms embellishes this street sign

Practical points

WHAT'S HAPPENING Dublin is an exceptionally friendly city and most people will be only too happy to help you out. Dublin Tourism Centre (tel: 01 605 7799; www.visitdublin.com; *open:* Mon–Fri 9–6; later in high season) is in Suffolk Street. It is usually crowded, but there are many leaflets to pick up, not all of which are free. Walking tours around the city are also advertised here, and can be fun and informative. Another useful start to city orientation is the Dublin Experience show at Trinity College, on view during the summer months.

If you are short of time, plan carefully and cut out extraneous attractions. Some of the big sights close for part of the weekend or on Monday, and Dublin Castle is occasionally shut altogether. Ask before you set off. Things not to miss are the Castle, Trinity College and the National Museum and Gallery. Try to catch some of the Georgian architecture around Merrion Square and St. Stephen's Green, and the two cathedrals to the west of the city. If you can, visit Kilmainham Gaol and Hospital, and walk in Phoenix Park. Art lovers will want to find Hugh Lane's Gallery, and, if the lighter side of culture appeals, head for the Guinness Brewery and Storehouse. Choose a promising-looking day for excursions to Howth or Dalkey; the best beaches lie around Killiney Bay or Sandymount (some dangerous currents). There is also a magnificent stretch of sand on North Bull Island.

If you happen to be in Dublin during a big match, you'll certainly be aware of it. Gaelic games are played at Croke Park, north of the city centre. The All-Ireland Hurling and Football Finals take place in September. St. Patrick's Day (17 March) is a fine time to be here, with parades and other happenings, although celebrations are smaller than in New York and Boston, for example. To find out what's going on, get a listings magazine (the best is *Big Issue*).

CITY TRANSPORT A bus map is worth getting. Although the central areas are reasonably compact, hopping on a bus can be welcome. The routes, if not always the schedules, are more or less adhered to. Most of them start from Busáras, the main station, just north of the river near the Custom House, or from the streets near College Green. If you plan to do much exploring, it is worth getting a pass lasting one or several days. The words *An Lár* on the front of a bus indicate it is going to the city centre. For longer trips, contact Bus Eireann's offices at the central bus station in Store Street. A branch of Thomas Cook (118 Grafton Street, tel: 01 677 1721) can answer general travel inquiries. For youth travel and student discounts, contact the USIT office on Aston Quay. The new Luas tram service runs right through the heart of the city.

For travel to the nearest coast, the DART (Dublin Area Rapid Transit) route, a single rail line between Greystones and Howth, is an entertaining excursion with fine coastal views. You can catch the DART trains at Connolly, Tara Street or Pearse stations. For train services farther afield (between Dundalk and Arklow), you should head for the main station, Connolly. Heuston Station serves the western and southern regions.

Taxis can be hailed in transit, but they also queue on some of the main streets, and are fairly expensive. Parking is always difficult and costly in the city centre. Never leave anything remotely valuable in your car.

CRIME The problems of urban life have caused a sharp rise in street crime generally, exacerbated by drug and alcohol abuse. Conspicuous visitors are easy prey. Don't carry too much money, and don't stray into unknown areas off the main tourist trail. The streets west of St. Patrick's Cathedral, or many north of the river, are not advisable for unscheduled sauntering.

ROCK 'N' STROLL
Self-guided walks around Dublin inevitably focus on its Georgian architecture or literary associations, or perhaps pub crawls for the thirsty. An alternative themed walk is the Rock 'n' Stroll Guide, which leads its followers to the principal places in Dublin associated with the contemporary music scene. Revisit The Chieftains' first gig at the Gresham Hotel, Mary Black's stamping ground at the Olympia, or U2's launch pad in Mount Temple Comprehensive School! Pick up the tour guide in any tourist office.

85

O'Connell Bridge, at the heart of the city

EASTERN COUNTIES The counties immediately around Dublin constitute the Pale, the area most strongly influenced by English rule from Norman times onwards. What lay beyond the Pale was less easily subjugated and often perceived (accurately) as a threat to English interests. The pull of the capital ensures these eastern counties still receive a steady flow of visitors, though scenically (with the exception of Wicklow) they are not Ireland's most exciting regions. There are, though, a good many reasons to spend time here. They are enormously rich in history, layer upon layer of it from prehistoric to recent times. The famous passage graves at Newgrange are Ireland's best-known neolithic site. Then there are Celtic High Crosses, the evocative monastic settlement of Glendalough, many later abbeys and churches, castles, and several of Ireland's grandest houses and gardens. Horse lovers will want to visit the Curragh at Kildare and the nearby National Stud. For walkers, the heather moors and wooded glens of the Wicklow Mountains bristle with opportunities. If you are thinking of a beach holiday in Ireland, the drier, sunnier climate of the southeast makes a seaside stay a reasonable gamble instead of a long shot. The best beaches in this region are in County Wicklow.

County Louth is the smallest of the 32 counties of Ireland. Inland, it echoes the drumlin country of those other border counties, Cavan and Monaghan, a gentle, placid landscape of little hills and lakes. Its easterly section is more dramatic, a precursor of the Mountains of Mourne that loom enticingly across Carlingford Lough. The Cooley Peninsula, setting for one of Ireland's greatest epics (*Táin Bo Cuailgne*—the Cattle Raid of Cooley), makes a fine excursion, where the lakeshore village of Carlingford is one of the most delightful low-key holiday bases, managing to avoid (for the most part) the strains of other border towns such as Dundalk or Monaghan. Drogheda, Louth's other main town, seems to have weathered its Cromwellian torments more resiliently than most and amply repays a stop, or even a stay. All around it, stretching into County Meath, is a rich cluster of prehistoric and Celtic sites, great abbeys and castles,

The gentle aspect of the Wicklow Mountains

THE LITTLE GENTLEMAN IN BLACK VELVET

This favourite Jacobite (supporter of the deposed King James II of England) toast during the reign of Queen Anne is still drunk in certain nationalist and Catholic circles. The 'little gentleman' is the mole that is alleged to have killed William III. When, while out riding in England on 21 February 1702, his horse, Sorrel, stumbled on a mole-hill and threw him, badly fracturing his collarbone. The king died in London two weeks later. If this sounds a heartless tradition, the anti-Catholic toasts of the Orange Order are much more savage. The 19th-century British prime minister, Sir Robert Peel, apparently drank to these in his early life, and became nicknamed 'Orange Peel' by the Irish.

the Hills of Slane and Tara suffused with legends and national symbolism. The Boyne River is a place of pilgrimage for many tracing the progress of that famous battle of 1690 along alternate banks, although this was only one of numerous skirmishes between Jacobite and Williamite troops in those troubled years.

DUBLIN'S HINTERLANDS Closer to Dublin, the coast is studded with small fishing ports, most fairly dull. Howth and Malahide are the ones to visit—the first for its breezy headland views and castle gardens, the second for an interestingly furnished castle and art collection. The capital's immediate hinterland is County Kildare, where the rolling, springy grassland provides pasture and an exercise track for dozens of fine-boned thoroughbreds. This is the heart of Ireland's bloodstock industry, one of the more solid mainstays of Ireland's economy. Keen followers of horse-racing may want to time their arrival carefully to coincide with one of the big annual races. Naas (the county seat) holds its big race meeting in April, at Punchestown Racecourse. The Curragh, famed for horse-racing since time immemorial, hosts all of Ireland's classic events—the Oaks, the Derby, and the St. Leger.

Naas, Kildare's county town, is near enough to all this to benefit from horse-borne prosperity and far enough from Dublin's suburban tentacles to have a spirit of its own. It makes one of the best places to pause and plan a route. If horses aren't your scene, you can search for Round Towers and Celtic High Crosses, follow the great canal routes that crisscross the county, or investigate the mournful Bog of Allen, where there is an interesting interpretative centre explaining the significance of bogland ecology: Bog of Allen Mature Centre, Lullymore, near Rathangan (tel: 045 60133). Kildare's most important stately home is Castletown; one of Ireland's largest houses, Castletown is built in the Palladian style.

South of Dublin lies County Wicklow, one of the capital's favourite 'lungs'. A glance at its topography soon indicates why—the Wicklow Mountains reach a significant altitude by Irish standards (Lugnaquillia is Ireland's third-highest peak at nearly 1,000m/3,039ft) and contain

The lonely Vale of Glenmacnass in the Wicklow Mountains just south of Dublin. Glenmacnass means 'the valley of the sons of Neasa'

some very beautiful and unpopulated scenery. The coastline, too, has attractions—breezy headlands and great sweeps of sand stretching from Bray southward, the best being Brittas Bay south of Wicklow Head. A journey over the central heights is most rewarding; choose one of the routes around the Sally Gap and take in the awe-inspiring views around Glencree and Glenmacnass, or seek out the hidden lakes of Tay and Dan. Powerscourt Gardens and Russborough House shouldn't be missed; ensure you time your visit to find them open. The other 'unmissable' is Glendalough, a collection of ancient monastic buildings in a gorgeous setting. Wicklow's impressive range of sights also includes the great gardens of Kilruddery and Mount Usher, and Charles Stewart Parnell's house at Avondale, now a forest park and museum to his memory. There is no shortage of excellent accommodation or restaurants in County Wicklow; its nearness to Dublin ensures a steady year-round trade and the county exudes a quietly prosperous air.

The most famous parts of the Boyne Valley and the holiday resorts of the east coast are also pretty well equipped, and County Kildare has a number of good places to stay or eat. The less popular regions of Louth and Meath, however, offer rather patchy choices and a fair amount of forward planning is necessary to stay anywhere pleasant. If you have time to spare, it's worth reaching Carlingford.

The tower of Trim Abbey, as seen from the town's castle

LEINSTER TABOOS
In ancient Ireland, the lives of kings and other notabilities were hedged in by taboos, doubtless going back into the mists of prehistory. Death was the inexorable outcome of these being violated one by one, a subject beloved of the dramatic storytellers of medieval Ireland. Five taboos recorded for the king of the Leinstermen included those forbidding him from:
- travelling widdershins (counterclockwise) around the Wicklow Hills on a Wednesday;
- sleeping between Dublin and the Dodder River with his head facing to one side;
- setting up camp for nine days on the plains of Cualu (Bray);
- travelling alone on the road to Dublin on a Monday;
- riding on a dirty, black-hooved horse over the plain of Mullaghmast (County Kildare).

The meaning of the interwoven spirals, found on several stones at Newgrange, remains unclear

THE BOYNE VALLEY

Drive

From prehistory to 1690 along the Boyne Valley

A drive through the past from prehistoric times to Ireland's most significant battle site, whose divisive echoes reverberate more than 300 years later in the streets of Belfast and London. (It is recommended that you follow the precise route of this drive on a detailed, large-scale map.)

Head north from Drogheda on the R132. Clearly signed to the west are the High Crosses and Round Tower of **Monasterboice** (see page 106). Looping back south again by the Mattock Valley, watch for signs to the remains of **Mellifont Abbey**, in a maze of quiet lanes (see page 105). About 6.5km (4 miles) west of **Drogheda** (signed off the N51 from the town) is the historic **King William's Glen**, site of the famous Battle of the Boyne in

1690. An orange and green sign by the river marks the main site of conflict. A marked trail from the Townley Hall Estate (the extensive grounds of a Georgian mansion) leads to a viewing place above the battleground showing where the opposing armies camped, and where William's army crossed the river from the north at two separate points, taking the forces of James II on the southern banks by surprise. An explanatory diagram and display board outlines the battle manoeuvres. It is worth getting a leaflet or map (available from local tourist offices) showing the battle sites if you want to explore in detail, since dodging back and forth across the river can be disorientating. The battle route passes the Boyne Navigation Canal, part of a grand scheme to connect Ireland's major waterways.

The battle was a historical landmark for many reasons, a minor point of interest being that it was the last conflict in Europe in which opposing monarchs played an active military role; William III himself narrowly escaped death from a sniper's bullet on the morning of the battle. His soldiers used sprigs of leaves to

A mural on a cottage near Drogheda celebrates the famous battle

distinguish themselves from the Jacobite forces, since they wore no clearly recognizable uniforms. As they crossed the river they played the Orange marching tune *Lillebulero*. Gradually, James's forces were pushed back south towards **Duleek**, where one of Ireland's oldest stone churches once stood. St. Ciarán's was built in the 5th century soon after Christianity first reached Ireland. The remains now visible date from later centuries. The final skirmish of the Battle of the Boyne took place at Duleek, and William is thought to have spent the night after the battle near there. Buried in the churchyard is Lord John Bellew, a Catholic who died at the subsequent Battle of Aughrim. He was shot in the stomach and is said to have died bravely, facing his enemies.

Farther west lie some of Ireland's most important neolithic remains, including the passage graves of Dowth, Knowth and Newgrange, collectively known as **Brugh na Boinne** (see pages 108–109). Besides the main tombs, at least 40 other burial places are believed to lie in and around this fertile farmland within a strategic bend of the Boyne River. Some of these sites have not yet been excavated, although from the Newgrange tomb several strange humps and mounds are clearly visible in the surrounding landscape.

Kells (formerly known as **Ceanannus Mór**), up the Blackwater Valley, is best known for the *Book of Kells*, a splendid illuminated manuscript now housed in Trinity College Dublin (see page 73). Many other antiquities and sacred sites are clustered along the Boyne Valley around **Slane**, **Navan**, **Tara**, seat of the High Kings of Ireland, and **Trim** (see their respective entries throughout this chapter; the Hill of Tara is on page 107). Castles dating from more recent times are scattered throughout the region. Trim itself has an enormous fortress, the largest dating from Norman times. The evocative ruins of **Bective Abbey** are also worth looking for on the peaceful meadows by the river between Trim and Navan.

This simple church at Kells dates from the first millennium

▶▶ Avoca
863B

Avoca, a pretty hamlet of neat white cottages in a wooded setting by the meeting of the Avonbeg and Avonmore rivers, is the home of Avoca Handweavers. They produce some of Ireland's most energetically marketed craft products from a group of whitewashed buildings containing the oldest surviving handweaving mill in Ireland, dating from 1723. The business was built up over 40 years by the Wynne sisters, who claim to have invented the car blanket! Bright tweeds of natural fibres are manufactured (mostly on modern machinery) and made into hats, suits and voluminous cloaks. High-quality Avoca products can be found all over the country. Bus tours converge to watch weaving demonstrations, enjoy good lunches or teas in the café, and (perhaps) take something home with them.

Avoca Handweavers give daily demonstrations of their craft

▶▶ Avondale
863B

Deep in one of County Wicklow's most beautifully wooded areas is the Georgian birthplace and home of the 19th-century politician Charles Stewart Parnell, now a museum dedicated to his memory. Parnell was one of Ireland's greatest campaigners for democracy and land reform. Though at first regarded by the English as a dangerous revolutionary because of his association with the Irish Land League, he eventually won Gladstone's abiding respect and persuaded many people that Home Rule was a viable option for Ireland. His career foundered abruptly after his long-standing liaison with the wife of a fellow Member of Parliament became public knowledge (see panel). Soon after divorce proceedings were instituted, Parnell was ousted from his political position and died of strain and ill-health. A film relates the background to Parnell's life story and the history of the house, which is interestingly furnished and contains many touching mementoes and political cartoons. Some of his eloquent love letters to Kitty O'Shea are framed on the walls, as is the extensive Parnell family tree, many of whose members died tragically of madness, vaccination, fevers or grief.

The grounds were taken over by the state in 1904 as a forestry school. Much research on arboriculture is conducted there and the forest park is full of fine and flourishing trees of many different species. Walks lead through the 200ha (500-acre) park by the riverside.

PARNELL AND KITTY O'SHEA

Parnell fell in love with Kitty, wife of Captain Willy O'Shea, by whom she had three children. It was not a successful marriage, however, and the two spent long periods apart, constantly impecunious. She first met Parnell outside the House of Commons in London, and the attraction was instant. Within a short time the two were secretly living together, and Parnell fathered her remaining children. O'Shea put up with the situation at first, hoping for the inheritance from Kitty's wealthy aunt. When his chances were dashed, he sued for divorce. (See also pages 42–43.)

▶ Bray

Bray is a convenient place for Dublin's citizens to get a breath of sea air, though it cannot be described as the most exciting piece of Ireland's coastline. It is the southerly terminus of the DART suburban railroad line from Dublin, so is easily reached without a car. The best views are from Bray Head, the final projection of the Wicklow range, from where the Great and Little Sugar Loaf mountains can be seen. North of Bray is the long sandy beach of Killiney Bay.

Bray has literary associations with James Joyce, who lived briefly at 1 Martello Terrace, which featured in *A Portrait of the Artist as a Young Man*. It is now privately owned and not generally open to the public. A more accessible place of interest is **Kilruddery House and Gardens▶** (tel: 01 286 2777; *open:* May, Jun and Sep. *Admission: expensive*) to the south of the resort, a rare example of 17th-century landscaping. Ponds, avenues, parterres and hedges are laid out with mathematical precision. The house dates from the 1650s (extensively remodelled in the 1820s) and contains many interesting features—Grinling Gibbons carving, Chippendale furniture and a water-powered stable clock.

▶▶ Carlingford

The most enjoyable place on the Cooley peninsula (see page 96) is Carlingford, between the green slopes of Slieve Foye and the blue waters of the lake, with the Mourne Mountains beyond. This delightful village is by far the best base in the area, with several excellent, inexpensive pubs and guesthouses. For its modest size, it has some imposing monuments, indicating that it was a place of some significance during the Middle Ages. King John's Castle stands on the north side of the harbour, a massive D-shaped fortress dating from the 13th century. Its opposite number is Greencastle, on the Northern Irish side of the lake. In the village itself are Taafe's Castle and the Mint, both fortified houses, and the old town hall, or Tholsel, an arched gateway.

Avondale House is famous as the birthplace of Charles Stewart Parnell. In the surrounding Forest Park you may be fortunate enough to catch sight of an otter

DROGHEDA ALE

'Of one part of its manufactures, every traveller must speak with gratitude—of the ale namely, which is as good as the best brewed in the sister kingdom…And while satisfying himself of this fact, the philosophic observer cannot but ask, why ale should not be as good elsewhere as at Drogheda: is the water of the Boyne the only water in Ireland whereof ale can be made?'

William Makepeace Thackeray (1842)

The banner of a local fishermen's guild now in the Millmount Museum, Drogheda

▶▶▶ Castletown House 862C

Celbridge, Co. Kildare, tel: 01 628 8252, www.heritageireland.ie
Open: Apr–end Sep Mon–Fri 10–6, Sat–Sun 1–6; Oct Mon–Sat 10–5, Sun 2–5; Nov–end Mar Sun 2–5
Admission: moderate

This huge stately home is rated as one of the finest examples of Palladian (classical) architecture in the Republic. It has many intriguing features, and has been extensively restored by the Irish Georgian Society. It was built in 1722 for William Connolly, Speaker of the Irish House of Commons, who made a fortune from forfeited estates after the Battle of the Boyne—it is hardly surprising that local attitudes to the house have been somewhat ambivalent. Designed by Alessandro Galilei in the style of an Italian villa, it contains wonderful plasterwork by the Francini brothers, and a sumptuous Pompeiian Long Gallery with splendidly hideous Murano chandeliers. The extensive grounds feature clipped yew trees and a folly obelisk. Though no longer lived in, its contents clearly reveal the character and tastes of its former owners. Lady Louisa Connolly, who married in 1758 at the age of 15, was one of its most influential collectors and decorators. An extravagant woman in some ways, she appears more compassionate and socially aware than many of her class, declaring when faced with the gargantuan banquet menus of the time, 'It can never be right or useful that one set of people should be gorged with food and the other part in want.'

▶▶ Drogheda 862D

This was originally a Viking town, later expanded into one of Hugh de Lacy's principal Norman strongholds, although little remains of the old town walls. In 1412, the two parts of the town on either side of the Boyne were united by charter to become the largest English town in Ireland; something of this ancient medieval pattern can still be seen in the hilly streets. The Millmount to the south side is topped by an 18th-century military barracks and fort, with a view of the northern part of the town and the viaduct.

Drogheda stands at the lowest bridging point of the Boyne River, just a short distance from the site of the famous battle of 1690. Wartime violence was nothing new; in 1649 Drogheda saw one of Cromwell's bloodiest assaults. Women and children who took refuge in one of its churches were burned alive and the defending garrison, driven south of the river to the hilltop Millmount Fort, were massacred after their surrender. The garrison commander, an English royalist, was battered to death with his own wooden leg. 'I think that we put to the sword altogether about 2,000 men', Cromwell wrote smugly. 'It is right that God alone should have all the glory.' Today the Millmount Fort houses a strangely peaceful collection of items in the excellent, privately run **Millmount Museum▶▶** (tel: 041 983 3097; *open*: Mon–Sat 9.30–5, Sun 2–5. *Admission: inexpensive*)—medieval guild banners, old trade machinery and tools and a coracle made of willow and leather. Other sections of this garrison have been converted into craft studios and a restaurant.

Over the river again, several buildings in the densely packed main town catch the eye: the 1224 Magdalene Tower, last remnants of a Dominican friary; the fine 13th-century St. Laurence Gate, surmounted by two drum towers; the little chapel of the Siena Convent; and the Tholsel, an 18th-century town hall now used as a bank. The two churches of St. Peter's are also worth a look, the Protestant one for its grim 'cadaver' gravestone, the Catholic one for the famous shrine of St. Oliver Plunkett (see panel on page 114), primate of all Ireland, whose blackened head was rescued from the flames after his execution at Tyburn (London) for high treason (his crime was simply unrepentant Catholicism).

Despite these somewhat grisly memories, Drogheda is an attractive place, with some good music pubs (notably Carberry's on North Strand and McHugh's on Lawrence Street) and it makes a convenient base for exploring the rich heritage of the Boyne Valley.

DROGHEDA AND CROMWELL

The atrocities committed by Cromwell's troops are well documented in many sources, although the precise number of casualties is hard to establish. Yet the municipal records of Drogheda on both the day before *and the day after* the alleged massacre in 1649 deal with the vexatious topic of street lighting, and make no mention of Cromwell's frightful conduct, even in cowed acquiescence. It is indeed an odd omission. There is no doubt that some of Cromwell's actions have been exaggerated for propaganda purposes, though he amply earned his hated reputation in Ireland.

95

Castletown House, considered by some to be the finest 18th-century mansion in the Republic

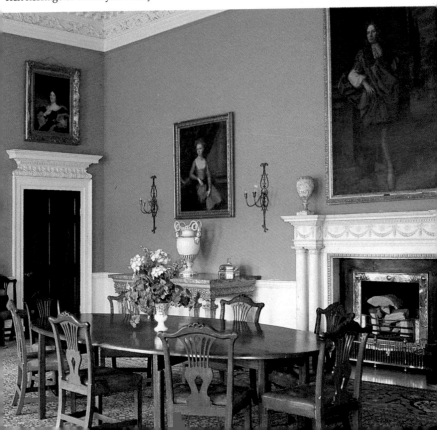

THE LONG WOMAN'S GRAVE

Near the Windy Gap on the Cooley Peninsula a plaque relates the strange tale of the Long Woman's Grave. A man courted a tall Spanish beauty, telling her he owned all the lands that could be seen from a high place. She married him and came to Ireland, then asked him to show her his inheritance. He brought her to the Windy Gap, where the views are closely obstructed by cliffs. She died of shock and is buried in the Long Woman's Grave.

Colimore Harbour in Dalkey, not far south of Dun Laoghaire

▶ Dundalk
862E

Dundalk is a border town, uncomfortably close to the most sensitive section of the Northern Ireland frontier. However, it is able to boast a few features of interest, the most noteworthy building being its **Cathedral of St. Patrick▶** (*Open:* daily, 8–6), a pastiche of King's College Chapel, Cambridge, that has rich mosaics inside. A museum and interpretative centre, which are housed in an old 18th-century distillery, relate the history of County Louth.

Just outside of the town, there is a huge bird reserve at **Dundalk Bay▶**, where thousands of wading birds can be found searching for food and shelter among the mudflats. North of the town, a few minutes' drive takes you into the lovely scenery of the hilly, granite **Cooley Peninsula▶▶**, attractive in its own right, but also overlooking tempting views of the Mountains of Mourne across the lough that divides the Republic from Northern Ireland. Cooley is associated with one of Ireland's best-known myths, the Cattle Raid of Cooley, in which Queen Maeve, who is jealous of her husband's prize white bull, attempts to take the brown bull of Cooley by force. Cuchulainn, the Hound of Ulster, becomes the hero of the hour, but is mortally wounded during the battle (see pages 27–28). Curiosities on the Cooley Peninsula include the giant Proleek Dolmen, accessible via a footpath from the Ballymascanlon House Hotel and the Windy Gap, a mountain pass closely hemmed in by cliffs and crags, and scene of an incident in the Cattle Raid epic.

Dun Laoghaire's coat of arms clearly shows the town's seafaring connections

▶ Dun Laoghaire 863C

Visitors from abroad have difficulty either spelling or pronouncing the name ('Dun Leary') of this major entry port into the Republic. Its former name (Kingstown) commemorated the English George IV, who visited in 1821. Its Irish name refers to an earlier monarch, the 5th-century High King of Tara, Laoghaire, who allowed St. Patrick to set up his mission in Ireland. When the harbour was constructed by the Scot, John Rennie, in the early 19th century, its vast granite piers were the largest in the world. Besides its commercial traffic, Dun Laoghaire is a prestigious yachting centre. Apart from catching ferries, visitors stray to this Victorian town of brightly painted houses to look at the **National Maritime Museum▶** (tel: 01 280 0969; *open:* May–end Sep Tue–Sun 1–5. *Admission: inexpensive*), in the former Mariners Church on Haigh Terrace, which houses a French longboat captured at Bantry, County Cork, in 1796, and the old optic from the Baily Lighthouse on Howth Head.

The **James Joyce Martello Tower▶▶** (tel: 01 280 9265; *open:* Apr–end Oct Mon–Sat 10–1 and 2–5, Sun 2–6; Nov–end Mar by appointment. *Admission: expensive*) at Sandycove is another place of interest. Joyce spent a brief and disturbing time here with the poet-surgeon, Oliver St. John Gogarty, who later appeared as Buck Mulligan in *Ulysses*. Apparently, one of the guests had a nightmare and fired several shots into the fireplace of the room where they were sleeping. Gogarty then shot at a row of saucepans above Joyce's head, shouting 'Leave him to me!' Joyce left the next morning. The Martello Tower houses a small museum of Joycean memorabilia. The gunpowder magazine (*Open:* Apr–end Oct) now houses the Joyce Library and Joyce's death mask, made on 13 January 1941. Close by is the Forty Foot Pool mentioned in *Ulysses*, a natural seawater swimming hole where nude bathing was once permitted, for men only. Nearby **Dalkey▶** (pronounced Dawkey) is an attractive resort with ancient fortified mansions and summer boat trips to Dalkey Island, a bird sanctuary and home to a herd of wild goats.

A detail from the Christ in Majesty *sculpture, in Dun Laoghaire*

97

THE VANISHING STONE

The antiquarian, W. F. Wakeman, noted in 1893 that a 'celebrated inscribed stone, which was supposed to mark the grave of an Irish monarch, gradually disappeared from the *Rightfert*, or 'King's Cemetery', at Glendalough. Bit by bit it was sold to tourists by the lying 'guides' (so called) who infest that time-hallowed spot'.

TRADITIONAL FARE

An unsubstantiated story tells how Grace O'Malley, the famous 16th-century pirate queen from the west of Ireland, came on a visit to Howth and found the gates of the castle barred against her. She then abducted the young heir, and promised to return him only on condition that a place should always be laid at the family table for any unexpected guests—a practice still scrupulously followed to this day.

▶▶▶ Glendalough   862B

Glendalough, tel: 0404 45325, www.heritageireland.com
Open: mid-Mar to mid-Oct daily 9.30–6; mid-Oct to mid-Mar daily 9.30–5; last admission 45 minutes before closing
Admission: inexpensive

This collection of monastic remains is one of the most important in Ireland. Bus tours visit it from Dublin, and the crowds have brought about a tawdry rash of souvenir shops, pubs and cafés in the local villages, along with plenty of guesthouses and hotels. Once away from this, however, the utter peace and beauty of the location are captivating, perhaps more than the ruins themselves. It is easy to see why St. Kevin (see page 115) sought solitude here in the 6th century, but his plans were somewhat thwarted. Beset by acolytes and lovelorn women, he eventually set up a large religious settlement here, which was attacked by Vikings in later centuries and overrun by English forces in 1398, after which its influence declined.

The ruins stand around two lakes in a beautiful wooded valley sheltered by great spurs of the Wicklow Mountains. The main concentration can be seen near the Lower Lake, by the visitor centre, where traffic converges. This modern building contains an exhibition of religious antiquities and an audio-visual presentation of monastic life in Ireland. From there you can take a guided tour or make your own way around the remains. The famous sites are the well-preserved 30m (100ft) Round Tower and the intact church often called St. Kevin's Kitchen because of its chimneylike bell tower. Against the backdrop of the wooded slopes, this assembly of quaint stone rooflines and pencil spires is unforgettable. Also visible are the

One of the most famous, and most visited, of Ireland's Round Towers can be found in the beautiful wooded setting of Glendalough

shells of the roofless cathedral and the Priests' House, and many crosses and gravestones. Farther up the valley (a pleasant walk or short drive) near the more spectacular and peaceful Upper Lake are various minor sights—a beehive cell, an early fort and another ruined church. St. Kevin's Bed is a suitably masochistic rocky ledge high on a cliff face (safely accessible only by boat) where the saint used to sleep. Keen walkers have an excellent choice of routes in this area (a national park information point is open in summer, and there are several local hostels).

▶▶ Howth   863C
This is now little more than a suburb of Dublin, but its attractions are still easily appreciated, particularly at the coast. Howth (it rhymes with 'both') Head gives fine views of Dublin Bay, the Wicklow Mountains and Boyne Valley beyond. In the bay is the rocky bird sanctuary and monastic island of Ireland's Eye, to which you can take a boat trip in summer. Cliff paths lead around the coastline, through Howth village and its ruined abbey, and past Baily Lighthouse. The partly ruinous, 15th-century Howth Castle is inland, near the Deer Park Hotel, and has fine rhododendron gardens. A small transport museum can be visited near the DART railway station, featuring Howth's famous open-topped tram. Howth's pubs, hotels and fish restaurants make it a pleasant outing from Dublin.

▶▶ Kells   861D
North of the Boyne lie several fine monastic buildings. Kells (formerly known as Ceanannus Mór), up the Blackwater Valley, is best known for the *Book of Kells* (see page 73). A facsimile copy is in the modern Church of Ireland occupying the site of St. Columba's 6th-century monastery. A Round Tower, five High Crosses (the best is the South Cross, carved with biblical scenes) and a simple two-storey church all date from the first millennium.

Howth remains a working fishing port, and has a good range of fish restaurants

Both this High Cross and the Round Tower have lost their summits, but Kells small oratory remains intact

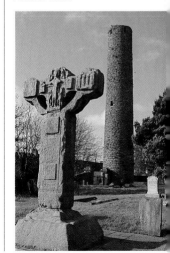

Eastern Counties

100

Kildare, popular with canal enthusiasts

HIGH CROSSES

South Kildare contains several well-preserved High Crosses. The best are at Moone and Castledermot. The Moone example stands over 5m (16ft) and depicts biblical scenes (lane signposted near post office). There are two crosses at Castledermot, again carved with scriptural themes. Both sites stand in the ruins of ancient monasteries.

CANAL TRIPS

County Kildare is traversed by two great canal systems, the Royal and Grand canals, which connect Dublin with the interior lakelands and the Shannon and Barrow rivers. They were major arteries of trade during the Industrial Revolution until the 1801 Act of Union stifled Ireland's economic development. The place to find out more about the canals is Robertstown. There, trips run from the restored Old Canal Hotel (exhibition), which was built in 1803 to serve canal-borne passengers; candlelit dinners with music are sometimes held in summer.

A range of shoes is on offer to Kildare's four-footed residents

▶▶ Kildare

The county town, Naas, has a villagelike air: gaily painted shopfronts, old pubs and, of course, a betting shop cluster around its market square by the sturdy tower of **St. Brigid's Cathedral▶** (*Open:* daily 10–6. *Admission: inexpensive*), dating from the 13th century, but much altered since. Stained-glass windows depict Ireland's great saints—Brigid, Patrick and Columba. During the 5th century, Kildare was one of the few religious houses in Ireland exclusively for women. The cathedral is flanked by a tall **Round Tower▶▶**, which you can climb in summer for views of this rolling horse country (tel: 045 521 229; *open:* May–end Sep daily 10–1 and 2–5. *Admission: inexpensive*). Immediately outside town is the wide, springy, gorse-speckled plain called the Curragh, which will stir the heart of any racing *aficionado*. The Curragh is Ireland's largest military camp, where the armoured vehicle that carried Michael Collins to his fatal ambush in 1922 is on display.

If you are at all interested in horses, visit the **Irish National Stud▶▶**, based at Tully just outside the town (tel: 045 521 617; *open:* mid-Feb to mid-Nov daily 9.30–6. *Admission: expensive,* includes Japanese Gardens). Visitors can tour the buildings and see the horses being exercised and groomed, or at ease in fenced paddocks. These animals enjoy a standard of living many humans would envy. The stallions work from January to July; the rest of the year is their 'holiday'. They have to perform as stalwartly in the covering sheds as they ever did on the racecourse.

The stud was set up in 1902 by the British, and transferred to the Irish state in 1943. Its eccentric founder was Colonel William Hall Walker, who believed that the stars influenced the horses' form. The stallion boxes are built with lantern roofs to allow heavenly bodies their full effect on the horses. Every time a mare foaled, Colonel Walker would cast its horoscope and race or sell the progeny accordingly. The system, it is said, was uncannily successful.

Spring and early summer are the most interesting times to visit, when you will see new foals with the mares. The foaling area contains a special unit in which orphan foals can be safely fostered. Later in the year the Sun Chariot Yard holds promising yearlings whose paces are just about to be tested. Veterinary research is carried out at the stud, along with all aspects of the complex and rarified science of horse breeding. The animals are not pets and should not be approached; apart from their extreme value, they can be fierce and may bite or kick, and mares with foals can be particularly savage.

The ornamental lake near the stable units provides mineral-rich drinking water for the horses, said to encourage good bone structure. Also in the grounds are the ruins of the Black Abbey, dating from the 12th century, along with the **Irish National Stud Horse Museum▶**, dedicated to all aspects of the equine species, and with plenty of racing memorabilia.

Next to the Stud are the **Japanese Gardens▶▶** (same hours as National Stud), considered by many to be Europe's most beautiful. The gardens symbolically depict man's progress from birth to eternity via a series of landmarks representing disappointments and failures on the road to enlightenment and final happiness. On the way, visitors pass such features as the Marriage Bridge, the Hill of Ambition and the Tunnel of Ignorance. The intricate landscaping makes the gardens seem much bigger than they really are. They were created by the Japanese gardener Eida and his son between 1906 and 1910. A garden centre sells bonsai trees, and there are tearooms.

TWO BODIES
A saint's relics were of huge importance to the economy of a monastery because of the pilgrims who came to venerate them, and strife between monasteries for the possession of such relics was by no means uncommon. One recorded instance concerned the relics of St. Abban, a south Leinster saint. His medieval *Life* tells of a struggle between the monks of Killabban (his County Kildare birthplace) and those of his monastery at Maganey for the possession of his body. The former claimed it because they were his first followers, while the latter based their claim to it on the fact that the saint had lived and died among them. Divine Providence, however, stepped in and settled the matter satisfactorily by bestowing an identical body of the saint on each of the communities!

101

The elegant Japanese Gardens next to the National Stud

The English and the Irish probably come closer to understanding each other through their mutual love of horses than in any other way. Ireland is currently estimated to have about 55,000 horses, including 15,000 racehorses.

LAYTOWN RACES

The much loved and highly unusual Laytown Races are held just once a year in either July or August. The course is a gently shelving beach of soft sand in a little coastal resort in County Meath, near Drogheda. As soon as the tide goes out, the six-furlong track is quickly marked and the horses thunder across the strand amid a lively seaside atmosphere of candy-floss stalls and paddling children. The competitors race not only each other, but the advancing tide! Sadly, a serious accident in 1994 cast a shadow over Laytown's future. Races are still held, however, but with more safety measures.

102

A focal point of Ireland's racing country is Punchestown racecourse, County Kildare

A land of horses Ireland is the heart of the racehorse industry, where many of the world's best thoroughbreds are reared and trained. It also has facilities for every type of equestrian sport: flat-racing, steeple-chasing, show-jumping, eventing or trekking. Equestrian centres abound, and fox hunting is alive and well. For other aspects of the horse world, turn up at the jolly Connemara Pony Show (Clifden, August), the fashionable Dublin Horse Show (August) or the horse fairs in Buttevant (County Cork, 12 July) and Ballinasloe (County Galway, October), where all classes of horseflesh change hands amid an arcane code of palm-slapping and luck money (a small amount that the seller gives so the horse's new owner will have 'good luck' betting on his purchase).

Irish breeding Horses thrive in Ireland's mild climate and lush, unpolluted pastureland. The grass overlies a base of limestone, which produces the calcium needed for healthy bones. The native Irish horses are Connemaras, those cheerful animals that survive on saltmarsh grasses and seaweed in the far west. Romantic legends tell how Spanish Arab horses escaped from Armada vessels shipwrecked off the Galway coast in the 16th century and intermingled with the native stock, producing a taller, faster and more elegant breed. The two other distinctively Irish equines are the powerful draft horses, used to plough fields and draw carts, and the charismatic creature of the turf, the long-limbed thoroughbred. Crossbreeding between draft and thoroughbred produces the sturdier but athletic animals used for hunting or show-jumping.

The lure of the turf Horse-racing is more than a mere sport in Ireland; it is a passion, consuming and generating vast sums of money. On-course betting turnover amounts to about 3 115 million a year, and thousands are avid studiers of form. The breeding industry turns over staggering amounts, aided by favourable government tax breaks. Racing, however, was known in Ireland many centuries ago. The legendary Red Branch knights of Ulster raced, as did later Gaelic warriors, although it was then mainly a sport of kings. The Normans and Elizabethans loved it; Cromwell, with his characteristic lack of *joie de vivre*, tried to ban it as the work of the devil—possibly one of his least popular moves in Ireland. During the 18th century racing was all the rage, and two neighbours in County Cork coined a new phrase with their epic cross-country dash between the spires of Buttevant and Doneraile churches—'steeple-chasing'.

Today, racing 'over the sticks' still has a great following, although not nearly as much money is involved as in flat-racing. Jumpers are usually gelded, so when their sporting days are over they cannot retire gracefully to sire lucrative strings of winning progeny, as flat-racers do. Nonetheless, the courage and stamina needed of both horse and rider in steeple-chasing make it an exciting and highly respected sport.

Ireland has nearly 30 racecourses, and meetings are held somewhere on approximately 245 days of the year, including Sundays. They vary enormously from state-of-the-art Leopardstown, just outside Dublin, to the quaint Laytown Races (see panel). Ireland's most celebrated flat-racing venue is the Curragh in County Kildare, 2,300ha (5,700 acres) of gorsy plain where visitors will see strings of racehorses testing their paces on the springy turf. The great national hunt (steeple-chasing) courses are at Fairyhouse (where the Irish Grand National is held), Punchestown, Navan and Galway. You can find full details of the racing calendar in any Irish paper, or from the tourist board. The most valuable race is the Irish Derby; the winner, whose progeny will be closely watched for hereditary swiftness, commands a guaranteed place in the annals of racing history.

The tack room at one of Ireland's many riding schools; this is at Donacomper, near Celbridge in County Kildare

103

RACING IN IRELAND
Racing in Ireland is a popular sport with many of the 27 racecourses holding festivals at various times during the year. Summer is predominantly a flat-racing season, with the major races being held at the Curragh, Co. Kildare or Leopardstown, in the southern suburbs of Dublin. National Hunt racing continues throughout the year, and among the most popular venues are Punchestown, Co. Kildare, which hosts a three-day festival meeting in spring; Fairyhouse in Co. Meath, which plays host to the Grand National; and Galway, which has a six-day meeting in the summer.

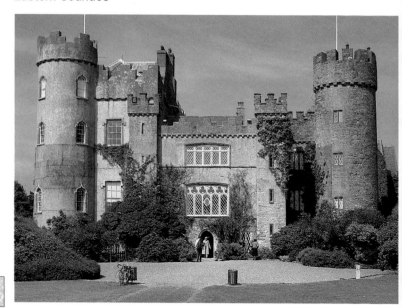

Inside Malahide Castle highlights include the Oak Room, full of intricate panelling from the 16th and 17th centuries

NEWBRIDGE
Beyond Malahide, in Donabate, lies the former home of the Cobbe family. Designed by George Semple, Newbridge is an 18th-century house set in wooded parkland (*Guided tours* available). The drawing room is an authentic example of Georgian decor, and the areas 'below stairs' contain original utensils and equipment. More unusually, the much-travelled Cobbes built up a charming little museum of curiosities from many foreign places. Craft workshops and period transportation displays are on show in the courtyard.

►► Malahide Castle   863C

Malahide, Co. Dublin, tel: 01 864 2184, www.malahide.ie
Open: Apr–end Oct Mon–Sat 10–5, Sun 11–6, Nov–end May Mon–Sat 10–5, Sun 11–5. Admission: moderate

With the exception of a brief spell under Cromwell, this romantic-looking building was the seat of the Talbot family for nearly 800 years before it was bought by Dublin County Council in 1976. The Talbots were Jacobite supporters and fared badly in the Battle of the Boyne. It is said that the 14 cousins who sat down to breakfast at Malahide on the morning of the battle were all dead by nightfall. The tour of the building enables you to see its transition from a simple fortification to a charmingly domestic country house in elaborate Gothic style; the present turrets and battlements are ornamental. It contains many original furnishings, mostly 18th-century and a fine collection of portraits that now form Ireland's National Portrait Gallery. The structure dates from several periods, the oldest section being its 14th-century tower. The beautiful gardens around the castle contain a remarkable botanical collection; beyond lies an expanse of well-kept parkland. In the castle yard is the **Fry Model Railway Museum►**, with engines and rolling stock handmade by a Dublin railway engineer, Cyril Fry. The O-gauge railway is an amazing scale model with stations, bridges, barges, the Liffey River and the Hill of Howth.

► Marino Casino   863C

Malahide Road, Marino, tel: 01 833 1618,
www.heritageireland.com. Open: Jun–end Sep daily 10–6; Apr Sun and Thu 12–5; May, Oct daily 10–5; Feb–end Mar, Nov Sun and Thu 12–4. Admission: inexpensive

If you are on your way to Malahide or Howth, this little Georgian gem is worth tracking down in Dublin's northern suburbs. The Casino has nothing to do with gambling, but was built for Lord Charlemont (who lived in what is now the Hugh Lane Municipal Art Gallery, see page 56) as an exuberant bit of neoclassical frivolity, a skittish aside to a villa in which he planned to house some of the works of art he brought home from a grand tour. The villa no longer exists, but the Casino survives, flamboyantly decorated with urns concealing chimneystacks. Nearby Marino Crescent (also known as Folliot's Revenge) was built out of spite to block Lord Charlemont's view of the sea. The backs of the houses were made particularly hideous, with ill-proportioned windows and scruffy sheds.

▶ **Maynooth** 862C

If you are touring west of Dublin you will probably drive through Maynooth at some point, a pleasant Georgian town with a ruined castle and, nearby, the famous seminary and lay university of St. Patrick's College (tel: 01 708 3576; *open:* by appointment. *Admission free*) that contains an ecclesiastical museum. During the Reformation the college was suppressed, but reopened in 1795 after the repeal of the harsh Penal Laws against Catholics. The town's main square is in Victorian Gothic style and was designed by Augustus Pugin. Close by is the large estate of Carton House, a fine Georgian mansion built for the dukes of Leinster in 1740.

▶▶ **Mellifont Abbey** 862D

Mellifont Abbey, Colon, tel: 041 982 6459
Open: May–end Sep daily 10–5
Admission: inexpensive
Remains of the first Cistercian church in Ireland, founded in 1142, are in a maze of quiet lanes by the Mattock River. Built by St. Malachy, Archbishop of Armagh, it was heavily influenced by the French Cistercian monastery at Clairvaux, where St. Malachy had stayed and befriended the abbot, St. Bernard. View the ruins from the parking area, or pay a small entrance fee for a closer look. The ruin's most striking section is the Romanesque octagonal lavabo, or washing place, about half of which is still standing.

A TASMANIAN CONNECTION
The late Lord Talbot de Malahide was also the owner of another Malahide, in Tasmania, where his relatives still live. Inspired by his family's interests there, and by his own fascination for botany, he wrote the definitive multivolume work on the plants of Tasmania. He also introduced to the Irish Malahide garden plants from his antipodean property, as well as others from Africa, North and South America, China, Australia and Mexico—which makes it a botanist's paradise.

105

Portraits from the National Gallery in Dublin now hang in the imposing setting of Malahide Castle

Mount Usher Gardens make the most of their position on the Vartry River

The Hill of Tara, once a site of pagan importance, is one of many such places to have been 'Christianized'

▶▶ Monasterboice
862D

North of Drogheda, off the N1, is one of the best examples in Ireland of a carved High Cross. This is the 10th-century Cross of Muiredach, nearly 6m (20ft) high, which bears numerous biblical scenes in deep relief, such as Cain slaying Abel, David and Goliath and the Last Judgment. The west face is devoted to the life of Christ, including the arrest in the Garden of Gethsemane and the risen Christ returning to meet St. Peter and St. Paul. At the bottom of the cross is an inscription in Gaelic saying 'A prayer for Muiredach by whom this cross was made'. Two other more eroded High Crosses can be seen on the site, along with a fine Round Tower and a pre-Gothic sundial. Two ruined 13th-century churches stand within the enclosure.

▶▶▶ Mount Usher Gardens
863B

Ashford, Co. Wicklow, tel: 0404 40205, www.dublingardens.com Open: mid-Mar–end Oct daily 10.30–5.30. Admission: moderate

These lovely gardens stand in 8ha (20 acres) of land on the banks of the Vartry River. Water forms an essential part of the scenery, with cascades and bridges visible in just about every section. It is possible to get utterly lost if you forget which way the water is flowing. The grounds were laid out by Edward Walpole, a Dublin businessman, and his sons from 1868 as a wild garden, and contain about 5,000 species, including many rhododendrons and eucalypti. The gardens offer fine displays of colour throughout the summer. The maples in late September and October are especially striking. Several craft and clothing shops stand by the entrance, where there is a tearoom.

▶ Navan
862D

Navan occupies a strategic site on the Boyne. Not compelling in itself, it makes a good base for seeing several places in the area. Within the town, the most interesting sight is **Athlumney Castle►**, over the bridge. This 15th-century tower house was apparently burned down by its last owner, Sir Lancelot Dowdall, a devout Catholic who refused to let it fall into William's hands after the Battle of the Boyne. He is said to have watched his home blaze all night from the opposite banks, then set off into exile.

About 13km (8 miles) south of the town is one of Ireland's most famous antiquities, the **Hill of Tara►►►** *(tel: 046 25903, www.heritageireland.ie; open:* May–end Oct daily 10–6. *Admission: inexpensive).* This shows evidence of occupation from many different periods, and was the symbolic seat of the High Kings until the 11th century. Its history is steeped in legends, but archaeological evidence suggests that some grim events must have taken place there. Various ring forts can be seen, although some were damaged in recent years by British Israelites searching for the Ark of the Covenant (see panel). The site has probably always been associated with religious cults of some kind, but its influence waned after the arrival of Christianity. It was from this hill that King Laoghaire and the Druids first noticed St. Patrick's defiant fire on the nearby Hill of Slane.

The Hill of Tara is now just a grassy flat-topped hill grazed by sheep, reached by a field path from the parking area. It rises only 90m (300ft) or so from the surrounding land, but the views over the plains are very extensive. Various inconclusive mounds and earthworks indicate the locations of the old palaces, banquet hall, and Bronze Age burial sites and many artefacts have been unearthed. Tara's most significant event in modern times was a mass meeting called by the nationalist leader Daniel O'Connell (see page 42), which is said to have attracted over a million people. This alarmed the British government, which suppressed O'Connell's activities and thus put one more nail in the coffin of a peaceful Anglo-Irish settlement.

A Hill of Tara interpretative centre has been established in an old church on the hillside, which really helps visitors to get to grips with the complex history of Tara and to identify the many different earthworks.

Today, visitors to the Hill of Tara are more inclined to appreciate the views than dig vainly for the Ark of the Covenant

107

THE ARK OF THE COVENANT

In 1899, the purchase of a book on Charing Cross Road in London led a group known as the British Israelites to the belief that the Ark of the Covenant lay buried on the Hill of Tara. One of them, a Mr. Groome, went off to Ireland to excavate in furtherance of his biblical quest. When he found nothing, some locals took pity on his disappointment and placed some Roman coins where he would dig on the morrow and where, inevitably and to his own delight, he duly discovered them the next day. But after a singular lack of success in locating what he had set out to find, he packed his bags and returned to England. The Ark remains undiscovered on the Hill of Tara—or anywhere else.

The entrance to the passage-grave, with the roof-box above the lintel

The sparkling white of the quartzite lends added drama to Newgrange

▶ ▶ ▶ Newgrange   862D

*Bru na Boinne, tel: 041 988 0300, www.heritageireland.com
Open: Jun–mid-Sep daily 9.30–7; May daily 9.30–6.30;
mid-Sep–end Feb daily 10–4.30; Mar, Apr daily 10–5
Admission: expensive*

Newgrange is unquestionably one of Ireland's most important archaeological sites, and perhaps the most spectacular passage-grave (the tomb takes the form of a long passage covered by a vast mound) in Western Europe. Dating from *c*3000BC, it is possibly 1,000 years older than England's Stonehenge. The tumulus stands in a sloping field above the road, overlooking the glittering snake of the Boyne and a vast sweep of quiet farmland. It is easily spotted because the front retaining walls of the grass-covered mound are faced with brilliant white stones of quartzite. The nearest source for these stones is the Wicklow Mountains, south of Dublin, so thousands of tons of material must have been dragged huge distances. Egg-shaped grey stones are studded at intervals among the white ones, though the original pattern of these (if there was one) is a matter of speculation. The mound itself measures about 100m (330ft) across, and is about 10m (35ft) high at its central point. Over the years it had collapsed, but was reconstructed during the 1960s, using careful measurements to determine its precise dimensions. In front of the mound is a low entrance formed by slabs of rock, and above it another rectangular opening, the roof-box. This sophisticated device is constructed with a narrow slit in the stone so that once a year, for about 15 minutes on the morning of the winter solstice, the rays of the sun illuminate the interior of the tomb. All around the edge of the tomb is a low wall of large boulders, some carved with spiral shapes. The significance of these is unknown; they may have been purely decorative.

There are several inscribed stones at Newgrange; this one is at the back of the mound

You can walk all around the mound (the white wall does not go all the way) to see what remains of a circle of standing stones. A guided tour takes you into the inner stone chamber of the tomb, from which three recesses lead; the dovetailed structure of the vaulted roof still keeps the water out. Mysterious patterns are carved on the inner stones, some invisible from outside and presumably for some cult purpose. Stone basins contained the bones of the cremated dead with offerings of beads and pins. At the end of the tour a light is switched on to re-create an approximation of the solstice phenomenon.

Newgrange is open all year and is besieged by school groups and visitors in high season. During the winter solstice (21 December) and several days around that date, access is virtually impossible; places are booked many years in advance to see the phenomenon within the tomb. Tourism at this sensitive site is carefully managed, but even so, erosion is occurring. The Office of Public Works has constructed an interpretative centre near the site with a model to reduce the pressure of visitor numbers.

Newgrange is by no means the only local antiquity. The nearby mounds of Dowth and Knowth also contain passage tombs. As you look from Newgrange over the lush pastureland enclosed by this sheltered bend of the Boyne, the shapes of numerous strange humps and tumuli are visible—these are other burial sites, about 40 in all, some of which have not yet been explored. The Irish name for this giant graveyard is *Bru na Boinne*, the palace of the Boyne. Its builders were a farming community who were apparently fairly settled and peaceful, clearing forests and raising stock. The looping Boyne River furnished them with a useful artery of communication and a natural defence barrier.

Many aspects of the tombs are puzzling, and myths and theories abound. The fatally wounded Diarmuid, lover of Gráinne, is alleged to have been brought here 'to put aerial life into him'. Other legends declare these tombs (inaccurately) to be the burial places of the Kings of Tara, while the sun-cult rituals echo those discovered in ancient Egyptian tombs, although these graves probably predate the pyramids by several hundred years.

TOMORROW NEVER COMES
In early Irish mythology, Newgrange was associated with the Dagda, the good god of the Celts, his wife Bóann (the divinized Boyne River) and his son Oengus—all supernatural beings belonging to the Tuatha Dé Danann (peoples of the goddess Danu), who had defeated the *Fir Bolg* people (see page 30) and had occupied Ireland before the Celts. The 12th-century *Book of Leinster* tells the tale of how Oengus used a verbal trick to get possession of the great mound at Newgrange from his father. The Dagda, it seems, was persuaded to let his son have it for a day and a night, and when he asked his son to return it the next day, Oengus replied that a day and a night meant forever—so he kept it. He probably argued, with impeccable Irish logic, that tomorrow never comes as every day is today.

DANIEL ROBERTSON

The terraces of Powerscourt Gardens were indelibly stamped by the unsteady hand of this gouty and eccentric architect who, in 1840, was commissioned by the 6th Viscount Powerscourt to draw up new plans for the garden. Apparently Robertson's *modus operandi* was to be trundled around the gardens in a wheelbarrow, directing staff while swigging intermittently at a bottle of sherry. Once the bottle was empty he ran out of ideas and all useful work for the day ground to a halt. Robertson's habits were expensive, and he was constantly in debt. Whenever the sheriff called, he used to hide in the copper dome of the house.

The Great Sugar Loaf Mountain forms a memorable backdrop to the gardens at Powerscourt

▶ ▶ ▶ Powerscourt   863C

Enniskerry, tel: 01 204 6000
Open: Mar–end Oct daily 9.30–5.30; Nov–end Feb daily
9.30–dusk. Admission: expensive

The pretty village of Enniskerry and the dramatic backdrop of the Wicklow Mountains add to the appeal of this vast estate, with its 1.6km (1-mile) long drive. James I granted the land to the 1st Viscount Powerscourt, Sir Richard Wingfield, in 1609. A magnificent house was designed by Richard Castle, whose Palladian handiwork can be seen all over Ireland. Unfortunately, the great edifice had just been restored when it burned to a shell in a disastrous accident in 1974. The house now has a new use: It houses an exhibition on the history of the estate, shops and a terrace restaurant, which overlooks the gardens. There is also a garden centre. All that can be seen now are the splendid **gardens**, laid out on the south-facing slopes in front of the house that overlook the Great Sugar Loaf Mountain. They were first created in the mid-18th century soon after the completion of the house, but redesigned in the 19th century by the redoubtable Daniel Robertson (see panel) with classical parterres and Italianate statuary. They contain glorious lakes with spouting fountains and winged horses and magnificent specimen trees that grow to a prodigious height in this mild climate. Unusual touches include a Japanese garden (1908) on reclaimed bogland sporting little scarlet bridges, a pet cemetery dedicated to many faithful friends (Jack, Sting and Taffy), mosaic terraces made of beach pebbles from Bray and neat kitchen gardens.

An additional attraction about 5km (3 miles) away (separate entrance charge) is the **Powerscourt Waterfall▶▶**, which plunges about 120m (400ft) in a mare's-tail plume down a jagged rock face (see panel opposite). There are excellent local walks around the valley below. To justify the entrance fee, take a picnic and make an outing of it.

▶▶ Russborough House *862C*

Blessington, tel: 045 865239
Open: May–end Sep daily 10.30–5.30; Apr, Oct Sun 10.30–5
Admission: moderate

Apart from a wonderful collection of paintings, Russborough House is also the home of some unusual dolls

Like nearby Powerscourt, this grand Palladian mansion shows the Anglo-Irish ascendancy in the Pale at its most confident and powerful. It was designed by the ubiquitous Richard Castle (and, after his death, Francis Bindon) for the 1st Earl of Milltown, a wealthy Dublin brewer. The structure is palatial: Two huge semicircular wings stretch from the main body of the building to two side pavilions. Inside, the grandeur continues in magnificent plasterwork by the Francini brothers. Some of it, like elegant cake icing, swirls around exquisite oval sea scenes by Claude Vernet, commissioned specially for the house.

Today the house is owned by the nephew of Alfred Beit, the German co-founder (with Cecil Rhodes) of the De Beer Diamond Mining Company. Besides a multitude of antiques, tapestries and valuable porcelain, his fabulous collection of art (strong on Spanish, Dutch and Flemish schools) is now held at Russborough. At least, some of it is, for Russborough has suffered two major burglaries. The first was in 1974 when, in a *cause célèbre* that hit all the headlines, Dr. Bridget Rose Dugdale stole 16 paintings for her IRA lover (the haul was recovered, undamaged, later). In May 1986, another break-in occurred and this time the owners were not so lucky. Now the house is under a fair degree of surveillance and some important works have been donated to the National Gallery in Dublin. There is, however, still plenty that makes the house well worth a special visit. The grounds consist of woodland and a large artificial lake (actually a reservoir).

Nearby **Blessington▶▶** is one of the most charming villages in the Wicklow Mountains and a popular base for tourers. Its wide street is flanked by tall trees and dignified Georgian buildings. Dame Ninette de Valois, founder of London's Sadler's Wells Ballet Company, was born nearby.

A DRAMATIC DISPLAY
When King George IV announced his intention of visiting Powerscourt in 1821, a path was hurriedly laid out from the great house to the waterfall in the grounds, and an artificial lake with sluice gates created at the top of the fall to make a more dramatic cascade for the king to admire. But the delights of the luncheon table in the mansion gave His Majesty insufficient time to visit the waterfall, and when the sluice gates were subsequently opened, the great onrush of water destroyed the wooden platform on which the king should have been standing. So the British monarchy has reason to be thankful to Powerscourt—and a good lunch!

Skerries is so-called because of the islands lying just off the coast; the name means 'sea rocks' in Gaelic

THE ROAD TO SLANE
The reason, it is said, why the road from Dublin to Slane was made so straight (unlike most in Ireland) was to minimize the time it would take King George IV to reach his mistress in Slane Castle when he visited in 1821.

A shield set into the walls of Slane Abbey

▶ Skerries   863D

This is one of the biggest resorts on the northeast coast, mostly visited by Dubliners. The strange indentations at Red Island are claimed to be the footprints of St. Patrick. Boat trips to St. Patrick's Island enable visitors to explore a ruined church where a national synod was held in 1148. Just south is the pretty fishing village of Loughshinny.

▶▶ Slane   862D

The town was built on the instructions of Viscount Conyngham in the 18th century, around a crossroads. For its modest size it has considerable historic interest, and is a pleasant grey-stone place of agreeable Georgian proportions. The estate of Slane Castle (tel: 041 988 4400, www.slanecastle.ie; *open:* late-May to early Aug Mon–Thu 12–5. *Admission: expensive*), former home of the Conynghams, can be glimpsed from nearby roads. Open-air rock concerts have been held in the castle grounds, but it is not generally open to the public. The Marchioness Conyngham was rumoured to have been George IV's last mistress, and he apparently spent a good deal of time there. Near the riverside is a mill. The four identical Georgian houses set at equal angles to the crossroads in the village centre have given rise to one of those appealing Irish tales that are almost certainly untrue.

The houses were supposedly built for four quarrelsome spinster sisters whose exasperated brother became so fed up with their wranglings under one roof that he insisted they live separately. Whether or not the story is true, the houses are fine examples and deserve a close look.

A humble labourer's cottage (now a museum) a short distance from the centre of Slane was the birthplace of the lyric poet Francis Ledwidge. A plaque outside displays one of his most haunting verses, written after his friend Thomas MacDonagh was executed for his part in the Easter Rising of 1916:

'He shall not hear the bittern cry
In the wild sky, where he is lain,
Nor voices of the sweeter birds
Above the wailing of the rain.'

Ledwidge himself was killed soon after this—at Flanders, fighting on the British side. He was only 30 and is now lamented as a great loss to literature, though his work was not widely read at a time of such political upheaval.

Outside the village is the **Hill of Slane▶**, on which the ruins of a monastery stand. The site is famous as the place where St. Patrick lit Easter fires to challenge the pagan king, Laoghaire, who had forbidden flames to be kindled within sight of his palace at Tara (see page 107).

▶ Straffan 862C

This village on the banks of the Liffey has two visitor attractions, although both are open only in high season. The **Butterfly Farm▶▶** (tel: 01 627 1109; *open:* Jun–end Aug daily noon–5.30. *Admission: expensive*) is the only one of its type in Ireland, with tropical species fluttering about in a hothouse full of exotic plants. The **Steam Museum▶** (tel: 01 627 3155; *open:* Jun–end Aug Wed–Sun 2–6; May and Sep by appointment only. *Admission: expensive*) documents the history of the steam age in Ireland, showing how it revolutionized industrial as well as agricultural practices such as butter churning and corn threshing. Working steam engines are on display, including Richard Trevithick's prototype steam-powered road vehicle. The engines stand in the courtyard of an 18th-century house. Phone in advance to attend a 'live steam day'. Straffan is also home to Ireland's most glamorous club, the **Kildare Hotel and Country Club** (tel: 01 627 3333. *Admission: expensive*), where Arnold Palmer designed the K Club, one of Ireland's most prestigious 18-hole golf courses and home to a future Ryder Cup—where Europe's top 10 golfers take on their counterparts from the US. The K Club is owned by multimillionaire Michael Smurfit, and the hotel itself is a fine example of an early 19th-century, mansard-roofed manor built in the French style.

GARRICK CASTLE
Standing near the Boyne a short distance upriver from Slane is the ruined castle of Garrick. Close by was a weir and, so the story goes, fish caught in a net there touched a wire connected to the castle kitchen, so that the cook would know when to serve up the freshest of salmon on the menu.

113

Slane Abbey was founded in 1512 for four priests, four clerks and four choristers

Christianity reached Irish shores during the late 4th century, not with Roman fire and sword, but through the persuasive urgings of an extraordinary band of missionary monks who brought the glad tidings to the pagan Gaels. Many of these early Christian teachers and founders of monasteries are now Irish saints.

ST. OLIVER PLUNKETT (1629–1681)

One of the most interesting of Ireland's saints was canonized as recently as 1976. St. Oliver Plunkett, Archbishop of Armagh and Primate of All Ireland, had the misfortune to live during the troubled years of the 17th century, when Catholicism was rigorously suppressed by English authorities. He was on friendly terms with the Protestant clergy of Ulster, who had a high regard for his sincerity and achievements, but false allegations by Titus Oates in 1678 over a 'popish plot' to bring French soldiers into Ireland resulted in his arrest, although the charges were blatantly absurd. On 1 July 1681, he was executed in London for 'treason', his offence being simply that he was an unrepentant Catholic. At his trial the Lord Chief Justice declared, 'The bottom of your treason was your setting up your false religion, than which there is not anything more displeasing to God'. Plunkett's severed head was rescued from the flames and brought back to Ireland. It lies in a shrine in the Catholic Church of St. Peter, Drogheda.

Saintly lives Innumerable saints are encountered on any visit to Ireland. Most of them are obscure (who now remembers St. Gobnet or St. Lurach?) and the patterns of their lives are often very similar—they renounced the world, founded monasteries and did good works. The achievements of these early monks, however, are hard to overestimate. The trials they endured, the distances they travelled in uncharted terrain and their dazzling artistic talents are truly staggering. Christianity was indeed a faith that moved mountains. The Christian message was mainly interpreted by men, just as it is now, and attitudes to women were extremely misogynistic. Just a few intrepid women saints braved this exclusive and hostile masculine preserve, among them St. Brigid, who founded one of the earliest of Ireland's nunneries at Kildare.

In today's Ireland, the saints still play an active role in the lives of many devout Catholics. You will find candles burning at every shrine, votive offerings in sacred places and eager pilgrims praying for their intercession in everyday affairs or for the perpetual forgiveness of sins. Factual evidence about most of the early saints is sparse. Their lives are but shadowy and wreathed in legends or miraculous tales. Some of them are composite figures or even Christian incarnations of pagan Celtic gods. The most famous Irish saint, of course, is St. Patrick, the most effective of all the early missionaries (see page 226 for details of his life and places associated with him).

St. Columba (c521–597) Also known as Columcille, St. Columba was born at Lough Gartan in Donegal. He was a high-ranking member of the O'Neill clan, a scholar, poet and natural leader. After training as a monk at Moville and Clonard, he founded the monasteries of Derry and Durrow, possibly also Kells. In 563 he left Ireland with 12 companions to found a monastery in Iona, an island off the Scottish coast, but retained his links with Ireland. He was a charismatic figure, tall and striking, well educated, persuasive and ardently committed to his cause. Some of his actions seemed less than saintly. This endearingly human paragon was, by all accounts, a thief and a cheat—stealing a ceremonial cross from a neighbouring church and secretly copying a psalter he borrowed from a friend. This resulted in the deaths of thousands at the Battle of the Books (see panel on page 210).

St. Ciarán (c521–545) The founder of the great monastery of Clonmacnoise, St. Ciarán had an auspicious pedigree as a Christian leader—he was the son of a carpenter. His first monkish years were spent on the Aran Islands with Enda, the islands' most famous saint. Later he went to Scattery Island, in the mouth of the Shannon, and finally to Clonmacnoise farther upstream, where he died soon afterward. Apparently he aroused such jealousy among his fellow clerics that they prayed he would die young—and he did! But his good works lived on, and the influence of Clonmacnoise spread far and wide, surviving until 1522, despite many Viking raids.

St. Brendan the Navigator (c486–575) This famous Irish saint was the founder of a monastery at Clonfert in County Galway, and also Ardfert in Kerry. His missions took place mostly in western Ireland, but he is best remembered as a great traveller. His epic voyage is chronicled in the 10th-century account, *The Navigation of St. Brendan*, in which he set sail with 12 disciples in search of an earthly paradise in the Atlantic Ocean. The journey lasted over seven years, and it has been suggested that his account of 'crystal columns' (icebergs?) and 'curdled seas' (migratory eels in the Sargasso?) may pinpoint him as the first to cross the Atlantic. St. Brendan's supposed voyage was imaginatively re-created in similar conditions by the modern explorer Tim Severin, and the wood-and-leather boat he sailed across the Atlantic in 1976 can be seen in the history theme park of Craggaunowen, County Clare (see page 183).

Clonmacnoise, founded by St. Ciarán, was for centuries the intellectual capital of Ireland

115

This little church at Glendalough is familiarly known as St. Kevin's Kitchen as the small bell tower resembles a chimney

ST. KEVIN (died c618)
Founder of the great monastery at Glendalough, County Wicklow, St. Kevin came from a noble Leinster family and was educated by monks from childhood. After his ordination he adopted a hermit's existence at Glendalough. His quest for solitude was in vain, however, for crowds of disciples soon gathered around him and he became the leader of a great and influential community. He is alleged to have murdered a woman who attempted to seduce him, shoving her from his rock-ledge cave into the lake below. The tale conveniently bolsters the early fathers' belief that women were the source of all corruption.

The stark silhouette of the Yellow Steeple; nearby stands a section of Trim's town walls

MICHAEL DWYER'S ESCAPE
The year 1798 witnessed great upheavals against English rule, especially in the southeast. During the harsh winter of 1798–1799 the Wicklow-born rebel Michael Dwyer took refuge in a cottage in Derrynamuck, in the Glen of Imaal. More than 100 English soldiers surrounded it, but he declined to surrender, although he requested that the owners of the house be freed. The army allowed this, then battle commenced. A fellow rebel, Sam McAllister, sustained a broken arm and could fight no longer, so offered to sacrifice himself to give Dwyer a chance to escape. He showed himself at the door and drew the English fire. He was immediately killed, but while the soldiers were reloading their muskets, Dwyer was able to slip away. The cottage is now a museum.

CAPTAIN ROBERT HALPIN
Robert Halpin (1836–1894) was one of Wicklow Town's most prominent citizens. His main achievement was as commander of the *Great Eastern*, the iron steamship that laid the first transatlantic telegraph cable. A granite obelisk commemorates him in the town, and a plaque at the church of St. Lavinius, but for further insights, head for his former home, Tinakilly House, 3km (2 miles) north of town, now a luxury hotel and restaurant.

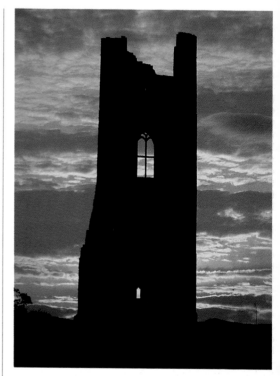

▶ **Trim** *862D*

Trim Castle is one of the most imposing Anglo-Norman fortresses in Ireland, and as it stands in the centre of the town by the Boyne River, it is easy to get a good idea of its size and layout. The ruins cover about a hectare (2.5 acres) and include a vast keep flanked by rectangular towers. Sections of curtain wall are interspersed with battle gates. The original castle was built by Hugh de Lacy in 1172, although the present structure dates from a later period. The ruins are freely accessible. Nearby are the ruins of the Royal Mint and a gaunt skeleton called the Yellow Steeple, dating from the 14th century, the last remnants of an Augustinian abbey, destroyed in 1649.

Bective Abbey▶▶, between Navan and Trim, is one of the earliest examples of a Cistercian foundation in Ireland. Hugh de Lacy was buried here in 1195, and it was obviously a place of some significance (its abbot sat in the English House of Lords). Most of the surviving ruins date from the 15th century and stand in a gloriously peaceful setting in a field by the Knightsbrook River.

▶ **Wicklow** *863B*

The county town of this much-visited area is small and unassuming, but it makes a pleasantly unstressful base, as its name, meaning 'Viking meadow', suggests. Its history, however, has been far from untroubled. In AD432, St. Patrick had an unfriendly reception when he landed at Travilahawk Strand. One of his entourage had his teeth knocked out and became known as Mantan (the toothless one). Irish clans (O'Byrnes and O'Tooles) slugged it out with the Anglo-Norman Fitzgeralds for centuries, and after the rebellion of 1798 many of the participants were tried in the town's courthouse; those who evaded capture took to the hills. Wicklow's main features of interest are the scanty remains of the Black Castle by the road above the harbour, a fine headland for coastal walks, a ruined 13th-century friary and a heritage centre in the town gaol (local history and genealogical research). The Protestant **Church of St. Lavinius▶** (*Open:* daily 10–6. *Admission free*) topped by a Byzantine dome, has several unusual details, including a Romanesque doorway and a fine roof. In Norman times the slopes to the Vartry River were planted with vines, a testimony to Wicklow's comparatively sunny climate. The harbour area is oddly severed from the main town; beyond it stretches a long, shingly beach trapping a brackish lagoon (Broad Lough), which makes a sheltered habitat for wildfowl.

▶▶▶ The Wicklow Mountains   *862B*

These wild hills on Dublin's doorstep are a great boon to city dwellers. From the southern suburbs you can gaze at them on clear days; by public transportation or a car they take just half an hour to reach. If you have time enough you can even walk there on the 132km (82-mile) Wicklow Way, starting just outside Dublin in Marlay Park. The route is not very clear in places and the mountains can be dangerous in misty conditions. The rounded hills of ice-eroded schist and granite enfold a strange mixture of bleak, awesome glens and boggy plateaux, interspersed with welcoming Shangri-La valleys like Glendalough or the Vale of Avoca. The improbable cones of the Great and Little Sugar Loaf mountains protrude suddenly from the surrounding contours, their granite caps more resilient than the rest. The wildness and emptiness of the mountains made them good hiding places after the 1798 rebellion, and during those troubled times they were full of insurgents. One of the main arteries through the region, the military road linking Rathfarnham and the garrison at Aghavannagh, was constructed by English forces in yet another attempt to impose control on recalcitrant Ireland.

THE DUKE OF WELLINGTON
A monument in Emmet Street, Trim, commemorates Arthur Wellesley, who lived here as a boy before becoming, as the Duke of Wellington, the victor at Waterloo. He had been born in Dublin in the same year as his great adversary, Napoleon. But he had very low regard for the capital city of his birth, if we can judge by the answer he gave when asked what he thought of Dublin: 'If a man is born in a stable, that does not make him a horse'.

117

Wicklow was one of the bases used by the Vikings on the east coast of Ireland

Southeastern Counties

Killimor · Banagher · Kilcormac · Clonaslee · Bracknagh · Rathangan
Cadamstown · Portarlington · Kilda
Woodford · Portumna · Birr · Kinnitty · Mountmellick · Monasterevin
Carrigahorig · Birr Castle · Slieve Bloom Mts · M7 · Irish Na Stud, Ja Gard
D · Borrisokane · Shinrone · Portlaoise · Fontstown
Mountshannon · Lough Derg · Roscrea · Mountrath · Castletown · Stradbally · Athy
Scarriff · Portroe · Cloughjordan · Ballyroan · Ballylynan
462m · Nenagh · Moneygall · Borris-in-Ossory · Timahoe · Castlederm
Killaloe · Ballina · Toomyvara · Donaghmore · Ballacolla · Abbeyleix · Arless
Silvermines · Templemore · Clonmore · Rathdowney · Ballinakill · Clogh · Newtown
694m · Templetuohy · Durrow · Carlow
C · Newport · Borrisoleigh · Johnstown · Ballyragget · Castlecomer · Brow Dol
Cappamore · Holycross · Freshford · Urlingford · Oldleighlin · Bagenalstown (Muine Bheag) · Leighlin
Caherconlish · Doon · Clonoulty · Thurles · Kilmanagh · Kilkenny · Dunmore Cave · Paulstown
Pallas Green (New) · Cappagh White · Holycross Abbey · Ballingarry · Bennett's Bridge · Goresbridge
Herbertstown · Oola · Rock of Cashel · Killenaule · Callan · Kells Priory · Gowran · Bor · Dungarvan · Graiguenamanagh
Hospital · Tipperary · Golden · Cashel · Stonyford · Black
Galbally · 918m · Fethard · 721m · Knocktopher · Thomastown · Inistioge · St M
B · Ballylanders · Galty Mts · Cahir · Newton · Slievenaman · Kilmaganny · Jerpoint Abbey · Ballyhale
Swiss Cottage · Clonmel · Knocklofty · Kilsheelan · Mullinavat · Rosbercon · New
Mitchelstown · Ballylooby · Mitchelstown Caves · Ardfinnan · Comeragh Mts · Carrick-on-Suir · Glenmore · John F Ker Arbor
Kildorrery · Ballyporeen · Clogheen · Knockmealdown Mts · 792m · Mooncoin · Dunbrod Abbey
Glanworth · 653m · Mount Melleray Abbey · 727m · Kilmeadan · WATERFORD · Arthurstc
Castletownroche · Ballyduff · Cappoquin · Kilmacthomas · Reginald's Tower · Passage East · Dunca
Fermoy · Lismore · Lemybrien · Kill · Waterford · Fethard
Rathcormack · Conna · Tallowbridge · Bunmahon · Annestown · Tramore · Dunmore Eas
A · Watergrasshill · Tallow · Dungarvan · Hook Head
Dungourney · Clashmore · Ring (An Rinn) · Mine Head
Passage West · Midleton · Killeagh · Youghal · Ardmore
Fota Island · Castlemartyr · Cloyne · Youghal Bay
Cobh · Shanagarry
Carrigaline · Whitegate · Ballycotton

1 · 2 · 3

118

An attractive thatched cottage at Kilmore Quay; throughout modern Ireland, you are more likely to see whitewash than thatch.

Far right: Ship's figurehead in the maritime museum found in the old Lightship, Kilmore Quay

Southeastern Counties

SOUTHEASTERN COUNTIES In contrast with the scenic wildness of western Ireland, the landscape of the southeast is mostly low-lying and docile. Rich pastureland watered by brimming rivers extends gently to a quiet coastline of long sandy beaches, estuarial mudflats of wading birds and low cliffs fringing deep bays. Ireland's most fertile farmland lies in the Golden Vale, making Tipperary one of the most prosperous inland counties. There is a great deal to see and do, although to reach all its scattered attractions you will need a car. The sunny, drier climate of southeastern counties attracts both Irish and foreign visitors for summer holidays, and there is an excellent choice of beaches.

Tacumshane, near Kilmore Quay, has the rarity of a thatched windmill in working order

TRAVELLING PEOPLE
There are about 3,000 itinerant families in the whole of Ireland, amounting to a population of around 20,000. Many live in illegal roadside camps for a few weeks before moving on. Notices discouraging 'travellers' can be seen as you approach many towns and villages. The origins of the true 'traveller' may date back to the 18th century, when many families were dispossessed by the harsh Penal Code, and took to the roads as tinsmiths (hence the old term 'tinker') and dealers. They ranged far and wide, gathering together at events such as the Ballinasloe Horse Fair, where their 'king' was elected. Today's travellers represent a considerable social problem, for large groups of itinerants prove unpopular even among a race as tolerant as the Irish.

TOWN AND CULTURAL ATTRACTIONS Development here remains low-key; Tramore is the largest built-up resort, offering amusement parks and a costly multimedia attraction themed on the Celts. If this atypical brashness doesn't appeal, it is easily avoided. The southeast's other resorts are all small and villagelike, even the county town of Wexford. Waterford is the only 'towny' place, a thriving port and commercial centre where derricks unload cargoes on the wharves and industrial complexes hum. Most famous is the crystal factory about 2km (a mile) out of town. This is the largest of its kind in the world, and its annual turnover is astounding. There is no shortage of visitors on the free guided tours, even if few leave clutching a chandelier (see page 143).

The other sizeable towns of the area are medieval Kilkenny, a smart visitor town with enough attractions to act as an excellent base, and Tipperary's prosperous county town, Clonmel, where Georgian influences are more noticeable. Carlow, however, is disappointing: neither the town nor the county have much to detain you.

County Tipperary's great visitor honeypot is the Rock of Cashel. Bus tours flock to this atmospheric outcrop of limestone in the middle of lush plains to admire the majestic ruins clustered on its summit. If abbeys and monasteries interest you, this is a good area to explore—the great settlements at Holycross (County Tipperary), Duiske, Jerpoint (both County Kilkenny), Dunbrody and Tintern (both County Wexford) are some of the finest. Castles, too, stud the bridging points in these great river valleys—no significant town is without some bristling fortress or other. Cahir, Kilkenny, Lismore, Nenagh and Enniscorthy are among the most impressive.

SPORTS AND FITNESS BREAKS As well as for seaside breaks or conventional touring, the southeast is a splendid area for exercise. The flatter coastal terrain makes walking and biking holidays less strenuous than in some parts of the country, though inland the hill ranges of the Comeragh, Blackstairs, or the splendidly named Knockmealdown Mountains have plenty of visual drama. The South Leinster Way through Carlow and Kilkenny takes in some of the most beautiful scenery around the Nore and Barrow rivers. The Munster Way meanders along the borderland of Tipperary and Waterford over the spectacular high point known as the Vee Gap and the lovely valley of the Nire. You can link the two routes (they meet at Carrick-on-Suir), or pick up the Kildare Way along the Barrow River towpath from Graiguenamanagh. Bird-watchers should head for the reclaimed Wexford Slobs, Hook Head Peninsula or the Saltee Islands.

For fishing holidays the region is excellent; the rivers teem with brown trout, salmon and all kinds of other fish, particularly the Blackwater River. Dungarvan and Dunmore East are the best centres for deep-sea fishing. Lough Derg in the far northwest of County Tipperary is another good location for water sports, including cruising, though the main centres are in Clare or Galway (Killaloe, Mountshannon and Portumna). Equestrian sports are popular in this horsey country; hacking (hiring horses) and fox-hunting can be arranged. Tipperary breeds some of Ireland's finest racehorses, and the interest in racing is evident from no fewer than four racecourses, while greyhound racing centres on Clonmel. Competitive sport is a passionate preoccupation throughout Ireland, but the traditional games of Gaelic football and hurling are played in Tipperary with special enthusiasm. It is no surprise to discover the Gaelic Athletic Association (GAA) was founded here by the sportsmanlike Archbishop of Cashel.

A TURBULENT HISTORY The Vikings held sway over this region for many years, finding those broad estuaries and inviting harbours easy landings from which to torment the native Celts with pillage and nose taxes ('Pay up or we'll cut your nose off!'). Following their example, Strongbow invaded Ireland for the Anglo-Normans via Waterford in 1169, ostensibly to aid Dermot MacMurrough in regaining his Leinster throne. In return, Strongbow received the hand of Dermot's daughter, the first dynastic alliance between Irish and Norman. But the Normans stayed on and their power grew. The Gaelic MacMurrough Kavanaghs resented the curtailment of their influence, and remained a thorn in the English side, rebelling every so often with unexpected ferocity. Cromwell finally broke their resistance and is unaffectionately remembered in this part of Ireland for his slaughter of hundreds of unarmed citizens at Wexford. The southeast was relatively peaceful through the 18th century, but the surface calm disguised many ill feelings. When a confrontation with the yeomanry fanned smouldering passions in 1798, the people of Carlow and Wexford erupted in fury, wielding pikes in a brave but hopeless stand against English cannon fire at the decisive battle of Vinegar Hill, Enniscorthy.

121

The Vee Gap, near Mitchelstown in County Tipperary, looks especially dramatic in 'Irish weather'

Ardmore's Round Tower; it is one of the finest (and latest) in Ireland

ARDMORE'S ROUND TOWER

'The tower…is said to have been built by St. Declan in one night; that when it had arrived at its present height, a woman coming to gather herbs, looking up, asked the Saint what he was doing, upon which he threw down his trowel and killed her, and coming down he threw her upon the top of the tower, where a part of her remained till a few years ago. It is certain, however, that the tower was never raised higher than it is, which it is said it would have been, had not the woman interrupted the Saint in his pious work.'
P. D. Hardy: *The Holy Wells of Ireland* (1836)

▶▶ Ardmore 1182A

Ardmore (roughly 13km/8 miles east of Youghal) is an attractive little resort at the foot of high cliffs, where simple hotels and a guesthouse or two command awesome views over the bay. A blue-flag award for its clean beach and a 'tidy town' commendation indicate a sense of local pride. One of its best-known residents is the popular novelist Molly Keane. An ancient place, Ardmore saw the foundation of Ireland's earliest Christian settlement when St. Declan arrived here from Wales, some 30 years before St. Patrick. His bell and vestments were miraculously borne across the water by a glacial boulder, now tilted on a little spur of rock on the beach. It promises wondrous healing powers for all agile enough to creep beneath it.

Excellent views can be seen from the monastery. Most of the remains date from after Declan's time; a well-preserved 30m (100ft) Round Tower and cathedral are largely 12th century. The cathedral displays clear and vigorous carvings of biblical scenes, such as the Judgment of Solomon and the Weighing of Souls. Inside are several ogham stones (see page 16). St. Declan's Oratory is an older structure that may contain the saint's remains, the surrounding earth much pillaged for its restorative properties. St. Declan's Well and a ruined church where the saint spent his final years can be found along the cliff walk leading from the village.

▶▶ Cahir 1181B

The fortress in the centre of this small town on the Suir River is in fine condition after restoration work. **Cahir Castle▶▶** (tel: 052 41011; *open:* Apr–end Jun and mid-Sep to mid-Oct daily 9.30–5.30; Jun–mid-Sep daily 9–7.30; late-Oct–end Mar daily 9.30–1 and 2–4.30. *Admission: inexpensive*) dates mainly from the 15th century with later alterations, and was formerly a stronghold of the powerful local Anglo-Norman Butler family, dukes and earls of Ormonde. Queen Elizabeth I's favourite, the Earl of Essex, rammed a few cannonballs into its masonry in 1599, but it survived Cromwellian times little scathed. The huge walls enclose three separate 'wards', outer, middle and inner, the inner one guarded by a gate with a portcullis. Rooms in the keep are whitewashed and contain armour displays and period furnishings from the 16th and 17th centuries.

Cahir's fortunes waxed and waned through the centuries, but in peacetime it developed an important milling industry introduced by local Quakers. The town is something of a time warp and some of its shops and houses appear little changed for decades. One of them, Keating's Draper's Shop, traded in predecimal currency until it closed down a few years ago. Another agreeable feature of the town is its evident lack of religious or political bigotry. Protestants and Catholics used to worship simultaneously in its ruined church, separated only by a curtain wall. Somewhat unusually, in the main square is a war memorial dedicated to the many local men who fell in the Great War. Throughout most of the Republic the World Wars seem unmarked, and the people who gave their lives in these conflicts are forgotten.

The other curiosity in Cahir is the **Swiss Cottage▶** (tel: 05241144; *open*: May–end Sep daily 10–6; Oct–end Nov Tue–Sun 10–4.30; Dec–end Mar Tue–Sun 10–6; Apr Tue–Sun 10–5. *Admission: inexpensive*), just outside the town on the Clonmel road. This quaint thatched building with its eyebrow windows and corkscrew timbering looks like something out of Hansel and Gretel rather than the Swiss Alps. It was designed in about 1810 by the royal architect, John Nash, for the Butler family, in a then-fashionable genre known as a 'cottage *orné*', a sort of rustic summer-house or hunting lodge in which the wealthy gentry relaxed and amused themselves in what they imagined to be rural simplicity. The cottage was rescued from dereliction by enthusiastic conservationists and extensively restored, the original handpainted French wallpapers and fabrics have been faithfully copied, and it is now elegantly furnished with many fascinating period details.

St. Declan's Well, Ardmore

123

Cahir Castle was once thought to be impregnable, but Cromwell took the castle in 1650

At around 100 tons, the capstone of Brownshill Dolmen weighs heavy upon its supporting stones

An intriguing shop-front in Carrick-on-Suir

▶ Carlow   *1183C*

Though a county town, Carlow is disappointingly lack-lustre apart from a few nice old shop-fronts (Cigar Divan on Dublin Street is a fine example of authentic Victoriana). It lies on the east bank of the Barrow in the once tempestuous borderland at the edge of the Pale, old warehouses lining its former quays. Its castle, standing in the grounds of a mineral-water bottling plant, is perilously ruinous after the misguided attempts of a Dr. Middleton in 1814 to reduce the thickness of the walls in order to convert the castle into a lunatic asylum. Unfortunately he understood little of the explosives he was using for the purpose, and the walls were well and truly modified, becoming so unsafe that some parts later had to be demolished. Also worth a brief look in the town is the county museum which has various reconstructed farm interiors. The 19th-century Gothic cathedral is easily spotted by its unusual lantern spire, looking like a crown of thorns. It contains an elaborate pulpit and a finely sculpted marble **monument to Bishop Doyle**▶, or JKL (James of Kildare and Leighlin). The story goes that the artist, John Hogan, forgot to include the bishop's ring, and was so mortified by this omission that he committed suicide.

Some 3km (2 miles) east is the **Brownshill Dolmen**▶, clearly visible across a field, though it stands some way from the road. The tilted granite capstone is enormous, weighing around 100 tons, and is thought to be the largest of its type in Europe. It poises on its supporting stones as delicately as a ballerina. A fenced path leads from the parking place around the edge of the field.

▶▶ Carrick-on-Suir   *1182B*

A border town straddling the counties of Tipperary and Waterford, Carrick is noteworthy for its beautiful Tudor mansion. This is all the more remarkable because such buildings are a rarity in Ireland, in comparison with

Ormond Castle, one of the finest examples of an Irish manor house

literally hundreds of fortresses and abbeys. Despite its name, **Ormond Castle►►**, the house is completely unfortified, perhaps in misplaced expectations of less turbulent times (tel: 051 640 787; *open:* mid-Jun–end Sep daily 10–6. *Admission: inexpensive*). The building was commissioned by 'Black Tom', the swarthy-faced 10th Earl of Ormond, in anticipation of a visit by his cousin Queen Elizabeth I (who didn't come). Tom was a great favourite of the Queen's, a potent reason for an attempted poisoning by his rival, the Earl of Leicester, which he survived. Tom remained an ardent royalist and contributed greatly to the maintenance of English rule in Ireland during this troubled period.

Behind the grey-stone, gabled exterior pierced with many mullioned windows lies lovely stucco work, particularly fine in the 30m (100ft) Long Gallery where royal coats of arms surmount the fireplace. The timber roof contains no bolts, only carpentry joints. Marks can be seen in the attic-room beams, where garrisoned soldiers would stick their knives before retiring for the night.

There is probably no truth in the legend that Anne Boleyn (Queen Elizabeth's mother) was born at Carrick. Today the town is much prouder of a more recent hero, Sean Kelly, the bicycle racer, who was ranked number one in the world throughout the late 1980s. He won many of the sport's major events. A square in the town is named after him.

Just outside Carrick (on the N24) a well-signed thatched roadside showroom indicates the factory of **Tipperary Crystal►** (tel: 051 641 188; *open:* Mon–Fri 10–3.30). Visitors are welcome to look around the production plant and, of course, buy the hand-decorated glassware. The founders of this enterprise learned their trade at the much more prestigious Waterford factory, but were laid off during hard times and used their severance pay to set up a rival company, using similar techniques. Prices are slightly lower and Tipperary Crystal has been successfully competing with Waterford—a gratifying piece of vengeance for those laid-off workers.

A LITERARY RANSOM
The Butler family of Carrick Castle had many notable warriors, but it also included men of letters, particularly one Émonn mac Risderd Butler. He employed scribes to write for him, and one of their manuscripts, dating from the middle of the 15th century, is now preserved in the British Library in London. So highly prized were his manuscripts that two were given to the Earl of Desmond in ransom for Émonn's life after he had been defeated in the Battle of Pottlerath in 1462.

GAELIC ATHLETIC ASSOCIATION
This largely rural movement was first founded in 1884 in Thurles, 16km (10miles) north of Cashel, under the sponsorship of the Archbishop of Cashel, Thomas William Croke (1824–1902). The GAA's purpose was ostensibly to popularize traditional Irish pastimes such as hurling, handball and Gaelic football, and today it remains Ireland's most important sporting association. Though not party political, it has proved a fertile recruiting ground for Republican activists, and in the past has been suspected of IRA sympathies.

The Rock of Cashel rears up from the fertile plains of County Tipperary

▶▶▶ **Cashel**   *1182B*

Rock of Cashel, tel: 062 61437
Open: mid-Mar to mid-Jun daily 9–5.30; mid-Jun to mid-Sep daily 9–7; mid-Sep to mid-Mar daily 9–4.30
Admission: moderate

Stories tell how the devil bit a huge chunk out of the Slieve Bloom Mountains, then spat it out in disgust here in the Golden Vale when he saw St. Patrick preparing to build a great church. This erratic outcrop of limestone among the patchwork plains of rich cattle pasture looks almost freakish enough to justify such a tale. The Rock of Cashel is a mere 61m (200ft) high, but approached from below, the craggy outline of towers and gables crowning the hilltop looks most ethereal, especially in certain conditions of light or weather. Close up, the romantic image fades a little under the pressure of tourism. It is one of Ireland's most popular sights and is always besieged by visitors in high season. The little town of Cashel has managed to avoid the worst excesses of commercialized religiosity, however, and remains a pleasant country town.

Cashel has long been a place of great significance, and rivalled Tara as a royal seat for the kings of Munster from the 4th century AD. St. Patrick arrived in about AD432 and converted King Aengus, who became Ireland's first Christian ruler. Among many legends associated with this event, St. Patrick is alleged to have used a shamrock leaf to illustrate the nature of the Holy Trinity. During Aengus's baptism, St. Patrick accidentally drove his sharp crozier through the king's foot, but the king did not complain and his wound was discovered only after the ceremony, when he said he had assumed the suffering was some sort of initiation rite, emulating the pain of Christ.

The buildings visible on Cashel date mainly from the 12th and 13th centuries. Earliest of these structures is probably the **Round Tower▶**, well preserved, with an entrance doorway 3.5m (12ft) above ground level. **Cormac's Chapel▶▶**, ornately carved with beasts and human figures, begun in 1127, is in excellent condition and displays the Irish Romanesque style clearly. A sarcophagus in the chapel is said to be the tomb of Cormac, the bishop-king of Munster, who presided during Cashel's great time of influence in the 12th century. The roofless 13th-century **St. Patrick's Cathedral▶▶**, the largest building on the Rock, with tall lancet and quatrefoil windows and a later central tower on Gothic arches, witnessed a particularly unpleasant act of Cromwellian barbarism when Lord Inchiquin besieged the town in 1647. The citizens fled to sanctuary in the cathedral, whereupon turf was piled up around the walls and set on fire, roasting hundreds of unfortunate townspeople to death. Attempts were made to repair the building but it declined, and in 1749 Cashel's main place of worship was moved to the town. The **Hall of the Vicars▶**, a 15th-century residence for privileged members of the choir, at the foot of the Rock, has a museum with St. Patrick's cross and coronation stone. The Brú Ború heritage centre promotes Celtic studies and performing arts.

In the town, a small **folk village▶** attracts many visitors (*Open: Mar–end Apr 10–6; May–end Oct 9.30–7. Admission: moderate*). It features reconstructions of 18th-century buildings and displays artefacts of the period. The **GPA-Bolton Library▶▶** in the grounds of the Protestant Cathedral is an unusually gripping collection of old tomes; it contains over 12,000 volumes, including part of Chaucer's *Book of Fame*, printed by Caxton and a collection of church silver (tel: 062 61944; open: Feb–end Sep Mon–Fri 9.30–5.30. *Admission: inexpensive*). Take a look at **Cashel Palace▶**, a splendid brick edifice, former home of the Archbishop of Cashel and now a luxury hotel (see Hotels and Restaurants, page 272). Visitors can take advantage of the basement Buttery Restaurant, one of the best places in town for a hearty meal or quick snack.

127

St. Patrick's Cross

MILER MAGRATH
Buried in the cathedral at Cashel is Archbishop Magrath, a noted pluralist who enjoyed the best of both worlds. Born around 1523, he began his religious life a Franciscan friar, soon becoming Catholic Bishop of Down and Connor, an office he later combined with being Protestant Archbishop of Cashel. At his death (1622) he had amassed 70 parishes, four bishoprics, two wives and numerous offspring.

Inside the museum at the Rock of Cashel

CHARLES BIANCONI

This adopted citizen of Clonmel was born at Tregolo in northern Italy on 24 September 1786. He was dispatched to Ireland by his father to avoid a scandal at the age of 16 after he had fallen in love with a neighbour's daughter who was destined for a marriage with the nobility. On 6 July, 1815, he began a one-horse cart service between Clonmel and Cahir, which rapidly grew into a thriving mail-coach business and reputedly the world's first public transportation system. His vehicles were known as 'bians' (after Bianconi) and ran thousands of miles each day all over Ireland, despite competition from the railroads. His headquarters were in Hearn's Hotel on Parnell Street and he became mayor of Clonmel twice.

The attractive harbour at Dunmore East continues...

▶▶ Clonmel · 1182B

Clonmel is Tipperary's county town, a prosperous and pretty place with plenty of life and, if home-grown novelist Laurence Sterne's writings are anything to go by, some whimsical goings-on. Sterne lived during the 18th century and is best known for his novel, *Tristram Shandy*. Other novelists have connections with the town; Anthony Trollope worked for a while in the local post office and George Borrow, the 19th-century traveller and writer, was at school here. There are no outstanding sights in the town, but it has lots of pleasant shops and eating places and stands on the edge of some extremely picturesque touring country. The **circular drive▶▶** to the south, along the Nire and Suir valleys, is well worth taking on a fine day. So are trips into the unspoiled Comeragh Mountains.

The town was once an important stronghold of the powerful Butler family. Its Main Guard replaced the court-house destroyed in the Cromwellian siege. The West Gate dates from 1831 and stands on the site of an earlier medieval gateway. Near St. Mary's Protestant church are sections of the old 14th-century walls that defended the town against Cromwell for longer than any other Irish town. Several churches have eye-catching, 19th-century, 'streaky bacon' coloured brickwork.

Clonmel is famed for its field sports, notably fox-hunting and hare-coursing (sending dogs after hares). It is a great centre of the greyhound world and the slim animals can often be seen being exercised along the road, much as racehorses are in Kildare.

▶ Dungarvan · 1182A

A bustling fishing port and resort on the Colligan estuary, Dungarvan is surrounded by low cliffs and gentle hills. The setting is rather more appealing than the town itself, but it caters well to simple family stays with an excellent beach at Clonea Strand. The centre of the town is Grattan Square, flanked by stately buildings. Down by the harbour a maze of tiny alleyways laces between warehouses towards the quayside, where several attractive old inns serve good seafood. Old Market House contains a museum of local history, where the sad tale of the *Moresby*, shipwrecked in Dungarvan Bay, is recounted. Close to the town the remains of Dungarvan's Castle, built by King John, can be seen, and on the east bank of the Colligan is an Augustinian abbey overlooking attractive **Helvick Head▶▶**. The drive around the bay to this headland leads through the tiny Gaelic-speaking village of **Ring▶▶**, with some fine coastal views on the way.

▶▶ Dunmore East · 1183A

This substantial village at the seaward end of Waterford harbour is now a popular resort and sailing centre, but tourism is a secondary interest. Dunmore has its own *raison d'être* dating from 1813, when it was chosen as Waterford's mail packet station. Bright fishing boats crowd the pretty harbour of what is obviously still a well-used port. Visitors are warned that they approach the waterside at their own risk; ropes and steel hawsers bestrew the workmanlike quays. The setting is lovely—red sandstone cliffs, topped with vivid emerald turf and golden gorse, catch the sun, while beneath lie sheltered coves of soft sand. A lighthouse guards the headland. The picturesqueness has encouraged an influx of well-heeled visitors and the village has been used more than once as a film location. Waterford residents retire or escape here in spacious architect-designed bungalows, and more transient holiday-makers stay in thatched homes. The core of the old community is still visible closer to the harbour, in a pleasing assembly of well-kept Georgian and Victorian cottages. The village boasts an exceptionally good range of reasonably priced accommodation and unpretentious eating places, and is an excellent place to stay to explore Waterford City or any of this attractive coast.

MASTER MCGRATH
At a fork in the road 5km (3mi) northwest of Dungarvan stands a splendid commemorative monument—to a greyhound. It was erected by local sportsmen to Master McGrath, winner of the Waterloo Cup three times (1868, 1869 and 1871) and victor in all but one of the 37 courses he ran. Doubtless they were keen to honour both his triumphs and the bets he won for his backers.

...to be the mainstay of the local economy

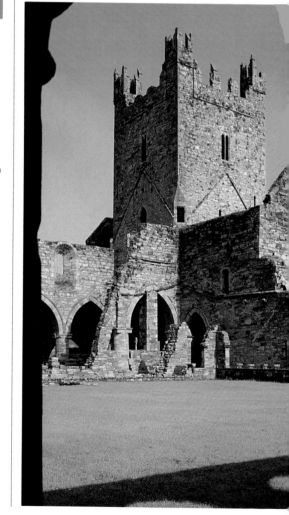

From the County Wexford Museum in Enniscorthy

AN IMPOSTOR
The Round Tower that dominates the Irish National Heritage Park at Ferrycarrig gives the impression that the hill on which it stands was the site of an early Irish monastery, to which Round Towers normally belonged. However, a plaque in the wall gives the game away; the tower is a 19th-century copy commemorating the men of Wexford who died in the Crimean War (1853–1856).

In its heyday, Jerpoint Abbey was surrounded by a small town, but few, if any, traces of this now survive

▶ **Enniscorthy** *1194B*

The market town of Enniscorthy on the banks of the Slaney River is remembered for a terrible battle in the troubled year of 1798. On 21 June about 20,000 rebels, including many women and children, armed with agricultural implements and metal bayonets or swords, gathered on Vinegar Hill just outside the town. They had held it for nearly a month, but English troops under General Lake, finally losing patience, strafed the insurgents with continuous cannon fire. Exactly how many were killed is not known, but the massacre remains vivid in the minds of Irish people. The Battle of Vinegar Hill effectively marked the end of the 1798 uprising, but Enniscorthy played an active anti-British role in the Easter Rising of 1916. A fascinating collection of items connected with the battle can be seen in the **Wexford County Museum**▶▶ (tel: 054 35926; *open:* Jun–end Sep daily Mon–Sat 10–1, 2–6, Sun 2–5.30; Feb–end May, Oct, Nov daily 2–5.30; Dec, Jan Sun 2–5.30. *Admission: inexpensive*), housed in the sturdy square-towered castle. This impressive Anglo-Norman building was briefly leased to the Elizabethan poet and politician, Edmund Spenser, during his inglorious period of office in Ireland. From the castle you can see the slopes of Vinegar Hill, golden with gorse most of the year, and crowned with the stump of an old windmill that served as the rebels' HQ. The town is the centre of the southeast's soft-fruit industry, and every July a Strawberry Fair is held. Enniscorthy's other noteworthy building is its Gothic cathedral of St. Aidan's, designed by Pugin.

A few miles up the road lies **Ferns▶**, now a village but formerly the capital of Leinster. Its ruins are the remains of a 13th-century castle and an Augustinian abbey.

▶▶ Ferrycarrig
1194B

Just where the Slaney River broadens into tidal mudflats west of Wexford is the **Irish National Heritage Park▶▶**, which re-creates aspects of life in Ireland through about 9,000 years of history up to the Anglo-Norman period (tel: 053 20733, www.inhp.com; *open*: daily 9.30–6.30. *Admission: expensive*). Full-scale models of lake settlements, ring forts, burial places and a complete Norman castle lie hidden among hazel groves and reed beds in a large park. This is 'theme-park Ireland', but it is well done, informative and naturalistic, helping to put into context many of the scattered antiquities you will find as you travel around Ireland. The visitor centre has an audio-visual presentation.

▶ Holycross Abbey
1182C

Holycross, tel: 050 443241
Open: daily 9–5 and during services. Admission free
Holycross Abbey is set in peaceful water meadows by the Suir River. It was founded in 1169 and restored in the 15th century. It fell into decay until 1971, when much rebuilding and interior whitewashing made it usable again as a parish church. The abbey's great treasure that attracts thousands of pilgrims to its wall shrine is an alleged splinter of the True Cross, thought to have been given to Murtagh O'Brien, King of Munster, by a 12th-century pope. The Ulster clan chiefs O'Donnell and O'Neill stopped off to pray here on their way to Kinsale, but fate was against them (see page 162). The interior contains a rare wall painting of a Norman hunting scene and some fine stonework.

▶▶ Jerpoint Abbey
1183B

Thomastown, tel: 056 77 21755
Open: Mar–end May and mid-Sep to mid-Oct Wed–Mon 10–5; Jun–mid-Sep daily 9.30–6.30; otherwise obtain key from theon-site caretaker. Admission: moderate
These evocative Cistercian ruins seem to have a much more authentically medieval ring about them than somewhat commercialized Holycross, the stone tower and battlements erupting suddenly on a quiet bend south of Thomastown. Peer through the gaps in the walls, but if the visitor centre is open it is worth the modest entrance charge to wander around the cloisters and chancel for a close-up of the vivacious carvings of medieval figures and beasts on capitals and tombs. The **glassworks▶** at Jerpoint produce a plainer style than most Irish crystal factories.

131

Characterful figures adorn the tombs at Jerpoint Abbey

The Long Gallery in Kilkenny Castle includes portraits by Van Dyck and Lely

DUNMORE CAVE
These caverns can be found just north of Kilkenny town in craggy limestone farmland, with an entrance lying down a long flight of steps. One has a thick stalagmite pillar and lots of tiny ceiling straws like icicles. A collection of items and geological material is on display at the visitor centre by the ticket office. One grisly find included the bones of more than 40 people, many of them women and children, who are believed to have taken refuge in the caves, perhaps to elude the Vikings. Their undamaged bones suggests they died of starvation or may have been suffocated by smoke.

▶▶▶ Kilkenny   1183C

One of Ireland's most delightful towns, Kilkenny stands on a bend in the Nore River. It is packed with history (in summer, with visitor traffic, too) and its medieval heritage is particularly well preserved. Discerning visitors will find a number of high-quality craft studios and good restaurants. One of the most popular times to come is during the Arts Week festival in the last two weeks of August. The beautiful countryside around Kilkenny makes it an excellent touring base. The most striking building is the **castle▶▶** (tel: 056 77 21450, www.kilkenny.ie), a stronghold of the Butler family until the 20th century, a Norman fortress that gradually became more domesticated through the centuries. It saw conflict, however, when anti-Treatyites occupied it briefly during the Civil War in 1922. After massive restoration, the castle is once again on show. The hammer-beamed picture gallery, lined with portraits and elaborate ceiling decorations, is the best room. The well-proportioned 18th-century buildings opposite the castle have now been converted into an imaginative enterprise called the Kilkenny Design Centre, where local artists produce high-quality crafts. A large retail outlet fronting the street supplies some of the best goods on sale in Ireland and is an attractive place to do some shopping, though prices are steep.

Kilkenny's historical importance formerly rivalled Dublin's, and several significant political events took place there. The Statutes of Kilkenny, passed in 1366, were a notorious and crude attempt to assert English authority in Ireland by what was essentially a form of apartheid. The Anglo-Norman settlers were prevented from intermarriage or social intercourse with the native Celtic Irish, on pain of death. Gaelic names were banned, the language was suppressed and the native population was forced to live outside the city walls. Understandably, the Irish grew restless at this repressive regime. After the Reformation had suppressed even their religious beliefs, the 'Old English' and Gaelic aristocrats (both Catholic factions) formed an uneasy alliance called the Confederation of Kilkenny, a parliamentary assembly that aimed to resist the ferociously unjust anti-Catholic laws imposed by Protestant England. Cromwell's invasion brutally put a stop to this and thus drove an iron stake through the heart of Anglo-Irish integration, which, if left to itself, would, over time, probably have resulted in a harmonious community.

Many other interesting buildings are scattered through the old town. **St. Canice's Cathedral**▶ ▶ (tel: 056 77 64971) is its most notable church and one of the finest 13th-century buildings in Ireland, despite Cromwell's use of it to stable his horses in 1650. The monuments of the black limestone known as Kilkenny marble are particularly impressive—one female statue wears a traditional Irish cloak. Next to the cathedral are a **Round Tower**▶, which can be climbed for splendid town views, and the valuable **St. Canice's Library**▶ containing many rare early volumes. St. Mary's Cathedral is the Catholic counterpart built in 1849. Other medieval churches include the Black Abbey, the ruined St. John's Priory and St. Francis's Abbey.

One of several Tudor buildings is **Rothe House**▶ ▶ (tel: 056 22893). This stone mansion belonged to the merchant John Rothe and his growing family of 12 children, which necessitated the addition of several wings rambling around cobbled courtyards. The restored building has now become a museum run by Kilkenny Archaeological Society. The Tourist Information Centre is housed in a **Tudor almshouse**▶ (tel: 056 77 51500, www.southeastireland.com) built by lawyer Sir Richard Shee in 1594. A *son-et-lumière* presentation is held upstairs. The Tholsel (town hall) and courthouse date from the 18th century.

ALICE KYTELER
The medieval home of Dame Alice Kyteler is now a popular old tavern in Kilkenny. In 1324, she was charged with witchcraft and the poisoning of her four husbands, all of whom had died painfully in quick succession, leaving Alice somewhat wealthy. Whether there was any truth in the accusation is unknown, but Alice was a sly character, and she fled to Scotland, leaving her poor maid, Petronella, to take her place at the stake.

KELLS PRIORY
The countryside south and east of Kilkenny is pretty. If you head south you will find the romantic remains of Kells Priory, a walled monastery looking like some medieval city standing in a sloping field. A short way south of the tiny medieval village are a Round Tower and a High Cross.

133

St. Canice's Cathedral

THE VEE GAP

Drive

The Vee Gap

A roller-coaster drive between southern Tipperary's two ranges of hills, with panoramic views of fertile plains.

From the mundane agricultural town of **Tipperary**, an important dairy farming centre, a scenic route is marked via the **Glen of Aherlow▶▶**. A road through dappled woodland meanders up to a sharp hairpin bend, giving a breathtaking vista down the Aherlow Valley. This beautiful glen is about 16km

(10 miles) long, following the course of the Aherlow River. Shortly afterwards it joins the Glen of Aherlow road, with grand glimpses of the Slievenamuck Hills to the north and the shallow-pitched ridge of the Galty Mountains on the southerly side. The highest summit is Galtymore Mountain, at 919m (3,015ft). The Cahir Way and numerous forest trails lead through the hills, past ancient cairns and glacial tarns. The region is noted for its traditional farmhouse cheeses, Galty bacon and sausages, hams and even venison. **Mitchelstown▶** is a good place to buy these products.

From **Bansha** the N24 leads southeast to **Cahir▶▶** (see pages 122–123). At Cahir the minor R668 runs down towards the old market town of **Clogheen▶**, where you can

134

join the spectacular **Vee Gap Drive►►** through the Knockmealdown Mountains. The Vee road winds steeply up through larch and rhododendron, and at its most dramatic loop several safe parking bays offer irresistibly photogenic views. Far below, the Suir Valley and the Golden Vale of emerald fields lie as flat and placid as an embroidered quilt beneath vast skies. Black-and-white cattle graze amid a sprinkling of farmsteads. Just south of these viewpoints the road climbs over heather-, bracken- and gorse-covered slopes to the V-shaped pass that forms the boundary between Tipperary and Waterford counties. A tarn is visible below the road, and a couple of stone shepherds' shelters. Beyond the pass, the road descends past **Mount Melleray Abbey** (see page 136) to **Cappoquin**.

► Kilmore Quay
1194A

Just offshore lie the Saltee Islands, Ireland's largest bird sanctuary. Boats run from the harbour from May until mid-July, the nesting season for thousands of seabirds. The pretty village of thatched and whitewashed cottages vies with Kinsale by hosting a seafood festival in July—the Wooden House pub is one of the better bars offering traditional music. An old lightship moored in the harbour contains a small maritime museum. The westerly sandspit of Ballyteigue is another important nature reserve, with rare plants.

►► Lismore
1181A

The **castle►►** (tel: 058 54424), looming above the dense woodland of the Blackwater Valley, is one of Ireland's most evocative fortresses. Built by Prince John in 1185, it was extensively remodelled in the 19th century, when Joseph Paxton (designer of the Crystal Palace in south London) was commissioned to re-create a Tudor-style residence for the 6th Duke of Devonshire from the medieval ruins. It was planned on an opulent scale; the gorgeous **gardens** are open to the public during the summer (although you can't see inside the castle). Sir Walter Ralegh lived there for a time, later selling it to Richard Boyle, father of the famous pharmacist who was born in the castle. It also functioned as an archbishop's palace, eventually passing in 1753 to the Cavendish family, the Dukes of Devonshire, whose Irish seat it remains to this day. For many years Lismore Castle was the home of Fred Astaire's sister, Adele, who married a Cavendish.

The other main buildings of interest in Lismore are the two cathedrals. **St. Carthage's►►**, the Anglican one, is mostly 17th century, its notable features including the splendidly carved MacGrath tomb dating from 1548 and two bright lancet windows by the pre-Raphaelite artist, Sir Edward Burne-Jones. The Catholic Cathedral, built in 1881, contains many ornate decorations in Italian Romanesque style.

An award-winning **heritage centre►►** (tel: 058 54975) has appeared in Lismore's stone courthouse. An excellent audio-visual production on the history of the town and area dwells particularly on its importance as a monastic settlement and university in the 7th century. Today Lismore is proud of another local celebrity, the travel writer Dervla Murphy, who acquired her wanderlust by cycling around this beautiful wooded valley where she was born.

SURPRISING LISMORE
Lismore Castle is a place of surprises. James II, on looking out of the window over the Blackwater River in 1689, was so amazed at the drop that he started with a fright; the spot is pointed out to this day. In 1814, when workmen were repairing the castle, they found a crozier dated around 1100 in a wall and a later medieval manuscript containing the lives of early Irish saints. Both were probably hidden when the castle was besieged and burned in 1645. They are now in the National Museum, Dublin.

135

A figurehead at the Maritime Museum, Kilmore Quay

▶ ▶ ▶ Mitchelstown Caves   1181B

Burncourt, tel: 052 67246, www.mitchelstowncaves.com
Open: daily 10–6
Admission: moderate

These caves are believed to be the largest system of river-formed limestone caverns in Ireland. Though privately owned, they remain pleasantly uncommercialized. You buy your ticket at a roadside farmhouse, and the 3km (2 miles) tour around a small section of the caves is conducted on an amateur family basis. Minerals in the rocks have caused spectacular colourations. The caves served as a hiding place for the Earl of Desmond during the 16th century. Occasional special events take advantage of the acoustics.

▶ Mount Melleray Abbey   1182B

Mount Melleray, tel: 058 54404
Open: daily 9–6. Admission free
This austere, grey monastery was founded in 1832 by the Cistercian order, who have industriously turned a barren hillside into fertile and productive land. The community of mostly Irish monks was expelled from its original home in France and granted land here. Visitors are welcome in the main church and can stay in the guest lodge by prior arrangement. Just south of the monastery is a grotto shrine where miraculous visions of the Virgin have been seen, and the faithful gather to light candles and pray.

▶ New Ross   1183B

The main reason for visiting the otherwise quiet town of New Ross is for the unique experience of boarding a full-scale replica of a Famine emigrant sailing ship. The Dunbrody Historic Emigrant Ship (tel: 051 425239, www.dunbrody.com; *open:* Apr–end Sep 9–6; Oct–end Mar 10–5. *Admission: inexpensive*), is a hauntingly beautiful

Mitchelstown Caves lie in a limestone trough between the Knockmealdown and Galty mountains, and are the unexpected home of a very rare spider, Porrhoma Myops

The J. F. Kennedy Arboretum, near New Ross

1845-style, sea-going, three-masted barque. The quayside visitor centre has an interesting exhibit on life on the boat. New Ross is a very old settlement, founded in the 13th century by Strongbow's son-in-law, William le Marshall, on an ancient monastic site. Part of the ancient city gates remain. The waterfront can be pleasantly explored from a boat deck; river cruises up the Barrow are organized in summer on the Galley Cruising Restaurant. There are also many rewarding excursions, particularly north, towards Inistioge and St. Mullin's. Flower-dappled lanes wander through ancient villages studded with crumbling castles and abbeys. Sparkling rivers snake through the meadows and the gentle contours of the Blackstairs Mountains, brown, green or heather-coloured, rise in the background.

The drive northwest through the beautiful Nore valley leads past **Inistioge►** to **Thomastown►►** and **Jerpoint Abbey►►** (see page 131). Inistioge is a picturesque little town, with linden trees planted in its main square beside the bridge, a pretty riverfront and a jumble of 18th- and 19th-century houses on the lane twisting up from the town centre. There are ruins of a Norman castle and an Augustinian monastery. Thomastown, once a medieval walled town of importance, is now a lovely place with mellowed grey-stone buildings and a few ruins. The **Kilfane Glen and Waterfall►** is an 18th-century woodland garden. Return to New Ross via **Graiguenamanagh►►** and **St. Mullin's►** (see page 141). Graiguenamanagh, in a spectacular position beside the river, is a little market town, famous for **Duiske Abbey►** (*Open:* daily 9–5 and during services. *Admission free*), a much-restored 13th-century Cistercian foundation, once the largest in Ireland. The effigy of a knight stands beside the abbey's entrance.

South of New Ross lies the **J. F. Kennedy Arboretum►►**, occupying an area of forest and landscaped gardens with about 5,000 types of specimen trees and shrubs (tel: 051 388171; *open:* May–end Aug daily 10–8; Apr, Sep daily 10–6.30; Oct–end Mar daily 10–5. *Admission: inexpensive*). Nature trails lead through the grounds and visitors can drive to a viewpoint on the summit of Slieve Coillte. Much botanical and arboreal research is carried out there.

IRISH-AMERICAN PRESIDENTS
Two recent US presidents have roots in southeast Ireland. President John F. Kennedy's great-grandfather was born in a cottage in Dunganstown, just south of New Ross in County Waterford, and descendants of the family still live there. A memorial arboretum to President Kennedy has been planted close by. President Ronald Reagan's folk probably hailed from the tiny, one-horse town of Ballyporeen, near Mitchelstown in County Tipperary. President Reagan visited Ballyporeen in 1984 and brought great fame to it.

'*As long as Ireland produces men with sense enough to leave her, she does not exist in vain.*' George Bernard Shaw's remark is unkind, but apt. Irish-born people or, more broadly, people of Irish descent, have had a most disproportionate influence in many fields, particularly in the arts, media, sports and politics. But they have often shown this after they have left the island.

Top: Ireland's most famous 20th-century exile, James Joyce

138

THE FLIGHT OF THE WILD GEESE
After the final victory of William III's forces at the Battle of Limerick in 1691, many Jacobite officers accepted the terms of surrender at the Treaty of Limerick and sailed away down the Shannon to join the armies of Catholic Europe (perhaps with the hope one day of returning to defeat the old enemy). Among these aristocratic mercenaries was the hero of the Battle of Limerick, Patrick Sarsfield, Earl of Lucan. Like the earlier Flight of the Earls in 1607, this exile of leaders dealt a great blow to Gaelic power in Ireland. Their estates and castles were quickly snatched by Protestant settlers.

A constraining influence Many periods in Ireland's history have worked against pioneering spirits; the long doldrum since the Irish Free State was formed in 1922 is one of the most noticeable of these in recent times. After English shackles were shaken off, Ireland had everything to play for—high ideals, a young and vigorous population and a new nation to form. Under de Valera's rule and the constricting influence of a peculiarly oppressive form of Catholicism, Ireland remained fossilized in a twilight zone of romantic mythology, social divisiveness and economic gloom. Many people have left Ireland since, ironically for the land whose rule they have so roundly rejected.

Artists and Ireland Artists and writers have deserted Ireland for centuries in search of havens where their work would receive a better reception than in the reactionary climate of their birthplace. Since World War II, the Irish government has tried to stem the tide by offering artists (including writers) tax-free status in the Republic. The hugely successful novelist Frederick Forsyth was one of the most notable acceptors of this bribe, though other writers found it odd that a government should encourage literary enterprise with fiscal measures and then censor it on religious or moral grounds. An enormous number of Irish writers have made their homes abroad. One, Cecil Day-Lewis, even became an English poet laureate. The novelist Edna O'Brien, herself an exile in London from Tuamgraney, County Clare, described the claustrophobia of Irish provincial life. 'Hour after hour I can think of Ireland, I can imagine without going too far wrong what is happening in any one of the little towns by day or by night.' For a visit, for a holiday, the pace of Ireland is refreshing, endearing, delightful. However, for a lifetime, many have found it stultifying.

Enforced emigration Reasons for the steady departure of Irishmen to lands abroad range from general 'grass is greener' aspirations to the most dire and desperate emergencies. Most drastically, the Famine years of the late 1840s resulted in massive emigration, mostly from the west. Whole communities were decimated and many have never recovered. In earlier times, religious persecution was often the spur, famously in the exile of leading Catholic families after the confiscation of their lands

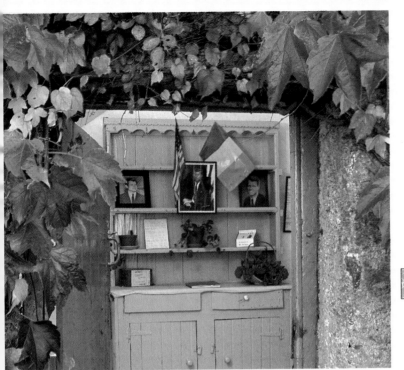

(The Flight of the Earls in 1607, see pages 34–35), or after defeat in battle ('The Wild Geese', after the Battle of Limerick in 1691, see panel). The Ulster Presbyterians emigrated in great numbers in the late 18th and early 19th centuries in order to seek their fortunes in the New World. One of the best places to learn all about this fascinating phase of Irish history is at the **Ulster American Folk Park** in County Tyrone (see page 234).

The Kennedy homestead in the J. F. Kennedy Arboretum near New Ross shows what early American homesteads looked like

Influential exiles To see evidence of Ireland's influence abroad, you need look no further than the list of US presidents. Over a quarter of them are of Irish descent—mostly of Ulster Protestant stock. More recently, John F. Kennedy and Ronald Reagan have partly redressed the balance with their origins in counties Waterford and Tipperary. Canada has had Brian Mulroney as prime minister. Today more than 40 million US citizens can claim Irish ancestry.

The excellent Ulster American Folk Park near Omagh, County Tyrone, Northern Ireland

Irish representatives overseas can be found in just about any field you care to mention: John Field, the composer; John Philip Holland, inventor of the submarine; James Hoban, architect of the White House; the writers F. Scott Fitzgerald and Eugene O'Neill; Sir Hans Sloane, founder of the British Museum; John McEnroe, the tennis star—and a host of others whose influence can be found across the globe.

▶ Oldleighlin 1183C

A few minor sights make this village worth a brief stop. One is the squat crenellated tower of the 13th-century Anglican church known grandiosely as St. Lazerian's Cathedral, with, nearby, a 7th-century monastery and Lazerian's well, which attracts many pilgrims. The simple cathedral has a Gothic door and two fonts. Leighlinbridge to the east, as its name suggests, is a bridging point over the Barrow (the original bridge here dates from 1320). The scanty remains of the Black Castle can be seen on the east bank, one of the earliest Norman defences in Ireland.

▶▶ Ring of Hook 1183A

The quiet peninsula on the east side of Waterford Harbour is a strange low-lying place full of deserted villages and migrant birds. The straight, empty roads lead through Ballyhack, where a small shuttle ferry cuts out the long trek inland via New Ross, then through **Duncannon**, a peaceful small seaside resort with a sandy beach and a reputation for fine sea fishing. Military remains indicate its former strategic importance; a fortress built by the Anglo-Normans stands by the waterfront, strengthened to guard against the Spanish Armada in the late 16th century, and during Napoleonic times the British built three Martello Towers to deter the French. The big house here, Loftus Hall, was built by the 4th Marquis of Ely for his bride-to-be, Victoria, the Princess Royal, who called off her engagement for mysterious reasons. It later became a hotel, capitalizing on a ghostly legend that the Devil once escaped through the roof here after a game of cards, leaving cracks that are impossible to repair (a good excuse for leaving them alone, anyway!).

At the craggy, desolate tip of the peninsula stands an ancient lighthouse, the oldest in Ireland. Warning lights for shipping have been kept here for some 1,400 years, but the present, zebra-striped version dates from Norman times. Even earlier than that, a Welsh monk called Dubhand is thought to have kept a form of lighthouse by hoisting a cauldron of burning pitch to a high platform. On stormy days the sea sends dramatic columns of spray through blow holes in the rocks. During high season some enterprising families seek out

140

BY HOOK OR BY CROOK
The origin of this phrase is much disputed, but Cromwell is alleged to have used it when he was planning his assault on Waterford, declaring he would take the city 'by Hook ...' (on the eastern side) '... or by Crook' (just below Passage East on the west side of the harbour).

The lighthouse on Hook Head has ancient origins; it was built by one Raymond le Gros in 1172. The sea at Hook Head is also noted for the beauty of the corals found growing on the limestone

these quiet beaches around Fethard and Booley Strand; at other times of year you can enjoy them almost unchallenged. The village of Slade is especially charming and is a well-known scuba-diving centre. The remains of some 18th-century salthouses can be seen on the pier (where salt was extracted from seawater by evaporation).

A cannon still guards the busy port of Rosslare

141

▶ Rosslare
1194B

Well known as a ferry terminal for traffic from Normandy and Wales, Rosslare is actually 8km (5 miles) north of its harbour. It is a popular seaside resort capitalizing on its long, sandy beach and relatively sunny climate. However, there is little of interest in the place, except perhaps for golfers (it has an excellent links course).

Just south of Rosslare is Our Lady's Island, connected to the mainland by a causeway, where the ruins of an Augustinian priory and a Round Tower can be seen (the tower leans more precariously than that at Pisa). There is an annual pilgrimage to the Marian shrine from 15 August to 8 September. Some pilgrims crawl around the site on their knees; others walk with one foot in the water.

▶ St. Mullin's
1183B

A monastery was founded here in the 7th century by St. Moling, a monk of high birth and apparently artistic talents. The watercourse that he dug with his own hands to power a mill is still there, but the monastery buildings have disappeared and the remains date from medieval times. In the churchyard are a penal altar, used surreptitiously when Catholic services were banned, and the graves of several Leinster kings, including the warrior Art MacMurrough, scourge of the Anglo-Normans. St. Mullin's is scarcely worth visiting for its remains alone, which are minimal and hard to track down, but the village itself is at a most beautiful spot by a stream with the Blackstairs Mountains rising behind. Many places around here, or in Graiguenamanagh (see page 137), upstream where the more impressive monastery of Duiske Abbey stands, are ideal for walks and picnics.

CAPTAIN MYLES KEOGH
Captain Keogh, from Leighlinbridge, was an adventurous soul. He fought for the pope in the 1860s when Garibaldi was uniting Italy, then joined the American Civil War on the Union side. His third military adventure was with Colonel Custer's 7th Cavalry, where he fought gallantly at the Battle of Little Big Horn against the Sioux Indians in 1876. He was apparently one of the last to die and as a mark of respect was not scalped after the battle. His horse Comanche was the only survivor on the army's side.

142

Waterford City has been a bustling centre since the Vikings settled there in the middle of the 9th century

WATERFORD MUTINY
The citizens of Waterford were a fairly pugnacious lot, it seems. Mayor Briver had to be rescued by his wife in 1641 when a riot took place. Mrs Briver wrote that when she heard swords being drawn against her husband, 'I ran oute into the streete without hatt or mantle and laid my handes about his necke and brought hem in whether he wud or no'. Later this same mayor lost three fingers from his hand—bitten off by an angry mutineer.

▶▶ Waterford   1183B

Waterford is by far the largest town in the southeast and one of the few prospering industrial centres in the Republic. It is most famous for its glassworks, benefiting again after suffering badly during the last recession. Other industries include light engineering, electronics, paper manufacture and brewing. Some visitors find the overtly workmanlike quaysides a turnoff after rural towns in Ireland, but Waterford has a grand history and plenty to explore.

Waterford is essentially a Viking city, with many reminders of this period of its history among the buildings lying immediately behind the waterfront. **Reginald's Tower▶** (tel: 051 873501; *open:* Easter–end Oct daily 10–5.15; Nov–Easter Wed–Sun 10–4.15. *Admission: inexpensive*), was built in 1003 as part of the old city walls by a certain Reginald (an unlikely sounding name for a Danish city governor), and served subsequently as royal residence, fortress, mint, prison and air-raid shelter. It is now the Civic and Maritime Museum, containing many municipal documents and regalia.

The most interesting churches are **St. Patrick's** Catholic church of 1750, well restored after being used as a corn store during penal days, and the Protestant **Christ Church Cathedral**, built in 1770 and containing a weighty colonnade of Corinthian columns and fine stucco ceiling decorations. A grim memorial to James Rice, a mayor who died in 1490, depicts the process of posthumous decomposition in graphic detail. The Catholic **Holy Trinity Cathedral** also has a remarkably sumptuous interior.

Later civic buildings worth a glance are the 1849 courthouse with a massive classical portico, the **city hall▶** (tel: 051 873 501) of 1788 with magnificent Waterford crystal glittering in the public assembly rooms, and the **Chamber of Commerce▶** (tel: 051 875 788. *Admission free*), a town house of 1795 with a spectacularly beautiful stairwell.

Housed in the old granary beside Merchant's Quay, **Waterford Treasures▶** (tel: 051 304500; *open:* Apr–end Sep Mon–Sat 9–6, Sun 11–6; Oct–end Mar Mon–Sat 10–5, Sun 11–5. *Admission: moderate*) is a heritage centre and city museum in one. The audio-visual displays guide you through 1,000 years of Waterford history.

A visit to the crystal factory on the N25 Cork road, near the city centre, is the most popular visitor activity Waterford has to offer. Free factory tours take place every weekday during the mornings. At busy times of year you should reserve a place.

The tours are indeed interesting and take about 40 minutes (a good plan for a wet day: to reserve a place contact Waterford Crystal on 051 332500, www.waterford-visitorscentre.com. *Admission: expensive*). You are taken around each stage of manufacture. Basic ingredients of glass are silica and potash; lead crystal also requires a significant quantity of lead oxide in powder form (safety regulations must be strictly adhered to with this toxic substance). The lead gives the glass its qualities of brilliance and capacity to refract light, and also makes it very heavy. The ingredients are heated to about 1,200°C (2,200°F) over many hours, then hand-blown and skillfully shaped before cooling. Finally the glass is cut with deep grid-like patterns, the air filling with minute particles and the screech of carborundum and diamond wheels. You will see Waterford crystal in grand houses throughout Ireland; today, a modern version of one of those glittering droplet chandeliers costs several thousand Euros.

The plant now covers a site of about 15ha (38 acres). By far the largest market for Waterford crystal is the United States, and American tastes are therefore strongly reflected in the ornate designs. Waterford now has many home-grown rivals throughout Ireland, although Waterford still claims the edge for its high quality (no inferior produce is ever sold; it is simply smashed and melted down again), its purity of colour and its deep cut. Certainly, if you want to find out about crystal, this is the place to do it. Prices start at over €25 for a tiny liqueur glass.

THE HISTORY OF WATERFORD CRYSTAL

The history of Waterford glass started in the late 18th century, when George and William Penrose set up a factory there in 1783. It flourished for 68 years, before the disastrous economic conditions of 1851 caused its closure. A century later, Waterford once again became home for a glassworks, modest at first, but expanding to prodigious dimensions within only 40 years.

143

A master cutter concentrates on his task

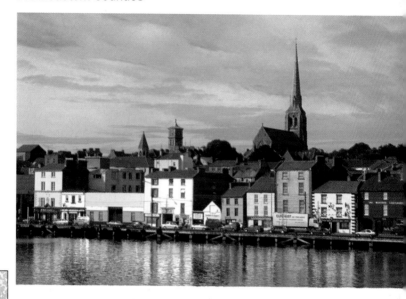

The county town of Wexford lies where the estuary of the River Slaney meets Wexford Harbour

WEXFORD OPERA FESTIVAL
This event has been held during October at the Theatre Royal for over 40 years, now attracting opera buffs from far and wide, as well as many international stars. It tends to favour rare or neglected works, and so has a pleasantly off-beat, avant-garde tinge. If you manage to get tickets, you may of course discover why some of these works are rare and neglected! For all that, it's the social event of the year in Wexford, festive but unsnobby, where local people dress up and drink champagne. Book well ahead for seats; they are gold dust (box office tel: 053 22400). If you can't get a ticket, many other events will be going on, too—concerts, revues, recitals, jazz in pubs, etc. Many travel companies offer package tours to the opera festival.

►► **Wexford** *1194B*

For all its bloody history, Wexford has a peaceful air. First glances may suggest it is all too dull, basking in its muddy estuary like some somnolent reptile. But it is by no means moribund. Present traces of a proud past are admittedly vestigial, but a bustling small-town charm and sense of life outweigh any initial disappointment. If you catch it during October when the acclaimed opera festival is in full swing, you will be left with no doubt that Wexford rates itself pretty highly, and why not, achieving full-page write-ups as it does in all the national papers?

The Viking name *Waesfjord* (harbour of the mudflats) is appropriate. The Slaney River and several tributaries empty their silt-laden waters into the sea there, and Wexford's practicality as a deepwater port has long since been overtaken by its rival in the next county, Waterford. But the mud is not all bad. North and south of the town, large areas on either side of the estuary provide a habitat for many thousands of wading birds. The **Wexford Wildfowl Reserve**►► is a must for ornithologists (tel: 053 23129). The 'Slobs', as the mudflats are known locally, are 'polders', or reclaimed land lying lower than sea level. Follow the signs for the reserve from Wexford's coastal exit roads and you will reach a research station with a visitor centre, a lookout tower, identification charts and hides (like hunting blinds). Entrance is free. The neighbouring dunes around Raven Point are also an important nature reserve with rare plants and insects.

The town itself straggles along the waterfront, several blocks deep. The helpful tourist office can be found right in the centre of the seafront, where Crescent Quay takes a bite from the shore. The bronze statue outside commemorates Commodore John Barry, the brilliant naval officer who avenged his Irish ancestors by emigrating to Philadelphia and trouncing the English during the Revolutionary War. Wexford is best explored on foot (historic walking tours are advertised) when narrow alleys and one-way streets provide no obstacle. The old centre of town is a cheerful mix of agreeable pubs, old-fashioned shops and plenty of decent down-to-earth eating places. The main historic monuments are the **Westgate Tower▶** (tel: 053 46506), dating from 1300 (*The Wexford Experience*, a short film, is shown inside), and the remains of **Selskar Abbey▶**, where the Anglo-Irish treaty was signed after the Norman invasion, and where Henry II spent many Lenten hours atoning for the murder of St. Thomas à Becket. A couple of modern Gothic churches can be seen, interesting only because they are virtually identical. In the Bull Ring Cromwellian troops slaughtered 300 hapless citizens as they prayed for mercy. Many others were put to the sword in one of the most appalling massacres of the Ironside invasion. When Ireland rebelled again in 1798, Wexford's inhabitants were among the most vigorous pike-wielders, as the statue in the Bull Ring indicates.

Two other sights are well worth a visit if you are in the vicinity of Wexford. The **Irish National Heritage Park▶▶** is described on page 131 (see **Ferrycarrig▶▶**). Towards Rosslare is another museum, in the massive Gothic-revival building called Johnstown Castle, constructed as a private residence around the core of a 15th-century tower house. This contains the **Irish Agricultural Museum▶▶** (tel: 053 42888); the rest of the building serves as an agricultural college. It is the largest collection of its kind in Ireland, full of attractive displays of intriguing implements like furze rooters, barley hummlers and turnip knives. The veterinary section displays fearsome horse gags and drenching horns. Little workshops have been re-created showing how the tools would have been arranged and used by wheelwrights and coopers, among others. There are also displays of ancient domestic appliances and butter-making equipment. The grounds around this imposing castellated and mullioned grey-stone building are beautifully landscaped and open to the public.

145

The Irish National Heritage Park

Southwestern Counties

Map labels (grid D, top):

Kilkee · Cooraclare · Killadysert · Kilrush · Killimer · Loghill · Loop Head · Mouth of the Shannon · Ballylongford · Tarbert · Glin · Shana · Ballybunion · Glin Castle · Ballyduff · Athea · Ardag · Kerry Head · Causeway · Listowel · Newcast West · Ballyheige · *Feale* · Duagh

Grid C:

Ballyheige Bay · Rough Point · Abbeydorney · Abbeyfeale · Ardfert · 357m · Kilkinlea · Mullaghbaretr Mts · 409m · 953m Cnoc Breánainn (Brandon Mt) · Brandon Bay · *Tralee Bay* · Stacks Mts · Br · 828m Beenoskee · Tralee · Kilmalkedar · Camp · 852m · Castleisland · Gallarus Oratory · Anascaul · Slieve Mish Mts · Scartaglen · Newma · Na Blascaodaí (The Blaskets) · Castlemaine · Farranfore · Ballydesmon · An Daingean (Dingle) · Inch · Milltown · Boherbue · Ceann Sléibhe (Slea Head) · Kerry County · Killorglin

Grid B:

Báan Daingin (Dingle Bay) · Glenbeigh · *Laune* · *Lough Caragh* · Beaufort · Killarney · Millstreet · Killarney Leane · *Lough Leane* · Rathmore · Doulus Head · 1041m National Park · Muckross · Poulgorm Bridge · Valentia Island · Carrauntoohil · Muckross · Derrynasagart Mts · Caherciveen · Macgillycuddy's Reeks · 840m · Carriganimmy · Mangerton Mt · Ballymakeery · Kilgarvan · Kenmare · Béal Átha an Ghaorfthaidh (Ballingeary) · Macr · Sceilg Mhichíl (Skellig Rock) · Waterville · Sneem · Tahilla · Inchigeelagh · *Lee* · Kil · Staigue Fort · Parknasilla · 707m · Ceann Bhólais (Bolus Head) · Knockboy · Caherdaniel · Lauragh · *Kenmare River* · *Cabhá Mts* · *Bandon* · Scariff Island · Ardgroom · Glengarriff · Imaccullin Gardens · Dunmanway · Bat · Derrynane · 686m · Adrigole · Bantry · Cod's Head · Allihies · Castletown Bearhaven · Drimoleague

Grid A:

Dursey Island · Bear Island · *Bantry Bay* · Durrus · Leap · R · Muntervary or Sheep's Head · *Dunmanus Bay* · Ballydehob · Glandore · Ca · Dron · Stone · Goleen · Toormore · Schull · Skibbereen · Castletownshend · Mizen Head · Crookhaven · *Roaringwater Bay* · Baltimore · Lough Hyne · Toe Head · Cape Clear · Clear Island · Fastnet Lighthouse

1 2 3

RAIN IN THE WEST?

'When the glass is up to thirty
Cork and Kerry will be dirty;
When the glass is high O very
There'll be rain in Cork and Kerry;
When the glass is low, O Lork!
There'll be rain in Kerry and Cork.'

'Thirty' refers to high barometric pressure, normally assuring dry weather!

SOUTHWESTERN COUNTIES Ireland's southwestern corner ranks high with most visitors, and for many people the counties of Cork and Kerry represent the best that Ireland can offer, with striking scenery, charming towns, a mild climate and many places of interest. There is a huge variety of things to do and see for just about anyone, young or old, active or sedentary. To see much of it, you will need your own transportation, as elsewhere in Ireland. If you prefer to see things slowly and in more detail, that could mean a bicycle or a Romany (Gypsy) caravan. If you can afford to pamper yourself, the region has a fine collection of country house hotels (including a few stately homes) and many excellent restaurants.

FUNGI THE DOLPHIN
This half-tame creature has captured the hearts of thousands in the past few years. His behaviour suggests he may have escaped or been released from a marine park at some stage. He cavorts in Dingle Bay (Báan Daingin) to the delight of all onlookers and the great pleasure of the tourist authorities, and has apparently no fear of humans or their boats. He will frolic beside wetsuited swimmers, jump over boats, and really gives the impression that he enjoys company. Fungi seems to have become completely fixated by his human visitors and will chase off any rival dolphin who encroaches on his territory. Boat trips from Dingle harbour virtually guarantee a sighting in summer.

Page 146: Slea Head, Dingle

The predictable, but pleasant, face of tourism on the Muckross Estate near Killarney

Events such as Kinsale's annual gourmet festival raise both standards of cuisine and the region's popularity with international visitors. The high quality of local ingredients helps; seafood, good beef and rich dairy products now available everywhere belie the terrible sufferings of the southwest during the Famine years.

The massive emigration from these counties to the New World has resulted in a backwash of third- or fourth-generation visitors migrating back to the land of their forebears searching for roots. Shannon Airport welcomes transatlantic visitors, who converge on Limerick and Killarney. Many foreigners from continental Europe approach via Cork and some have settled there permanently, adding new influences to the area's restaurants and bringing fresh artistic talents with them.

A WARM WELCOME English attempts to subjugate this old Irish province of Munster produced a mass of fortifications all along the coast, ever-watchful for Catholic plots from Spain and France using Catholic Ireland as an unlocked back door from which to invade Britain. Today, however, the tricky Anglo-Irish interface leaves little mark here.

The southwest has two of Ireland's largest cities, Cork and Limerick. These are certainly worth seeing, but the rural areas are far more appealing. The coastline is, in places, particularly beautiful, and generally more exciting than the lush inland scenery, cut by its great easterly flowing rivers. An exception is Killarney's National Park, a high spot in any itinerary. Less well known, but also worth exploring, is the forest park of Gougane Barra, on the remote inland borders of Cork and Kerry. It is a place of wildlife, of tumbling streams and the hermitage of St. Fin Barre. Founded probably in the 6th or 7th century, although the ruins beside the modern church date from

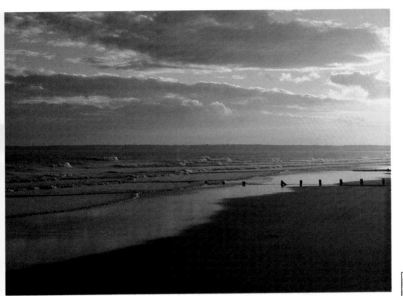

Youghal beach, Cork

the 18th century, the hermitage of Cork City's patron saint is set on an islet in the beautiful Gougane Barra Lake, the source of the Lee, which eventually reaches the sea at Cork. The county of Limerick is the Cinderella of the three, with little to lift its flattish landscapes from mediocrity. Killarney and Blarney are perhaps the only blatant examples of mass tourism in the region. Elsewhere, the tourist scene is low-profile. Kinsale, Kenmare, Dingle (An Daingean), Youghal and Bantry all make charming and much classier bases for exploring the coast.

A MILD AND VERDANT LAND Few would argue that the islet-strewn peninsulas that trail westwards to the Atlantic are the places to visit for the best scenery, where the blue water of never-distant sea sets off the brilliant rain-washed emerald of fields and mountains. There the pace of life is slow and gentle, and the ambience profoundly Irish, perhaps most noticeably in the Dingle peninsula, one of the largest Gaeltacht (Irish-speaking) regions. Traditional Irish music can be heard all over the region, particularly in Dingle and some of the villages of south Cork, such as Leap and Clonakilty.

The influence of the Gulf Stream keeps frost permanently at bay and, although Atlantic storms can be severe, sheltered regions lend themselves to superb subtropical gardens and a great range of flora and fauna. Even the least botanically minded can scarcely fail to be impressed by the lush fuchsia hedges dripping scarlet all summer, the rhododendrons in profusion or the arbutus trees that grow wild in the valleys of Iveragh. Water lilies and rare bog plants colonize the reedy pools of Cork's quieter peninsulas. The southwest is a good place for birdwatchers, too—the region is first landfall for the myriad exhausted migrants in spring and autumn on Clear Island or the wild Skellig Islands, the moors, mountains and lakes of Kerry, and the sheltered, muddy estuaries around Timoleague on the south Cork coast.

ROSE OF TRALEE FESTIVAL
This is held in the last week of August and is a great attraction for the region. Six days and nights of merriment take place, including pipe bands and parades. The main event is a beauty contest that any woman of Irish origins can enter. Visitors from around the world compete for the honour of being crowned Rose; details from the Festival Office in Lower Castle Street, Tralee (tel: 066 7121322).

▶ ▶ ▶ **REGION HIGHLIGHTS**

Bantry House *page 151*
Blarney Castle *page 151*
Clear Island *page 152*
Cobh *page 153*
Cork *pages 156–157*
Dingle Peninsula *pages 158–159*
Killarney National Park *page 160*
King John's Castle *page 167*
Kinsale *pages 162–163*
Ring of Kerry *pages 170–171*

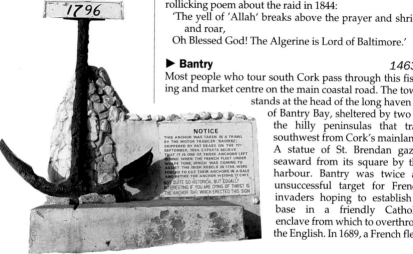

The enormous, conical, whitewashed beacon near Baltimore acts as a marker for boats

An enterprising bar in Bantry has erected this elaborate and informative advertisement for its wares

1796

NOTICE
THIS ANCHOR WAS TAKEN IN A TRAWL
BY THE MOTOR TRAWLER "SAOIRSE",
SKIPPERED BY PAT DEASY, ON THE 11th
SEPTEMBER, 1964. EXPERTS BELIEVE
THAT IT IS ONE OF THOSE ANCHORS LEFT
BEHIND WHEN THE FRENCH FLEET UNDER
WOLFE TONE, WHICH WAS COMING TO
ASSIST THE IRISH REBELS IN 1796, WERE
FORCED TO CUT THEIR ANCHORS IN A GALE
AND RETIRE. THE ANCHOR WEIGHS 17 CWT.
NOT QUITE SO HISTORICAL BUT EQUALLY
INTERESTING IF YOU ARE DYING OF THIRST IS
THE ANCHOR BAR WHICH ERECTED THIS SIGN

▶ Baltimore
1463A

Baltimore combines salty fishing-village charm with a sturdy castle and several good restaurants. Trips are also available to Sherkin Island, where there is a 15th-century friary, and to the Fastnet Lighthouse on the outermost scrap of Irish territory. In June 1631, Baltimore witnessed a curious and tragic incident when Algerian pirates stole into the harbour and attacked the village, killing a number of residents and abducting about 200 as slaves to North Africa. Some believe the raid may have been orchestrated by the fierce O'Driscoll clan to frighten off English settlers. If so, it worked: many of them moved upstream where they felt less threatened. The poet, Thomas Davis, wrote a rollicking poem about the raid in 1844:

'The yell of 'Allah' breaks above the prayer and shriek and roar,
Oh Blessed God! The Algerine is Lord of Baltimore.'

▶ Bantry
1463A

Most people who tour south Cork pass through this fishing and market centre on the main coastal road. The town stands at the head of the long haven of Bantry Bay, sheltered by two of the hilly peninsulas that trail southwest from Cork's mainland. A statue of St. Brendan gazes seaward from its square by the harbour. Bantry was twice an unsuccessful target for French invaders hoping to establish a base in a friendly Catholic enclave from which to overthrow the English. In 1689, a French fleet sailed in, offering support for James II, only to be rebuffed by Williamites. In 1796, the revolutionary Wolfe Tone arrived with another French fleet (see panel), but was driven back by fierce storms. An alert local landowner, Richard White, sent urgent warnings to the English forces and was rewarded for his loyalty by a peerage.

His descendants still live in **Bantry House**►► (tel: 027 50047, www.bantryhouse.ie; *open:* Mar–end Oct, daily 9–6. *Admission: expensive*), one of the most beautifully sited houses in Ireland. The terraced Italianate gardens overlook a gorgeous sweep of Bantry Bay, and the house's sumptuous rooms are full of fascinating contents. The hospitable present owners offer a classy brand of B&B in a separate wing of the house, and another attraction is the **Bantry 1796 French Armada Exhibition Centre**►► in a renovated side courtyard. This lively museum recounts the history of Wolfe Tone's failed rebellion and displays articles recovered from the wreck of the frigate *La Surveillante*, which sank during the storms and was excavated in 1982.

Minor diversions in the town itself are a museum of local history and the **Kilnaruane Pillar Stone**►, carved with mysterious early Christian symbols.

►► Blarney   1474B

Everyone has heard of Blarney and, when bus tours clog the village, it seems as if everyone has come to see it, too. Visitors come for two reasons— to kiss that stone in **Blarney Castle**►► (tel: 021 438 5252, www.blarneycastle.ie; *open:* May, Sep Mon–Sat 9.30–dusk, Sun 9–5.30; Jun–end Aug Mon–Sat 9–7, Sun 9–5.30; Oct–end Apr Mon–Sat 9–dusk, Sun 9.30–dusk. *Admission: expensive*) and to visit the large gift and craft centres nearby. Why the Blarney Stone exercises such fascination is hard to fathom, but the belief that kissing it endows you with Irish eloquence is certainly appealing.

The stone is an oblong block of limestone set high among the battlements of a fine 15th-century tower house, once a stronghold of the MacCarthys, former kings of Munster and lords of Blarney. A Cormac MacCarthy supposedly strung Queen Elizabeth I along with promises and prevarications, until she exclaimed in exasperation, 'Blarney, Blarney!' What he says he does not mean,' and thus the word entered the language. To reach the stone, you must clamber up the tower steps (more than 120 of them), join the inevitable line (in high season, at least), and then lie down and lean backward over a sheer drop. It looks awkward but is actually quite safe, even without the two strong-armed retainers there to grab your ankles. The stone is swabbed down regularly to prevent transmission of any nasty ailments. Some locals will offer to take your photograph while you are kissing the stone, but be warned, it isn't a flattering angle (see above)!

The lush water gardens by the Lee River and the 19th-century Rock Close (a rock garden with fanciful wishing

WOLFE TONE'S INVASION
On 16 December 1796, a French Armada of 43 ships set sail from Brest, bound for Ireland. The French intended to aid Wolfe Tone's rebellion and to deal a blow to the British. From the start, it was a disaster, storms disrupting communications between the fleet. Only 16 battered crews reached Bantry Bay with Wolfe Tone. On Christmas Eve he was ready to attack, but decided to wait for Hoche, the French commander. By the next day his chance of a landing had gone; savage gales had blown the ships out of the bay. Tone wrote in his journal, 'We were close enough to throw a biscuit ashore…The elements fight against us'.

151

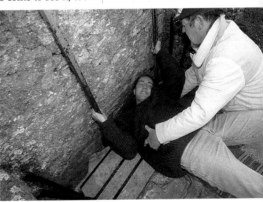

Whatever one gains from kissing the Blarney Stone, one loses one's dignity

FASTNET LIGHTHOUSE
This perches like a fairy-tale castle on its rocky bastion to warn shipping off the treacherous coast. Recreational sailors use it as their westerly target during the biennial Fastnet Yacht Race, starting from Cowes on the Isle of Wight.

There's more to Blarney than the stone

THE SINKING OF THE LUSITANIA
Speculation about this has made disturbing reading. In World War I the ship, sailing from New York to Liverpool, was sunk off Cobh by the Germans, who claimed that she was carrying arms as well as civilians. This was denied, but evidence now suggests that it was true. More disturbing is the theory that the Allies contrived the episode to hasten US entry into the war. The German government had placed advertisements in New York papers warning passengers not to take the sailing, implying that the vessel was not a random wartime target. Both suspicion and casualties were increased by the unusual absence of patrolling British warships. She sank in 20 minutes, leaving passengers floundering in the water. Some survived by clutching floating debris, one sitting in a cane chair. The submarine that had sunk the ship did nothing to save passengers, although knowing many were US civilians, and not a remotely legitimate target.

steps and druidical associations) make an attractive foil for the romantic ruin, and behind the castle is an elaborate Scottish baronial mansion called **Blarney House** (visitable on a joint ticket), furnished in Victorian style.

In the village, craft and knitwear shops catch the purse strings, the most advertised being Blarney Woollen Mills, now a colossal hypermarket with a restaurant, hotel and large parking area. The smaller shops are more enjoyable than this bargain basement, but there's certainly a wide range of merchandise from all over Ireland.

►► Castletownshend   1463A
The literary cousins, Edith Somerville and Violet Martin, lived in Drishane House and are both buried in the greystone church of St. Barrahane, where Edith was organist. They are better known as Somerville and Ross, authors of the *Irish RM* stories. The village is pretty, its main street sloping steeply up from the quayside. If you careen down it too fast you are in danger of hitting a tree carefully preserved in the middle of the road. Nearby is an excellent, quaint old pub called Mary Ann's. The Townshend family still live in the local castle, where an idiosyncratic B&B evokes the atmosphere of the *RM* books.

►►► Clear Island   1462A
The frayed coastline at Ireland's bottom left-hand corner disintegrates into a scattering of islets around Baltimore. From there, or from Schull further along the coast, you can take a boat to Ireland's most southerly community, Clear Island, where the Irish-speaking population of fewer than 200 is greatly outnumbered by the birds. An observatory enables visitors to delight in the multitude of streaming migrants—all kinds of gulls, shearwaters, storm petrels and rare songbirds, even an occasional disorientated albatross. Other sights pale beside the birdlife: the well and church dedicated to St. Ciarán, born here in the 6th century, a wind-driven electricity generator financed by the EU and a small heritage centre. It is possible to stay on the island, although amenities are spartan.

▶▶ Cobh

1475B

For many Famine emigrants, the scenic panorama of **Cork Harbour**▶▶ and the colourful houses of Cobh must have been their last glimpse of the Emerald Isle. Many perished en route in the dreaded 'coffin ships'. The name Cobh (pronounced 'cove') means 'haven' in Irish. Besides emigrant ships, Cobh berthed some of the great transatlantic liners, including the ill-fated *Titanic* and the *Lusitania*, torpedoed offshore on 7 May 1915, with the loss of 1,198 lives (see panel). Many victims are buried in the local cemetery. Cobh's history is presented in **The Queenstown Story**▶▶ (tel: 021 481 3591; *open:* May–end Oct 10–6; Nov–end Apr 10–5. *Admission: moderate*) at a local heritage centre. Today Cobh is a fishing port, seaside resort and sailing centre, its well-restored buildings great character. **St. Colman's Cathedral**▶▶ (tel: 021 481 3222; *open* daily at varying times. *Admission free*) is the most striking landmark, set high on the hilltop, its spire honed to an impossibly slender point. It was designed by Pugin in 1868 and is an exuberant masterpiece of Victorian high Gothic. Harbour trips are available in summer.

In the estuary at the mouth of Cork harbour and connected by bridges to the mainland, **Fota Wildlife Park**▶▶ (tel: 021 481 2678; *open:* mid-Mar–end Oct, Mon–Sat 10–5, Sun 11–5; Nov–mid-Mar Mon–Sat 10–3, Sun 11–3. *Admission free* for gardens and arboretum; wildlife park: *expensive*) can be reached via the Cork–Cobh railroad line. Here cheetahs and wallabies are bred and there is an important arboretum with rare specimen trees.

BUILT TO LAST?

A 16th-century tower house at Castlehaven near Castletownshend was built by the O'Driscolls, who gave it to the Spaniards before the Battle of Kinsale in 1601. When the Spanish were defeated, they yielded the castle to the English. Before *they* could occupy it, the O'Driscolls retook it and were about to blow it up when in turn they were surprised by the English, who prevented the destruction. It survived until 1926, when Edith Somerville, one of the literary combination of Somerville and Ross, was out for a walk; she heard a rumble and found that the castle had collapsed into a heap of rubble behind her.

153

St. Colman's Cathedral sits perkily on top of the Georgian seafront

The Anglo-Saxon bishop and historian known as the Venerable Bede remarked on Ireland's clement weather: 'Ireland is far more favoured than Britain by latitude, and by its mild and healthy climate...there is no need to store hay in winter...and no lack of vines.' The typical Irish 'soft day' of gentle drizzle and sunshine is ideal for plants, and Ireland contains a fine collection of gardens of all types in which many rare species flourish.

154

STRAWBERRY TREE
This plant is most closely identified with Killarney and the lush countryside of south Kerry, where it grows to prodigious heights. It is also known as the arbutus tree, *Arbutus unedo,* and has waxy white flowers and dark green glossy leaves. It flowers in the autumn and is then hung with slow-ripening strawberry-like fruits. A song of 1890 commemorates the tree:
My love's an arbutus
By the borders of Lene,
So slender and shapely
In her girdle of green.

ILNACULLIN GARDENS
Annan Bryce, a Belfast-born MP, purchased Ilnacullin from the British War Office in 1910. His dream to build a mansion and lay out gardens on this bare island off Glengarriff in County Cork was ambitious: the soil was shallow and infertile, the terrain exposed. To realize his project he enlisted the help of Harold Peto, an advocate of the Italian style of garden design and architecture in an age when less formal wild gardens were all the rage. Ilnacullin is a blend of both styles, containing a wide range of oriental and southern hemisphere plants and many architectural features complementing the splendid natural setting.

A long tradition In early Christian times a major activity of any monastery was gardening—mostly for food or medicines, but also for decorating churches. With the arrival of the Normans horticulture became much more complex and widespread, with new and varied foodstuffs. Sir Walter Ralegh's foreign travels introduced important plants from the New World—tobacco, cherries and, of course, the potato. His friend, the Earl of Cork, laid out one of Ireland's first Renaissance pleasure gardens in the estates of Youghal. During the latter part of the 17th century gardening was on a grand scale, influenced by the gardens of Versailles, designed by Le Nôtre. Exotic plants began to arrive from abroad and Dutch immigrants brought innovative botanical techniques. The 18th century was a great age for gardening, as for most aspects of civilized living, passing from baroque formality to the naturalistic landscapes of 'Capability' Brown. The Royal Horticultural Society of Ireland was founded in 1816.

During Victorian times botanical tastes diversified, many gardeners concentrating less on design and more on accumulating specimens; several important botanic gardens were planted at this time. Two great gardeners of the age were Daniel Robertson (see page 110) and William Robinson, who introduced a new style of 'natural' gardening based on a close observation of landscape. Many smaller, intimate gardens appeared, too, some influenced by the English style of Gertrude Jekyll—two gorgeous creations are Heywood (County Laois) and Butterstream (County Meath). During the early 20th century a passion for oriental gardens developed; the Japanese Gardens at Tully, Kildare, are one such example (see page 101).

Period landscapes One of Ireland's most interesting gardens, historically, is Kilruddery, outside Bray (see page 93), which retains its 17th-century canals, parterres and statuary. Representing an earlier era, the lovely gardens around Lismore Castle were laid out in Jacobean times. Greatest of the Georgian gardens surround houses such as Florence Court, County Fermanagh (see page 230) and Castletown, County Kildare (see page 94). A fascinating late 18th-century example is Emo Court, County Laois, where lawns dotted with neat, clipped yews and statues provide a foil for James Gandon's neoclassical mansion.

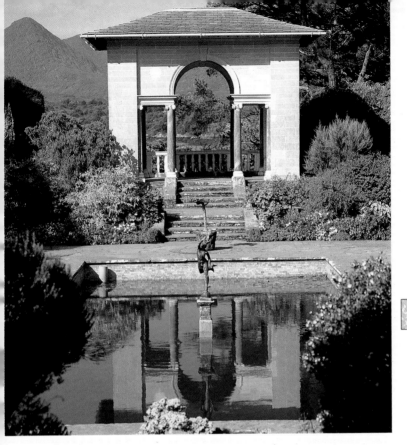

Spectacular gardens Despite its latitude, Ireland has some celebrated gardens in the north, several in the care of the National Trust, among them Mount Stewart and Rowallane (see page 231). In the southwest, Anne's Grove near Castletownroche represents some of the best work of William Robinson—shrubs, magnolias, rare mallows and water plants flourish in hedged compartments and walled gardens. The Italianate gardens of Bantry House, set by the sea, are a must for keen gardeners, too, as are the castle gardens of Timoleague and the grounds of Muckross House in Killarney's National Park, where vast rhododendrons and exotic trees (including the strawberry tree, see panel) grow against a mountain backdrop. Derreen Gardens, on the road between Kenmare and Castletown Bearhaven, luxuriate in woodland with many subtropical species, tree ferns mingling with bamboo and eucalyptus. Nearby are the gardens of Dunloe Castle, with more rare trees (Chinese swamp cypresses and the pungent 'headache tree', *Umbellularia californica*). One of the most enjoyable of all the southwest's gardens is Harold Peto's masterpiece, Ilnacullin, on an island reached by boat trips from Glengarriff, in County Cork (a landing charge). On a fine day in May or June, this Italian garden of Grecian temples and an orderly jungle of flowering shrubs makes a marvellous excursion (see panel opposite).

Bord Fáilte produces a useful leaflet with information about Ireland's best gardens.

Ilnacullin Gardens on Garinish Island

The glorious colours of Rowallane Gardens

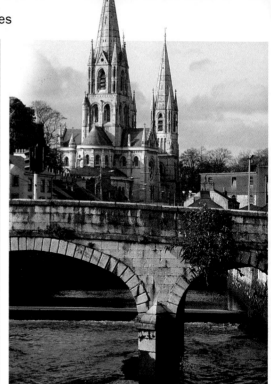

St. Fin Barre's Cathedral looks down over the southern branch of Cork's Lee River

THE *EXAMINER*
Cork's daily newspaper seems to epitomize the independent spirit of the city. The *Examiner* (just called 'the paper' locally) is a distinguished piece of journalism that has gone national. The first edition appeared in August 1841, shortly before the potato famine. Many of the population were illiterate and certainly too poor to afford newspapers, so it was a brave venture. The first edition proclaimed it devoted 'to the welfare and interests of the whole community', and that it seems to be, read by all classes of society. It survived attacks by anti-Treaty demonstrators in 1922 when the machinery was smashed, and has never lost a day's printing through strikes, wars or technical problems.

►► Cork   *1474B*

Cork has no compelling sights, nor is it especially beautiful, and an initial reaction to the Republic's second city may be one of disappointment. Nonetheless, visitors generally go away well pleased with the place, perhaps infected by the vehement enthusiasm of its inhabitants for their city. The way *not* to enjoy Cork is to drive through panicking about the check-in time at the airport or harbour. A map shows why the city, the first bridging point on the Lee estuary, is a bottleneck. Traffic is invariably congested during working hours, and parking is regulated: Leave the car in one of the official parking areas and walk.

Cork takes pride in being the cultural and economic centre of the southwest, constantly challenging Dublin's supremacy. It has always favoured ousting British rule, becoming known as 'rebel Cork' after supporting Perkin Warbeck (a Flemish impostor who, in 1492, claimed to be Duke of York), and was a base for the Nationalist Fenian movement in the 19th century. Its prosperity was based on trade in hides, textiles, butter and wine. Industries such as shipbuilding and engine manufacturing are no more, replaced by skills such as the computer business. The centre's streets reveal Cork's mercantile past—tall 18th-century bow-fronted houses and fine warehouses.

The centre is built on reclaimed marshes ('Cork' comes from the Irish meaning 'marshy place') and the older part of the city is on an island embraced by two arms of the Lee River. The land rises steeply towards the heights of Shandon; several imposing church spires pierce the skyline, Victorian Gothic being the prevailing style. **St. Fin Barre's►** (tel: 021 496 3387) was designed by William

Burges in a flourish of white limestone steeples. Inside it is richly decorated, with angels gazing down from a starry apse. On the Shandon side of town is **St. Anne's Church►►**, which soars to a red and white pepper-pot tower surmounted by a golden weather vane in the shape of a salmon. It houses the famous eight-bell carillon immortalized in the corny ballad known as 'The Bells of Shandon'. You can climb the tower and, for a fee, 'play' the bells. The nearby neoclassical **Shandon Craft Centre►** (tel: 021 450 7487) contains several craft studios, making jewellery, ceramics and traditional porcelain dolls.

On the island, Cork's commercial heart beats along the main thoroughfares of Grand Parade and St. Patrick's Street. Old-fashioned department stores flank trendy clothes boutiques, but the newer and most chic shops are around the pedestrianized area near St. Paul's Street. Classy Donegal rainwear and equestrian clothing are also sold in these side streets. To the west lie elegant Georgian malls and the university. The **Cork Public Museum►►** (Republican history features prominently, tel: 021 427 0679) is in the grounds of Fitzgerald Park by the Mardyke Walk, an attractive riverside breathing space.

Cork has plenty of nightlife, from raucous pub discos to avant-garde theatre. Its opera house (not a pretty sight) is a 1960s addition to municipal culture; other arts venues are the **Triskel Arts Centre►** (tel: 021 427 2022) and the **Crawford Art Gallery►** (tel: 021 427 3377, and worth a visit just for its restaurant—see Hotels and Restaurants, page 281). At the end of October, the city is thronged for its acclaimed international jazz festival. Eating in Cork is a pleasure, with plenty of choice, from imaginative, cheap organic foods to gourmet French cuisine. The **English Market►** off Princes Street has excellent food stalls. Accommodation in Cork ranges from civilized Georgian town houses to well-run, good-value hostels.

►►► Dingle Peninsula   *1461C*
See pages 158–159.

ELIZABETH ALDWORTH
This young lady from County Cork achieved fame as the only woman ever to be accepted into the bizarre and secretive world of Freemasonry. The local lodge met at her family home in Doneraile (her father was a Mason), but naturally she was always banished during the proceedings. One day in 1712 curiosity got the better of her and she hid in a clock-case to find out what went on, but she was discovered. Once the Masons got over their anger, they decided the only way to keep her quiet was to enroll her, and so she became the order's one and only female member. Her grave is in St. Fin Barre's Cathedral.

157

BETTER THINGS TO COME
'Limerick was, Dublin is, and Cork shall be The finest city of the three.'
Recorded in 1859 as 'the old prophecy'.

The Coal Quay open market in Cork City

THE DINGLE PENINSULA

Drive

The grandeur of the Dingle Peninsula

A tour of this remote, Irish-speaking westerly extremity offers many things: superb coastal scenery with peaceful beaches and scattered islands; grand mountains and lush, fuchsia-splashed countryside; a fascinating assortment of antiquities; and a lively scene of music and excellent seafood

The shrine at Slea Head

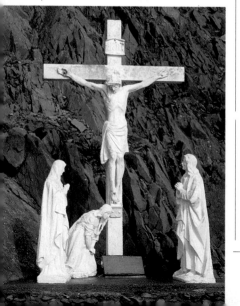

restaurants based on the charming fishing port of Dingle (An Daingean).

Starting points for this drive are Castlemaine (north of Killorglin) or Tralee. For scenic drama go clockwise (although the scenery at first is quiet) with good dune beaches at Inch and small hamlets like **Anascaul►**; the strange, secretive tarn (small mountain lake) to the north, **Anascaul Lake►**, is worth a brief detour.

Dingle (An Daingean)►► is the peninsula's main tourist centre, constantly lively during the summer. It is by no means undiscovered, as anyone arriving during its festival season (July–August) will note, but it never seems as overcrowded or touristy as Killarney, and it's a great deal classier. Off-season, though, many of its good restaurants, craft shops and hotels are closed and no boat trips run. The town is extremely well kept, with restored shop-fronts and colourful inn signs. The harbour is particularly appealing, its bright fishing vessels moored in a lovely natural haven. In former centuries smuggling was a major source of income.

Beyond Dingle is **Ceann Trá (Ventry)►**, where you may see upturned *currachs* (canvas-covered canoes) on the beach. Follow the road marked Ceann Sléibhe (Slea Head) Drive around Ireland's most westerly point. The whole area is riddled with forts, souterrains, standing stones and crosses; you need a good detailed map. On the hillsides you will pass a number of strange little stone huts known as beehives or *clochans*. There are more than 400 in the area altogether. Some farmers may charge you to visit these, and the more perfect specimens may have been reconstructed from the original stones as storage places (or for their more recent value as visitor attractions). **Dunbeg▶▶**, near Ventry, is one of the best sites (an Iron Age clifftop fort with beehive huts nearby).

If archaeology does not thrill you, the scenery certainly will, especially when the wild **Na Blascaodaí (The Blasket Islands)▶▶** appear as you round the **Ceann Sléibhe (Slea Head)** promontory. The Blaskets are now occupied by a handful of summer visitors, including the former Irish prime minister, Charles Haughey, and there are plans to renovate some of the abandoned houses. The last native inhabitants moved to the mainland in 1953, the local women no longer willing to confine their marriage prospects within this tiny community. The Blaskets have inspired a thriving literary tradition: Maurice O'Sullivan's *Twenty Years a'Growing* and Tomás Ó Crohan's *The Islandman* are two of the best-known accounts of island life. Summer boat trips visit the islands from **Dún Chaoin (Dunquin)▶**, where the film *Ryan's Daughter* was made. The Blasket Centre at Dún Chaoin contains an exhibition on island life.

Towards the ragged northwest of the peninsula are two interesting historic monuments. One is the **Gallarus Oratory▶▶**, a tiny but perfectly preserved church built of neatly packed unmortared stones. It dates from between AD800 and AD1200 and still keeps the rain out, although its roof-line is sagging slightly. A short distance up the road is **Kilmalkedar▶**, another early church from about the 12th century, roofless but bearing fine Romanesque carvings in purplish stone. By returning to Dingle again, you can start the final dramatic leg of this drive, over the **Connor Pass▶▶▶** (most spectacular on a clear day), past the 953m (3,127ft) summit of Mount Brandon. Once over the pass, you see **Brandon Bay▶▶** opening in a fantastic geological model of lakes, rivers and rock-strewn contours. The seafaring monk St. Brendan set sail from these shores in the 5th century. In 1976, Tim Severin recreated this voyage in a similar craft of wood and leather to discover whether St. Brendan could have reached America before Columbus (see the Craggaunowen Project, page 183). The northern coastal strip, back at sea level, is a quiet and pleasant drive past long stretches of beach and farmland.

Dunbeg promontory fort, Ventry, dates from between 400BC and 50BC

ROSS CASTLE

Ross Castle is a fine ruin dating from the 15th century; a tower house and later dwelling house still remain containing 16th- and 17th-century furnishings. Home of the local chieftains, the O'Donoghues, Ross Castle was the last place in Munster to fall to Cromwellian forces in 1652. The story goes that General Ludlow, hearing of a superstition that Ross Castle would never be taken by land, bought ships to sail up the lake, whereupon the defenders, hitherto defiant, immediately gave up their arms.

From Ross Castle, it is possible to take boat tours of the lake (these are non-stopping) or, alternatively, to hire a rowing boat for a landing on Innisfallen Island. Here, against a landscape of gentle valleys and dark woods, are the ruins of Innisfallen Abbey dating from AD600.

KATE KEARNEY

A well-known pub on the way up to the Gap of Dunloe, Kate Kearney's Cottage is named after the colourful local beauty who dispensed illegal *poteen* (home-brewed liquor) to travellers passing through the gap during the mid-19th century. She was apparently in constant trouble with the law, but was finally vanquished by the potato blight that made *poteen* distilling impossible. One night, she simply vanished.

KILLARNEY ENVIRONS

▶▶ **Killarney** *1463C*

Every visitor to the southwest has to see Killarney. The town itself, however, is disappointing. Once a seemly little place with a soul of its own, it is now given over wholly to tourism. It becomes hopelessly congested in summer, is very commercialized and, apart from the tall-spired Catholic **cathedral of St. Mary's▶**, designed in flamboyant high Gothic in 1842, has no outstanding features of interest. However, the immediate surroundings of the **Killarney National Park▶▶▶** (tel: 064 31947) are not to be missed and, if you can evade the milling tour buses and wheedling 'jarvey-men' (pony-trap drivers), it takes on the grandeur of genuine wilderness. Macgillycuddy's Reeks, Ireland's highest mountains, lie just outside the National Park, but are clearly visible on fine days. Killarney is the usual starting and finishing point for the popular excursion drive known as the Ring of Kerry (see pages 170–171), although if you have your own transportation you can just about avoid the town centre. The tourist office, however, is very helpful with maps and detailed local information. The Kerry Way is a 56km (35-mile) footpath leading through the mountains from the National Park towards Glenbeigh on the Iveragh peninsula.

Once out of the town, the choices for exploration are bewildering. To the south (the east shore of Lough Leane) lie the Muckross estate and various well-known beauty spots on the Kenmare road up to the pass called Moll's Gap. On the way, you may be diverted by the 15th-century **Ross Castle▶▶** (tel: 064 35234, see panel) by the lakeshore, and **Muckross Abbey▶**, a 15th-century ruin surprisingly well preserved after a Cromwellian visit in 1652. The main attraction, however, is **Muckross House▶▶** (tel: 064 31440) and the surrounding gardens and parkland. No cars are allowed within the estate, but you can park near the house. To explore the extensive grounds, you can either accept a ride from one of the jarvey-men (negotiate the fare carefully before you set off) or hire a bicycle. Muckross House is a furnished 19th-century neo-Tudor mansion designed by William Burn. Attached to it is a folk museum, where craftsmen demonstrate their trades and there are several reconstructed farmhouses. The lakeside gardens have wonderful rhododendrons and azaleas, best in early summer. The Meeting of the Waters is a popular spot between the Upper Lake and Lough Leane, where arbutus trees flourish in the mild climate. Lake boats 'shoot the rapids' there, and close by is the **Torc Waterfall►►**, plunging 20m (66ft) down a mountainside. All these make excellent picnic sites if you can avoid the crowds.

Beyond Muckross House the road winds on through woods, heather moors and mountains, becoming ever more beautiful, but you'll need to be careful at hairpin bends and tunnels. **Ladies' View►►** is a place to pause for an unforgettable vista across the lakes of the National Park toward the Gap of Dunloe. (The 'ladies' were Queen Victoria and her ladies-in-waiting, who presumably caught this view on a fine day and were duly impressed.)

The **Gap of Dunloe►►►** is Killarney's other great visitor attraction, a rugged glacial pass between the mountains, providing magnificent views of tarns and cliffs. It lies on the west side of the lake and is reached by heading north from the centre of Killarney. Once again, the jarvey-men will be only too happy to stir their bored nags into action from the centre of town, but you will save time and money by driving at least as far as touristy Kate Kearney's Cottage (see panel opposite). From there vehicular traffic is banned, so you must walk or hire a pony or jaunting car. Most of the visitors head no farther than the Gap itself, but if you want more seclusion you can continue on foot through the lonely Black Valley down past Lord Brandon's Cottage (a tea-shop) to the lakeshore and pick up a boat past the caves of Middle Lake and over to Ross Castle.

KILLARNEY WILDLIFE
Ireland's last wolf was killed near Lough Leane in 1700, and the wild mountain landscape of the National Park, backed by Macgillycuddy's Reeks, has always been home to many species of wildlife, some quite rare. A herd of red deer may be found there, together with wild goats, Japanese sika deer, otters, badgers, foxes, hares and hawks. The remote Black Valley attracts many birds. Whooper swans, with their shiny black legs, yellow-and-black bills and whooping, buglelike call, visit every winter; hooded crows and the rare chough can also be seen.

161

Ladies' View, near Killarney, justly one of Ireland's most famous panoramas

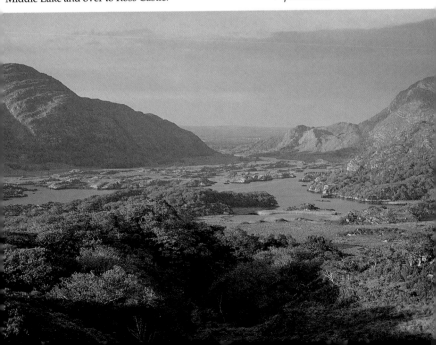

▶ ▶ ▶ Kinsale   1474A

Kinsale has attractions out of proportion to its modest size and so is very popular, though it has managed to maintain a more exclusive image than Killarney. Its setting is seductive, with tall slate-roofed houses sprinkled among the steeply wooded estuary slopes of the Bandon River. Its historic interest and fishing-village charm make it an appealing place both to stay and to eat (see panel). From Kinsale you can easily explore both Cork City and the glorious coastal or inland scenery of south Cork. It is also a notable sailing and fishing centre.

During 1601–1602, a Spanish force occupied Kinsale and was besieged by English troops. Irish allies of the Spaniards were routed, a significant step towards the establishment of the English order (and the decline of Gaelic power) in 17th-century Ireland. Soon afterwards the main players in this struggle, the O'Neill and O'Donnell clan chieftains, fled to Europe and abandoned their lands to English settlers. The town was spared a Cromwellian hammering, wisely backing the winning side. Later that century, James II landed at Kinsale with French forces in an attempt to regain his throne, and from here he finally left Ireland, defeated. Kinsale became an important English naval base, and Desmond Castle (now a heritage centre) held many French prisoners in Napoleonic times. The town is proud of its history, which is well recorded in the local **museum▶** (tel: 021 477 7930; *open:* Wed–Sat 10.30–5, Sun 2–5. *Admission: inexpensive*), a Dutch-style 17th-century town hall in the centre of town. Some of its most interesting exhibits relate to the sinking of the *Lusitania* (see page 152).

Of Kinsale's two fortresses the more interesting is **Charles Fort▶▶** (tel: 021 477 2263; *open:* Easter–end Oct daily 10–6; Nov–Easter daily 10–5. *Admission: moderate*), on the east side of the estuary, built in the late 17th century to guard the harbour entrance. One of the best-preserved examples of a star fort in Europe, you can clamber over the ramparts (keep an eye on children) and visit a military exhibition. On sunny days the signposted Scilly Walk is a wonderful stroll along the edge of the sea to the village.

Kinsale fishermen tend their nets

From Kinsale to Mizen Head is by no means undiscovered, but seems far less obligatory and overdone than excursions such as the Ring of Kerry, when you take your place in a convoy of tour buses. Meandering along tiny coastal roads through small villages, and undoubtedly getting lost amid Irish signposting, is one of the most delightful ways to enjoy the Emerald Isle.

The Old Head of Kinsale is a lonely headland on which stands a ruined fortress; offshore is the wreck of the *Lusitania* (see page 152). From Timoleague to Clonakilty—the Seven Heads peninsula—is a massively convoluted shoreline. **Timoleague**▶▶, known for its beautiful gardens, is also remarkable for its skeletal Franciscan abbey. There the coast is utterly peaceful, but beautiful. Wading birds paddle in the estuary, and the shores are full of unusual plants. **Clonakilty**▶ is an engaging place. There's little to see, but it has a lively feel, the main street lined with painted shop-fronts and old-fashioned bars. Traditional music, street theatre, festivals and crafts add to its attractions. Outside town is the birthplace of Michael Collins (see page 43), whose exploits are recounted in O'Donovan's Hotel. Seemingly endless, unspoiled sand graces the vast beach at **Inchydoney**▶▶.

The drive through the fuchsia-splashed villages of Ross Carbery, Glandore and Unionhall is glorious; creeks and lagoons mirror wooded slopes and fishing cottages with sandy coves tucked biblike under their chins. Leap is famous for Irish music, which is based at Connolly's Bar. Beyond lie the pretty village of **Castletownshend**▶▶ (see page 152), tidal Lough Hyne and a scatter of islands in Roaringwater Bay. After **Skibbereen**▶ are the colourful villages of **Ballydehob**▶, **Schull**▶▶, **Goleen**▶ and the spectacular 220m (722ft) cliffs of **Mizen Head**▶▶, guarded by an O'Mahoney strong-hold. Barleycove is a fine beach. To the north, Sheep's Head peninsula is a lovely tour if time permits. The Beara peninsula is unfairly neglected in favour of the Ring of Kerry, but is as rewarding and less crowded. Highlights include the rugged copper-mining country around **Allihies**▶ and the **Healy Pass**▶▶.

A MODERN SHRINE
Between Glandore and Ross Carbery, and not too difficult to search out, is the Drombeg Stone Circle, a good example from the early Bronze Age. Charred bones were buried in the middle of this stone circle. Nearby is a *fulacht fiadh*, or cooking trough, which would have been heated with stones from a fire.

163

The lighthouse at the Old Head of Kinsale

Many of Ireland's historic houses fell into decay or were destroyed during the 20th century, but a heartening number have survived, and those too large to make comfortable family homes have been converted for other purposes. Some of them are now splendid hotels, giving many visitors a chance to experience a grandeur granted at one time to only a privileged few.

A CRICKETING PRINCE IN IRELAND
Set in glorious countryside beneath the Twelve Bens in Connemara, but far, far away from any cricket pitch, is Ballynahinch Castle, now a comfortable hotel. At the beginning of this century, when still a private residence, it was owned by Prince Ranjitsinhji, a characterful Indian nobleman who played cricket for England on many occasions.

164

*Top: Bantry House
Below: Ashford Castle, County Mayo*

A taste of the past These hotels are all highly individual, but fall into several types. The ultra-wealthy favour the great baronial castles (mostly more or less latter-day fakes, but nonetheless with some interesting history and contents, and palatial comfort). There is the legacy of the Georgian era, spanning 170 of Ireland's most prosperous years. These may be mansions in rolling parkland or pleasingly modest rectories. Then there are Victorian properties with famous family histories. Just a few examples can be mentioned; for further suggestions see Interesting Places to Stay (pages 242–243) and Hotels and Restaurants (pages 269–283).

Grand castles Shannon Airport attracts many well-heeled transatlantic visitors who desire nothing more than to stay in a real Irish castle. This need is satisfied by several large, expensive, luxury hotels within easy reach. Nearest, 13km (8 mile) from the airport, is **Dromoland Castle**, a vast mock-Gothic mansion on a 150-ha (370-acre) estate. The estate dates back to the 16th century, when it was the seat of the O'Brien family, descendants of the great High King, Brian Ború, but the original house was replaced in the 1820s and the interior has been given a New York-style facelift by society decorator Carlton Varney. **Ashford Castle** is another Hollywood dream also under American ownership, this time on Lough Corrib, predictably furnished in sheer luxury and with superb grounds. Once the home of the Guinness family, it incorporates a 13th-century castle and a later French-style château in its opulent 19th-century shell. Also within reach of Shannon is **Adare Manor**, past seat of the earls of Dunraven. Again it is Victorian and grandiose with vast mullions and fireplaces and colossal state rooms. On a somewhat smaller scale is **Markree Castle** in Sligo, home of the Cooper family since 1640, and last altered substantially in 1802. Its hotelier owner is a member of the original family and an accomplished restaurateur. The castle has welcomed literary lights such as Lady Gregory and W. B. Yeats. **Waterford Castle** has a special brand of seclusion. It is set on an island in Waterford harbour and reached only by private car ferry. The core is a genuine 17th-century castle, with oak panelling, antique furniture and tapestries.

Elegant country houses One of the earliest period houses in Ireland now open as a hotel is **Assolas Country House** in Kanturk, County Cork. This peaceful place was built about 1590, but is now largely 17th-century in style, with gorgeous gardens and fishing rights. If Georgian elegance is to your taste, one fine example is **Enniscoe House**, near Crossmolina (Mayo), a mid-18th-century mansion with fascinating period features. The perfectly proportioned façade conceals an earlier structure with a different layout of floor levels and room sizes. Its owner, Susan Kellett, is a descendant of the original family. **Carnelly House** (Clare) is also Georgian but was built in Queen Anne style by Francis Bindon. The tall windows, Francini ceilings and Corinthian pillars give a gracious air to this creeper-covered brick house. **Cashel Palace** is an exceptional building of the same period (1730) and for 200 years was a bishop's palace. It stands beneath the Rock of Cashel and has an ancient mulberry tree on the lawn. **Coopershill** in County Sligo dates from 1774, but echoes earlier times in its utterly relaxing rooms. Regency-period **Marlfield House** (1820) is in Gorey, Wexford. This formed part of the Courtown Estate, later the seat of the Earl of Courtown and a great focus of social life. It retains the tradition of lavish hospitality amid elegant and sumptuous furnishings.

Adare Manor, County Limerick

TINAKILLY HOUSE, WICKLOW
This is one of the most interesting Victorian houses in Ireland. It was built in the 1870s for Captain Robert Halpin, commander of the *Great Eastern* steamship that laid the first telegraph cable linking Europe and America. Halpin was granted a substantial pension by a grateful government and retired here to this grand mansion in 3ha (7 acres) of sheltered gardens by the sea. Unfortunately he barely lived long enough to enjoy it. After a danger-ous life of shipwrecks and dubious escapades in the American Civil War he succumbed to blood poisoning at 58, after cutting his toenails! A splendid staircase, mahogany inlaid doors, Italian fireplaces, oil paint-ings and seafaring memo-rabilia preserve something of the atmosphere of this flamboyant house and its larger-than-life owner.

LOUGH GUR

Limerick's countryside is not especially noteworthy, but there is one little jewel tucked away in the southeast. Lough Gur is a beautiful crescent-shaped lake around which evidence of early civilizations has been found. Antiquities include a wedge tomb and a large stone circle at Grange. Cartloads of remains were discovered after the partial draining of the lake in the 19th century. An interpretative centre has been set up overlooking the reedy lake, with a visitor centre and museum in two replica thatched *crannóg* huts of the neolithic era.

166

King John's Castle is unusual in that it has no keep

▶ Limerick

1474D

Limerick is a significant city in terms of industry and population, currently vying with Galway for third place in the Republic. It has a rich historical background and plenty of interesting sights, and, as a result of its strategic location at the lowest bridging point on the Shannon, most visitors to the southwest wind up here at some point during their stay. With relatively dull scenery on its doorstep, Limerick's attractions as a long-term base are limited. Until recently, it was a run-down and oddly surly city with a high rate of unemployment and crime. (Readers of Frank McCourt's memoirs, *Angela's Ashes,* will know just how rough and depressed Limerick once was.) However, energetic multimillion-pound efforts to revitalize the centre are at last showing some success, particularly around its historic quaysides. Wharves and warehouses have been transformed into new business premises, its Norman and Georgian heritage is now carefully restored, and the air of neglect has been banished with attractive shops, restaurants and cafés. It is certainly worth half a day's time, more if you are interested in Irish history. Limerick was originally a Viking settlement, due to its strategic location at the mouth of the Shannon. Brian Ború, High King of Ireland, eventually conquered the Danes, many of whom settled down quite happily in Ireland and intermarried with native Gaels. The Norman era was important for Limerick. The Normans expanded the town and built huge fortifications with curtain walls, King John's Castle being one of the most impressive. In Cromwellian times it suffered terribly under the onslaughts of General Ireton, Cromwell's son-in-law and commander of Ireland, who besieged the city walls for more than six months. Later that century, Limerick was one of the last Jacobite bastions after the Battle of the Boyne, the hero of the period being Patrick Sarsfield, who made a daring raid on William's ammunition wagons and supply trains.

Eventually, however, Limerick capitulated, and the infamous Treaty of Limerick was signed in 1691. Few incidents in Ireland's history illustrate the role of 'perfidious Albion' more clearly than this. Within two months the English reneged on their promises to grant the Catholic population religious and property rights and instituted draconian measures against them. **The Treaty Stone►**, on which the agreement was signed, became a symbol of all that was hateful about English rule. It can still be seen at the west end of Thomond Bridge, now sandblasted clean in an attempt to erase the memories. Today Limerick is a vehemently Catholic and nationalist city.

Within the town centre the most notable monument is **King John's Castle►►** (tel: 061 411 201), near Thomond Bridge. First built in 1200, it still looks the part of a medieval Norman fortress, though much restored after its 17th-century battering during the Siege of Limerick and subsequent alterations. The tower is the oldest section and housed a British garrison until the birth of the Irish Free State in 1922. An excellent and imaginative visitor centre now reconstructs the story of Limerick and its castle, while outside in the castle yard lie re-creations of various curious engines used in medieval siege warfare—find out what the mangonel and trebuchet were and how they worked.

For more history, Limerick's **City Museum►** (tel: 061 417 826) in two restored 18th-century houses documents the city's prosperity in Georgian times, when it produced fine silverware and lace. Even more worthwhile is the **Hunt Museum►►** (tel: 061 312 833), outside the centre in the university campus area at Plassey. The art historian and antiquarian, John Hunt, donated a magnificent collection of Celtic and medieval art, including the Antrim Cross and a Bronze Age shield. Only the National Museum in Dublin can better it for early Celtic and medieval art. **St. Mary's Cathedral►** (tel: 061 416 238), in the centre, is the city's most appealing religious building and its oldest, founded in 1168 but dating mainly from the 15th century. Unexpectedly in this strongly Catholic city, it is a Protestant church. Its most interesting features include black oak choir stalls with carved 15th-century misericords (see photograph and caption, above right).

An ornately carved misericord from St. Mary's Cathedral. They were so-called because they afforded clerics some form of rest when standing through lengthy services (misericordia is Latin for pity). They perched on these small seats, rather than standing unsupported

Inside St. Mary's Cathedral

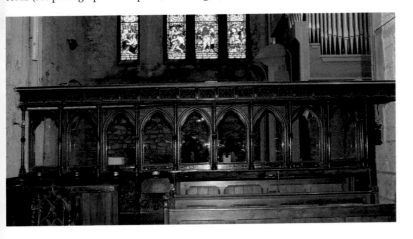

Old Midleton Distillery even had its own fire engine

THE MOUTH OF THE SHANNON
W. M. Thackeray thought the undulating grounds that border the Shannon estuary enjoyable, if not beautiful: 'though the view is by no means a fine one, I know few that are pleasanter than the sight of these rich, golden, peaceful plains, with the full harvest waving on them and just ready for the sickle.'

WHISKEY
Whiskey (*uisce beatha—the water of life*) has an interesting pedigree. It was probably invented by Irish missionary monks with their arcane knowledge of the Middle Eastern alembic, a still used for making perfumes. Thirteenth-century soldiers were fortified with a dose of the stuff before battle and Queen Elizabeth I herself is said to have been partial to a drop—probably a taste acquired from Sir Walter Ralegh, who was presented with a handsome 32-gallon cask of whiskey by the Earl of Cork. In introducing tobacco and possibly whiskey, it seems Ralegh was responsible for popularizing more than one addictive substance!

▶▶ Old Midleton Distillery   *1475B*
Midleton, tel: 021 461 3594, www.whiskeytours.ie
Open: Mar–end Oct daily 10–6 (last tour at 5); Nov–end Feb tours only, daily 11.30, 2.30 and 4. Admission: moderate

In the pleasant little town of Midleton, an impressive 18th-century industrial complex of stone mills and warehouses has been restored to enlighten visitors about the fine art of whiskey distilling. The Jameson Heritage Centre is an entrepreneurial venture by Irish Distillers, emulating the successful Northern Irish attraction at Bushmills. For a fee (which includes a tasting) you can tour the modern distillery together with the Old Midleton Distillery, in use for 150 years from 1825 to 1975. The world's largest pot still, with a capacity of more than 178,200L (40,000gal), stands by the reception building. Despite the heritage centre's name, it was the brand known as Paddy, rather than Jameson's, that was distilled in Midleton from the 19th century; John Jameson's whiskey was always produced in Dublin.

▶ Rathkeale and environs   *1474D*
Castle Matrix▶▶ (tel: 069 64284; *open:* mid-May to mid-Sep daily 11–5, rest of year by appointment. *Admission: moderate*), just outside Rathkeale, is a 15th-century tower house containing an important collection of documents connected with the Flight of the Wild Geese, the exodus after the Battle of Limerick. The farmland of west Limerick and the Shannon estuary is tame compared with the grandeur of Cork or Kerry, but if you have been around the Dingle peninsula you could well find yourself driving through it. A few sights are worth a detour. **Ardfert**▶, north of Tralee, has some restored monastic remains. The beach nearby is Banna Strand, where Roger Casement's abortive adventure took place (see page 43). Hugging the Shannon coast is **Glin Castle**▶▶ (tel: 068 34173, www.glincastle.com; *open:* May–end Jun daily 10–noon and 2–4, rest of year by appointment. *Admission: expensive*), seat of the Knights of Glin and a fine 18th-century house with Victorian Gothic additions (open only to group tours). Part of the house is a B&B where you can stay in luxurious accommodation. Further along, and probably the most worthwhile stop of all, is **Foynes Flying Boat Museum**▶▶ (tel: 069 65416; *open:* Apr–end Oct daily 10–5. *Admission: moderate*), in the terminal of the original Shannon Airport. During the 1930s and 1940s, Foynes

was the operational headquarters for seaplanes travelling to and from the United States, and with its fascinating collection of film footage, instruments, photos and logs, the museum is a must for any aviation buff. **Adare▶**, a notably pretty village of thatched cottages on the main Limerick road, contains the ruins of three ancient abbeys and of 12th-century Desmond Castle. Adare Manor, a lavish Gothic mansion, is now a country house hotel.

▶▶ Youghal   *1475B*

Youghal stands by the winding Blackwater estuary, right on the border between counties Waterford and Cork. Pronounced 'yawl', this ancient walled seaport has a rich history and several interesting buildings. Its resilient, salty character is striking, and in 1956 it impressed the director, John Huston, sufficiently to use it as a film location for *Moby Dick*. Its most illustrious resident was Sir Walter Ralegh, once mayor of the town. A Potato Festival is intermittently held to commemorate Ralegh's supposed introduction of the Virginian tuber to Irish shores. A citizen with a more genuine claim to the town's attention was Richard Boyle, father of the famous scientist who formulated Boyle's Law and builder of the almshouses in the town. The **Youghal Heritage Centre▶▶** (tel: 024 92447) is a great introduction to the complex history of the town and its environs; an audio-visual display and guides to walk you through the town are available. **St. Mary's Collegiate Church▶** (tel: 024 92350) is Youghal's most impressive building, containing many tombs and effigies, including one to the fantastically wealthy Earl of Cork and his 16 children (by three wives). Other privately owned buildings to look for are the Georgian **clock tower▶** bridging the main street; the tower house, **Tynte's Castle▶**; and the **Red House▶**, a Dutch-style merchant's house. The **town walls▶▶** are some of the best examples in Ireland, with large sections still in fairly good condition. Another good reason to pause in Youghal is its excellent seafood restaurant, Aherne's (see Hotels and Restaurants, page 281).

ROSE OF TRALEE

The pale moon was rising
above the green
mountain,
The sun was declining
beneath the blue sea;
When I strayed with my
love by the pure crystal
fountain,
That stands in the beautiful Vale of Tralee.

She was lovely and fair as
the rose of the summer;
Yet 'twas not her beauty
alone that won me;
Oh no, 'twas the truth in
her eyes ever dawning,
That made me love Mary,
the Rose of Tralee.

William Mulchinock

The lighthouse at Youghal

THE RING OF KERRY

Drive

The spectacular Ring of Kerry

Perhaps the most popular of all tourist routes in Ireland, this drive offers a mix of dramatic scenery, sights and eating places, some geared towards the bus-tour trade. Allow a full day to see everything.

Sneem caters well to tourists

Many of the tour buses that ply this route start from Killarney, so if you have your own transportation you stand less chance of being held up in traffic convoys if you do the Ring clockwise, starting in **Kenmare▶▶**. There are advantages either way; if you prefer to save the best till last, follow the bus route. As a variation, you could take the high mountain road that runs down the spine of the Iveragh peninsula through Macgillycuddy's Reeks. Several roads connect this with the coastal route. From Kenmare, the coastal road begins pleasantly enough through Templenoe and Blackwater Bridge, with peaceful estuary views to the south. At Parknasilla the lush gardens of the Great Southern Hotel give some idea of how mild the climate is, with palms and tender shrubs growing profusely. **Sneem▶** is a pretty village of colour-washed houses clustered around the village green. Farther on, don't miss **Staigue Fort▶▶**, perhaps the best example of a stone *cashel*, or ring fort. It probably dates from about 500BC and its stout walls must have been a sturdy defence for the inhabitants huddled within. Now all you will find are a startled sheep or two perched on the walls. An honesty box requests a small fee to compensate the farmer for 'trespass'. On the southwest tip of the Ring is the Derrynane Estate at **Caherdaniel▶**, where the Irish statesman Daniel O'Connell lived. The wooded grounds are part of a **national park►►**, and encompass lovely rock-and-sand beaches and dunes. The house is now a museum commemorating O'Connell.

Waterville►► faces the Atlantic gales bravely, its short holiday season attracting many visitors to a long sandy beach. Golf and fishing are additional attractions. As you approach Waterville you may spy a brief but unforgettable glimpse of the jagged **Sceilg Mhichíl (Skellig Rock)►**, some way out to sea. These inhospitable islets provided a penitential home for Celtic monks who founded St. Finian's Abbey there in AD560. Oratories, crosses and beehive huts are among the ruins visible on Skellig Michael, the larger island. Little Skellig is a notable haven for seabirds, especially gannets. Boat trips run in summer from various points along this coast, but landings on the islands are now very limited because of erosion and damage to the sites, not to mention bad weather. Choose a calm day in these waters! The **Skellig Experience►►**, an interpretative centre near the modern bridge at **Portmagee►** (tel: 066 947 6306; *open:* mid-Mar to mid-Nov daily 10–6. *Admission: moderate*) linking mainland Kerry with Valentia Island, provides lots of multimedia information about the hardy Skellig monks, the local seabirds and various aspects of coastal life. A guided cruise among the Skellig Islands is available.

Valentia Island► is a strange place of tame hills and a domesticated patchwork of walled fields and fuchsia hedges. The first transatlantic telegraph cable to the United States was laid from there in 1866. Knightstown is the main village, with fishing and tourism its principal concerns. If you decide to stay overnight, you can enjoy some excellent traditional music and dancing there.

Cahersiveen►, on the mainland, was the birthplace of Daniel O'Connell. From here the north coast road leads past grand mountain slopes and sea vistas to the town of **Glenbeigh►**. A detour inland past the lushly wooded slopes of Lough Caragh makes an interesting variation to the coast road, which is fairly unexciting from here as far as **Killorglin►**.

171

Looking across Valentia Harbour

Western Counties

RED MARY

Máire Rua (Red Mary)
O'Brien, who lived in the
17th century, was appar-
ently a perfectly harmless
person, although one tale
described her as a woman
of great lust who had
many suitors. Before
giving her hand, she would
demand that a suitor
should prove his worth by
riding her fierce stallion—
which then promptly raced
out over the Cliffs of
Moher and deposited his
rider in the Atlantic below.
All perished except one,
who succeeded in bringing
the stallion back to Máire
Rua whereupon she
closed the gates of her
castle. In trying to leap
over the gateway the
horse died, thus explain-
ing the name of her
castle—Leamaneagh
(*Léim an Eich*, or horse's
leap), though neither
history nor legend records
that she married the
brave horseman.

*A Celtic cross is
silhouetted against the
darkening sky on
Inishmore, the largest of
the Aran Islands*

CONNEMARA PONIES

The qualities of this versatile breed make it popular with horse-lovers all over Britain and Ireland. At most times of year they can be seen roaming the harsh terrain of Connemara, surviving on a diet of brackish grass and seaweed. In August many are brought to Clifden for the Connemara Pony Show to be examined by local dealers. Resilience is an obvious characteristic, but these ponies are also good-tempered and easily taught. A subtle mixture of Arab blood lends style to the sturdy native stock and, when well groomed and smartened up, they are handsome, elegant creatures in any show ring.

Dún Aengus, on Inishmore, the most imposing ruin in the Aran Islands

IRISH CABINS

During the early 19th century standards of living in Connaught were extremely poor due to overpopulation and the oppressive land laws of the time. A description in 1823 gives an idea of how many people lived: 'a room fifteen feet by nine, no window, no chimney, not even the sign of a fireplace, a mud floor sunk considerably below the level of the road by the side of which it stands, originally ill made and in this wet season covered by almost one foot of water, in one corner are a few lighted sods of turf which, while they afford but little warmth to the wretched group around them, fill the room with volumes of smoke'.

WESTERN COUNTIES Oliver Cromwell's famous declaration that Irish rebels could go 'to Hell or to Connaught' suggests he didn't think much of this western region. In times when soil fertility and accessibility were important considerations, these rain-swept, isolated outposts of barren limestone or waterlogged bog must have held few attractions. Famine struck western Ireland particularly hard and emigration from counties Galway, Clare and Mayo has been high. Until the 18th century, British influence was minimal, and the area is still firmly Gaelic in outlook, its population mostly in tiny, scattered rural communities rather than towns and villages. The traditional Irish spirit is evident in local speech, music, crafts and sports. Now, it is the west's very distinctiveness that many visitors find so appealing, and, above all, its scenery. These three counties encompass a colossal variety of landscapes and sights. Scenic highlights are unquestionably the ghostly grey-white expanses of bare limestone in the Burren and the wild coast and mountains of Connemara, where the Twelve Bens loom over flattering mirrors of water amid moorland and blanket bog. Mayo, to the north, is quieter and less popular, although its peaceful scenery has always appealed to a discerning minority. Achill Island is one of its loveliest (and most visited) spots. Céide Fields, near Ballycastle, is an imaginatively displayed neolithic settlement long preserved in peatland (tel: 096 43325 and ask for visitor information).

VISITOR ATTRACTIONS Tourism, low-key at first, has boomed and become much more commercialized since the opening of Shannon Airport, near Limerick. This is still an important, though no longer mandatory, stop for all transatlantic passenger aircraft flying into Ireland. Worryingly, the importance of tourism to the region's economy may threaten some of its most sensitive sites. The Office of Public Works planned to build a new visitor centre in one of the most remote parts of the fragile Burren. This plan, at least, was rejected by the Irish Supreme Court, but there will doubtless be others.

Off-season (Oct–Apr) most of the west is quiet, with everything except the busiest attractions being closed and less choice of accommodation available. In order to tour the area in any depth, it is essential to have a car. If you are unable to drive, the best base is rapidly expanding Galway City, which offers plenty to do all year round and opportunities for nearby excursions. One of the most interesting trips is to the Aran Islands—it is advisable to stay a day or two, if you can, and see them all. The west provides ample opportunities for golf, riding, fishing and relaxing.

The ideal time to visit the Burren is May or June, when its fantastic variety of flowers are at their best. For birdwatching, however, spring and autumn are good times, particularly on the Cliffs of Moher and Downpatrick Head. Inland, huge expanses of water also attract thousands of wildfowl. Pontoon, between loughs Conn and Cullin, is an especially good place to watch them. So, too, are the lonely bogland and mountains of the Connemara National Park and the strange turlough lakes of Counties Galway and Clare—one month, a sheet of water, the next, just a vivid emerald patch of freshly watered vegetation, brilliant with flowers, as the giant underground aquifers steadily fill.

Knappogue Castle in County Clare runs medieval banquets in season

CURRACHS

These traditional rowboats, with no keels, are made of tarred canvas stretched over a light wooden frame (originally made of hazel rods and cowhide). The stern is flat, the prow high, so the boats ride high in the water and are extremely buoyant in the roughest seas, though very fragile. Most carry three oarsmen. They are carried to and from the water's edge upside-down over the crew's heads to avoid damage by rocks, which gives a very strange insectlike impression to a spectator. They are still used for inshore lobster fishing and collecting seaweed, but the popular sport of *currach*-racing on the west coast of Ireland also helps to keep these unusual craft afloat. (See photograph on page 194.)

Typical Aran cottages, with the ubiquitous dry-stone walls marking the field boundaries

▶▶ Acaill (Achill Island) 1721D

Mayo's western seaboard seems on the verge of disintegration, its straggling peninsulas anchored to the mainland only by a thread. Achill is the largest of these semi-islands, a rough triangle with sides about 24km (15 miles) long, linked to Curraun (itself a peninsula) by a modern road bridge over Achill Sound. Its quiet beaches and spectacular mountain scenery make it an appealing destination; touring, by car or bicycle, surfing and fishing are the main activities and in summer boats make trips to coastal caves or in pursuit of the harmless basking sharks that haunt this coast. A rash of uniform visitor cottages threatens to blight the island's beauty. Keel is the main village, boasting shops, simple accommodation and a splendid sandy beach, with some dramatic formations known as the Cathedral Rocks at its farthest end. The most scenic parts of the island can be seen from the Atlantic Drive (signed from the main road near the bridge), which leads past awesome cliffs, heather and gorse moors and white cottages sprinkled against dark rocks. Beyond Keel, the road stretches towards Achill Head, rearing towards the Atlantic like a sea monster.

▶▶▶ Oileáin Árann (Aran Islands) 1721B

The cracked limestone terrain of the Aran Islands, lying about 48km (30 miles) out in Galway Bay, links them geologically with the Burren, in County Clare. The islands are flattish, but tilt towards massive sea cliffs in places. Making a living on these bleak rock platforms, virtually treeless and exposed to the full brunt of Atlantic storms, has always been a struggle. Large areas have no natural depth of soil and the islanders have created fields from a mixture of sand and seaweed compost, protecting them with an intricate network of dry-stone walls.

Today's dwindling population of islanders (about 1,500) subsist on their age-old livelihoods of fishing and farming and, increasingly, on tourism. Many speak Gaelic, and a very few still wear traditional Aran dress. The canvas fishing boats called *currachs* are used, although now they often have outboard motors. The Arans have inspired a strong

Traditional shop-front, Bunratty Park

CASTLES AND ABBEYS

The Shannon region has many ancient buildings, often carefully restored to achieve full tourist potential. Besides well-known Bunratty, there are tower houses at Knappogue, a MacNamara stronghold and Dunguaire, near Kinvarra. Less touristy are Aughnanure, on Lough Corrib and Portumna, on Lough Derg. Some of the best monastic sites include: the Franciscan friaries of Quin and Ennis; Clonfert, which has a lovely Romanesque doorway; Ballintober, founded by a Connaught king; Ross, near Headford; and the remains at Kilmacdoagh, with its leaning Round Tower and cathedral. Cong Abbey, in Mayo, housed the great processional Cross of Cong, now in Dublin.

177

tradition of literature and oral storytelling; J. M. Synge set his play *Riders to the Sea* here and the film, *Man of Aran*, made by the Irish-American director, Robert Flaherty, in 1934, depicted the harsh life on the island.

Most visitors, on a day-trip to one island, only get a faint whiff of Aran's cultural background; by staying in the islands' simple accommodation, you will absorb far more. Two ferry companies serve the Aran Islands from Galway City, Rossaveal and Doolin (County Clare). Aer Arann flies tiny aircraft to all three islands from Galway. All transportation services may be affected by weather.

Inis Móir (Inishmore)►►► is the largest and most visited island. You can explore by bicycle, on foot, take a minibus or a pony-trap ride along its 11km (7- mile) spinal road. Inishmore has a wealth of ancient monuments, notably one of Ireland's outstanding prehistoric sites, the remarkable cliff fort of Dún Aengus. Three concentric horse-shoe rings of stone perched atop mighty cliffs seem an odd place of refuge, so exposed to the elements and with a sheer drop to the roaring sea below. Its precise age and purpose are still a mystery. The smaller islands are **Inis Meáin (Inishmaan)►►** and **Inis Oirr (Inisheer)►►**, both of which have small fortresses, churches and folk museums to visit.

►► Bunratty Castle and Folk Park — 1733A

Bunratty, tel: 061 361 511, www.shannonheritage.com
Open: 8 Sep–end May, daily 9.30–5.30; Jun–end Aug daily 9.30–7. Admission: expensive

Bunratty, on the main visitor route from the west coast to Shannon Airport, is now a highly commercialized venture, dragging in bus tours by the thousand for 'medieval' banquets and 'traditional Irish nights' of fiddle music and Irish stew. For all that, the 15th-century castle is genuine enough and well worth seeing.

Set in the castle grounds, the Folk Park re-creates rural Irish life at the turn of the 20th century by means of a series of 'typical' village buildings of the sort you will rarely see in Ireland outside folk theme parks. There are also exhibitions, gift- and tearooms and the famous tourist pub, **Durty Nelly's►**, obligatory viewing for any tour.

STONE GATES

Despite there being a high density of fields and walls on the Aran Islands, wooden gates are very rare, since trees are scarce. The islanders' answer is to use small gaps in the wall, filled with stones. When access is needed the 'gate' is dismantled and then reassembled. Some gates are topped with a branch of thorn to dissuade the occupant of the field from pushing the gate over. See above for a typical example.

THE BURREN

Drive

The eerie beauty of the Burren

A moon buggy may seem better suited to this eerie landscape than a car. Geologists, botanists and antiquity-hunters will be in their element.

From a distance, parts of this treeless limestone plateau in north Clare look bleak, but a closer exploration reveals that the area is astonishingly rich in plant life, playing host to more than 1,100 of the 1,400 species found in Ireland. Although the stone surfaces have been scraped clean by the elements, every crack and hollow contains some fragile vegetation. Alpine species flourish next to those from Mediterranean shores: rare saxifrages, gentians, maidenhair ferns and orchids. The best time to visit the Burren for flowers is in May or June.

Within a couple of hours you can drive across the Burren on the major road from Ennis to Ballyvaughan and get an idea of the landscape of ancient domed hills and grey-white 'flagstones'. But this moonscape reveals its real charms only to the sharp-eyed observer on foot, so take a picnic and leave your vehicle at some stage. Walkers on the Burren should wear sensible footwear and take great care. A 32km (20-mile) marked trail, the Burren Way, runs from Ballyvaughan towards Doolin.

Bloody cranesbill, which grows commonly all over the Burren

Ballyvaughan▶ ▶ is an attractive centre from which to explore the Burren; other bases with accommodation are **Killinaboy**▶, **Corofin**▶ and **Ennistymon**▶. The southern section of the Burren is characterized by seasonal lakes called *turloughs*, which ebb and fill as the region's water table changes. Gradually, rainwater falling on this limestone plateau finds its way underground into a maze of caves and subterranean channels. Most are too dangerous for novice investigations, but one has been opened and is worth a visit: **Aillwee Caves**▶ ▶ (tel: 065 707 7036, www.aillweecaves.ie; *open:* Mar–end Jun and Sep–end Oct daily 10–6; Jul–end Aug daily 10–7. *Admission: moderate*) south of Ballyvaughan, is a

commercial operation, but the cavern itself is left reasonably natural apart from pathways and illumination. Near the cave entrance a shop sells local cheeses and other produce.

Parts of the Burren are reasonably fertile, yet others seem inhospitably bare, a shock after the lushness of most of Ireland. For centuries before the advent of tourism, the population of the Burren lived in poverty.

The best way to find out more about the Burren's unique flora and geology is to visit the **Burren Centre**▶ ▶ (tel: 065 708 8030; *open:* Jun–end Aug daily 9.30–6; Mar–end May and Sep–end Oct daily 10–5. *Admission: moderate*) at Kilfenora, by **St. Fachtnan's Cathedral**▶ ▶. Other sights to look for as you cross the central spine of the Burren are ancient tombs, such as the 4,500-year-old **Poulnabrone Dolmen**▶, or the **Gleninsheen wedge-tomb**▶, easily spotted beside the R480 near Caherconnell. The ruins of **Leamaneh**▶, a 17th-century mansion owned by the O'Briens, are a prominent landmark near Kilfenora.

Another curiosity is a weatherworn *sheila-na-gig* on the ruined church at **Killinaboy**▶. These carvings of female figures in indelicate poses were perhaps an ancient fertility symbol, or a dire warning of the sins of the flesh.

179

A strange stone structure in the area known as the Burren

There are no snakes in Ireland, as every Irish schoolchild knows. But its national parks, national nature reserves, bird sanctuaries and forest parks provide a remarkably varied collection of habitats for a vast number of other species, including creatures that are now very rare in Britain, such as corncrakes and otters.

180

THE BURREN

This unusual terrain soaks up the rays of the sun and releases it gently throughout the winter, keeping temperatures a vital fraction higher than the surrounding area. It supports an amazing variety of plants, including many fragile, low-growing types that would be swamped in the average meadow. Species to look for include the deceptive fly orchid (resembling an insect), gentians and alpine saxifrages. Mountain avens and wild thyme grow everywhere on the Burren, forming colourful sheets in early summer. Needless to say, visitors are requested not to pick or uproot any of the area's plants.

Fly orchid

An unspoiled land Ireland is a predominantly rural country, but like everywhere else, is steadily becoming more built up. Land use is changing, usually to the disadvantage of native flora and fauna, but there are still huge tracts of unspoiled countryside where ancient farming patterns prevail. Migrant birds return year after year to safe haunts, rare orchids and obscure insectivorous plants flourish in specialized niches and lichen grows thick on walls or tree trunks in unpolluted air. Birdwatchers and botanists, or anyone who appreciates country life, will much enjoy a break in Ireland. Remember your binoculars and a reference book for identifying unusual species. If you plan to walk any of the long-distance footpaths of Ireland, or visit specialist regions like the Burren, check what to look for at an information or visitor centre before you set off. Bord Fáilte's leaflet, *Ireland Naturally*, outlines the main nature reserves and places of interest.

Abundant wildlife Practically any part of Ireland offers the keen-eyed naturalist a good selection of species, but a number of locations are especially noted for unusual wildlife. Ireland has fewer mammals than Britain (no moles, for instance), but those that are there can often be found more abundantly. Otters colonize many rivers and streams, even quite near towns. Pine martens, red deer and red squirrels can be found in the newly designated forest parks. The last remaining native woodlands can be seen in the national parks of Killarney and Glenveagh.

Exotic plants If you are interested in plants, the best region to head for is the mysterious limestone wilderness of the Burren in County Clare (see panel and pages 178–179). Other areas special for plants are the sand-dune habitats, such as the Raven National Nature Reserve in County Wexford (wild asparagus, round-leafed wintergreen and lesser centaury) and the lush, subtropical oceanic lands of Kerry and Cork, where wild fuchsias bloom and the strawberry tree grows to unusual size. Mosses and ferns thrive in the moist, mild air. Ireland's boglands support a unique ecosystem of wetland plants, including sundews and butterworts (see pages 24–25).

Rare birds Birdwatchers have an immense choice of habitats. There are many exciting coastal reserves, first landfall for rare migrants that cross the ocean to breed or winter in Ireland. Spring nesting seasons begin early for native birds, followed by an influx of species from Africa.

THE IRISH YEW
Every example of this tree ultimately comes from cuttings taken from the mutant discovered in the gardens of Florence Court in County Fermanagh. The branches have an unusual upright habit instead of the normal spreading growth. The original tree was identified and first propagated in 1767 and the Irish yew is now planted widely in graveyards and formal garden settings.

MARINE RESERVES
For marine habitats, head for Strangford Lough near Belfast, or Lough Hyne in south Cork, where sheltered sea inlets have fostered unique colonies of creatures usually found in more tropical waters. Giant skate and basking shark glide through the narrow straits, carpeted with bright corals and sponges.

There are pine martens in the forest parks, but you will be lucky to see one

Corncrake

In autumn, rare American waders appear in ones and twos, and in winter great numbers of waterfowl fly in from northern Europe and the Arctic or Canada. Manx shearwaters glide close to Belfast towards dusk, with an eerie cry that once unnerved the Vikings and nest on Light House Island. Greenland white-fronted geese arrive in huge flocks on the 'slobs' (reclaimed *polder* mudflats) of Wexford. Puffins nest in a few rocky places on the west and southwest coast (the Cliffs of Moher, Clear Island or Puffin Island). Terns colonize the sheltered inland sea of Strangford Lough. Several of the most famous bird reserves are islands: Ireland's Eye, just off Howth near Dublin, the Copelands near Belfast and the wild Skellig Rock off the southwest tip of Cork. Clear Island and the Saltees are both accessible by boat at the most interesting times of year. Other good birdwatching locations are the quiet estuarial coast of Waterford and Wexford (particularly around Hook Head, Kinsale Old Head and Kilmore Quay), the muddy flats of Timoleague and the wild rocky fastnesses of Clare, Mayo, Rathlin Island and Donegal, where seabirds gather in vast numbers on cliff ledges, at spots such as Horn Head (Donegal), the Cliffs of Moher (Clare) or Downpatrick Head (Mayo). Inland, many of the larger lakes and river systems support huge colonies of waterbirds—godwits, avocets and swans. Birds of prey can be seen wheeling in lonely circuits around the Wicklow Mountains, the Slieve Blooms, the Sperrins (in the north) and Macgillycuddy's Reeks.

EDWARD SYNGE

During the dreadful Famine days, some Protestant landlords attempted to lure their starving tenants away from the Catholic church with offers of soup, education and other blandishments if they would convert. In Clare, Edward Synge was one such individual; he aroused such passionate antipathy that an attempt was made on his life. A stoutly bound leather Bible in his breast pocket diverted the bullet aimed at his heart, thus finally convincing many of his unbelieving flock that God was very definitely on his side! The Bible (complete with hole) is displayed at the Clare Heritage Centre in Corofin.

A justifiably famous Irish viewpoint shows Clifden in its glorious setting by the Twelve Bens, most of which are visible below. Leaving Clifden on the Sky Road (on a clear day) and looking back after a short while reveals the full panorama

▶▶ Clifden   1721C

The 'capital of Connemara' occupies a glorious position at the head of Clifden Bay, with the Twelve Bens mountain range a dramatic backdrop. Clifden is little more than a large village, but its location makes it a popular base, and it is now a major music and tourism centre. It is also an agricultural and market town, but much of the land around it is too poor to farm, and the region's income derives mainly from tourism. It has a range of affordable accommodation, lively bars and fine sandy beaches. An arts festival is held in late September, though a more traditional event is the August Connemara Pony Show.

Cottages and bungalows have sprung up all around the 19th-century core of the town, founded in 1812 by the local landowner, John d'Arcy, descendant of an Anglo-Norman family who converted from Roman Catholicism to avoid dispossession under the Penal Laws. He built the ruined Gothic castle visible from the Sky Road.

The best views of the town and the surrounding landscape are seen from the Sky Road, a narrow circuit around the Kingstown peninsula to the northwest. This scenic corniche skirts the hillsides, overlooking plunging vistas of white farms, emerald fields and sapphire sea.

▶▶▶ Cliffs of Moher   1722B

Sheer, dark walls of rock stretch dramatically for 8km (5 miles) along the coast of Clare, an even-topped curtain, in places as much as 200m (700ft) high. These remarkable cliffs are home to a variety of seabirds, including a colony of puffins. On clear days there are splendid views of the Aran Islands and the mountains of Connemara. A cliff path leads to the southerly extremity of Hag's Head, fenced as the cliffs are so friable. The rocks are basically limestone of the same sort as the Burren, but shale and sandstone have formed on top, and are subject to rainfall erosion and the pressure of many feet; keep back from the edge. You can park near the highly commercialized visitor centre (tel: 065 708 1171, www.shannonheritage.com; *open:* centre Jul–end Aug daily 9–8; Jun 9–7; May, Sep 9–6.30; Apr 9.30–6; Oct–end Mar 9.30–5. *Admission free*). Close by is a folly viewpoint built by the 19th-century politician Sir Cornelius O'Brien, where a telescope gives a close-up of the huge rock faces and sea stacks in the lazily moving waves.

▶ Corofin
1733A

This village amid the pretty lakes of the southern Burren is a fine base for exploring the area. Accommodation consists mainly of B&Bs, with one good private hostel in the centre. Even if you don't stay, visit the **Clare Heritage Centre▶▶** (tel: 065 683 7955, www.clareroots.com; *open:* mid-May–end Oct daily 10–6. *Admission: inexpensive*), housed in the former Protestant church. It has a moving exhibition connected with the Famine period, when this part of Ireland suffered particularly badly. In a building close by there is a genealogical centre, containing half a million baptismal records of more than 2,500 families. Descendants of émigré families come to find their roots (see pages 74–75).

▶▶ Craggaunowen Project
1733A

Kilmurry, Sixmilebridge, tel: 061 367 178,
www.shannonheritage.com
Open: May–end Aug daily 10–6. Admission: expensive
This historic reconstruction brings to life Ireland's pre-Christian past and is one of the best of its kind, well explained with a good visitor centre, coffee shop and picnic area. The art historian and archaeologist, John Hunt, restored the 16th-century tower house of Craggaunowen Castle during the 1960s. A Bronze-Age *crannóg* (island dwelling) stands in a reedy lake; other exhibits include a ring fort and a stretch of Iron-Age timber road. Also on display is the leather-covered boat called the *Brendan*, in which Tim Severin and his crew sailed the Atlantic in 1976–1977, in a putative repetition of St. Brendan's 6th-century voyage to the Americas (see page 115).

ALCOCK AND BROWN
John Alcock and Arthur Whitton-Brown were the first to fly the Atlantic nonstop, setting off in a Vickers Vimy biplane from St. John's, Newfoundland and crash-landing (fortunately unharmed) in Derryginlagh Bog, just south of Clifden, on 15 June 1919. They averaged a flying speed of about 160kph (100mph) and the journey took them more than 16 hours. A monument in the shape of a plane wing commemorates the flight, on a windy hilltop site overlooking the Connemara coast just off the Ballyconneely road, but it's not easy to find.

183

FUN ON JUDGMENT DAY
When two imaginative girls were growing up in Chile in the early 1900s, each wrote a poetic epitaph for the other, agreeing that whoever lived longer would place her poem on the other's tombstone. Subsequently both came to live near Corofin. When Audrey Douglas (née Sharman) died in 1968, she was buried in the grounds of the Church of Ireland church in the village (now the Clare Heritage Centre). Faithful to her pact, Vanda Cutler inscribed the following on the tombstone, visible for all to read:

Here, as ever, sleeping
    sound,
Lies our Audrey in the
    ground.
If she wakes, as wake
    she may,
There'll be fun on
    Judgement Day.

CONNEMARA

Inishturk
Inishbofin
Inishshark
Cleggan
Omey I
Kylemore Abbey
Letterfrack
Connemara National Park
Clifden
Mannin Bay
Ballynahinch
Ballyconneely
Slyne Head
Cloch na Rón (Roundstone)
An Caiseal (Cashel)
Glinsce (Glinsk)
Cill Chiaráin (Kilkieran)
An Gort Mór (Gortmore)
The Twelve Pins
An Mám (Maum)
An Teach Dóite (Maam Cross)
Maumturk Mts
Muckrea Mts
Killary Harbour
Aasleagh
Leenane
Partry Mts
Joyce Country
Jarconnaught
Oughterard
Aughnanure
Lough Corrib
Headford
Lough Mask
An Fhairche (Clonbur)
Neale
Cong
Shrule
Tuam
Kilmaine
Ballinrobe
Partry
Claremorris
Ballindine
Lough Carra
673m

0   5   10   15 km
0   5   10 miles

Drive

Mountains, beaches, untouched bogland and a fiord

If you're lucky with the weather, this magnificent drive offers superb coastal and mountain scenery, a 2,000ha (5,000-acre) national park and one of Ireland's best areas of blanket bog.

Connemara is the westernmost section of County Galway, beyond Lough Corrib. Inland are moors and looming hills, lakes and streams fringed by vivid green vegetation and a massively indented but placid coastline. One main road, the N59, leads through the centre of Connemara and around the northern area, but it's best to deviate from this for at least part of the way to take in some of the coast. If you start at Galway, take the main road for the first section (via Oughterard).

Oughterard▶▶ is some way inland, but is surprisingly a great fishing centre, serving the resort area of Lough Corrib, Ireland's second-largest lake (40km/25 miles long), which virtually splits the county in half. If you have time, a detour along the lush lakeshore towards Curraun is a pleasant option. From Oughterard it's a straightforward and beautiful trip

Roundstone, a quiet village on the peaceful Connemara coast

Dramatically sited Kylemore Abbey

past mirror-like pools to **An Teach Dóite (Maam Cross)**▶, where the monthly cattle fair is about the only sign of life. There you have a choice between exploring the mass of islets along the coastal peninsulas, or pressing on to the small, unremarkable settlement of Recess. Further on, stop at **Ballynahinch Castle**▶▶ (now a luxury hotel, see panel on page 164). A detour via the peaceful coastline of **Cashel Bay**▶▶ is a good alternative here. Sheltered from Atlantic gales and storms, this quiet bay sprouts luxuriant subtropical vegetation.

Cloch na Rón (Roundstone)▶ has a particularly attractive setting at the foot of Errisbeg with wonderful views of the Twelve Pins; its tourist industry is taking over from fishing. If you cut across the peninsula instead of following the coast you will see at close quarters one of the best remaining stretches of Irish blanket bog. It's a lonely road with some bad pot-holes, so drive carefully, especially towards nightfall. The bog is haunted by the ghost of a traveller murdered by two old women who offered him shelter—no advertisement for the local B&B trade!

Clifden▶▶ is the 'capital' of Connemara, a lively, popular town with magnificent scenery all around, best seen from the wonderfully scenic **Sky Road**▶▶, signed to the northwest. Just past the seemly Quaker village of **Letterfrack**▶▶ is the entrance to the

Connemara National Park▶▶ (tel: 095 41054, www.heritageireland.ie; *open:* Jul–end Aug daily 9.30–6.30; Apr–end May and Sep daily 10–5.30; Jun daily 10–6.30. *Admission free*), containing some of the West's finest mountain scenery. There's a visitor centre (*Admission: inexpensive*) with an exhibition on local natural history and bogland. Staff can suggest short hikes through the park; guided walks are organized in summer. For more challenging walking, follow one of the routes given in *The Mountains of Connemara; a Hill-walker's Guide*, on sale in local tourist offices. A little farther on stands **Kylemore Abbey** ▶▶▶ (tel: 095 41146, www.kylemore-abbey.com; *open:* Easter–end Nov daily 9–dusk. *Admission: expensive*), whose fairy-tale towers are reflected in a clear lake. Kylemore, a 19th-century folly, now houses a girls' boarding school, but welcomes visitors to its chapel, gardens, main hall and craft shops. The road to **Leenane**▶ is especially scenic, running past the long inlet called Killary Harbour. Leenane achieved cinematic fame as the setting for the film, *The Field*. A brief drive over the bridge to **Aasleagh**▶ gives a view of a series of waterfalls, a salmon leap and the gateway to County Mayo. If you want to return towards Galway from Leenane, a couple of routes wind through Joyce Country (so named because nearly everyone there has the

Oysters and Guinness at the International Galway Oyster Festival, held in late September each year

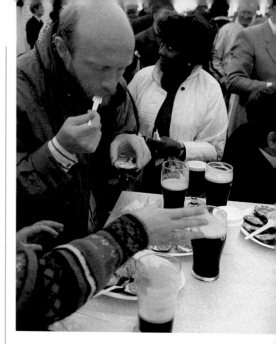

THE LYNCH MEMORIAL
This marble plaque over a Gothic doorway can be found near the Collegiate Church of St. Nicholas in Market Street. It commemorates a poignant, though almost certainly fictional, legend that a former city mayor, James Lynch FitzStephen, tried and convicted his own son, Walter, of killing a Spanish rival for the affections of his beloved. The boy confessed to the crime and Judge Lynch felt morally obliged to condemn his son to death as he would any other citizen guilty of murder. But no one would carry out the sentence, so he was forced to hang his son himself. After the execution the mayor retired into seclusion, a broken man.

CLADDAGH RINGS
These ornaments of silver or gold originated in The Claddagh, once a close-knit fishing community just outside Galway's old city walls, now a neat suburb. Claddagh rings depict two hands holding a heart surmounted by a crown, symbolizing a promise, or a hope, of eternal love and friendship. The precious heirlooms were handed down the female line and, depending which way the ring was worn, showed whether a girl was engaged, or still on the marriage market.

▶▶ Galway   *1733B*

Galway is in the midst of an economic and cultural renaissance. The little city in the west is now the fastest growing urban centre in the country. Despite its size, it has an intimate, villagelike atmosphere and everyone seems to know everyone else, although this may be an illusion, as much of its population consists of temporary visitors (tourists or students). Besides its prestigious 19th-century university, where students can take their degrees in Gaelic, Galway has several Irish-language schools. None of its sights is essential viewing, but the city seems to add up to more than the sum of its parts and is a good centre for entertainment and shopping (especially second-hand books and classy crafts).

There is always plenty going on, both low- and high-brow—a festival just about every month, an innovative theatre, concerts, lively pubs and restaurants. In short, it is perhaps Ireland's most enjoyable and upbeat city, full of vivacity and character, and increasingly frequented by younger visitors in search of 'good crack' (fun). It hosts high-calibre Irish folk groups and its sporting prowess is a source of pride, particularly in traditional games such as Gaelic football and hurling. The Galway Races (a six-day meeting in July) and its Regatta Festivals are some of the oldest regular events. Beside its own attractions, Galway is a good base for exploring local areas—Connemara, Lough Corrib, the Aran Islands and the Burren.

Galway's prosperity was founded on its strategic location at the lowest bridging point of the Corrib River, a waterway once used by many vessels, now mainly by the spring salmon that leap the falls by the **Salmon Weir Bridge▶▶**. Founded by the Anglo-Normans in the 13th century, Galway became known as the City of the Tribes, a reference to the 14 leading families who held sway quarrelsomely in its early history. In its heyday, Galway was a significant port and European trading centre; its traditional vessels, the elegant lateen-rigged Galway hookers, traded food and fuel for livestock from the Aran Islands, or smuggled contraband from France and the Channel Isles. By the western mouth of the river are the remains of a Gaelic-speaking fishing community known as **The Claddagh▶** (see panel). The cottages have now been replaced by tidier municipal housing, but old photographs and artefacts displayed in the city's **museum▶▶** (tel: 091 567 641) show how it looked. The museum is in a stone structure called the **Spanish Arch▶**, erected by the harbour to protect ships unloading Iberian cargoes of wine and brandy.

Up towards the centre of town, the most striking monument is the unattractive **Roman Catholic Cathedral of Our Lady Assumed into Heaven and St. Nicholas▶** (tel: 091 563 577), a vast limestone structure in neo-Renaissance style, all seeping copper and flashy marble. The amorous behavior of its former bishop (Eamonn Casey), which raised eyebrows in 1992, has failed to dent local faith. More attractive buildings lie in the medieval quarter of the city, where wandering through its delightful streets of well-restored shop-fronts and stone town houses is recommended. Sixteenth-century **Lynch's Castle▶**, now an Allied Irish Bank building, was once the seat of the Lynch family and its mullioned façade is decorated with exotic escutcheons and gargoyles. The dignified **Collegiate Church of St. Nicholas▶** (tel: 091 564 648) has seafaring associations, including a legend that Christopher Columbus prayed there. Eyre Square is a welcome space after the confinement of the tiny old lanes. Dedicated to President Kennedy, it contains several monuments, the most interesting being the crested Browne Doorway, a disembodied portal dating from 1627, removed from a grand mansion in 1905. Bits of the city walls are incorporated into the Eyre Square shopping centre. Nora Barnacle, James Joyce's wife, hailed from Galway and her house can be visited in the Bowling Green.

187

The beach at Salthill, west of Galway, looks south towards the Burren

Western Counties

MYSTIC VISIONS

Shrines and grottoes throughout Ireland, most still in constant use, declare the absolute faith many Irish people have in miracles, that is, in otherwise unexplainable religious experiences. These miracles can take the form of visions or statues that move, weep or bleed. The testimony of these people is often unshakeable, even under rigorous cross-questioning. Grotto shrines can be seen at Ballinspittle, near Kinsale and Mount Melleray, in County Waterford, among others.

Knock's position on the world pilgrimage trail was confirmed by the visit of Pope John Paul II in 1979

CROAGH PATRICK

The brooding, conical outline of this mountain dominates the skyline all around southwest Mayo. It is associated with St. Patrick, the site of his Lenten fast and legendary banishment of the snakes. Each year, on the last Sunday in July, pilgrims make an arduous ascent, some barefoot. On clear days, the summit gives magnificent views over Clew Bay to the Partry Mountains and Connemara. If you have sensible shoes, you can climb Croagh Patrick in a couple of hours. (See also page 226.)

▶ Knock   *1733D*

Knock's pedigree dates back over a century, when it was suddenly transformed from a humdrum little bog village into one of the most revered Marian shrines in Christendom. It is now the 'Lourdes of Ireland', with a vast new basilica, constantly thronged by pilgrims. Its present high profile in the Catholic world is due in large part to the energies of a local priest, Monsignor James Horan. He battled with the authorities for an airport which, despite early descriptions as 'a foggy, boggy white elephant', has greatly opened up the northwest region to visitor traffic since its eventual inauguration in 1986, seven years after Pope John Paul II made a celebrated visit to Knock. The commercialized religiosity of innumerable souvenir stalls may offend the purist, but today Knock attracts more pilgrims than ever, around 1.5 million a year.

On a stormy night in 1879, two village women saw a vision of the Virgin Mary, with St. Joseph and St. John, on the gable of the parish church. Unable to believe their eyes, they called other villagers, who also saw the vision before it gradually faded away. All 15 witnesses were interviewed and cross-examined by a commission of inquiry. Some 50 years later, three surviving witnesses were again independently interviewed and firmly maintained every detail of what they had seen, giving an unnerving veracity to their story.

The original church still exists, the gable where the vision had appeared now preserved behind a glazed oratory. It has fine features inside, notably stained glass by the ubiquitous Harry Clarke (1889–1931). The new church, designed to hold a congregation of many thousands, was completed in 1976. Though fairly hideous to an unpartisan eye, the hexagonal building contains interesting examples of modern art and architecture. Its

This Lisdoonvarna house has turned a few heads

32 ambulatory pillars each contain stone from a different Irish county and the windows represent each of the four provinces: Connaught, Leinster, Munster and Ulster.

Knock's religious significance dwarfs any other reason to come here, but there is a good little **folk museum▶** (tel: 094 88100, www.knock-shrine.ie; *open:* May–end Oct daily 10–6; Nov–Apr by appointment only. *Admission: moderate*) in the village, illustrating life in the west of Ireland and giving some background on the shrine.

▶▶ Lisdoonvarna   *1722B*

Ireland's only spa stands in this curious village on the edge of the Burren, emitting sulphurous and radioactive iodine-filled springs alleged to cure numerous ills. The bathhouse facilities may seem primitive, but the old-fashioned bathtubs and massage rooms have a certain historic fascination. Needless to say, the water tastes terrible.

Grandiose spa hotels and villas indicate the spa's one-time popularity, but today the village is more renowned for its Matchmaking Festival, held annually in September after harvest time. The festival has an honourable history: Wealthy farming families used to pair off their eligible sons and daughters via a 'matchmaker' for appropriate dowries of cattle or horses. Later the festival became a dating agency for the famously shy and sexually repressed bachelor farmers of rural Ireland, who often had few social outlets and little opportunity to meet potential brides. Many failed to marry until very late in life, if at all. These days, however, the festival has become a tawdry and depressing event, at which lonely singles turn up for a drunken grope and a one-night stand rather than a soulmate. Unusually in organized dating circles, the proportion of men is far higher than women (about three to one). There's plenty of good 'crack' (fun), though, and it's certainly worth a visit as a social curiosity. If you're on the lookout, you may get lucky!

At the **Burren Smoke House▶** (tel: 065 707 4432. *Open:* daily 10–7. *Admission: inexpensive*), signed from the village centre, fish is smoked, amid a choking salty fug of charring wood chippings. Here women deftly fillet and trim massive sides of salmon— both wild and farmed. A free video show explains the process. You can buy a variety of the products here, or try them in the Roadside Tavern next door.

MONSIGNOR JAMES HORAN
The guiding light behind Knock International Airport may ultimately be of heavenly origins, but its earthly inspiration took the shape of Mgr. James Horan, an indefatigable local priest. He first raised the idea of upgrading the grass airstrip to jumbo-jet capacity. After the Pope's visit to Knock in 1979, Mgr. Horan was convinced the shrine would draw vast numbers of pilgrims. Decried by many as a foggy, boggy white elephant, the airport nevertheless opened in 1986, soon proving popular with both visitors and pilgrims. Indeed, the Lourdes–Knock run is used by many French visitors wishing to fish in the lakes of the West!

CAPTAIN CHARLES BOYCOTT
The man whose surname has entered the English language as a word meaning 'to ostracize' was land agent for Lord Erne in County Mayo in the late 19th century. He lived at Loughmask House, on the lough's eastern shore. During the 1879–1882 Land War (Parnell's campaign to reduce land rents by 25 per cent) he was isolated by the local community 'as if he were a leper' for his refusal to cooperate. No one would work for him, or even speak to him and eventually he was forced to leave Ireland.

Thoor Ballylee, Yeats's retreat from the frantic events of 1920s Ireland

COOLE PARK

Yeats's patron lived there—the redoubtable Lady Augusta Gregory (1859–1932), a wealthy widow who encouraged many writers and artists at the turn of the century. The house fell into neglect after her death and was demolished during World War II, but the splendid grounds are now open to the public as a national park and are a marvellous place for walks and picnics. The 'autograph tree', a copper beech on which many famous visitors carved their initials, can be seen behind railings in the peaceful walled garden. In the park is the lake that inspired Yeats's poem *The Wild Swans at Coole*.

Setting the world to rights in Westport

▶▶ Thoor Ballylee   1733B
North of Coole Park, tel: 091 631 436
Open: Easter–end Sep daily 10–6. Admission: moderate

> An ancient bridge and a more ancient tower,
> A farmhouse that is sheltered by its wall,
> An acre of stony ground,
> Where the symbolic rose can break in flower.
>   (*Meditations in Time of Civil War*)

In 1917, W.B. Yeats found this evocative 'ivy-covered tower', conveniently close to his friend and patron, Lady Gregory, who lived at Coole Park. Thoor Ballylee was a fortified residence built by the Anglo-Norman De Burgo family during the 14th century. Then in his 50s and newly married to his young bride, George Hyde-Lees, Yeats purchased the derelict tower house for IR£35 and spent intermittent periods of the next decade there with his new family, converting the interior into simple but stylish living and sleeping quarters. The 'winding stair' image that repeatedly appears in his poetry refers to the stone steps leading up the tower. From the battlemented rooftop, views extend over the placid meadows by the nearby millstream to the Slieve Aughty Mountains. Many of Yeats's more mystical writings were produced there, notably *The Tower* and *The Winding Stair* (not generally his most admired work); by this stage his disillusion with the Irish political scene was taking effect and he sought relief in seclusion and mythology. By 1928, Yeats had abandoned the damp tower for warmer climes; he died in France in 1939. The Kiltartan Society took over the decaying tower in 1961 and restored it fully. The audio-visual show gives a good background to the poet, the house and the turmoil of the times.

▶▶ Westport   1722D

One of the most charming towns in Ireland's western region, Westport shows its Georgian origins clearly in its broad streets and river, which flows in tidy canals along a lime-fringed avenue called The Mall. It is set on an inlet of Clew Bay, where the Carrowbeg River flows into the sea. Many of its fine buildings remain, some carefully restored. The Protestant church is late Victorian (about 1880) and has charming art nouveau influences.

Westport was originally laid out as part of a great estate and, at the turn of the 18th century, prospered greatly from its textile industry. In 1801, though, the Act of Union made local businesses collapse as cheaper products flooded in from England. By 1825, Westport's linen industry was virtually finished. Today, Westport is a market town and fishing centre—it is a leading sea angling magnet, with a few good beaches nearby.

Westport House►► (tel: 098 25430/27766, www. westporthouse.ie; *open:* Mar–end Oct daily 11.30–5; Nov–end Feb Sat, Sun 11.30–5. *Admission: expensive*) stands in parkland just outside the town, near Westport Quay. Designed by James Wyatt and Richard Castle, it is the seat of the Brownes, Marquesses of Sligo, and is County Mayo's only stately home open to the public. Though highly commercialized in an attempt to meet the colossal running costs, it is still a remarkable house, beautifully furnished inside with Irish Georgian and Victorian silver and antiques, Waterford crystal, Chinese wallpapers and a fine collection of paintings, including a *Holy Family* by Rubens. The doors are of Jamaican mahogany (the 1st marquess spent time as a governor there, apparently one of its more benevolent rulers, freeing many slaves). The dungeons beneath the house date from an earlier dwelling, allegedly a castle belonging to the pirate queen, Grace O'Malley. These now provide but one of the many attractions and sideshows in the park and grounds, which include a zoo, a boating lake, a model railway and horse-drawn caravans. The Browne family has lived in Westport House for over 400 years.

Westport Quay, just outside the main entrance gates to the house, has several good restaurants and there is a range of accommodation in the town. A couple of summer festivals (arts in October and a street festival in July) and good music pubs are other reasons to head here. The Wyatt Theatre (in season) puts on some amateur productions of Irish drama.

'MY WIFE GEORGE'

W. B. Yeats was something of a pessimistic visionary at times, foreseeing the places he lived in going to rack and ruin after he left. On a plaque set into the wall of the tower at Thoor Ballylee, he inscribed the following verse:

I, the poet William Yeats,
With old mill boards and
    sea-green slates
And smithy work from the
    Gort forge,
Restored this tower for my
    wife George;
And may these characters
    remain
When all is ruin once
    again.

191

Westport House also has an attractive modern church in its grounds

Any glance at Ireland's antiquities—its great churches, the jewellery worn by the Celts, the intricacies of illuminated manuscripts like the Book of Kells—will show what a long tradition of sheer artistry exists there, what a delight in pattern, shape and texture. This continues today, encouraged strongly by tourism.

BOG-WOOD CARVINGS

An artist with a highly individual product is Michael Casey, who works at Barley Harbour in County Longford and has achieved an international reputation. He has made an art of carving bog wood (blackened timber preserved for thousands of years beneath boglands) into imaginative sculptures of figures or animals. It is a long process. First the wood has to dry out—taking almost two years. Then it is carved and finished carefully with sandpaper and beeswax to a remarkable sheen. The wood used is mostly yew, pine or oak.

The labour-intensive and highly skilled craft of lace-making, here practiced in Monaghan

Souvenir hunting Ireland's craft industries are a major source of revenue. They vary from huge enterprises employing hundreds of workers, like Waterford Crystal, to tiny artisan studios where one person practices wood-carving or jewellery-making. Some crafts are still cottage industries—much knitting or lace-making, for example, is still done at home. Most visitors will want to take at least one reminder of Ireland home and there is now a wide and attractive choice of souvenirs to suit all purses; shop around for price and quality. Prices can be high in Ireland with VAT at its currently high rates. If you live outside the EU, consider reclaiming this tax on anything valuable.

Many craft centres and even factories now welcome visitors and free tours are provided at several large enterprises, such as Waterford Crystal, Tyrone Crystal, Belleek Pottery, Foxford Woollen Mills in County Mayo, Donegal Parian China and Magee's tweed factory in Donegal Town. These are often elaborately set up with guided tours, audio-visual shows, refreshments and showrooms where you can inspect, and of course buy, the product. Packing and shipment arrangements can also be made if you live abroad.

Kilkenny is an attractive place to buy crafts. The Kilkenny Design Centre, set up in old stables opposite the castle, provides a high-quality outlet for many of Ireland's best producers.

Craft villages Smaller studios have developed (mainly in the west of Ireland, notably in Donegal, Connemara and Dingle) where economic conditions have justified a special focus of attention on employment opportunities. Artists can rent small workshops in these 'craft villages' to produce jewellery, knitwear, pottery, woodwork, hand-weaving, etc. Connemara marble, a greenish stone, is fashioned into innumerable souvenirs near Moycullen. Several potters in Cork and Kerry have been particularly successful; Stephen Pearce's modern pottery in terra-cotta colours with abstract stripes of white is a typical example. Produced at Shanagarry, east of Cork City, it is now available in fashionable stores in Dublin or the West End of London. Robin and Jane Forrester's Bandon pottery is also very popular—in blue with a fruit pattern.

Glass and crystal Few visitors will be able to take a stained-glass window home, but in many of the churches of Ireland you will see the work of artists Harry Clarke or Evie Hone, who brought about a revival of this craft in the earlier part of the 20th century. There are good examples at Carrickmacross in Monaghan, Ardara in Donegal and at Kingscourt, Cavan. Ireland's brand of deep-etched, brilliant lead crystal is most famously produced at Waterford, but now has many competitors—in Tipperary, Cavan, Athlone, Donegal, Tyrone and Galway. Jerpoint Glass, made in County Kilkenny, is plainer.

Linen and wool Textiles have always been a staple of Ireland's craft industry, linen and wool being the two main fibres used. Today's flax production is quite limited, but high-quality dish towels and tablecloths are available all over the island, subtly woven in damask patterns or more crudely stamped with shamrock motifs. Lisburn has linen trails and a linen museum. Centres of the lace industry are Carrickmacross and Clones in the border counties of Cavan and Monaghan (see panel on page 246) and Limerick. Both produce 'mixed lace', which is sewn onto cotton net. Genuine handmade lace is expensive. Knitwear is ubiquitous. The classic Aran sweater is now produced all over Ireland in many different designs.

One of Ireland's most famous products is tweed. Manufacture still centres on Donegal, where those classic, hard-wearing fibres in soft peaty colours are woven in factories such as Magee's. Other natural fabrics are woven by Avoca Handweavers (see page 92). They are one of the most high-profile of Ireland's craft enterprises, producing soft worsteds and mohairs in bright, jewel-like colours of blues and pinks, mostly for women's fashions.

Limerick, too, is renowned for its lace

STEPHEN PEARCE
Stephen Pearce's pottery is at Shanagarry, near Cork, and is open to visitors. Only three designs are made, each in a simple, yet sophisticated style, from local clay. One is a black-and-white glazed earthenware range called Shanagarry, another a terracotta range, and the third a blue-and-white design. There may be only three ranges of pottery, but in all these contain over 400 separate items.

GLASS FACTORIES
Many of Ireland's lead-crystal manufacturers welcome visitors to look around and watch the glass being blown and cut by hand. Most famous is Waterford (see page 143), but other companies such as Tipperary Crystal, Tyrone, Galway and Cavan will also allow visitors (contact local tourist offices for details). If you prefer a more modern, plain form of glass, one of the most interesting studios to visit is Jerpoint Glass, at Stoneyford in Kilkenny (tel: 056 24350).

193

Belleek Pottery dates back to 1857

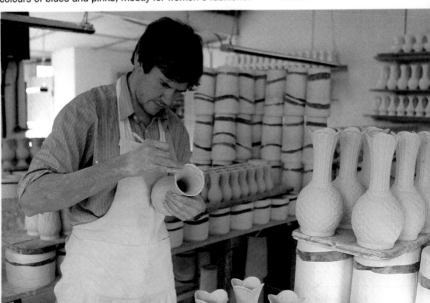

Northwestern Counties

LOUGH DERG

This lake, set in desolate bog and moorland east of Donegal, is a highly popular destination for pilgrims who converge in droves on a tiny island, ostensibly for inner peace and solitude, although Station Island is now virtually covered by buildings—an octagonal basilica and several hostels.

St. Patrick is said to have spent 40 days praying and fasting there, and now the island receives up to 30,000 visitors a year. During a three-day summer vigil of prayer and contemplation only black tea and dry toast may be consumed; no sleep is allowed on the first night. Pilgrims walk barefoot around the island's shrines. If this sounds like an interesting weekend break, be warned that penitents come here from all over the world. Book early to avoid disappointment!

A currach *turned upside down to dry out beside a stoney beach on Inishmore Island*

194

THE STOLEN CHILD

'Where the wave of moon-
light glosses
The dim grey sands with
light
Far off by furthest Rosses
We foot it all the night,
Weaving olden dances,
Mingling hands and
mingling glances
Till the moon has taken
flight;
To and fro we leap
And chase the frothy
bubbles,
While the world is full of
troubles
And is anxious in its
sleep.
Come away, O human
child!
To the waters and the wild
With a faery, hand in hand,
For the world's more full of
weeping than you can
understand.'

W. B. Yeats (1865–1939).
(See page 201 for The
Rosses.)

NORTHWESTERN COUNTIES Donegal's spectacular scenery is often considered the best in Ireland, although its location keeps it remote. Outside a brief, intense summer season, when visitors flit through like butterflies, these northern regions (counties Sligo, Donegal and Leitrim) can seem forlorn and windswept. All through the year clouds scud rapidly in from the Atlantic, bringing lashing horizontal squalls or drizzling sea mists. Just as suddenly these are followed by shafts of sunlight and vivid rainbows that transform its glens, cliffs, mountains and beaches into the landscapes of Irish travel brochures. Here, in these far-flung peninsulas, you will find that elusive rural idyll—softly domed ricks of hand-turned hay and whitewashed thatched cottages with scarlet doors. The postcard scene disguises a history of constant struggle against the elements and economic deprivation. In many of these areas emigration is chronic. Until an increase in US investment there was little industry other than the old cottage-based crafts of knitting and weaving, although these are now organized to catch the visitor's eye in villagelike studio complexes or factories such as Magee's of Donegal Town. Most of the region's income comes from tourism and not all the side-effects are beneficial. On some sections of coastline, insensitive development has resulted in a garish outbreak of modern white bungalows that bear little relation to their surroundings. Numerous seaside resorts amuse those hardy enough to chance the weather. Bundoran's tawdry image evokes a socially conservative era. Today, some of these splendid and unpolluted beaches have achieved a new cachet as outstanding surfing spots.

NORTHERN EXTREMITIES

Somewhat tenuously attached to the Republic by a thin isthmus of land between the coast and its severed Ulster neighbours, Donegal waves its tattered banner even farther northward than the Six Counties, constituting Ireland's northernmost extremity. Its cliffs at Slieve League are the highest in Europe and

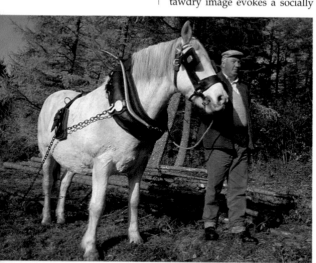

*The sturdy Irish Draught
is especially useful where
vehicles cannot venture*

several wild promontories make important habitats for sea birds. It scores not only with incomparable coastal scenery, but also with inland Glenveagh National Park, where massive glacial valleys carve through moors and blanket bog. Offshore lie several inhabited islands: Tory Island, where locals fish for lobster and paint naïve art; and Aranmore, more prosperous and biddable, welcoming visitors with holiday cottages.

Third-largest county after Cork and Galway, Donegal has the biggest Gaeltacht (Irish-speaking community) in Ireland and nationalist sentiments run high. This is the ancient Gaelic territory of Tir Chonaill—land of Conal. Even after the Flight of the Earls (see pages 34–35), the English never quite got their hands on Donegal's wilder regions, and after partition, though technically part of Ulster, they let it stay with the Republic. Road signs in rural areas may appear only in Irish. A significant proportion of the population on the eastern side of the county are Protestants, however, who look across the border from their prosaic farmland for their spiritual home.

LEITRIM AND SLIGO Farther south is Leitrim, which has a much lower tourist profile than Donegal, and few foreign visitors could pinpoint it on a map. It has pretty enough, but unspectacular, countryside, mostly mixed farmland, lakes and moors on undulating low hills, with just a few dramatic limestone ridges near Manorhamilton. Lough Allen, the first lake on the Shannon, virtually bisects the county and provides most of its recreational attractions in the form of boating and fishing. Carrick-on-Shannon, the county town, is now a well-established cruise-boat centre. Leitrim has few significant historic sights.

   Sligo, on the other hand, is rich in history, prehistory and mythology, with ancient burial places and cairns. The distinctive shapes of Benbulbin and Knocknarea loom above the town, redolent of antique Celtic legends. The poet W. B. Yeats has strong links with the county, the scene of his childhood and his last resting place. The landscapes and myths of Sligo weave throughout his best work.

197

The very Irish Errigal Mountain looms above the white marble church of Dunlewy, County Donegal

THE *ANNALS OF THE FOUR MASTERS*
During the troubled 17th century a Franciscan monk, Michael O'Cleary, and three lay Gaelic scholars wrote these chronicles of Irish history and mythology. The *Annals* cover the period from before the biblical Flood of Genesis to the year 1616, and are an important record of Ireland's Celtic heritage. They are now housed in the National Library in Dublin, where facsimiles of the originals are on display.

▶ **Ardara**   *1942D*

Knitwear and tweed are the main concerns of this small town at the head of a deep sea-lough (saltwater lake). Outlets vie with each other on the main street, but you can, if you prefer, head for any one of half a dozen or so factory shops where you can watch the manufacturing process in action and probably visit a bar or tea-shop at the same time. Prices are generally cheaper here than in most retailers. The annual Weavers' Fair in midsummer is a popular local festival with plenty of traditional music and good 'crack' (fun). A heritage centre has been set up in the old law courts. The Church of the Holy Family has a fine stained-glass rose window by the well-known artist Evie Hone.

▶▶ **Carrowkeel, Carrowmore,**
       and Creevykeel   *1942B–2C*

These confusingly named places are three of the most interesting and important prehistoric sites in the northwestern region. **Carrowkeel▶**, in the Bricklieve hills, is an ancient cemetery of circular mounds dating from the late Stone Age (2500–2000BC). There are some splendid views from the exposed hilltop site. **Carrowmore▶▶** (tel: 071 961534; *open:* Easter–end Sep daily 10–6. *Admission: inexpensive*), near Sligo, is the largest group of megalithic monuments in the whole of the British Isles. This site contains about 60 tombs, stone circles, dolmens and other antiquities, the earliest of which are alleged to predate the famous passage-grave at Newgrange (see pages 108–109) by 700 years. Many have been damaged or removed, and incredibly, in 1983, plans were drawn up—and luckily abandoned—to turn the site into a dump. **Creevykeel▶▶**, near Mullaghmore, is a fine example of a neolithic court tomb, dating from about 3000BC, with a double burial chamber surrounded by a wedge-shaped mound of stone. Polished stone axes, worked flints and some bronze Celtic artefacts found there are now in the National Museum in Dublin.

One of the crafts demonstrated at the Donegal Craft Village using traditional pottery wheels and tools

▶ **Donegal**   *1942C*

Surprisingly, Donegal is not the county town of County Donegal (an honour granted to the somewhat unprepossessing town of Letterkenny), but it is nevertheless an attractive and strategic base for exploring the northwest and, more especially, for shopping. Its main store, Magee's (see panel opposite), is one of the best-known places to buy Donegal tweed. A short way out of town, on the southern side, is a collection of workshops producing a variety of high-quality crafts—jewellery, handweaving, ceramics, batik and crystal (look for signs indicating the Donegal Craft Village on the N15, the main road from Ballyshannon). Several other factory shops can be visited in the area, including those at Ardara (see page 198). **Ballyshannon▶**, a garrison town to the south, specializes in the region's brand of china, known as Parian ware (because it resembles the clear, white Greek marble from the island of Paros). The **Donegal Parian China Factory▶▶** (tel: 071 98 51826, www.donegalchina.ie; *open:* May–end Sep daily 9–5.30; Oct–Apr Mon–Fri 9–5.30. *Admission free*) and visitor centre are on the Sligo road. On the Ballyshannon–Belleek road is Celtic Weave China, producing basketware rather similar to the traditional Belleek pottery produced over the border in Northern Ireland (tours of the factory are free).

Donegal (*Dún na nGall*) means 'fort of the foreigners', a reference to its history as a Viking stronghold. After the Vikings left, the town became the headquarters of Tír Chonaill, the territory of the O'Donnell clan. 'Red Hugh' O'Donnell built a fortress and a Dominican abbey there in the 15th century. Early in the 17th century, the Gaelic chieftains left Ireland in the exodus known as the Flight of the Earls (see pages 34–35), and their lands and castles were appropriated by English and Scottish settlers. Sir Basil Brooke took over Donegal Castle in 1610 and enlarged it to a comfortable, if well-defended, Jacobean home with mullioned windows and imposing fireplaces. Today the castle remains are Donegal's most interesting sight. Sir Basil set about making his mark on the town in other ways, too, and Donegal displays typical characteristics of Ulster planning, including a classic Diamond (actually a triangular 'square') in the city centre, where a monument stands to the Four Masters. To the south of town is a lovely stretch of coastline where several rivers flow into Donegal Bay. There the sun sets amid a maze of tranquil islets and sheltered creeks. St. Ernan's Island, reached by a causeway, is one of the best places to enjoy this scenery.

The Diamond, Donegal Town

MAGEE'S
This large department store on the north side of the Diamond is an Irish legend, still run by the family who established it in 1866 (the firm has passed to cousins of the original Magees, the Temples). In the late 19th century, handwoven Donegal tweed was produced on wooden looms, some of which are still in use. Magee's is the only company still weaving and tailoring handwoven tweed in Donegal. High-quality men's clothing and suit fabrics are produced under the Magee's label for worldwide export, in light worsteds as well as the hard-wearing, traditional tweed in the soft colours of the Donegal landscape. More than 600 work in two factories using advanced technology, and visitors are welcome for a short, free tour during opening hours. The upstairs café makes a good place for a coffee or light lunch.

THE ATLANTIC COAST

200

Drive

The Atlantic Coast

So complex is north Donegal's coast-line that any tour can take many varia-tions depending on how much time you have. Best views are from minor roads rather than the N56, but skirting the peninsulas is time-consuming, and roads may be poorly surfaced.

The highlights of the journey are the sculpted rocks at **Crohy Head▶▶** near Dungloe, the fiery headland known as **Bloody Foreland▶▶▶**, and the panoramic seascapes around **Horn Head▶▶▶** and **Rosguill▶▶**. If you still have time and a taste for this gorgeous scenery, **Fanad Head▶▶** by the calm fiord of Lough Swilly, or the pastoral **Inishowen Peninsula▶**, from which Malin Head relays weather

reports, are diverse and unspoiled. Inland, the beautiful and lonely routes through the **Glenveagh National Park▶▶** are well worth exploring (see page 203).

The weather in Donegal is always uncertain, but its very unpredictability is exhilarating, and compensations include amazing sunsets and glorious rainbows. Facilities for visitors along the Donegal coast are limited but steadily increasing.

The section between Dungloe and Crolly is known as **Na Rosa (The Rosses)►** (Na Rosa means 'the headlands'), a bleak, rocky and fragmented coastline, sometimes worn into stacks and arches. Inland, the terrain is poor, consisting of boulder-strewn bogland waterlogged by myriad tiny lakes and streams. If you have time, you may be able to take a summer boat excursion to **Árainn Mhór (Aran Island)►** (also known as Aranmore, but not to be confused with the Aran Islands off Galway Bay)—a 25-minute trip from Burton Port. Mostly bog and lakes, there are beaches and quiet walks. Boats now regularly visit **Toraigh (Tory Island)►** to the north, a treeless wilderness with 150 or so inhabitants who supplement their income from fishing by running a school of naïve art. Summer ferries leave from several local ports (such as An Bun Beag (Bunbeg) and Falcarragh), but you may be marooned in bad weather. Balor, Celtic god of darkness, is said to have lived on the island's eastern cliffs.

   Gaoth Doghaire (Gweedore)►, the next peninsula, is scenically austere but densely populated, with new cottages and even some industry springing up along the coast. The most scenic stretch is **Bloody Foreland►►**, a mass of red granite that glows a brilliant colour at sunset. The sheer, quartzite cliffs of **Horn Head►►** provide terrific views and a windy ledge for thousands of seabirds. Sheep Haven is particularly attractive, and several roads lead to popular resorts. Marble Hill Strand has a fine beach. **Dunfanaghy►** is the main resort, a gentle seaside village near an excellent sandy beach offering windsurfing and canoeing and a blowhole called **McSwyne's Gun►** that 'explodes' periodically in rough weather. Beyond Dunfanaghy look for **Doe Castle►►**, a 15th-century fortress rebuilt in Victorian times. Views from the battlements overlook a wide expanse of Sheephaven Bay. Lackagh Bridge provides another vantage point. Inland, the barren, rocky landscape is scattered with lakes. The next outcrop is **Rosguill►►**, where an 11km (7 miles) circular tour called the **Atlantic Drive►►►** is signed past dunes and beaches. Highlights of the **Fanad Peninsula►►** include the neat plantation villages of **Rathmelton►** and **Rathmullan►**, where 'Red Hugh' O'Donnell, Earl of Tyrconnell, was lured onto an English merchant ship for a drink, seized and taken to Dublin prison. On the **Inishowen peninsula►►**, don't miss the stone forts called **Grianan of Aileach►►**, **Fort Dunree►** (The Guns of Dunree) and **Malin Head►►** (see pages 206–207 for more details).

201

The splendour of the Donegal coast

Derek Hill gave Glebe House to the nation in 1980. It makes a short but worthwhile detour from the Glenveagh National Park

ARTHUR KINGSLEY PORTER
The castle of Glenveagh was once owned by the American art historian Arthur Kingsley Porter, a specialist in medieval sculpture. One day in 1939, he set off on a fishing trip in Donegal; later his boat was found abandoned on an island without a trace of its former occupant. Wagging tongues said he feigned his disappearance to escape an unhappy domestic life; claims that he had been spotted subsequently in the French port of Marseilles and as a Buddhist monk in the Himalayas have never been substantiated, and his real fate remains tantalizingly unknown.

One of the early-Christian standing stones in or near Glencolumbkille

▶▶ Glebe House and Gallery   1953D
Church Hill, tel: 074 91 37071
Open: Easter and May–end Sep Sat–Thu 11–6.30
Admission: moderate

This Regency building on Lough Gartan, a rectory dating from 1828, was for 30 years the home of the landscape and portrait artist, Derek Hill, who hailed originally from England. He furnished the house with immense taste and care, using a great mix of styles and art from all over the world, including Asian and Middle Eastern tapestries and ceramics, Victoriana and original William Morris papers and textiles. Donegal folk art is also well represented, and in the adjacent gallery are works by Picasso, Bonnard, Kokoschka, Renoir, Augustus John and other leading 19th- and 20th-century artists. A particularly interesting part of the collection contains works by the naïve school of painters on Tory Island, notably James Dixon. Temporary exhibitions are held in summer.

▶▶ Gleann Cholm Cille (Glencolumbkille) 1941D

The scenery is the great draw here; the drive along the north shore of Donegal Bay beyond the fishing port of Killybegs, past the grand cliffs of Slieve League, is thoroughly spectacular, through sheep-strewn moorland, heather and turf-cut bog to a boiling mass of rocks and sea stacks by the shore. A detour by the coast, for example to the picturesque Gaelic-speaking estuary village of Teelin, is especially recommended. Glencolumbkille, as its name suggests, has many other associations with St. Columba (Columbcille), the 6th-century saint from Lough Gartan who lived there for a time. On the saint's day (9 June), pilgrims conduct a barefoot procession.

A more recent benefactor, as yet uncanonized, was the energetic priest, Father James MacDyer, who made strenuous efforts to alleviate the area's chronic poverty and unemployment. He was responsible for setting up a number of collective enterprises to provide work. The most high-profile of these is the **Folk Village▶** (tel: 074 973 0017; *open:* Easter–end Sep Mon–Sat 10–6, Sun 12–6). *Admission: inexpensive*), on the edge of town. It is a small project using reconstructed cottages to simulate life in bygone Ireland. Three small dwellings are replicas of those typical in the area during the 1720s, 1820s and 1920s, furnished with items of the period. The reception building sells craft souvenirs from all over Ireland, and the Shebeen café offers a variety of curious beverages, including some made from fuchsia or seaweed. A 'famine pot,' filled daily with an unenticing brew of the type of corn porridge eaten during the hungry years, stands in the yard.

▶ ▶ ▶ Glenveagh National Park   *1953D*

Church Hill, tel: 074 91 37088, www.duchas.ie
Open: Feb–end Nov daily 10–6. Admission: free
Some 10,000ha (25,000 acres) of wild scenery make up this park of glaciated valleys and open moorland around Lough Beagh. Parts of the park are wooded with native oak and birch or imported rhododendron and spruce. The approach via Dunlewy at the foot of Mount Errigal gives some of the most spectacular views. Off the main road, an expedition to the Poisoned Glen (so called because of a toxic variety of spurge, a shrub that grows by the water-side) is worth taking. Beside Lough Beagh stands the estate of Glenveagh Castle, created during the mid-19th century by John George Adair, who built the mansion in about 1870. He is remembered mostly for the harsh eviction of all his tenants after the murder of one of his estate managers in 1861. He later emigrated to the United States. His wife returned to Glenveagh after her husband's death and created the glorious gardens around the castle.

During the Civil War, the castle was occupied by the IRA and the Free State Army, then restored by a benevolent American owner who later transferred the land to the Irish National Parks Service. The estate contains the largest herd of red deer in Ireland, believed to number about 600 at present. A visitor centre is located on the estate (free minibus service to the castle in summer).

TORY ISLAND

A story about the Tory islanders claims that in 1884 a British gunboat, *The Wasp*, was dispatched to reprimand the inhabitants and to collect unpaid taxes. The islanders apparently called upon the forces of Balor, the one-eyed Celtic god of darkness, by circling the wishing stones in the centre of the island, and the gunboat promptly sank with all but six hands.

203

Glenveagh Castle and gardens

The Irish film industry is undergoing a revival, attracting film-makers from around the world. Ireland has a great stock of cinematic talent, and its history and political troubles are providing inspiration for Neil Jordan and Jim Sheridan, two home-grown directors, but there are many delightful films in a lighter vein.

Top: John Wayne and Maureen O'Hara starred in The Quiet Man, *roughly a cross between* The Taming of the Shrew *and* Much Ado about Nothing, *set in rural Ireland*

204

Richard Harris in pensive mood in the immensely successful The Field. *Critics, however, could never quite decide whether the plot lived up to the dramatic scenery*

Ireland stars In many films, Ireland itself is the star of the big screen. Directors of many nationalities have used Irish locations for movies—even ones not set specifically in Ireland—the soft beauty of its landscapes overcoming the vagaries of its climate. Earliest films included *Life on the Great Southern and Western Railway* (1904) and *In the Days of St. Patrick* (1919). Better remembered is Robert Flaherty's *Man of Aran*, made in 1934. This documentary of the harsh lifestyle endured on the Aran Islands has now become a classic, though it was not accurate in all respects—shark fishing, for example, had not been customary on the Aran Islands for over 60 years. It is regularly shown in Kilronan, the largest community on Inishmore, during the summer tourist season. *The Dawn*, set in Killarney, was made in 1937 by Tom Cooper, a story of the Revolutionary War using highly effective location sequences. In 1947, a British film was made about the story of Captain Boycott (see panel on page 189), villain of the struggle for tenants' land rights during the 19th century, starring Cecil Parker and Stewart Granger.

A stunning backdrop Several films of the 1950s used Irish backdrops, too. Most notable of these was probably *The Quiet Man*, a John Ford movie of 1952 with John Wayne and Maureen O'Hara. Much of the filming was done around Cong, in County Galway, and some of the stars stayed at the local posh hotel, Ashford Castle. It's a rollicking love story of an American who returns to Innisfree to find a bride and good-naturedly perpetuates many Hollywood myths about the Irish. Yet another version of *Moby Dick* appeared in 1956, and the director, John Huston, chose the picturesque Cork town of Youghal for his harbour scenes. Rock Hudson is said to have sampled all the bars of Trim, County Meath, in 1955 during the filming of *Captain Lightfoot*, where the old Norman bridge played a leading role.

The National Film Studios were established at Ardmore in 1975, although lack of capital made this indigenous enterprise still largely dependent on foreign investment. Only

John Boorman's production *Excalibur* (both produced and financed in Ireland) could be described as an 'Irish film' of the 30 or so that were made there between 1975 and 1980. Stanley Kubrick used Caher Castle, Tipperary and Huntington Castle, in County Carlow, for *Barry Lyndon*, a gorgeously photographed, if rather static, version of Thackeray's tale about an Irish adventurer.

1980s to present Many more recent films have featured Irish locations. Stephen Spilberg used the beaches of Wexford to represent battle-scarred Normandy in *Saving Private Ryan*; *Far and Away* used the Temple Bar district of Dublin to represent 19th-century Boston; and *Educating Rita* found Trinity College a more suitable icon for an English university than either Oxford or Cambridge. *The Commitments* and *My Left Foot* (the moving story of a severely handicapped writer) were also set in Dublin. So was *The Lonely Passion of Judith Hearne* (though Brian Moore's novel was set in Belfast), a poignant tale of a genteel spinster music teacher, played by Maggie Smith, who falls for gold-digging ne'er-do-well—Bob Hoskins. Some of Neil Jordan's best-known films include *The Miracle*, *The Crying Game*, *Michael Collins* and *The End of The Affair*. *The Snapper* and *The Van*, by Stephen Frears (completing Roddy Doyle's 'Barrytown Trilogy' begun with *The Commitments*), are both set in Dublin. In sharp contrast, the lush location photography of *The Field*, filmed in the Connemara village of Leenane, provides the sort of Irish green that almost hurts your eyes. Leenane, full of tiny fields and looming hills, was a natural choice for this grim tale written by John B. Keane. John Hurt and Richard Harris starred, and once again, the film created a local legend, with many residents—and pubs—earning bit parts as extras. *Hear My Song*, starring Ned Beatty, is also set largely on Ireland's west coast. *December Bride*, a spare tale of nonconformist passion, is one of the few nonterrorist movies to be set north of the border.

RYAN'S DAUGHTER

The blockbuster in 1970 was unquestionably David Lean's emotive love story, *Ryan's Daughter*. For this an entire village was built on the beautiful far western tip of the Dingle peninsula, at Dunquin. Few vestiges of this remain today, but the film still lives on in the imaginations of local people, many of whom were used as extras, and for a while had a taste of Hollywood glamour. The story, by Robert Bolt, is set at the time of the Easter Rising and tells of an Irish woman who falls for a British officer, to the horror of all. The film had a star cast (John Mills, Sarah Miles, Robert Mitchum) and had great box-office success, if dismissed as overromanticized by the critics. Certainly Lean picked his set with care—Dunquin is a magical place.

Local extras stare down the street of the specially built village in Ryan's Daughter. *One critic, Pauline Kael, wrote of the film, 'Gush made respectable by millions of dollars tastefully wasted'*

FORT DUNREE (THE GUNS OF DUNREE)

A short way north of Buncrana is Fort Dunree Military Museum, an example of a coastal defence battery. The building was originally constructed in 1880 to guard the entrance to Lough Swilly. Martello towers augmented a series of heavy guns. At the beginning of World War I, a British fleet of 40 warships assembled at Dunree Head to protect the convoys that gathered here for the North Atlantic run. In 1917, a US base was established there, but 21 years later it was handed over to the Irish Republic and was last manned in 1952.

Some believe that the Grianan of Aileach was designed for sun-worshipping rituals, with hundreds watching the goings-on from the terraces

▶▶ Grianan of Aileach   *1954D*

This remarkable circular fortress lies about 13km (8 miles) south of Buncrana, perched on a hilltop and reached by a small winding lane. Aerial photographs of it, such as the one below, show the stone ring fort in an emerald pool of grassland amid scrubby tufts of brownish heather and gorse. The name means 'stone palace of the sun'. Similar *cashel* forts can be seen elsewhere in Ireland, such as Staigue Fort in County Kerry. Its precise age is disputed, some authorities dating it well before the Christian era (to about 1700BC), others rather later. Its suspiciously neat appearance is due to enthusiastic restoration during the 1870s by Dr. Walter Bernard, a Derry historian. The round enclosure measures about 23m (75ft) across, with walls 5m (17ft) high and 4m (13ft) thick. A single gate allows access to the interior, which contains four tiers of steps and various passages or storage places. It was recorded by Ptolemy in the 2nd century AD and was used as a stronghold by the O'Neill kings for several centuries before its gradual destruction. If you are lucky enough to visit it on a fine day the views from this hilltop are amazing, stretching for huge distances over Derry, the Fanad and Inishowen peninsulas and the Swilly estuary.

▶▶ Inishowen Peninsula   *1954E*

Ireland's most northerly point lies in the Republic on this ragged triangular headland, not in Northern Ireland as most people would expect. Lough Foyle and Lough Swilly virtually isolate Inishowen from the rest of the county. The interior is a mix of low white farms and cottages huddling against the wind, and grand brown mountains rising toward Slieve Snaght. The scenic 160km (100-mile) route around the edge of Inishowen takes in Malin Head, castles, churches, High Crosses and pre-Christian antiquities. None of these is essential viewing, but the tour, which takes a full day, is a dramatic and varied drive.

Buncrana▶▶ is the main centre, a popular holiday resort much favoured by inhabitants of Derry. Throughout the centuries it witnessed many clashes between English and Irish. Ireland's remote extremities were always feared (not without reason) as a potential Achilles' heel in English defences against invading Catholic forces from Spain or France, and any hints of disaffection were dealt with ruthlessly. In 1602, the O'Dohertys prepared to welcome a second Spanish armada here, and a couple of centuries later Wolfe Tone was held in Buncrana Castle after his abortive rebellion in 1798. Buncrana also has a Vintage Car Museum.

Malin▶ is a 17th-century plantation village built around a green, its most striking feature a long bridge of stone arches. Malin Head relays weather reports from the fishing village of Ballyhillin, sheltered from the worst of the storms by the rocky promontory. Several minor historical sights, such as crosses and stone circles, are clustered around Carndonagh.

▶ Letterkenny

1953D

Donegal's county town is now the main commercial centre of the Republic's northwest region and, as such, has several bustling shopping centres. It guards the lowest bridging point on the Swilly River, just before it widens into the scenic fiord known as Lough Swilly. There are few especially attractive views of this from the town itself, however, which is on the whole not all that interesting. Its main claims to fame are the longest main street in Ireland and the lofty spire of the Victorian neo-Gothic St. Eunan's Cathedral, which has a handsome altar of Carrara marble and rich stained glass. Look for the Four Masters carved on the pulpit. The Irish patriot Wolfe Tone was captured in Letterkenny in 1798 after his foiled invasion with French allies, and taken to Dublin under heavy guard. The county museum is housed in the old workhouse and the regional tourist office just out of town on the N56. Letterkenny makes a useful base for exploring inland Donegal, including the Blue Stack Mountains and the Glenveagh National Park.

INCH LEVEL

Inch Level, on Lough Swilly, at the base of the Inishowen peninsula, is the most important wetland habitat in the northwest and has international status as a bird reserve. Mute and whooper swans live here or visit it for part of the year. Brent and barnacle geese and other wildfowl migrate to Trawbreaga Bay in winter.

St. Eunan's Cathedral, Letterkenny, was built by Donegal masons using Donegal sandstone

207

208

▶▶ Lough Gartan   *1953D*

Donegal's local saint, Columba (or Colmcille/Columbcille in Irish), was born by the beautiful shores of Lough Gartan in AD521. A modern building on the eastern shore houses the **Colmcille Heritage Centre▶** (tel: 074 91 37306; *open*: Easter and May–end Sep Mon–Sat 10.30–6.30, Sun 1–6. *Admission: inexpensive*), which outlines the saint's life (see page 114) and the rise of Christianity in Ireland. An interesting feature is an exhibition on the preparation of illuminated manuscripts, using parchment and natural pigments. At the saint's alleged birthplace are two sacred stones around which various superstitions have spread. Pregnant women pray at the Natal Stone to ensure a safe delivery, while the Stone of Loneliness warded off the anguish of homesickness and was a place of pilgrimage for those about to emigrate.

▶▶ Parke's Castle   *1942B*

Fivemile Bourne, tel: 071 91 64149, www.heritageireland.com
Open: mid-Mar–end Oct daily 10–6. Admission: inexpensive

A fortified manor house with an interestingly chequered history stands by the calm waters of **Lough Gill**. Built in 1609 by an Ulster settler, Captain Robert Parke, it occupies the site of a much earlier tower house belonging to the O'Rourke clan, rulers of the kingdom of Breffni. The last unfortunate O'Rourke lord sheltered a shipwrecked Spanish Armada officer and was executed in London for treason. Features of the medieval structure can be seen in the later house. Beyond the outer defences near the water's edge lies a little beehive hut of stone. This is a sweatbox, or early Irish sauna, used to alleviate various ailments. Exhibitions and an audio-visual show about the castle and many local places of interest, including Sligo's range of antiquities, can be seen inside; free guided tours are available. From the jetty you can take a boat around Lough Gill, calling at the Yeatsian island of Innisfree (see panel).

Parke's Castle stands on the shores of Lough Gill, considered one of Ireland's most picturesque loughs. About 8km (5 miles) long, Lough Gill resembles a smaller version of the Lakes of Killarney

The eerie light of dawn on Lough Gill

▶ Rathmelton

1953D

This dignified plantation town is all stately warehouses and seemly Georgian buildings on a salmon river. It was built by Sir William Stewart for settlers during the early 17th century. The Leannan River was once an important waterway, and in earlier times Rathmelton was a significant port exporting grain, salmon, butter and linen (a more unusual product was iodine, made from local seaweed). A new heritage centre in the former Presbyterian meeting house displays information both on the town's history and on the founding of American Presbyterianism.

An exhibit from the Flight of the Earls Heritage Centre, Rathmullan

▶ Rathmullan

1953E

The eastern side of the Fanad peninsula, overlooking the fiord-like scenery of Lough Swilly, is the most appealing drive, and this fortified harbour village is one of the most interesting places to visit.

Before the battery was constructed by the English to ward off Napoleonic attacks, Rathmullan figured twice in Irish history. First, it was the place where 'Red Hugh' O'Donnell, the Ulster chieftain, was treacherously lured on board a disguised merchant ship for a convivial drink, only to find himself in chains on his way to Dublin Castle, where he languished for six years. Twenty years later, the earls of Tyrone and of Tyrconnell finally left Ireland from Rathmullan in the incident known as the Flight of the Earls (see pages 34–35). Initially they had hopes of raising support against the English from Spanish allies, but their plans came to nothing and they died in exile, leaving their great estates and castles to be occupied by Ulster settlers. A heritage centre in the old fort tells the history of this period. Another of Rathmullan's attractions is a country house hotel, Rathmullan House (see Hotels and Restaurants, page 282), one of Donegal's most comfortable bases, with a good restaurant.

The Dominican Friary, more usually known as Sligo Abbey

THE BATTLE OF THE BOOKS
A tragic storm in a teacup —but an important principle of copyright—lies at the heart of this curious incident, which took place at Cooldrumman, north of Sligo. In AD561, St. Columba borrowed a psalter from St. Finian and surreptitiously copied it. When St. Finian found out he angrily demanded the copy. St. Columba refused and the pair went to arbitration at the court of the High King, Diarmuid. He decided in favour of St. Finian, with the famous judgment, 'To every cow its calf; to every book its copy', St. Columba refused to accept the ruling and raised an army against St. Finian; more than 3,000 men were killed. St. Columba was the victor, but, stricken with remorse, he went to live in exile in Iona off the Scottish coast, where he died in AD597.

The eye-catching monument to W. B. Yeats, winner of the Nobel Prize for Literature in 1923, in Sligo Town

▶ Sligo
1942B

Sligo is one of the largest towns in the northwest, a lively market town and centre for music pubs and eating places, designed more for its own 18,000 inhabitants than for visitors. Colourful houses stand alongside the Garavogue River and the town still has many characterful old quarters and shops. Its literary associations give it a cultural cachet and it now draws an annual influx of scholars and students on the Yeats trail, especially during August when a Yeats summer school is held.

Sligo was sacked by the Vikings in 807 and, situated as it is on the fringes of Connaught and Ulster, later became a key location for warring clans. The Anglo-Norman Fitzgeralds held sway in the 13th century when the castle (now vanished) and abbey were built. Later the O'Conors and O'Donnells fought for supremacy, and in Cromwellian times the town was one of the last Jacobite strongholds. During the Famine the population fell drastically and massive emigration occurred.

Sligo's main sights are its 13th-century Dominican abbey, sacked in 1641, and its **museum and art gallery▶** (tel: 071 91 41623; *open:* Jun–end Sep Mon–Sat 10–5.30; Apr, May and Oct Tue–Sat 2–5. *Admission free*), which houses many documents relating to W. B. Yeats, together with paintings by his brother, Jack. The town has two cathedrals, the Church of Ireland St. John's, designed by Richard Castle in 1730 and the 19th-century Catholic cathedral. Hargadon's pub is a local institution. It now allows women inside, but otherwise firmly retains its old-world character and decor, with tiny dark booths and swivelling windows.

Outside the town loom the great hulks of Benbulbin 525m (1,722ft) and Knocknarea 330m (1,083ft), like upturned ships. Both hills can be climbed, but can be treacherous in the mist because of the deep fissures in the rain-eroded limestone. Benbulbin is the legendary death site of Diarmuid, who eloped with Gráinne. Knocknarea, to the southwest, is supposed to be the burial place of the warrior Queen Maeve (though she died elsewhere), and is surmounted by a massive cairn of 40,000 tons of rock.

YEATS COUNTRY

Drive

Yeats Country and Benbulbin

You're never far from **Benbulbin** on this tour. The coast is quiet and much broken; inland are lakes and pastures.

This area is called 'Yeats Country' as the poet passed much of his childhood and was eventually buried here (his adult life was mainly spent in Dublin and County Galway). Above Sligo Town the curious hulk of Benbulbin looms like a capsized ship, its flat limestone top scored by erosion. Off the N15 north of Sligo is **Drumcliff churchyard▶**, where Yeats's tomb lies. Minor roads from the N15 lead past the headland of **Rosses Point▶**. Farther up, follow the coastal turning to **Lissadell House▶** (tel: 087 629

6928, www.lissadellhouse.com; *open:* May–end Sep daily 11–6. *Admission: moderate*), 19th-century home of the Gore-Booth family. Sisters Eva Gore-Booth and Constance Markiewicz, friends of Yeats, took part in the Easter Rising. The house, in need of restoration, is surrounded by rampant vegetation. On the promontory of **Mullaghmore▶** is Classie Bawn (private), former home of Lord Mountbatten, who was killed in 1979.

From the resort of **Bundoran▶**, a well-marked drive to Manorhamilton passes typical limestone ridge scenery. From there, go west around the north shore of **Glencar Lough▶▶**, where a waterfall drops 10m (33ft) through ferny rocks to a pool (in Yeats's poem *The Stolen Child*). Return to Sligo, then strike east for a drive around **Lough Gill▶▶**, famous for the lake-isle, Innisfree. Summer cruises are available from Sligo, Dromahair or Parke's Castle (see page 208). Other sites on the lough are the ruined Creevelea Friary and the Deer-park Monument, a series of stone burial chambers dating from 3500BC.

Northern Ireland

Victorian homage to the art of drinking: the Crown Liquor Saloon in Belfast

Rathlin
Island

rick-a-Rede
e Bridge

Ballycastle

moy

Cushendall *Red Bay*
Garron Point

Carnlough
Glenarm

ckey
M2 Broughshane
Ballymena   **Larne**
Moorfields
Island Magee

Kells
Ballynure
stown **Ballyclare**   Ballycarry
Doagh   **Whitehead**
rim
Carrickfergus
st
M2
nal **Newtownabbey**
M5 **Holywood** **Bangor**
lin   Ulster Folk &   **Donaghadee**
BELFAST Transport Museum
ty   **Newtownards**
Dunmurry ■ **Mount Stewart**
Lisburn   **M1** **Comber** **Ballywalter**
Maze town **Carryduff** Greyabbey
Ballygowan Kircubbin
gan
Hillsborough Saintfield *Strangford* Portavogie
■ **Rowallane** *Lough*
Dromore
Ballynahinch **Killyleagh**
Banbridge **Portaferry**
Castle Ward Strangford
ghbrickland **Downpatrick**
Clough
Castlewellan
iland Dundrum Ardglass
Maghera Killough
Hilltown St John's Point
852m▲ **Newcastle**
wry *Slieve Donard*
Mourne
npoint *Mts*
Rostrevor Annalong
ath
Kilkeel
ford **Greencastle**

4   5

NORTHERN IRELAND For many years, the Troubles have been a significant factor in any decision to visit Northern Ireland. Yet, for over five years now a cease-fire has held while the politicians try to make a power-sharing agreement work. For the visitor Northern Ireland is, most of the time, in most places, as tranquil as anywhere in the South—and that makes it pretty quiet. In fact, the reduction in the military presence, and relative peace, has allowed the more 'normal' street crimes such as theft to reassert themselves. However, this doesn't mean you shouldn't keep your wits about you, particularly in sensitive zones such as west Belfast, Derry, Armagh or Newry.

The relief of Derry

Cars are best parked in official parking areas or otherwise in pay-and-display areas (where you buy a sticker allowing you to park for a certain length of time). Some towns and cities have signposted control zones where vehicles must not be left unattended, and illegal parking may cause a security alert. Outside the trouble spots, Northern Ireland feels, and is, entirely peaceful. Wherever they come from, visitors receive a warm welcome. Local people, whether Catholic or Protestant, are extraordinarily hospitable. Most of them are on perfectly good terms with their neighbours of whatever creed, and it is often baffling to imagine where the tension lies. The majority of people here are simply interested in getting on with their lives in peace.

SCOTTISH CONNECTIONS The closeness of Scotland to Ulster (a mere 20km/13 miles at its narrowest point) has always influenced the province strongly, even before the plantation years (see pages 34–35). Waves of invaders made the short sea crossing, most notably Edward Bruce, brother of the famous Scottish leader, Robert, who first arrived at Carrickfergus with his 'gallowglasses' (mercenaries) in 1315. Settlement hasn't always been one-way: During the 4th and 5th centuries AD, Irish Celts made their way to various westerly parts of Britain. But the people who returned during the reign of James I were mostly Scottish Presbyterians—tough, industrious and determined to the point of intransigence.

Northern Ireland has been supported since the plantation years by massive financial support from Britain, but its economic success could not have been achieved without the settlers' Protestant work ethic and resourcefulness. These characteristics show in the many pioneers who left Ulster to seek their fortune in the New World.

CROSSING THE BORDER
Don't pick up hitchhikers near the border. Before driving in Northern Ireland, check your insurance. If you have hired a car in the Republic you must inform the company when you pick up the car that you intend travelling in the North (and vice versa). Major hire companies are fully covered for North and South Ireland, and make no extra charge.

The 'Scotch-Irish' who emigrated to the United States of America have achieved an influence out of all proportion to their numbers. Presidents Kennedy and Reagan were of Irish Catholic stock, but about a dozen former presidents were of Ulster Scottish descent. Theodore Roosevelt was one of these, and his mother described her Antrim forebears in these telling terms: 'grim, stern people…relentless, revengeful, suspicious…also upright, resolute and fearless, loyal to their friends and devoted to their country'.

TOWN AND COUNTRY The scenery of Northern Ireland is its primary attraction and most tourism is concentrated in a few clearly defined rural areas: the Mountains of Mourne, the Glens of Antrim, the Causeway Coast and the Lakes of Fermanagh. Other less well-known areas such as Lough Neagh and the wild Sperrin Mountains are now becoming more popular destinations for walking and fishing, and several forest parks have been created. The Ulster Way is one of Ireland's best long-distance footpaths, leading through the province's most scenic and beautiful landscapes in all six counties. But it is the cities of the North, especially Belfast and Derry, that give a complete picture of the province and cannot be ignored if you want to see more than surface prettiness.

The North is particularly strong on museums and boasts a fine collection of stately homes and gardens (its Georgian houses are generally better preserved than in the Republic). In many ways Northern Ireland's landscapes are similar to the Republic's, however the North—for years the more prosperous region—has fallen behind economically, and this is reflected in the slightly jaded look of some of its infrastructure.

Checkpoints aside, it's easy to get around. Roads are generally good and the traffic regulations, like the telephone and postal systems, are the same as in the rest of the UK. The euro is accepted in some places, but most take only sterling.

215

The strange, regular formations of the Giant's Causeway make a fascinating viewpoint along the beautiful Antrim coast

BELFAST

Right: the welcome at Larry's Bar is warmer than the ghostly images might imply

▶ **Belfast** 2134B

Since Partition in 1921, Belfast has been the official capital of Northern Ireland. Stormont is now home to the new powersharing government. With a population of around 400,000, Belfast is much smaller than Dublin, and a large exodus of the younger middle classes during the past two decades to dormitory suburbs has unbalanced the city centre's demography, although it is still a transient home for over 8,000 university students. Apart from its two best museums, none of its sights is hugely compelling, but there is certainly plenty to do for a day or two, and the city has a highly distinctive atmosphere.

Few people unfamiliar with the city will immediately warm to the prospect of a stay there. Religious bigotry, sectarian violence and deliberately high-profile security measures have in the past given the impression to outsiders that Northern Ireland's capital is a war zone. Like many things in Ireland, however, the reality is a surprise. If anything, Belfast has always been less of a risk for the average visitor than Dublin. In fact a return to normality and a massive reduction in security has seen the more 'ordinary' street crimes reappearing, which is a sad reflection on 'modern' Belfast. On the cutlural front, however, the city hosts one of the UK's liveliest and most acclaimed arts festivals at Queen's University each November, as well as an impressive year-round series of concerts, exhibitions, opera and drama. Restaurants along its Golden Mile are bustling and sporting events are flourishing.

The great engineering works that once made Belfast so prosperous are in sad decline, and unemployment figures in the province are among the highest in the UK. Its earliest industries included rope- and linen-making, cotton-spinning and printing. In 1859, the UK's largest shipyards were established here by the Yorkshire engineer Edward Harland and a marine draftsman from Hamburg, Gustav Wilhelm Wolff. Two vast yellow cranes with the initials 'H&W' still dominate the dockland skyline as powerfully as any cathedral and are affectionately known as Samson and Goliath. The decision to close these mighty shipyards

Like Dublin, Belfast lies close to hills, in this instance Cave Hill, north of the city

217

was a great psychological blow to the city, as well as an economic one. Other firms closely associated with Belfast are Shorts, the aircraft manufacturers and Gallahers, the tobacco giant.

Belfast's setting is often praised more than the city itself. The name derives from the Gaelic *beal feirste*, meaning 'mouth of the sandy ford', and Belfast stands at the head of a deep seawater lake surrounded by unspoiled hills, the Lagan River cutting through its heart. Belfast has abundant parks and open spaces, all documented by the tourist authorities (pick up leaflets in their office on North Street). Within minutes fast roads can take you beyond the city to scenic areas such as the Ards Peninsula or Strangford Lough; it is a slightly longer trip to the Mountains of Mourne or the Glens of Antrim.

The city's commercial centre and university area lie close to the river on its western side; prosperous residential districts are to the east and south. On the far west of town, beyond the dividing pale of the Westlink motorway, are the notorious sectarian ghettos that have given the city its worst reputation. The overcrowded run-down areas of Ballymurphy, Falls and Shankill are depressing and can easily be avoided. To some, however, they are fascinating, and intrepid visitors venture

Belfast's City Hall was designed by Crumwell Thomas in 1906; the staircase in the entrance hall is lit by seven stained-glass windows depicting scenes from the city's history

218

there to see their vivid and sometimes highly artistic displays of street mural propaganda. If you want to visit these areas, you can take one of the black cabs that assemble in lines at the edge of the city centre, plying strictly within either Catholic or Protestant territory. To see the Catholic Falls area (Andersonstown), pick up a cab at Castle Street; to visit Shankill, go to North Street. On the Falls route you will pass the last remnant of the notorious Divis Flats, some of the saddest housing in Europe and St. Peter's Catholic Cathedral in 19th-century Gothic. The Peace Line is a barricade of iron dividing Protestant and Catholic areas. On the

The City Hall, in the background, is built around a central quadrangle

THE *GIRONA*

Legend has it that one of the strange formations along the Causeway Coast confused the sailors of the Spanish Armada, fleeing after their defeat, who believed it to be Dunluce Castle (3km/2 miles west). The galleass *Girona* was wrecked in 1588 at Port-na-Spaniagh with all but five hands—a loss of about 1,300 lives. Artefacts salvaged from the ship in 1967 are now on display at Belfast's excellent Ulster Museum, including cannon, rings, coins and a quaint gold salamander ornament, set with rubies.

The Palm House at Belfast's Botanic Gardens is one of the oldest examples of a structure made of cast iron and curved glass, dating from 1839 to 1852

THE RED HAND OF ULSTER

A grisly myth explains the presence of a hand on Ulster's coat of arms. Two great warriors raced each other to the shores of Ulster; whoever touched land first would be king. Neck and neck they sped, until at the last moment one pulled ahead. The other, desperate to win, struck off his hand with his sword and hurled it ashore, so claiming victory. The red hand still stands on the province's coat of arms, a fittingly gory symbol.

The Grand Opera House had fallen into such disrepair that it closed in 1971, eventually reopening in 1980 after five years of restoration. Since then it has sadly become a victim of terrorist bombs, being badly damaged in both 1991 and 1993

Protestant side, murals can be seen all along the Shankill and Donegall roads, the most famous image being King William on a white steed, rearing from the waters of the Boyne.

MAIN SIGHTS

Belfast is essentially a Victorian city, modelled on those robust mercantile centres such as Liverpool and Manchester across the water. The poet John Betjeman found much to admire in the city's civic architecture, notably its **Custom House▶** near the docks (not open to the public), several palatial bank buildings near the High Street and the **City Hall▶▶** (tel: 028 9027 0456. *Guided tours* are available Wed mornings) on Donegall Square, a flamboyant structure of white Portland limestone. Inside, the City Hall has many interesting features and rich decorations of marble and glass. Donegall Square contains gardens, statues and several other noteworthy buildings, such as the **Linen Hall Library▶** (tel: 028 9023 1707), with a fine collection of volumes in its old-fashioned interior. The Albert Memorial Clock, on Victoria Street, was built in 1865 by William Barre and depicts Prince Albert in the robes of the Order of the Garter. The tower now leans slightly from the vertical.

Also in the city centre (large parts of which have been pedestrianized) is **St. Anne's Cathedral▶** (tel: 028 9032 8332), on Donegall Street. Belfast's Anglican cathedral is austere neo-Romanesque, enlivened inside by mosaics and a floor made of stone from all parts of Ireland. Sir Edward Carson, architect of Partition, is buried there. **St. Malachy's▶▶**, in Alfred Street, was built in 1844, the plain red-brick exterior of this Roman Catholic church disguising a glorious inner riot of plasterwork n Strawberry Hill Gothic style. **Sinclair Seamen's Church▶** in dockland is another of Belfast's most striking churches, with a jaunty nautical theme. The oval **First Presbyterian Church▶**, opened in 1783, has an unusual interior designed by Roger Mulholland. For a truly unforgettable flavour of Belfast, head for the Martyrs' Memorial Free Presbyterian Church, also east of the river, where the Reverend Ian Paisley presides each Sunday.

Belfast has some extremely florid architecture, which is particularly apparent at the start of its Golden Mile, stretching along Great Victoria Street towards the university. The **Crown Liquor Saloon▶** (tel: 028 9024 9476) is a splendidly ornate, gaslit Victorian pub now in the care of the National Trust, all coloured marbles, tiles, mirrors and panelled booths. Good Irish food is served, but lunchtimes can be busy. The **Grand Opera House▶▶** (tel: 028 9024 1919) is a beautiful Victorian theatre, badly damaged in bomb attacks in 1991 and 1993. It contains a typically lavish auditorium and presents performances of many kinds. Of the same era, but in a different style, is **Queen's University▶** (tel: 028 9033 5252) on University Road. The main building boasts an impressive facade of Tudor Gothic red brick and stone mullions. Close by are the **Botanic Gardens▶▶** (tel: 028 9032 4902) in Stranmillis Road, a beautiful oasis of lawns and gardens sloping down to the river. Its two main structures are the **Palm House▶** and the **Tropical Ravine House▶**.

On the grounds of the Botanic Gardens is a modern building housing what is certainly one of Ireland's best museums. The **Ulster Museum▶▶▶** (tel: 028 9038 3000) has a varied and extensive collection, though anything but wearisome. Schoolchildren delight in its dinosaurs; others may prefer its sparkling minerals or exquisite ceramics. The sections devoted to Belfast's industrial heritage are excellent, as is its clear and unpartisan summary of Ulster's history. One of its most

Queen's University, with its Tudor-style building, was founded in 1849

221

Belfast's tropical jungle can be found at the Botanic Gardens, south of the city

Belfast Castle (completed in 1870) was built in the style of Balmoral, the Queen's Scottish residence, and designed by W. H. Lynn

Flamingos cope with unfamiliar weather at Belfast Zoo

popular sections contains treasures and artefacts from the Spanish Armada ship, *Girona*, wrecked on the Causeway Coast. It has a fine collection of paintings, too, including some interesting 18th-century representations of the Giant's Causeway by Susanna Drury.

Outside the city centre lie several other sights. **Belfast Castle▶** (tel: 028 9077 6925), some way north on the lower slopes of Cave Hill, is a Victorian Scottish baronial house, with attractive gardens and fine views of the harbour area. Belfast's **zoo▶** (tel: 028 9077 6277) is pleasantly set in former gardens near to the castle and is just one of many parks and open spaces in and around the city boundaries. **Lagan Valley Park▶▶** (tel: 028 9049 1922) is one of the largest of these parks, with 16km (10 miles) of towpaths and locks. Close by there is a prehistoric earthwork called **The Giant's Ring▶**. On the A20, 6.5km (4 miles) east, is **Stormont▶** (tel: 028 9052 0700), a grand, classical building, which once housed the Northern Ireland parliament and now serves as administrative offices. It stands proudly at the top of a sweeping drive through neat parkland. The Scottish baronial Stormont Castle nearby contains the office of the Northern Ireland secretary of state, the British cabinet minister (senior member of the British Parliament) responsible for the province. Both can be viewed only from outside for obvious reasons. See page 235 for details of Ulster's Folk and Transport Museum in Cultra, on the Bangor road.

If you want to stay in Belfast, the best area to head for is the university area to the south of the city centre. In the seemly residential streets of Stranmillis, Malone and Botanic there are a number of moderately priced guesthouses—safe, clean and respectable. Several well-known hotels in the central areas have been terrorist targets in the past.

▶▶ Armagh   2123B

Armagh has often been the scene of battle, and today, this close to the border, security precautions are in force. County Armagh is predominantly Catholic, especially in the south, but the city itself is a Protestant stronghold. The two rival cathedrals, both dedicated to St. Patrick, scowl at each other from two of Armagh's seven small hills. The Protestant one has to be kept locked for security reasons, but instructions for obtaining the key are posted on the door. Solid, squat and square, it is mostly 19th century, in perpendicular Gothic style, with a fringe of grotesque heads around its otherwise plain exterior. It is the burial place of Brian Ború, the warlike king who finally drove the Vikings out of Ireland. The Roman Catholic cathedral, completed in 1873, stands proudly twin-spired at the top of a long flight of steps. The interior is astonishingly ornate—walls and roof covered with rich mosaics of saints and angels. The Mall, a broad, tree-lined square, is surrounded by some of Armagh's finest Georgian buildings, including the courthouse and the Royal Irish Fusiliers and County Museums. Armagh's most unusual sights are the 18th-century **Observatory**▶ (tel: 028 3752 4725) and neighbouring **Planetarium**▶▶, where computer displays and models track down heavenly bodies. **Navan Fort**▶, now just a huge mound to the west, was the ancient palace of Queen Macha, a site that rivalled Tara and the court of Ulster's chivalrous Red Branch Knights.

▶ Carrickfergus   2134C

The main landmark of this small seaside town is its vast Norman **castle**▶▶ (tel: 028 9335 1273), still mostly intact, on a basalt ledge by the shore. Displays of its history are housed inside, and today the castle plays amiably to the gallery by hosting medieval banquets and a Lughnasa festival in August. William of Orange entered Ireland via these shores in 1690 and a Williamite trail can be followed around the town. Just to the east is the **Andrew Jackson Centre** (tel: 028 9366 6455), an 18th-century cottage with re-created period interiors and displays relating to the seventh US president, whose parents lived nearby.

223

There are few remaining signs of Eamhain (or palace of) Macha, at Navan Fort, County Armagh. The site is thought to be 4,000–5,000 years old, and is associated with Cuchulainn, the Ulster hero

BULLETS, OR ROAD BOWLS
This ancient game is played along the local roads near Armagh (a version of it can also be seen in Schull, County Cork). A heavy iron ball, about the size of a baseball, is hurled along the lanes and the aim is to reach the end of the winding 4km (2.5-mile) course in the fewest number of throws. Betting is fierce. Ask for details in local pubs if you want to see a game—most take place on Sunday afternoons. The first Sunday in August is championship day.

The fine, underrated city of Derry

THE SIEGE OF DERRY
Catholic James II expected a welcome from Derry's governor when his troops arrived in 1688, but 13 Protestant apprentices, fearing reprisals, stole the city's keys and locked the gates against the Jacobite forces. Supporters of William III, who had deposed James II as King of England, joined the apprentices' cause and flocked into the city. They remained under siege for 105 days, the longest siege in British history, during which time the population was reduced to eating a grisly diet of rotting horsemeat, dogs and rats. More than 7,000 of the 30,000 crammed within Derry's walls died from starvation and disease. Yet when offered the chance to capitulate, the defenders merely raised a crimson standard signifying 'No Surrender'—which has since become the rallying cry of the Protestant Unionist cause. The courage of the apprentice boys is still celebrated in Loyalist marches. Eventually William's soldiers raised the siege and James's troops retreated.

▶▶ Derry (Londonderry)   *2122C*

This historic city, nestled in the Foyle Valley, is now officially known by its original name, Derry, although its Loyalist population still refers to it as Londonderry—an allusion to James I's gift of the city to the livery companies of London. (To add to the visitor's confusion, the county name remains officially Londonderry.) Derry's notorious Bogside district has seen much unrest, for it is there that Catholic/Protestant tribalism is most sharply polarized. Catholics, unwillingly stranded right on the Republic's border, have suffered much discrimination under gerrymandered Protestant control, while Loyalists find it impossible to cast off their atavistic siege mentality. On a freestanding gable-end near the Bogside (once an IRA no-go area and the scene of 'Bloody Sunday', when 13 Catholic civilians were killed in 1972 during a civil rights march) are the giant words 'You are now entering Free Derry'. Protestants reply a few streets away with the defiant slogan 'No Surrender'.

For all its political ill-feelings, Derry is a fascinating city, retaining intact the **17th-century walls**▶▶ that have played such a significant role in its history. These sturdy ramparts, 8m (25ft) high and up to 9m (30ft) thick, have never been breached. Five of the cannons that defended the city during its long siege stand above Shipgate Quay. Walkways lead along parts of the city walls, giving excellent views of both the inner city and the lower city with its great modern bridge spanning the Foyle River. Within the walls are an extraordinary little enclave of old-fashioned shops and bars, the Protestant cathedral of St. Columb in 'Planters' Gothic' style and a typical Ulster central square known as the **Diamond**▶. A hopeful sign of constructive community spirit is the Derry Craft Village, showcasing modern artisanry.

▶ Downpatrick   *2135A*

In contrast to Derry, the market town of Down has lengthened its name, in honour of its most distinguished visitor, St. Patrick (see page 226). Down Cathedral stands in the highest part of the town amid seemly Georgian buildings. It is small, mostly 18th century and, perhaps surprisingly, is Anglican, not Catholic. Inside, the original Regency box pews have been preserved.

Not far down the hill is Downpatrick's other major sight, the **Down County Museum**▶▶ (tel: 028 4461 5218), set in the local gaol. The **St. Patrick Heritage Centre**▶▶ (tel: 028 4461 5218) is well worth seeing for a coherent version of what is known of the saint's life and times (detailed film and exhibition). There are also very good local history and wildlife sections. The old prison cells can also be visited. These grim, dark, cramped rooms once housed the leader of the United Irishmen, Thomas Russell, who was convicted and executed here in 1803 for his part in Robert Emmet's rebellion (see pages 38–39).

From Downpatrick the landlocked sea inlet called **Strangford Lough**▶▶ and the **Ards peninsula**▶▶ can be explored. Both of these shore roads are attractive, especially the easterly one, but to reach this it is necessary to take the car ferry across the straits between Strangford and Portaferry, where the tides rush with great force. The lake is an important wildlife habitat supporting many unusual species. To find out more details about this remarkable ecosystem, simply stop at Portaferry's **aquarium**▶ (tel: 028 4272 8062), Exploris, near the quayside, which is devoted to local marine life. At Strangford, on the western side of the straits, is **Castle Ward**▶▶, built in a jarring mixture of styles (see page 230).

The gruesome figure of Death makes an appearance at the Derry Festival, held in February/March

225

St. Patrick is remembered in this stained-glass window (1937) at Down Cathedral

St. Patrick is Ireland's patron saint, and one of the best-known saints in Catholic hagiography. His importance to the island is evident from the number of places associated with him and from the many Patricks, Pats or Paddys (including a whiskey) named after him.

THE SHAMROCK
This plant, *trifolium minus*, is a trifoliate, or cloverlike plant, thought to have been used by St. Patrick to illustrate the doctrine of the Trinity. It is one of Ireland's national emblems, traditionally worn on St. Patrick's Day (17 March).

The saint is reputed to be buried in Downpatrick's cathedral graveyard, though the evidence for this is shaky. The rough granite slab that marks his 'tomb' dates from about 1900 and was placed over the site of a large pit excavated by relic hunters eager to find his bones. Downpatrick is, nevertheless, the best place to learn about St. Patrick (visit the heritage centre in the Down County Museum).

St. Patrick, son of a minor Roman official, was born in western Britain at the turn of the 5th century AD. He was captured by Irish raiders at the age of 16 and spent six years in Ireland in slavery, working as a shepherd on Slemish Mountain, County Antrim. Eventually he escaped to France, where he trained as a cleric. Haunted by a vocation to convert the Irish to Christianity, he returned in about AD432 and spent an energetic 30 years preaching and founding churches, mostly in Ulster, Leinster and Connaught. In AD433, he challenged Laoghaire, High King of Tara, by lighting the paschal (Easter) fires on top of the Hill of Slane against the pagan king's express command. Laoghaire was so impressed by Patrick's fiery sense of purpose that he let him continue his mission unhindered.

In County Mayo, the mountain Croagh Patrick is sacred to his memory. Legend has it that here the saint rang his bell and the snakes of Ireland fled. Of course there never were any snakes, but the mountain remains shrouded in mystery (and often mist) and is visited annually by countless devout pilgrims. The jewelled shrine said to contain St. Patrick's bell is held in the National Museum, Dublin.

The summit of Croagh Patrick—St. Patrick's mountain—appears to be perfectly conical from some angles

▶ Enniskillen   *2121B*

This appealing little town owes much of its attractiveness to its setting on an island where the two sections of Lough Erne constrict to their narrowest point. Several routes converge on Enniskillen's strategic location and at busy times it can be a traffic bottleneck. Nevertheless, it makes a good base for exploring Fermanagh's lakeland, where boat trips, fishing and several islands offer many diversions. In the town the main places of interest are the quaintly turreted Watergate and the castle, which contains two museums. One is a heritage centre devoted to Fermanagh life and customs, the other a museum dedicated to the Royal Enniskillen Fusiliers and Dragoons. The town's military associations with these famous regiments have made it a terrorist target. In 1987, Enniskillen suffered one of the IRA's most infamous attacks, when a Remembrance Day ceremony was bombed; 11 people were killed, 61 injured. Parking control zones are enforced within the town centre.

Many boat trips operate from various points on Lower Lough Erne (the northern lake), where several islands can be visited. **Boa Island▶**, **White Island▶** and **Devenish Island▶** all have interesting Celtic or early Christian antiquities. Reached via the pretty lakeshore roads, Castle Archdale Country Park and Castle Caldwell Forest Park have good woodland walks and picnic sites. Near Enniskillen are the grand houses, Castle Coole and Florence Court (see page 230).

At the far western tip of the lake, straddling the border with the Republic, **Belleek▶▶** is famous for its pottery. Guided factory tours can be arranged and a museum and visitor centre display its wares. Belleek pottery is extremely elaborate, delicate and expensive: Clay is extruded in thin strands which are laid over each other in complex lattice patterns to form the classic 'basketware' style. The results command high prices.

The Belleek Pottery

227

MARBLE ARCH CAVES
These caverns, 14km (9 miles) southwest of Enniskillen, are among the best in Ireland. The 90-minute tour takes place partly on foot, partly by boat. The impressive formations are given the usual fanciful names. Near the exit is a nature reserve where the Cladagh River emerges through a gorge into a bluebell wood.

Marble Arch Caves

CARRICK-A-REDE ROPE BRIDGE

If you arrive on the Causeway Coast between April and September, be sure to visit this curiosity linking the mainland with the salmon fisheries on Carrick-a-rede Island. The bridge is put up each spring and provides an exhilarating 18m (60ft) walk along planks with wire handrails, swaying alarmingly 24m (80ft) above a rocky cleft. You cross at your own risk (inadvisable in high winds), but the trip looks a lot more terrifying and perilous than it actually is, and it's great fun.

OLD BUSHMILLS DISTILLERY

In 1608, Sir Thomas Phillips was granted a licence to distill whiskey in the village of Bushmills, south of the Causeway Coast. Continuing the tradition today, Old Bushmills is the oldest continuously run (legal) distillery in the world. Now it is also a visitor attraction, offering tours (*Guided tours* Jul–end Aug Mon–Sat; Sep–end Jun Mon–Thu morning and afternoon, Fri morning only), with tastings of course (hot toddies in winter). Two blends and one malt are made. Reserve a place in high season (tel: 028 2073 1521).

The Giant's Causeway; the other end of Finn MacCool's construction is on the Scottish island of Staffa, where there is a similar (but smaller) causeway

▶ ▶ ▶ Giant's Causeway 2123D

This extraordinary phenomenon is Northern Ireland's most famous landmark, studied by the Royal Geographical Society as long ago as 1693. Visitors have flocked here from far and wide ever since. The Causeway is set on a cliff-lined coast of outstanding natural beauty and is now in the care of the National Trust. In April 1987 it was declared Ireland's only World Heritage Site.

The Causeway is a complex series of promontories, but the most spectacular section consists of about 37,000 polygonal columns of dark basalt, many tawny with lichen, packed so neatly together that it is easy to imagine them as building blocks of some supernatural hand. Most columns are hexagonal, forming a honeycomb pattern, but some have five, seven or as many as ten sides. They measure about 30cm (1ft) across and may reach a height of 12m (40ft). Besides classic 'threepenny-bit' stacks are other extraordinary formations, some like bulbous eyes, others like ramparts. All were formed about 55 million years ago, after a volcanic eruption poured molten basalt out above the chalky bedrock, crystallizing into these regular structures as it cooled. Legends have arisen about the origins of the Causeway; the main one tells how the Ulster giant, Finn MacCool, built it to walk across to Scotland.

At the top of the cliffs, a large modern visitor centre contains an interesting exhibition about the Causeway and the local history and wildlife. During high season a minibus shuttles visitors down the steep path to the Causeway, but this rather spoils the magic of the place; the best way to enjoy it is to walk along the North Antrim Cliff Path. Off-season, when no other visitors are around and the waves crash on these bleak, dark rocks, the Causeway is memorable.

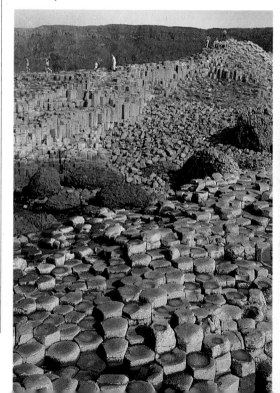

THE GLENS OF ANTRIM

Drive

The Glens of Antrim

Road access to the glens is from the A2 from Ballycastle to Larne. The area is good for walking, with the Ulster Way running along the coast past all the glens. From Larne, **Glenarm►►**, heavily wooded with forest trails and picnic sites and **Glencoy►**, near Carnlough, are the first glens you reach. Farther north is the most popular of the glens, **Glenariff►►**, described by William Thackeray as a 'mini-Switzerland', with waterfalls and a forest park.

Cushendall►►, the 'capital of the glens', has a number of minor sights, including a sandstone tower (the Curfew, or Garrison Tower), once used as a lockup for 'riotous persons', the ruined 13th-century Layde Old Church and Ossian's Grave, a Stone Age burial mound dating from 3000BC. The pretty conservation village of **Cushendun►►** sits at the foot of **Glendun►**, wildest of the glens. North of Ballyteerim is the Tornamoney Cashel, a stone fort dating from AD500–1000.

The properties and landscape owned by the Northern Ireland branch of the National Trust (NT) are an impressive collection. Besides the well-known set pieces such as Castle Coole and the Giant's Causeway, the National Trust also protects many minor and surprising sights—a lively Victorian pub in Belfast, a printing press and a beetling mill (used in the old linen industry) in County Tyrone, the curious rope bridge at Carrick-a-rede in County Antrim and several follies and castles.

JOINING AND MEMBERSHIP

230

For an annual fee members of the National Trust (or National Trust for Scotland) gain free admission to almost all the properties managed by the Trust throughout the UK Contact the National Trust, P.O. Box 39, Bromley, Kent BR1 3XL, UK (tel: 020-8315 1111).

Country Houses The grand Palladian mansion of **Castle Coole▶▶▶** (tel: 028 6632 2690), home of the earls of Belmore, is the most impressive house of its age in Ireland. A masterpiece by James Wyatt, completed in 1798, the house contains magnificent plasterwork and carved doors of ancient mahogany. Entrance to the landscaped parkland is free.

Ardress House▶ (tel: 028 3885 1236), in parkland near Portadown, dates from the 17th century. The interior contains paintings and good plasterwork. Livestock and farm implements are on show outside; visitors may explore the gardens.

Not far away from Ardress House is **The Argory▶▶** (tel: 028 8778 4753), very little changed since its construction in the 1820s. It has many original contents and a pretty, early-Victorian sundial garden. The interior is still lit by a rare acetylene gas plant surviving in the laundry yard. The surrounding wooded countryside offers many fine walks.

On the shores of Strangford Lough is **Castle Ward▶▶** (tel: 028 4488 1204), a mansion that clearly displays the diverse tastes of its 18th-century owners, Lord and Lady Bangor. He liked classical style; she favoured Gothic. Architecture was not all they disagreed on and eventually they separated. Despite its disparity of styles, the house and contents are of great interest, giving a vivid impression of Victorian life (see the laundry and the playroom). Within the 280ha (670-acre) estate are a 17th-century tower house, a wildfowl collection and an exhibition about Strangford Lough.

Florence Court▶▶▶ (tel: 028 6634 8249) is a particularly fine mid-18th-century Palladian (classical) house. The seat of the earls of Enniskillen, it was superbly restored after a disastrous fire in 1956. Splendid plasterwork is the main feature and is best preserved on the staircase and dining-room ceiling, which quick-thinking workmen saved from collapse by drilling holes to drain flood water. The grounds contain a water-powered

WELLBROOK BEETLING MILL (▶235)

The last stage of manufacturing linen is known as beetling, when flax fibres are hammered to produce a smooth surface. The cultivation of flax was Northern Ireland's largest industry and many deserted mills can be seen. West of Cookstown, in County Tyrone, is Wellbrook Beetling Mill (above) where the machinery is still in working order.

sawmill and a 220-year-old Irish yew tree, said to be the parent of all Irish-type yews. The 3rd earl's fossil collection is exhibited in one of the side pavilions.

A thatched 'long-house' dating from about 1691, **Hezlett House▶** (tel: 028 7084 8567) in County Londonderry was probably first used as a parsonage. Its most unusual feature is the cruck-truss (curved timber) roof. Inside, it is simply furnished in 18th-century style and contains a display of early building and joinery methods. Farther south is **Springhill▶** (tel: 028 8956 1861), former home of the Conynghams, a military family of Ayrshire origins. The edifice dates from the 17th century (with later additions). Outbuildings house a costume museum, while the gunroom contains weapons from Vinegar Hill and the siege of Derry.

Gardens There are two fine gardens in County Down. **Mount Stewart Gardens▶▶** (tel: 028 4278 8387) were created by the wife of the 7th Marquis of Londonderry in the 1920s. The mild microclimate created by neighbouring Strangford Lough enables many rare and tender plants to flourish. The house is richly furnished and contains political memorabilia. One forebear was Viscount Castlereagh, the 19th-century politician who signed the Act of Union. The county's other horticultural attraction is at **Rowallane▶▶** (tel: 028 9751 0131). This plantsman's garden was created over the first half of the 20th century on a drumlin (smooth glacial hills) site of 20ha (50 acres) and contains specimens from all over the world. Its pride and joy are the azaleas and rhododendrons in May and early June, but the gardens are worth seeing throughout the opening season from April to October.

GRAY'S PRINTING PRESS
Strabane, in County Tyrone, was an important centre of the Irish printing industry in the 18th and 19th centuries. The National Trust now preserves the only surviving printers, Gray's (*Open:* afternoons only in season; closed Thu and Sun) on Strabane's Main Street. John Dunlap, printer of the American Declaration of Independence and publisher of America's first daily newspaper, *The Pennsylvania Packet,* is said to have learned his trade here, as is James Wilson, grandfather of President Woodrow Wilson. Visitors may inspect an impressive array of decorative printing presses, all kept in working order, and other antique printing equipment.

231

Mount Stewart House and Gardens, County Down

With only one road leading through the Mountains of Mourne, they can only be properly appreciated on foot

BESSBROOK
This neat little town northwest of Newry was built during the 19th century by a Quaker linen manufacturer, John Grubb Richardson. It was designed to house his flax-mill workers, whose living conditions must have been much better than many of their colleagues at other mills. They may have regretted the absence of a pub, however. The tidy, slate-roofed houses are grouped around two village greens.

▶▶▶ **The Mountains of Mourne**   *2134A*

These wild, steep-sided granite hills present an unforgettable aspect when seen across Carlingford Lough from the Republic. They reach to an average height of about 600m (2,000ft) and are largely inaccessible except on foot, though the range is ringed by roads. Greencastle is a notable landmark near the entrance to Carlingford Lough. It changed hands many times and now stands gaunt and ruined near the rocky shore. Other places of interest along the coastal route are the marine park and restored 19th-century corn mill at Annalong and the Murlough National Nature Reserve, a stretch of sand dunes by Dundrum Bay providing an important habitat for many birds.

There is not much to recommend the town of Newry as a base to stay. If you want to explore the Mourne area, choose one of the eastern coastal resorts or stay in the delightful village of Carlingford over the border in the Republic. **Newcastle▶** is the main tourist centre for the Mourne Mountains. The resort, though pleasantly set, is of no great interest, but it has a good sandy beach and a wide range of accommodation. There are many walks in the nearby forest parks of Tollymore and Castlewellan.

Slieve Donard is the highest Mourne peak (852m/2,796ft) and it is said that on rare, clear days you can see all the countries of the British Isles from its summit (a relatively safe and easy climb), where there is also a hermit cell. At one time the mountains were a remote and ungovernable area inhabited by smugglers. A maze of ancient tracks lead through open moorland and upland pasture that make excellent walking country. For good maps and information, head for Newcastle's tourist office or the Mourne Countryside Centre at 91 Central Promenade. Rock climbing is popular on the steeper cliff faces. The most accessible section is a well-marked route called the Silent Valley that leads up to two reservoirs serving the Greater Belfast region. A visitor centre stands here and shuttle buses take people from the parking area to Ben Crom Reservoir (other traffic is banned). The upper sections of the Mourne hills are characterized by tiny fields and dry-stone walls. The Mourne Wall is the largest of these, 35km (22 miles) long and more than 2m (6ft) high, enclosing the water catchment area around the Silent Valley. Many semiprecious stones have been mined in the mountains around Hare's Gap.

The Ulster Way Northern Ireland is excellent for walking, and its interconnected paths form a magnificent 700km (435-mile) long-distance footpath through all six counties. For most of the way it hugs the perimeter of the province fairly closely, ducking inland across the Sperrin Mountains and briefly touching the shores of Lough Neagh. Obviously some sections are more scenic and easier to follow than others. The paths running through the Mountains of Mourne, the Glens of Antrim, the Causeway Coast and the Lakes of Fermanagh are the most popular and most clearly marked, and it is in these well-known tourist areas that you can most easily find accommodation. At various points the Ulster Way links with other routes leading through the Republic. Near the border areas it is advisable not to stray from the marked paths.

For the most part walking in Northern Ireland is safe and straightforward; no special equipment is needed apart from a good map and sensible footwear and clothing. Route guides and detailed maps are both available from various sources, notably the Sports Council for Northern Ireland, House of Sport, Upper Malone Road, Belfast BT9 5LA (tel: 028 9038 1222). The Youth Hostel Association of Northern Ireland (22 Donegall Road, Belfast BT12 5JN, tel: 028 9032 4733) also organizes rambling and hiking holidays throughout the year.

SPERRIN HERITAGE CENTRE

The fascinating history, wildlife and geology of the Sperrin Mountains is well documented in this visitor centre which can be found between Cranagh and Sperrin, 12km (7 miles) east of Plumbridge (*Open:* weekdays 11–5 and Sun afternoons; longer in high season). Nature lovers can enjoy the sight of rare mammals and birds of prey in these glaciated hills on the northeastern border of County Tyrone. The Sperrins also contain significant deposits of gold. Commercial exploitation is causing concern to environmentalists, but small-scale panning expeditions are arranged for visitors. Multimedia presentations include a holographic storyteller and 3-D slide shows, and weary walkers along the Ulster Way may welcome its excellent coffee shop.

233

Newcastle nestles under the shadow of the Mountains of Mourne

ULSTER-AMERICAN PRESIDENTS

A dozen Americans of Ulster stock have made it to the White House, 11 as presidents, including three first-generation emigrants. Some of the more memorable include: Andrew Jackson, whose family came from Boneybefore, outside Carrickfergus; Ulysses S. Grant, the Civil War hero, with roots in Aughnacloy in County Tyrone; Woodrow Wilson, whose thatched ancestral home is at Dergalt near Strabane; and Theodore Roosevelt, whose maternal family hailed from Antrim. The 12th man was Major General Robert Ross, fighting for the English, who burned down the White House in 1814. Ulster émigrés also produced two prime ministers of New Zealand and a South Australian governor.

234

Past centuries are imaginatively re-created at the Ulster American Folk Park

▶▶▶ Ulster American Folk Park   2122C

Omagh, tel: 028 8224 3292, www.folkpark.com
Open: Apr–end Sep Mon–Sat 11–6.30, Sun 11–7; Oct–end Mar Mon–Fri 10.30–5. Admission: moderate

This theme park near Omagh, County Tyrone, has been set up with a generous endowment by the Mellon banking magnates who founded Pittsburgh, Pennsylvania. Thomas Mellon left Ulster in 1818 with his family and became vastly prosperous. The park has been re-created in the peaty bogs around his birthplace at Camphill, a modest whitewashed cottage, and traces the progress of those early Ulster émigrés from the Old World to the New. A guided walk takes visitors from a large reception and exhibition centre through birch groves. In the first section, reconstructed buildings create the atmosphere of a typical 18th-century Ulster village—a blacksmith's forge, a weaver's cottage, a dour Presbyterian meeting house where interminable sermons were preached. Costumed staff cook up griddle cakes over open peat fires, spin wool and organize 'lessons' in the village school (quill pens are used). One of the more imposing buildings is Hugh Campbell's house, where extracts from his journal of 1818, written during his emigration voyage, can be read: 'During the night every moveable in the ship was put in motion by the great heaving…buckets full of all kinds of filth were hurled in the greatest confusion through the steerage to the great offence of our smelling organs!' On 12 July he wrote, 'This day the anniversary of the Battle of the Boyne was commemorated by a certain part of our passengers to the no small annoyance of another part', which suggests that not much has changed in the intervening years. Visitors then pass through the Emigration Gallery, a replica emigration ship (complete with sound effects of creaking timbers and roaring seas) and onto the New World, where typical log barns, wagons and farmsteads of the early settlers can be seen. Of its type, this theme park is highly successful without sacrificing historical authenticity. A café, craft shop and genealogy library are also on site.

▶▶▶ Ulster Folk and Transport Museum 2134B

Cultra, tel: 028 9042 8428, www.magni.org.uk
Open: Jul–end Sep Mon–Sat 10–6, Sun 11–6; Mar–end Jun
Mon–Fri 10–5, Sun 11–6; Oct–end Feb Mon–Fri 10–4
Admission: expensive

This museum is located about 8km (5 miles) east of Belfast in the extensive grounds of Cultra Manor on the Bangor road. Typical Ulster buildings have been re-erected or reconstructed here. The exhibits include urban terraces, shops and cottages, farmhouses, a flax mill, forge and school. Inside, demonstrations of local crafts such as spinning and weaving take place. An entertaining exhibition of domestic, social and agricultural life in Ulster can be seen in the gallery that functions as an introduction to the park. The transportation galleries on the opposite side of the main road house the entire Belfast Transport Museum and include many exhibits from horse-drawn carts to the ill-fated De Lorean sports car (see panel). The Irish Railway collection is one of the best sections. Local engineering heroes, such as Harry Ferguson, receive due attention, as do the great Belfast transport firms such as aircraft manufacturers Shorts and shipbuilders Harland & Wolff—one of their commissions was the *Titanic*.

▶ Wellbrook Beetling Mill 2123C

20, Wellbrook Road, Corkhill, Cookstown, tel: 028 8674 8210;
www.nationaltrust.org.uk
Open: Jul–end Aug (and Easter week) daily 1–6; mid-
Mar–end Jun, Sep Sat, Sun 1–6; first week in October Sat,
Sun 1–5. Admission: moderate

This 18th-century water-powered linen hammer mill is a testament to the history of linen making in Northern Ireland. Here the final stage in the production, known as beetling, took place and demonstrations using the original hammer show how a sheen was beaten into the cloth. Guided tours are conducted around the mill and costumed interpreters explain the various processes. The mill is located in a lovely wooded glen with many good walks.

The Ulster Folk and Transport Museum

The pioneering spirit lives on at the Folk Park

DE LOREAN
The famous gull-winged sportscar venture funded by public money to create employment in Belfast caused a major crisis in the Thatcher years when the enterprise crashed spectacularly, amid accusations of business malpractice and fraud. Investors and employees suffered greatly, and confidence in Northern Irish manufacturing projects took a sharp nosedive.

Lakeland Counties

THE CHILDREN OF LIR

According to Irish myth, the second wife of King Lir (not to be confused with Shakespeare's Lear) became inordinately jealous of her four step-children and turned them into swans, condemning them to roam for 900 years over the waters of Ireland—300 on Lough Derravaragh (Westmeath), 300 on the Sea of Moyle (the waters between Ireland and Scotland) and 300 on the Bay of Erris (Mayo). After their long enchantment the swans assumed human forms, but as ancient, wizened creatures who expired almost immediately.

Waiting for the racing results at Birr, County Offaly

▶ ▶ ▶ **REGION HIGHLIGHTS**

Birr Castle Gardens
pages 240–241

Boyle Abbey *page 241*

Clonmacnoise
pages 244–245

Lough Key Forest Park
pages 241 and 246

Slieve Bloom Mountains
pages 246–247

Strokestown Park House
page 250

Lakeland Counties

Castle Island on Lough Key (County Roscommon) is named after a 19th-century folly

SIONNA AND THE SALMON OF KNOWLEDGE

This legend echoes the story of Adam and Eve. Sionna, granddaughter of the great King Lir (see page 236), desired the gift of knowledge, which was granted to men alone. She went to Connla's Well to search for the Salmon of Knowledge. Whoever ate the salmon would acquire its wisdom. As Sionna tried to trap the fish, it lashed its tail and the well overflowed. Sionna was swept away and drowned in the Shannon Pot (the source of the Shannon in Cavan).

GRAND CANAL

Until the early 19th century the Grand Canal, running from Dublin through these lakeland counties to the Shannon River at Ballinasloe, was a most important transportation route, and it carried freight until 1959. The heyday of the Royal and Grand Canals, however, occurred before the Act of Union in 1801, which effectively destroyed Ireland's ability to compete with the Industrial Revolution in Britain. Horses would gallop along the towpaths, hauling barges at speeds of up to 16kph/10mph. In recent years many canals have enjoyed something of a renaissance, thanks to their recreational use.

LAKELAND COUNTIES These small, watery counties—Cavan and Monaghan near the Northern Ireland border, and Westmeath, Laois, Offaly, Roscommon and Longford—form the geographical heart of Ireland, yet are usually portrayed as places to get *through* on the way to somewhere more interesting. Initially they are unprepossessing. Dreary main roads blast through on radial routes from the capital, often slow with heavy traffic. Closer exploration of these unsung plains is surprisingly rewarding, however. There are historic towns, abbey ruins and grand houses to visit and masses of outdoor activities. Highlights include Strokestown House, Birr Castle Gardens and the monastic ruins of Clonmacnoise.

Facilities for visitors are limited compared with parts of the more popular western or southeastern counties. Budget accommodation, especially campsites or hostels, is scarce, but the area has some highly distinctive country house hotels, offering good value. These central counties also offer a less stereotyped picture of the Emerald Isle. Visitors are welcomed with true Irish hospitality, with no pressure to buy sweaters or shamrock table linen.

WATERLANDS The landscape seems at first monotonous—a shallow saucer of endless unremarkable arable and pasture land, broken up by a maze of lakes and river systems. Few grand vistas can be seen; the eyeline generally stops at the first broken hedge. The small-scale, piecemeal landscape appears intimate and domesticated, although its most significant geographical feature, the Shannon River, is the longest in the British Isles, carving its ponderous course through the brimming flood plains and water meadows of several counties. It provides many things—scenic interest, wildlife habitats, an important navigable waterway and a profitable playground for fishermen and boat lovers. As if more water were needed, long canals slice through the bogs, the Grand Canal in the heart of Offaly and the Royal Canal linking Dublin with the Shannon. These waterways and the massive lakes of the Shannon and its major tributaries are extensively exploited for recreational use. Myriad smaller pools dot the wavering horizons of Monaghan and Cavan. A practiced topographical eye will quickly identify this borderland area as drumlin country, where glacial deposits have been left in distinctive ridges, or eskers (the only geological term to be derived from the Irish language) and pear-shaped hills (drumlins) forming a classic 'basket of eggs' landscape.

Laois has the highest hills, the Slieve Blooms, which rise to a modest maximum of 527m (1,729ft). Amid these low-lying plains, however, they seem grand indeed and the long-distance footpath called the Slieve Bloom Way attracts many walkers.

SETTLERS, INVADERS AND BANDITS
Patterns of settlement are complex. Invaders and adventurers throughout the centuries tramped across these mournful boglands to find out what lay beyond, and the fierce clans who established themselves here posed a constant threat to the Anglo-Normans walled up in the Pale around Dublin. The area is full of castles, dour planters' churches and the estates of great families. In Elizabeth I's time many estates were confiscated from their original Gaelic owners and parcelled out to Scottish and English landlords.

The wild border counties of Monaghan and Cavan harbour further resentment. Once part of the old kingdom of Ulster, they were torn from their ancient allegiances by Partition. Complex geography makes a national frontier virtually impossible to police and parts well deserve the sobriquet 'bandit country'. The bizarre course of the boundary between North and South seems to epitomize, by its perverse loops and twists, the irrationality of the present dividing line. There is not much reason to linger on this section of the border and, while here, it is prudent to adopt the local habit of remaining tight-lipped on political opinions.

BOG BUTTER
Butter has always been eaten in Ireland in great quantities. In medieval times it was sometimes flavoured with garlic or onions. Before the days of refrigeration, it was discovered that Irish peat-bogs conserved food remarkably well, and caches were often buried in wooden barrels where they were safe from plunderers. It developed a distinctive cheesy flavour but would last for hundreds of years. Bog butter from long ago is still occasionally unearthed during turf cutting.

239

The ruined 13th to 16th-century Castle at Dunamase

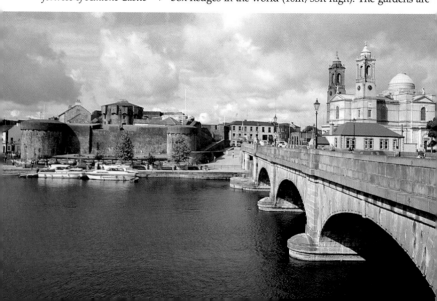

BIRTHPLACE OF COUNT JOHN McCORMACK WORLDS FAMOUS TENOR.

JOHN MCCORMACK

A legend in his own lifetime, John McCormack (1884–1945) is still regarded as one of the greatest lyrical tenors in recorded history and, fortunately, he lived in an era when his voice could be captured on early gramophone disks. He quickly achieved fame and was internationally recognized in Italy, England and the United States. He spent his fortune from his repertoire of popular music on his other two oddly varied passions: horse-racing and the Catholic Church. For his charitable services he was awarded the unusual honour of being made a Papal Count.

The Anglo-Norman fortress of Athlone Castle

▶ Athlone
2362C

The 'capital of the Midlands' stands at one of Ireland's most central points, midway along the Shannon and an important rail, road and river junction on the border between Leinster and Connaught. The town was besieged and badly damaged by Williamite forces after the Battle of the Boyne, when the defeated Jacobites retreated here and were finally routed at nearby Aughrim. Its strategic location necessitated a stronghold, and one of its most significant historic buildings is a **13th-century castle**▶▶ (tel: 090 649 2912; *open:* May–end Sep daily 10–4.30; Oct–end Apr by appointment. *Admission: moderate*) in the market square, whose curtain walls, towers and keep are still intact. The castle is used as the setting for a museum of local history; its most interesting section is an exhibition on the famous tenor, John McCormack, who was born in the town. Recordings of McCormack's voice can be heard on his own 78 rpm gramophone. Elsewhere in the town is his birthplace, on a narrow street called The Bawn. Apart from the castle, a handful of abbey ruins and a fine Jacobean house (Court Devenish) dating from 1620, there is no very pressing reason to visit Athlone, but it makes a good base for boat excursions on Lough Ree and its various islands. Of these, Inchclearaun and Inchbofin both have churches and Early Christian grave-slabs; Inchclearaun is also associated with the legendary warrior Queen Maeve, who met her death here bizarrely, struck by a missile of cheese!

▶ Birr
2362B

This pleasant, quiet Georgian town was formerly known as Parsonstown, after the family name of the earls of Rosse, whose seat is **Birr Castle**▶▶ (tel: 0509 20336, www.birr-castle.com; *open:* Mar–end Nov daily 9–6. *Admission: expensive*). The building is 17th-century Gothic and not generally open to the public, but the 40ha (100 acres) of gardens are open all year and well worth a visit. They contain many rare specimen trees and shrubs and the tallest box hedges in the world (10m/33ft high). The gardens are memorable in spring and autumn, when flowering trees, bulbs and colourful foliage are at their best. Walks lead beside the lake and rivers, around which the grounds are landscaped. The most fascinating feature of Birr Castle, however, is a remarkable early telescope, recently restored to its former glory. Built by the 3rd Earl of Rosse in the 1840s, it was then the largest and most powerful in the world, its 183cm (72in) lens enabling the aristocratic astronomer and his son, the 4th earl, to study the spiral nebulas and measure the heat of the moon. Massive supporting walls hold the instrument in place; taped information provides background history. The stable block at the castle is home to Ireland's Historic Science Centre, which has exhibitions of astronomy, photography and engineering.

The grounds of Birr Castle straddle the boundary between counties Offaly and Tipperary

241

▶ Boyle 2362D

The main reason to visit Boyle is to see the ruined **Cistercian abbey**▶ dating from 1161, founded by the same group of monks who built Mellifont. Although central and near one of the town's main streets, the abbey seems tranquil beside its rushing stream and a good proportion of it is still intact, despite innumerable attacks by warring Irish clans. The restored 16th- to 17th-century gateway contains an exhibition. The 12th-century church within the compound shows Gothic and Romanesque arches and interesting carvings.

A short distance east of Boyle is the **Lough Key Forest Park**▶▶ (tel: 071 966 2363, www.roscommon.ie; *open: daily dawn–dusk. Admission free*), part of the enormous Rockingham estate that once belonged to the King family (Edward King, drowned in the Irish Sea in 1636, was the subject of Milton's elegiac poem *Lycidas*). Rockingham originally belonged to the MacDermots, the local chieftains and Lords of Moylurg, but was handed to the King family in 1617. The big house in what is now the forest park was burned down in 1957, but King House, the family's town mansion in the main street, can be visited. Frybrook House is another fine Georgian mansion. With the Curlew Mountains close by and its excellent opportunities for walking and fishing, Boyle is an increasingly popular touring base.

AN IRISH ROMEO AND JULIET
Castle Island in Lough Key, near Boyle, is traditionally taken to be the burial place of two young lovers, Una MacDermot and Thomas Costello, the subject of a famous traditional Irish poem (*Úna Bhán—White Una*). Her parents would not allow the match and Thomas departed grief-stricken from her home, promising to return only if he were recalled before he crossed a nearby river. He tarried at the ford, but finally crossed, too late to learn that Una had died of a broken heart. She was buried on Castle Island, where Thomas used to swim his horse each night to lament his lost love until he collapsed lifeless over her grave. Two ash trees grew above the tomb and entwined over this Irish Romeo and Juliet, united at last in death.

Ireland is one of the most hospitable countries in the world. Visitor accommodation is big business, and there is a vast range of places to stay at all price levels, from modest cottages to great castles. A genuinely warm welcome, a homelike atmosphere and an excellent breakfast are features of many of them.

DISTINCTIVE HOUSES

Cheaper options include Blanchville in County Kilkenny, Bruckless House in County Donegal, Ballycormac House in Tipperary and several Glebe Houses (once providing accommodation for Church of Ireland clergy)—those in Dowth, County Meath and Ballinadee, County Cork are highly recommended. More modest but excellent value are Fergus View, convenient for the Burren, Church Villa or Dunmore Lodge (both in Dunmore East, County Waterford), Kille House in County Galway, Hanora's Cottage in County Waterford, Larchwood House in Cork and Rosturk Woods in County Mayo.

The dining room at Tullanisk, near Birr, in County Offaly

Useful publications Anonymous business hotels or luxury castles will give you reliable hot water and TV, but little of the real Ireland of conversation and idiosyncrasy that you will find in more personally run places. To meet the increasing demand for places with something special, several useful listings have been made. Pick up the booklets in any tourist office. *The Blue Book* lists a fine range of country-house hotels and restaurants, often with some historic interest or culinary distinction. Staying in most of these places is a memorable, but generally expensive, experience.

The Hidden Ireland provides an even more interesting selection of homes offering hospitality (as opposed to commercially operated hotels). In many of these you may dine *en famille*, join a country-house party atmosphere, get to know the owners, or join in locally available sports such as hunting or fishing. All the places are rural and of some architectural distinction, many are fascinating and distinguished old houses filled with family mementos and antiques. *Friendly Homes of Ireland* is a personal choice (by John Colclough, a well-known journalist) of generally less expensive places offering family hospitality in interesting settings. (There is some overlap between these listings.) Many visitors base their whole holiday on these selected houses, and although not every establishment may be to your taste, they all have merit, and if you have little idea of where to start looking, are of great help.

The grand exterior of Roundwood House, Mountrath, County Laois

Here are just a few places offering exceptional and typically Irish hospitality—informal, effortless, unsnobby and warm. (For details see pages 269–283.)

Luxurious mansions At the more expensive end of the price range, **Hilton Park** in Clones, County Monaghan, overlooking extensive parkland that includes a golf course and three lakes, offers a splendid Anglo-Irish country-house stay. Fourposter beds, elegant furnishings and lots of memorabilia add to the interest of the house, home of the Madden family for some 250 years. Organic produce from the gardens appears on its excellent dinner menus. **Bantry House** in Cork is a magnificent stately home still owned by descendants of the White family, who lived there in 1796 and helped to foil Wolfe Tone's invasion. The Whites were addicted to European fine art and furniture and had the money to support their habit; so the house has an impressive collection of paintings and tapestries. Don't miss the view of the bay from the rear of the house, said to be one of the best in Ireland. Accommodation is provided in a separate wing of newly refurbished rooms, all very comfortable, overlooking the lovely Italianate gardens. Concerts are a feature. The state rooms are open to the public, so don't expect complete seclusion. Slightly less expensive is **Ballyvolane House** (also in County Cork), dating from 1728, elegantly remodelled in early Victorian times. It has lovely peaceful grounds, private fishing and excellent Irish country cooking. **Newbay House**, closer to the Wexford coast, is another cheerful, relaxing Georgian home in sweeping parkland. The high-Georgian Moyglare Manor, in County Kildare, is set on 5.5ha (14 acres) of rolling hills and pastoral meadows. Owner Nore Devlin decked the place out in period antiques and paintings. **Ballinkeele House** was designed by Daniel Robertson (of Powerscourt fame) in 1840 and is the ancestral home of the Maher family, who dispense effortless hospitality and excellent cooking amid 135ha (340 acres) of farmland. **Roundwood House** in Laois is one of the best of all Irish country houses for character and idiosyncratic charm. It is also one of Ireland's finest Georgian homes, in the Palladian style. **Tullanisk**, also in Lakeland (County Offaly) is the former Dower House of the earls of Rosse, who own Birr Castle.

BALLYMALOE HOUSE
This rambling, Georgian mansion with a Norman keep is in farming country east of Cork. Owned by the Allen family, produce from the 160ha (395-acre) farm is used to good effect, for Myrtle Allen is one of Ireland's most celebrated chefs, happy to pass on her skills in books, television broadcasts, and through the Ballymaloe cookery school, run by her son and daughter-in-law, Timothy and Darina Allen. The hotel has many facilities and is lavishly furnished, but retains the feel of a family home and is utterly relaxing.

243

Tullanisk, in the Birr Castle estate; guests are given free admission to the castle gardens

Clonalis House (1878), seat of the O'Conors

GOLDSMITH COUNTRY
The poet and playwright, Oliver Goldsmith (1728–1774) was born at Pallas, County Longford, and spent much of his childhood in Lissoy parsonage, near Auburn crossroads. - Villages most associated with Goldsmith's writings (particularly his long poem, *The Deserted Village*) include Tang, where he went to school, and Ballymahon, his widowed mother's home. Most of his adult life was spent in London, but he recalled his Irish childhood and the gentle, humdrum lifestyle of this rural area in idyllic terms. The Three Jolly Pigeons pub, immortalized in *She Stoops to Conquer*, can be seen on the Ballymahon road near Athlone.

▶ **Castlerea**   *2361D*

The town itself is not in the least riveting, but **Clonalis House**▶ (tel: 094 962 0014. Call for opening hours and tour price), on the south-western outskirts, is worth a look. Guided tours are given by the family owners, and you can even enjoy an unusual, if expensive, brand of aristocratic B&B in its palatial bedrooms, or rent one of the nearby cottages. Clonalis House is a late-Victorian mansion in fine parkland whose main interest exists in its contents and its inhabitants. It is a rare example of a clan house, the seat of an ancient Gaelic family that can, it claims, trace its line back through 60 generations to the Kings of Connaught and the last High Kings of Ireland. The O'Conors have owned the local land for the best part of two millennia and many castles and abbeys in the region are associated with the clan. The house is sumptuously furnished with antiques and is full of archive material and family memorabilia, including silver, porcelain, costumes and manuscripts. One of its most prized items is a harp belonging to the great 17th- to 18th-century harpist, Turlough O'Carolan.

▶ ▶ ▶ **Clonmacnoise**   *2362B*

Clonmacnoise, tel: 090 96 74195, www.heritageireland.ie
Open: mid-May–end Sep daily 9–7; Oct and mid–Mar to mid–May 10–6; Nov–mid Mar 10–5. Admission: moderate
These extensive and impressive monastic remains stand in velvety, emerald water meadows by a rushy bend in the Shannon River, a place of almost tangible stillness, especially at dawn or dusk when the few visitors who venture here are absent. In earlier centuries it was even more isolated by the river and surrounding bogland, and was accessible only by boat, or along the esker (see caption opposite) known as the Pilgrims' Causeway. Founded by St. Ciarán (or Kieran) in about AD548, this Celtic site became the most important religious establishment of its time in Ireland and was renowned as a place of art and learning throughout Europe. St. Ciarán himself died of plague at the age of only 33, just seven months after the monastery site had been established, but news of his good works eventually spread beyond Irish shores. Several ecclesiastical treasures produced here are now on display at the National Museum in Dublin. The gold and silver Crozier of Clonmacnoise, decorated with strapwork and animal patterns, is one of these. The *Book of the Dun Cow*, one of the earliest and most famous manuscripts in the Irish language, was also produced here.
  Clonmacnoise was once a royal city and the burial place of the High Kings of Tara and Connaught, including the last

244

High King, Rory O'Conor (see Castlerea, left). Like most settlements of its type, it suffered depredations at the hands of Vikings and Normans and was devastated by English forces in 1552. Still visible within its enclosing walls are the remains of a cathedral, eight churches, two Round Towers, many carved gravestones and several High Crosses. The most interesting antiquities are displayed in the visitor centre. The splendid Cross of the Scriptures, erected in the 9th or 10th century, depicts, among the usual biblical scenes, King Dermot helping St. Ciarán erect the first cornerpost of the monastery at Clonmacnoise.

The Nuns' Church stands beside a quiet lane outside the main enclosure and is reached via a path through the modern cemetery and out onto the road beyond. It is worth making the short excursion to this pleasant spot; the tiny church with its finely carved arches is sheltered by tall trees in a peaceful little meadow. It was built by Dervorgilla, Ireland's equivalent of Helen of Troy, whose abduction by Dermot MacMurrough provided the excuse for Strongbow's Anglo-Norman invasion (see pages 32–33). On the other side of the monastic buildings, not far from the parking area, vestiges of a Norman castle stand on the slopes by the river. Rossana Cruises are a popular way of visiting Clonmacnoise from Athlone.

THE DEAD AT CLONMACNOISE

'In a quiet water'd land, a land of roses,
Stands Saint Ciarán's city fair;
And the warriors of Erin in their famous generations
Slumber there.'

T.W. Rolleston (1857–1920); from the medieval Irish poem by Enóg Ó Gilláin.

Clonmacnoise, strategically sited on an esker beside the Shannon. (An esker is a winding ridge of gravel deposited by a meltwater stream running beneath a glacier)

245

Many of the sporting activities of this central region are based upon its rivers, lakes and forests. Several forest parks have been created, to allow for recreation and to increase the region's tourism potential. Some of these designated parks have become rather overdeveloped, with plentiful picnic tables and similar amenities. If you prefer a slightly wilder scene, head for the Slieve Bloom Mountains.

LACE-MAKING

County Monaghan is famous for its lace industry. Carrickmacross and Clones are the two main centres and, in both cases, the craft was introduced during the 19th century by local rectors' wives, partly as a means of relieving the area's chronic poverty. The fortunes of the industry waxed and waned as a result of changing fashions and periodic overproduction. Lace is still made by hand in these centres, although the genuine article is extremely labour-intensive and expensive. Carrickmacross lace incorporates hundreds of intricate fine loops. Clones lace is crocheted and often features small raised knots known as Clones dots.

Lace-making, County Monaghan

Forest parks Lying just outside Boyle, in the grounds of the former Rockingham estate, the **Lough Key Forest Park▶▶** (tel: 071 96 62363) extends over about 340ha (840 acres) along a lakeshore, and includes a cypress grove, deerpark, ice house, temple, bog garden full of peat-loving plants such as azaleas, and many marked paths. Boats tour the lake from Rockingham Harbour and rowboats can be rented. There are ring forts and islands to explore, and a vantage point called the Moylurg Tower can be climbed for good views. The gateway and lodge of the old estate still exist, though the main house, designed by Nash, was burned down in 1957.

Northwest of Cavan on the N3, the 240ha (593-acre) **Killykeen Forest Park▶** (tel: 049 433 2541) is set amid the complex puzzle of water and islets that forms Lough Oughter. Marked walks and nature trails allow visitors to enjoy fishing, birdwatching and exploring early fortifications.

Rossmore Forest Park▶ lies near Monaghan Town on the Newbliss road and consists of 280ha (692 acres) of gentle hills and lakes interconnected by forest walks through rhododendron plantations. Just beyond Newbliss is the Victorian Annaghmakerrig House, former home of theater director Sir Tyrone Guthrie, and now left to the nation as a centre for writers and artists. Visitors can picnic and walk in its beautiful surroundings.

Haunted by red squirrels, **Dún a' Rí Forest Park▶▶** provides 230ha (568 acres) of wooded walks southwest of Carrickmacross. From the hilltop parking area are views of the Mourne Mountains and a ruined Elizabethan fortress. A wishing well called Tobar na Splinnc is set into a rocky ledge above the Cabra River, and Sarah's Bridge supposedly commemorates a lady who was so startled by a belated proposal of marriage from a man she had been meeting for 30 years that she fell off and drowned!

Lough Muckno Leisure Park▶ is a former Georgian estate near Castleblayney. Set beside Monaghan's largest lake, it offers signposted walks through beautiful grounds of mixed woodland and gently undulating drumlins. Trailers and campers can be accommodated nearby.

The Slieve Bloom Mountains Though not particularly high, the **Slieve Blooms▶▶▶** rise quite dramatically from the low-lying boggy plains that surround them, their looming purple shoulders a backdrop to many a view in this area. It is said that they are named after Bladhma, an ancient

246

A view of the fields and hills of the Slieve Bloom Mountains

hero, who once took refuge from his enemies in these hills. Later, in Cromwellian times, the Slieve Blooms again became a place of hiding for men whose lands had been confiscated by the Parliamentary forces.

The slopes are rounded rather than steep, many covered in conifer plantations, and the high density of well-marked paths and tracks (so unusual in Ireland) make them ideal for walking. A long-distance footpath called the Slieve Bloom Way runs for about 32km (20 miles) around these hills, on a route past waterfalls and glens, through bog and moorland, conifer woods and an ancient (pre-Ice Age) river valley. Though the hills are mostly too gentle for really dramatic views, the slopes do in some places drop away sufficiently to reveal the great plains below stretching mistily into the distance. Look for the rare pine marten that haunts the mountains, together with Irish hares, fallow deer and mountain goats. Good starting points for the walk are Glen Barrow or the standing stone at Forelacka. Despite their unthreatening altitude (maximum 527m/1,729ft), these hills can be treacherously misty and waterlogged, so adequate footwear, clothing and equipment are essential.

BOATING
An excellent way to enjoy the peaceful Midland scenery is from the deck of a boat, and you can charter boats in many centres on the 480km (300 miles) of navigable lakes, rivers and canals in the region. Athlone, the nearest point to Dublin on the Shannon, is one of the most popular starting points for narrow boats, and the scenery spans flower-filled banks, gentle pasture and open bogland (Athlone Cruisers Ltd., tel: 0902 72892).

Lough Key, a perfect place to enjoy some of Ireland's finest fishing

THE SEVEN WONDERS

Fore is famous for its seven wonders:
1. The monastery on a quaking scraw (a thin covering of grass grown on a bog).
2. A mill without a mill-race.
3. Water that flows uphill.
4. An ash tree that won't burn.
5. Water that never boils.
6. The great stone above the old church door.
7. The holy man in a stone (an anchorite's cell).
Many stories are told to explain the origin of these, but the grains of truth in some should be mixed with pinches of salt in others.

▶ Monaghan *2374E*

This garrison town shows a strong Scots Presbyterian influence, with solid mercantile buildings and a central square known as the Diamond, similar to those in Derry and Donegal. Its position close to the Northern Irish border is not fortunate and, although it prospered from the linen industry introduced mainly by Ulster settlers in the 18th century, it has been a hotbed of unrest from time to time. Charles Gavan Duffy, one of its most famous inhabitants who eventually became premier of Victoria, Australia, characterized the town's political awareness by founding the Irish Tenant League and a nationalist newspaper called *The Nation*. The flamboyant 19th-century Gothic spire of **St. Macartan's Catholic Cathedral▶** lords it over the more sedate classical and Regency buildings of the town centre. In the Diamond, the elegant 1792 Market House, with its fine, carved decorations, is now the tourist office. The Rossmore Memorial, a huge Victorian drinking fountain, with eight grey marble columns and a sandstone canopy, also in the Diamond, necessitated the removal from here of the old 17th-century market cross, once a sundial, to another square in the town (Old Cross Square). The town's most interesting sight is its **County Museum▶** (tel: 047 82928, www.countymonaghan.net/links/htm; *open*: Tue–Fri 10–5, Sat 11–5. *Admission free*) on Hill Street near the tourist office, an award-winning collection of local history and art. One of its prize exhibits is the beautifully embossed processional Cross of Clogher, dating from about 1400.

▶ Mullingar *2373C*

This busy town is the centre of a prosperous commercial and cattle-raising area. The modern **Cathedral of Christ the King▶** (tel: 044 48391; *open*: daily 9–5.30. *Admission free*) contains two famous mosaics by a Russian artist, Boris Anrep and an ecclesiastical museum which houses the vestments of St. Oliver Plunkett (see page 114). North of Mullingar and near the underrated Lough Derravaragh is

St. Brigid's Chapel in Mullingar Cathedral

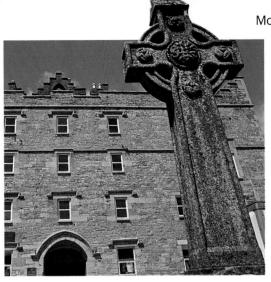

ADOLPHUS COOKE
Not far from Mullingar on the road to Delvin is the small village of Reynella, where the graveyard contains a strange tomb in the shape of a beehive. This is the grave of a celebrated local eccentric, Adolphus Cooke, who believed that one of his flock of turkeys was his reincarnated father. He also tried his favourite dog, Gusty, for the crime of repeatedly straying and cavorting with the common dogs of Mullingar. The setter was eventually reprieved when the hangman claimed that the dog addressed him in a foreign tongue, thereby proving Cooke's theory of reincarnation. Market Hall Museum in Mullingar contains a few relics relating to this extraordinary person.

249

Tullynally Castle► (tel: 044 61159, www.tullynallycastle.com; *open:* gardens, Jun–end Aug daily 2–6; May Sat, Sun and bank holiday weekends 2–6; guided tours daily 2.30–6. *Admission: moderate*) seat of the earls of Longford, with fine gardens. Inside is an interesting collection of domestic utensils and a celebrated private library, indicating the literary bent of the Pakenham family, whose scions include the present Lord Longford's gifted daughters, Antonia Fraser and Rachel Billington. Nearby is **Fore Abbey►**, founded in the 7th century by St. Fechin. This large religious community was destroyed many times during the Dark Ages, but a church dating from the 10th century survives, along with a 13th-century Benedictine priory built by the de Lacy family. The tea room and craft shop in the castle courtyard is open in May at weekends and bank holidays and daily during July and August.

► Roscommon   *2362C*

The huge **Norman castle►**, standing in fields on the edge of Roscommon, seems out of proportion to anything else in this little county town. It dates from the 13th century, though was much altered in later years, with refined Tudor mullions added in the 16th century. The quarrelsome O'Kelly and O'Conor clans seized it periodically, but its last definitive remodelling took place at the hands of Cromwellian troops and its drum towers now stand lopped and hollow around a rectangle of neatly mown turf. In the town are the **Dominican priory ruins►**, last resting place of the priory's 13th-century founder Félim O'Conor, a king of Connaught, whose tomb is decorated with effigies of gallowglasses (Irish or Scots mercenaries). The main street, with attractively restored Georgian and Victorian shops, bifurcates around a copper-domed Georgian courthouse (now a Bank of Ireland branch). Nearby is the castellated county gaol, where Roscommon's redoubtable lady hangman carried out her civic duty (see panel). Another curiosity is James J. Harlow's Funeral Requisites and Furniture Stores, a beautifully restored hardware shop and bar crammed with household gadgets and nostalgic examples of advertising.

LADY BETTY
Roscommon's condemned prisoners faced a female executioner during the 18th century. Condemned to death herself, allegedly for the unwitting murder of her only son, she volunteered to step into the breach when the hangman was ill, on condition that her life be spared. She was subsequently appointed as the town's 'hangwoman' with a salary and accommodation at the prison, and there she remained for about 30 years, performing her grisly duty with apparent efficiency and detachment. She drew charcoal portraits on her walls of some of her clients, whom she dispatched from a hinged board outside her third-floor window.

RICHARD CASSELS OR CASTLE

This architect (1690–1751) was one of the formative influences on Anglo-Irish architecture during Georgian times. Among his great works are Powerscourt and Russborough in County Wicklow, Westport in Mayo, Newbridge in Dublin and Strokestown Park House in Roscommon. He came from a Huguenot family settled in Hesse-Kassel in Germany. He first arrived in Ireland in 1728 to work on a project in County Fermanagh and soon became known to Lord Burlington and his circle. Before long he was the most sought-after architect in Ireland. His style was Palladian, with heavy mouldings and muscular sculpted stonework. His name appears most often in its anglicized form—Castle.

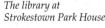

250

The library at Strokestown Park House

▶▶ Strokestown 2362D

Many Irish towns and villages reveal their Georgian origins in wide streets, but Strokestown's is certainly exceptional; originally modelled on Vienna's Ringstrasse, which had greatly impressed one of the local landowners, it is said to be the widest provincial main street in Ireland. The village is little more than an adjunct to the enormous **Strokestown Park House▶▶** (tel: 078 33013, www. strokestownpark.ie; *open:* Mar–end Oct daily 10–5.30; by appointment rest of year. *Admission: expensive*), which lies beyond the Gothic triple arch on this main street. Home of the Pakenham Mahon family, their 17th-century farmhouse was reconstructed by Richard Castle (see panel) in the 1730s in Palladian style for the Anglo-Irish politician, Thomas Mahon. Its most infamous proprietor was Major Denis Mahon, who presided over the Strokestown estate during the Famine years, and found himself so short of cash that he pressed his tenants to emigrate to the New World. Rumours spread that he was chartering the dreaded 'coffin ships' in which so many Irish emigrants perished, and he was shot dead near Strokestown in 1847. In 1979 the house was sold to an enterprising local garage firm, who gallantly resisted the mood of the times to let all traces of 'British imperialism' (including its superb Georgian heritage) lapse into ruin. The company restored the premises and parkland and established the Famine Museum commemorating the tragic events of the 1840s.

Strokestown Park House is one of Ireland's finest and most authentic Palladian buildings and gives a real flavour of the life and times of the Anglo-Irish families and their tenants. One of its many fascinating features is the galleried kitchen in the south wing from which the lady of the house could drop menus and instructions to the kitchen staff without troubling herself by any closer proximity. Tunnels allowing tradesmen and staff to perform their duties unseen link the main house to the kitchen and stables located in the wings.

At the far end of Strokestown, the **County Roscommon Heritage and Genealogical Centre▶** offers presentations on local history.

Arriving

Entry formalities British visitors entering the Republic or the North do not need a passport. The best advice, however, is to take it anyway. It provides a useful means of identification for changing money, renting a car or obtaining medical treatment. British nationals not born in the UK, or non-Caucasians, will find a passport cuts the red tape considerably.

EU and North American or Australasian visitors simply need a valid passport and can stay for up to three months. Other nationals should check to see if they require a visa.

In the North, British regulations apply. EU residents or those from English-speaking or Commonwealth countries can usually stay for up to six months with a passport or suitable identity documents.

By air Ireland's international airports are Dublin, Shannon, Cork, Belfast International (well linked by public transportation to the city centres) and Knock. If you are visiting western Ireland, Shannon makes a convenient landing point. Most European flights land in either Dublin or Belfast, but other airports are served from the UK. Flying time from London is an hour to Dublin or Belfast (90 minutes to Shannon, Cork or Knock). You can fly to Ireland from many regional UK airports. Dublin International Airport is 11km (7 miles) north of the city and has flights to Britain, mainland Europe and North America. Belfast International Airport is 32km (19 miles) west of the city.

The major airlines offer a range of tickets that can increase or decrease the price of any given seat by more than 300 per cent, depending on the day of purchase. As a rule, the further in advance you buy the ticket, the less expensive it is but the greater the penalty (up to 100 per cent) for cancelling. Check with individual airlines for details.

Charter flights offer the lowest fares but often depart only on certain days, and they are seldom on time. You may be able to arrive at one city and return from another; however, you may lose all or most of your money if you cancel your trip. Don't sign up for a charter flight unless you've checked with a travel agency about the reputation of the packager. It's particularly important to know the packager's policy concerning refunds in the event of a cancelled flight; some agents recommend that travellers purchase trip-cancellation insurance if they plan to book charter flights.

One of the most popular charter operators to Europe is **Air Transat** in the US (tel: 877/872-6728). Other companies advertise in Sunday travel sections of newspapers.

From North America, it can be a cheaper option to fly to London and reroute from there, although this will add time to your already long journey. In the United States and Canada there are many discount fares available. Aer Lingus, Continental and Delta operate scheduled services to Dublin; Aer Lingus also flies direct to Belfast. Boston–Shannon flying time is around five and a half hours.

Direct flights are also available from many European cities.

All Aer Lingus flights can be booked online at www.aerlingus.com. The following telephone numbers can be used to contact Aer Lingus:
● Republic of Ireland: tel: 0818 365 000
● UK: tel: 0845 084 4444
● US: tel: 1800 474 7424

By sea The Irish Sea is a notoriously uncomfortable crossing in bad weather. The main reason to opt for a sea crossing from the UK is to take a car, so cutting out the high costs of car rental in the Republic. Budget travellers may also use cheap rail/ferry or coach/ferry inclusive packages (student or youth reductions are considerable), though cheap air travel has severely dented even this market, and the Irish ferry scene has been marked by economic uncertainty in recent years. The main routes in the Republic are Holyhead to Dun Laoghaire (Dublin), Liverpool to Dublin, Pembroke or Fishguard to Rosslare, or Swansea to Cork; in the North you can travel from Liverpool or Stranraer to Belfast and Cairnryan to Larne. A fast catamaran service runs between

Stranraer and Belfast, Holyhead to Dun Laoghaire and Fishguard to Rosslare. Services also operate from Cork and Rosslare to certain ports in Normandy and Brittany. In summer you need to book in advance for a place on many crossings. Ask your rail or bus travel centre about combined train/ferry or bus/ferry fares. London to Dublin coach fares can be extremely cheap, though it can be a very tiring and lengthy journey. Getting to the North is more expensive. Slattery's (tel: 020 7482 1604) and Eurolines (National Express, tel: 08705 808 080) are the main operators, serving Ireland from many UK cities.

Quarantine Ireland is part of the British Isles quarantine area, which means that pets resident in Britain, the Channel Isles or the Isle of Man for at least six months can be taken to Ireland without requiring isolation. Animals from other places, of course, will be placed in quarantine. The following breeds of dog must be kept under tight control:
- American pit bull terrier
- English bull terrier
- Staffordshire bull terrier
- ban dog
- bulldog

Sited alongside working boats: the marina at Howth Harbour is fast filling up with elegant craft

- bull mastiff
- Doberman pinscher
- German shepherd (Alsatian)
- Rhodesian ridgeback
- Rottweiler
- Japanese akita
- Japanese tosa.

Camping and caravanning
Lists of caravan (trailer) parks and campsites are available from both national tourist boards; those in Bord Fáilte's brochure are regularly inspected and graded. All these sites have facilities, including mains water and electricity, showers, restrooms and sometimes restaurants and play areas.

Unofficial camping is widespread in Ireland, however, and as long as you have the landowner's permission and cause no disturbance you may camp in any field. You may be asked to pay a euro or two in tourist areas. Many hostels will allow cheap camping on nearby land with use of showers and kitchens. State-run forest parks in the Republic do not permit camping, whereas many in the North do.

Caravans can be rented, sometimes in conjunction with ferry deals. These vary from luxuriously furnished mobile homes to the picturesque, horse-drawn Romany (Gypsy) caravans of the Irish brochures (► 254 for more information).

253

Horse-drawn caravans If you want to rent a horse-drawn caravan, it is best to arrange third-party liability insurance. Expect to cover no more than 16km (10 miles) per day and stick to the quiet, flatter lanes of rural Ireland. Most caravans are four-berth. Don't expect luxury facilities aboard (bed linen and simple cooking utensils are provided, but no toilets, for example; take your own towels and matches for lighting gas burners). Before you set off, rental companies give you full instructions on routes and handling and looking after the horse. Prices for rental are seasonal and a deposit is required, and you will have to pay for each overnight stop on top of the rental for the caravan itself.

Riding horses can be rented to accompany the caravan to give another dimension to your holiday. Some of the best-known companies specializing in this kind of touring are Slattery's Horse-Drawn Caravans, 1 Russell Street, Tralee, County Kerry (tel: 066 712 2364), Clissman's Horse-Drawn Caravans, Carrigmore Farm, Wicklow (tel: 0404 48188, fax: 0404 48288) and Kilvahan Horse-Drawn Caravans, Portlaoise (tel: 0502 27048).

The road between Glengarriff in County Cork and Kenmare in Kerry

254

Car breakdown

If the car is rented, contact the rental company (their nearest contact number should be on your contract or other rental documents). Automobile Association (AA) members, or members of affiliated motoring organizations belonging to the AIT (*Alliance International de Tourisme*), may call on the AA rescue services (provided in the Republic by the Automobile Association of Ireland). Both the AA and the RAC operate a breakdown service for their members in Northern Ireland.

Car rental

Renting a car in the Republic is expensive; rates are among the highest in Europe, although they are cheaper in Northern Ireland. Tariffs vary and, as elsewhere, small local firms will often give you a cheaper deal than the major international companies. To offset this, the vehicle may in some cases be less road-worthy, pick-up points less convenient and service less efficient. You may also have to return the car to the pick-up point rather than dropping it off in another town (check drop-off charges in advance). The large companies are geared to a nationwide operation, so if you rent in Dublin and break down in Donegal you won't have a problem. Just phone the nearest office. Major companies also insure you automatically to drive on either side of the border, though you should always specify this when you accept the car; check the booking conditions and insurance cover carefully. Most multinational companies have offices at the main airports and ferry terminals, as well as in large cities. Rental charges at Northern Ireland airports, however, may be higher than renting with the same firm in the city. The tourist offices or the Automobile Association will be able to offer advice on approved companies.

Avis/Johnson & Perrott (based in Cork but with offices in most airports and cities) are the largest operators in the Republic, supplying cars for several major travel firms, airlines, etc. They provide clean, reliable cars and a good backup service.

Other large firms include Hertz, Murray's/Europcar and Budget. Rates are very seasonal. The cheapest way to book a rental car is to arrange an inclusive package deal in advance with a tour operator, airline and ferry company (fly-drive or rail/ferry-drive) rather than waiting until you arrrive in Ireland.

To rent a car you must have a valid driver's licence (an international licence with an English translation if you are a non-EU resident). Some companies specify age limits for drivers (usually a minimum of 21 or 23 and a maximum of 70 or 75). Make sure you take out collision damage waiver (CDW) as well as the standard third-party insurance. Manual transmission vehicles are usually supplied unless automatics are specifically requested. Almost all rental cars use unleaded fuel. The best-value deals include unlimited mileage.

Climate

No one goes to Ireland for a tan. It has a fine climate (mild, free from extremes, good for plants), but perhaps too much weather. As the pressure systems sweep in from the Atlantic, Ireland gets it all—and rain follows sunshine with immense rapidity. Ireland's 'soft days' of fine drizzle and low cloud are unavoidable, but it is unfortunate if you should happen to be touring the Ring of Kerry on one. Be prepared for the four seasons in a single day. The southeast is appreciably sunnier and drier than the west coast. July and August are the warmest months (average temperatures 10°C/50°F at night, 18°C/64°F during the day), but May, June or September may well be drier. Ireland has the added advantage of being less crowded in late spring and early autumn. It is impossible to predict fine days at any time of year. If the sun comes out, enjoy it while you can. If it rains, cover up or head for the pub. It probably won't last long.

Crime

In general, rural areas of both the Republic and Northern Ireland are extremely safe. The main problems occur in cities, particularly in the

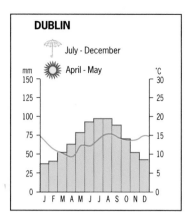

DUBLIN

July - December
April - May

ACHILL ISLAND

September - January
April - May

255

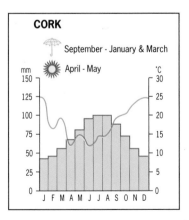

CORK

September - January & March
April - May

deprived areas of Dublin, where car theft is pervasive. Limerick also has a significant problem of violent crime and theft. Large gatherings (festivals, markets, horse sales and so

on) attract a criminal element, as anywhere, and it is sensible to take precautions with your belongings.
In particular, don't leave tempting valuables visible in a car. Personal violence or sexual assaults on strangers are fortunately rare, although women travelling alone should not take unnecessary risks (for example, by hitchhiking).

Customs regulations

EU travellers are able to import the following quantities of *duty-paid* goods for personal use only: up to 110 litres of beer; 90 litres of wine; and 3,200 cigarettes. *Duty-free* allowances (not available when travelling within Europe) are lower: 200 cigarettes; 1 litre of spirits; 2 litres of wine, 60ml of perfume and 250ml of toilet water, plus other dutiable goods to the value of €175 (tobacco and drinks allowances not available for travellers under 17). However, there are some restrictions on importing certain food items into both the Republic of Ireland and Northern Ireland (the latter if travelling from outside the UK). To obtain further information, get in contact with the Custom House either in Dublin (tel: 01 873 4555) or in Belfast (tel: 028 9035 2220).

The Irish are enthusiastic cyclists

Cycling

Cycling is without doubt one of the best ways to get around in Ireland, especially granted decent weather. The secondary roads are mostly empty, built-up areas limited, and open countryside all around. Most airlines will carry bicycles for free as long as you don't exceed your weight allowance. If you bring your own bicycle, take a spare tube and tyre with you, as Irish sizes are unusual. It is very easy to hire a bicycle when you arrive in Ireland. Raleigh (tel: 01 626 1333) is the biggest operator, with a nationwide organization of pick-up and drop-off points, but local dealers, hotels and hostels can provide them, too. It is advisable to rent cycle helmets, available in some places but not everywhere. Check brakes and tyres and get a pump and repair kit. Bicycles can be carried on long-distance buses and trains, but there is a charge. You can get leaflets on cycling from Fáilte Ireland or the Northern Ireland Tourist Board (NITB). Companies in Britain and Ireland arrange cycling holidays, with accommodation, transportation of luggage, lunches and guides, include: Celtic Cycling, Bagenalstown, County Carlow (tel: 0503 75282, www.celticcycling.com), Irish Cycling Safaris, UCO, Dublin 4 (tel: 01 260 0749, www.cyclingsafaris. com) and the Irish Travel Bureau,

Manchester (tel: 0161-976 3887, www.irishtravelbureau.co.uk).

Visitors with disabilities

A number of associations for people with disabilities give advice on travel and mobility problems. Registered drivers with disabilities may park free of charge with an orange badge. The national tourist boards both produce useful literature (Fáilte Ireland's *Accommodation Guide for Disabled Persons* is available free). Increasing numbers of hotels and guesthouses cater to people in wheelchairs and access to many sights, museums and other attractions, are being adapted. Addresses you may find useful:
● Comhairle (tel: 01 605 9000, www.comhairle.ie)
● Irish Wheelchair Association, 24 Blackheath Drive, Clontarf, Dublin 3 (tel: 01 833 8241, www.iwa.ie)
● Disability Action, 2 Annadale Avenue, Belfast BT7 3JR (tel: 028 9249 1011, www.disabilityaction.org).

Driving

Motorists drive on the left in Ireland, although driving habits can be erratic, particularly in rural areas. Hazards for the motorist include slow-moving farm vehicles, often without lights, that lurch suddenly into the roadway from field gates, or equally suddenly turn into farm entrances without signalling. Herds of cows, flocks of sheep, seemingly endless loose gravel and unexpected roadworks are all part of Irish driving. Farm dogs enjoy chasing passing cars. There is no need to swerve or brake for them; they know exactly how far to go. Poor public transportation networks and the importance of the pub in Ireland result in a high incidence of drivers on the roads with alcohol on board, though penalties for drinking and driving are severe. In short, a considerable amount of care is required at all times while driving on rural Irish roads.

Documents required A valid driver's licence is required (with an English-language translation if you wish to rent a car). Non-EU residents should obtain an international driver's licence from their country of origin.

If you do bring your own vehicle to Ireland, take the registration document with you, and also a letter of authorization from the owner if he or she is not travelling with the vehicle. Both the car and any trailer or caravan should carry an appropriately sized nationality sticker. Insurance is compulsory; a Green Card is a well-recognized international proof of cover.

Regulations Irish residents are not insured to drive non-Irish visitors' cars, other than a garage hand with written permission. A red warning triangle or hazard lights should be used if you break down. Use low-beam headlights in poor visibility. Front and rear seat belts should be worn at all times. Children under 12 must travel in the back. Offences such as speeding may attract an on-the-spot fine. Motorcyclists and passengers must wear helmets.

Speed limits In the Republic speed limits are defined in kilometres per hour and in the North in miles per hour.
In the Republic:
● 50kph (31mph) in built-up areas
● 100kph (62mph) in country areas unless otherwise indicated
● 120kph (7mph) on motorways.

In Northern Ireland:
● 48kph (30mph) in built-up areas
● 64–96kph (40–60mph) in country areas
● 113kph (70mph) on divided highways and motorways
In both the limit for vehicles with trailers is 64kph (40mph).

Roads In the Republic there are more and more stretches of motorway as roads are rapidly improved. There are three road classifications: National Primary (labelled N, plus a number between 1 and 50); National Secondary (N plus a number over 50); and Regional (R). These categories give little indication of how good the road actually is. Roads near large cities (Dublin, Cork, Waterford and Limerick) may suffer from congestion in rush hours. Elsewhere roadworks may cause

257

delays. Generally speaking roads are busier than in the past, and driving in Ireland is no longer such a relaxing affair. Roads in Northern Ireland are of equal quality, whether A-roads, motorways or B-roads.

Road signs In the Republic a single signpost may be cluttered with up to a dozen signs, in a mix of English and Gaelic. Distances are in kilometres on green Euro signs, but in miles on older black-and-white signs and even in Irish miles (equal to 2.05km or 1.3 miles) on some rare milestones, so the distance from your destination wavers as you travel! Part of the entertainment of driving in Ireland is finding your way in these circumstances, helped by local directions, often of the 'I wouldn't be starting from here' variety.

Fuel Unleaded fuel is now widely used on both sides of the border. Filling stations usually stay open till around 8pm (later in built-up areas) in the Republic and some are open 24 hours. In the North they stay open longer, some 24 hours.

Parking Several larger cities in the Republic have a disk parking system. Buy a disk from local shops or garages to allow you to park for a specified time. Elsewhere, multi-storey or pay-and-display parking areas are the norm. In Belfast and

other Northern Irish towns, park only in authorized places. Many towns have control zones where you may not leave a vehicle unattended. If you do, you may cause a security alert.

Crossing the border (See panel on page 214 for more details.) Since the 1997 cease-fire, border security measures have been relaxed, but there are still some checkpoints open. Be prepared to stop at checkpoints, state your destination and show identification. A passport is useful, especially if you have rented a car with Irish Republic plates. Make sure that your insurance covers you across the border.

Automobile Association Offices The main AA offices in Ireland are at:
● 23 Suffolk Street, Dublin 2 (tel: 01 677 9950)
● 12 Emmet Place, Cork (tel: 021 427 6377)

Electricity
The standard supply is 230 (240 in Northern Ireland) volts AC (50Hz), with mostly flat 3-prong sockets as in Britain (occasionally older round 2- or 3-prong ones may be found). North American appliances require both a transformer and an adaptor, which you should bring with you.

Embassies and Consulates
Embassies in the Republic:
● Australia: Fitzwilton House, Wilton Terrace, Dublin 2 (tel: 01 664 5300)
● Canada: 65 St. Stephen's Green, Dublin 2 (tel: 01 417 4100)
● UK: 29 Merrion Road, Dublin 4 (tel: 01 205 3700)
● United States: 42 Elgin Road, Dublin 4 (tel: 01 668 8777)

Consular offices for Northern Ireland:
● Australian High Commission: Australia House, The Strand, London WC2B 4LA (tel: 020-7379 4334)
● Canadian High Commission: Macdonald House, 1 Grosvenor Square, London W1X 0AB (tel: 020-7258 6600)
● New Zealand High Commission: New Zealand House, 80

Dublin has a good suburban rail system

DART DUBLIN AREA RAPID TRANSIT

← 14.10m →

Haymarket, London SW1Y 4TQ
(tel: 020-7930 8422)
● United States: Danesfort House,
223 Stranmillis Road, Belfast BT9
5GR (tel: 028 9038 6100).

Irish embassies abroad:
● Britain: 17 Grosvenor Place,
London SW1X 7HR
(tel: 020-7235 2171)
● Australia: 20 Arkana Street,
Yarralumla, Canberra 2600, ACT
(tel: 062 273 3022).
● Canada: 130 Albert Street, Suite
1105, K1P 5G4, Ontario
(tel: 613/233-6281)
● United States: 2234 Massachusetts
Avenue NW, Washington DC 20008
(tel: 202/462-3939/40/41/42). There
are also Irish consulates in Chicago,
Boston, New York and San Francisco.

Emergency telephone numbers
Dial 999 throughout Ireland for
police, fire, ambulance or rescue
services (covering coastal, mountain
and cave).

Health
There are no special health require-
ments or recommended vaccinations
for visitors to the Republic or to
Northern Ireland, and no particular
hazards or diseases.

EU residents are entitled to
reciprocal health care (bring Form
E111 or equivalent with you, obtain-
able from Post Offices). Make it clear
you want to be treated under EU
reciprocal arrangements if you need
medical attention.

If you are a British citizen you are
entitled to reciprocal free health care
in the Republic; in practice this may
be difficult to obtain unless you
have an E111, and you may not
find a doctor registered with the
Health Board Panel who is prepared
to treat you without charging.
British citizens are entitled to free
National Health Service treatment
in Northern Ireland.

It is advisable for any visitor to
take out adequate medical insurance.
A good travel policy will cover loss
and theft of property, cover you for
any legal emergency and get you
home if you're stuck. If you need
medical treatment, keep all bills
and medical receipts for any subsequent claim. Be sure to take some
convincing identification with you
when you ask for treatment, and
proof of insurance.

The International Association for Medical Assistance to Travellers
(IAMAT) offers a list of approved
doctors whose training meets British
and US standards.
In the **United States** contact: 417
Center Street, Lewiston, NY 14092
(tel: 716/754-4883).
In **Canada**: 40 Regal Road, Guelph,
Ontario N1K 1B5 (tel: 519/836-0102).
In **Europe**: 57 Voirets, 1212
Grandlancy, Geneva, Switzerland.
Membership is free.

*A detail from a mural at the Irish Life
Centre in Dublin*

259

Language

Everyone in Ireland speaks English, but officially the Republic is bilingual and Gaelic (Irish) is the first language in areas of Cork, Waterford and parts of the west (especially Dingle and Connemara) and northwest. Irish citizens can be heard in Irish if summoned to court, and it is an entry requirement for some universities. Radio, television and newspapers have features in Gaelic. In practice, you don't need to speak Gaelic, but you may find a warmer welcome if you try. Pronunciation is difficult, bears no resemblance to spelling and it is hard for a non-native to attempt some place-names without hearing an Irish speaker first. There are several dialects of Gaelic and pronunciation varies from place to place.

Lost property

Serious losses should be reported to the police, who should give you a copy of your statement if you wish to make an insurance claim. Inform your embassy if you have lost a passport, or a bank displaying the Eurocard symbol if you have lost credit cards or travellers' cheques

❑ Here are a few of the words and phrases you are most likely to come across:

Fáilte Ireland (Irish Tourist Board, literally 'Welcome Irealnd')—pronounced 'fawlcha'
Céad míle fáilte (literally, 'a hundred thousand welcomes')—'kay-d mille fawlcha'
céilí (Irish dance night)—'kaylee'
Gaeltacht (Irish-speaking region)—'gale-tackt'
Garda Síochána (police)—'gawrda sheekawnah'
poteen (alcohol distilled from potatoes, illegal and often dangerous)—'potcheen'
sláinte (good health)—'slawn-cha'
slán (goodbye)—'slawn'
Taoiseach (Prime Minister)—'teeshock'
uisce beatha (whiskey, literally 'water of life')—'ishka baha'
Most importantly, on entrance doors to public toilets, *Mná* means women and *Fir* means men.

And a few words that appear in place-names:
ard height (Ardmore, Ardglass)
ath ford (Athlone, Athlumney)
bal, baile, bally town (Ballymena, Ballinrobe)
carrick rock (Carrickfergus, Carrickmacross)
drom, drum ridge (Dromahair, Drumcondra)
dún fort (Donegal, Dungannon)
ennis, inis island (Enniskillen, Innisfree)
glen vale, glen (Glendalough, Glengarriff)
kil, cille church (Killarney, Kilkenny)
lios, liss mound, ring fort (Lismore, Lisdoonvarna)
rath fortified homestead, ring fort (Rathmullen, Rathkeale). ❑

The Irish seem very keen to get as much use as possible from their signposts, overloading them with countless signs—as seen here at Dromahair, County Leitrim

(keep a note of the numbers and your purchase receipt *separate* from the cheques in order to obtain replacements rapidly).

Media

Television broadcasting in the Republic of Ireland is operated by a state-sponsored body called RTE (Radio Telefís Éireann). It has five radio and three television channels (RTE1, Network 2 and the Irish-speaking TG4). There is also the privately owned TV3. You can receive them all over Ireland, including the North. In much of the Republic, you can pick up BBC (radio and television) and Ulster Television. Local radio, including many independent stations, offers blasts of Irish music, chat and lilting Gaelic (also useful for traffic and weather reports and events). British visitors will hear a new slant to Irish or world affairs, or the problems of the North, on Irish news broadcasts.

The main newspapers in the Republic are the *Irish Times* and the *Irish Independent*—both slim publications that are expensive by US standards, but a great insight into Irish life and politics. Another respected newspaper is the *Irish Examiner*, which comments on world affairs with *gravitas*. Sunday papers include the *Sunday Tribune* (good arts reviews and listings), *Sunday Independent* and *Sunday Business Post*. The *International Herald Tribune* and the *Wall Street Journal* are available in Dublin and major cities. The most widespread local paper in the North is the evening *Belfast Telegraph*. In the mornings you have a choice of the nationalist *Irish News* or the loyalist *News Letter*.

Money matters: currency
Republic of Ireland

The unit of currency is the euro. Notes come in denominations of 5, 10, 20, 50, 100, 200 and 500 euros; coins come in denominations of 1, 2, 5, 10, 20 and 50 cents and 1 and 2 euros.

Northern Ireland In the North the currency used is the pound sterling (as in the rest of the UK). Many shops in the North, especially in towns near

CONVERSION CHARTS

FROM	TO	MULTIPLY BY
Inches	Centimetres	2.54
Centimetres	Inches	0.3937
Feet	Metres	0.3048
Metres	Feet	3.2810
Yards	Metres	0.9144
Metres	Yards	1.0940
Miles	Kilometres	1.6090
Kilometres	Miles	0.6214
Acres	Hectares	0.4047
Hectares	Acres	2.4710
Gallons	Litres	3.7854
Litres	Gallons	0.2642
Ounces	Grams	28.35
Grams	Ounces	0.0353
Pounds	Grams	453.6
Grams	Pounds	0.0022
Pounds	Kilograms	0.4536
Kilograms	Pounds	2.205
Tons	Tonnes	0.9072
Tonnes	Tons	1.1023

MEN'S SUITS							
UK	36	38	40	42	44	46	48
Rest of Europe	46	48	50	52	54	56	58
US	36	38	40	42	44	46	48

DRESS SIZES						
UK	8	10	12	14	16	18
France	36	38	40	42	44	46
Italy	38	40	42	44	46	48
Rest of Europe	34	36	38	40	42	44
US	6	8	10	12	14	16

MEN'S SHIRTS						
UK	14	14.5	15	15.5	16	16.5	17
Rest of Europe	36	37	38	39/40	41	42	43
US	14	14.5	15	15.5	16	16.5	17

MEN'S SHOES						
UK	7	7.5	8.5	9.5	10.5	11
Rest of Europe	41	42	43	44	45	46
US	8	8.5	9.5	10.5	11.5	12

WOMEN'S SHOES						
UK	4.5	5	5.5	6	6.5	7
Rest of Europe	38	38	39	39	40	41
US	6	6.5	7	7.5	8	8.5

A Kilkenny pub sign

The Republic has the following public holidays:
● first Monday in May
● first Monday in June
● first Monday in August
● last Monday in October.

Northern Ireland also takes these days as holidays:
● first Monday in May
● last Monday in May
● Orange Day (12 July)
● last Monday in August

Good Friday is not a statutory holiday, but is observed as a holiday, albeit marked by religious devotion, in most parts of Ireland.

Opening hours
Times given below are general and subject to local variations. In the Republic, particularly in rural areas, shop hours may be erratic but shop-keepers are also flexible and may be willing to open up specially. In Dublin and Belfast, hours may be longer, with late-night shopping on either a Thursday or Friday.

Museums and other visitor sights vary greatly: The largest stay open all year; others close from mid-September or October until Easter. Summer opening hours are usually longer than in winter. Some museums close on Monday; to avoid disappointment *always* check with the tourist office before making a long journey.

Published times may be unreliable, or sights closed for renovation, or some other reason.

The following opening hours apply in the Republic:
● shops: Mon–Sat 9–5.30; many stores stay open late on Thu and Fri
● banks: 10–4 (*Closed* national holi-days). Many banks stay open until 5 on Thu in Dublin.
● post offices: Mon–Fri 9–5.30 or 6, Sat 9–1 (usually closed at lunchtime). Village post offices also close early one day a week
● pubs: Mon–Thu 10.30am–11.30pm, Fri–Sat 10.30am–12.30am, Sun noon–11.

Opening hours in the North are slightly different:

the border, will accept euros, but it's best to have a supply of both currencies ready if you are crossing the border.

Changing money This is best carried out at a bank; see **Opening hours**. Exchange facilities are also available at international airports, travel agencies, hotels and some tourist offices, although the rates may not be as favourable at these places. Most ATMs will accept American bank cards on the Cirrus or NYCE systems.

Credit cards Major credit cards (those bearing the MasterCard and Visa symbols) are widely accepted all over Ireland, particularly in shops catering to visitors. Charge cards, such as American Express and Diners Club, are also acceptable in some outlets (less so in the North). You can use Visa to withdraw cash from banks displaying the card's symbol. Smaller retailers or restaurateurs and bed-and-breakfast owners prefer cash.

National holidays
New Year's Day, St. Patrick's Day (17 March), Easter Monday, Christmas Day and St. Stephen's Day (26 December, known as Boxing Day in the North) are public holidays in both the North and the Republic.

- shops: Mon–Sat 9–5.30, with one midweek early closing day (Wed or Thu). Some close for lunch, while many Belfast stores open late (until 9) on Thu
- banks: Mon–Fri 9.30–4.30. Some banks close 12.30–1.30
- post offices: Mon–Fri 9–5.30, Sat 9–1. Some close for lunch, or, alternatively, all day Wed
- pubs: Mon–Sat 11.30am–11pm (some pubs in Belfast open until 1am on Fri and Sat); Sun 12.30–2.30, 7–10 (at the landlord's discretion).

Pharmacies (chemists)

Besides medicines, these places also stock cosmetics and photographic products. When closed, they display a notice outside giving the list of pharmacists that stay open late. In an emergency, contact the local hospital. Contraceptives (condoms) are more widely available than they were a few years ago (when they were illegal), with many pubs having dispensing machines in the men's restrooms.

Places of worship

Ireland naturally has many churches, though it may surprise visitors to see how many are Church of Ireland (Protestant), not Roman Catholic. This 'imbalance' is the result of the

The view from the Rock of Dunamase, County Laois

Penal Code (see page 36), which suppressed Catholic worship and encouraged Protestant church building. Some churches open only for services and are otherwise locked, but you can usually obtain the key by asking someone nearby where it is kept. If you cause no disturbance it is acceptable to slip in and out of a church during mass for a quick look around (don't barge about during the service, of course).

There are few non-Christian places of worship, but Belfast and Dublin have synagogues and Dublin a mosque as well (check with tourist boards for details). Marian shrines, such as the one at Knock, or grottoes like Ballinspittle, attract many pious Catholics, the majority of whom are women.

Police

In the Republic, the police are called the Gardaí (pronounced 'gardee'), wear blue-and-black uniforms and are unarmed.

In the North, the police force has been renamed the Police Service of Northern Ireland (PSNI) and they wear green uniforms. They carry arms, and police stations all over the North have very tight security. It's hoped the on-going peace talks will lead to nationalists as well as unionists joining this new police force to make it truly reflect the community's diversity.

263

Post offices

These are easily identifiable, even in the Republic, by the word 'Post' in green. The postal services in the Republic are expensive (postcards are cheaper than letters). In the North postal rates are the same as in the rest of the UK (a two-tier system is used: first and second class, the former purportedly buying speed). Post boxes are red in the north, green in the south. The correct stamps must be used either side of the border. The GPO in O'Connell Street, Dublin, is open longer hours than elsewhere, including Sundays and bank holidays. See also the opening hours section, page 262.

Public transportation

Local public transportation in the Republic is, in general, very limited, which is why you see so many young people hitchhiking. Things are better in the North, though it is still immeasurably more convenient to have your own transportation.

Air Regular air services connect Dublin with all parts of the country, and if money is no object, it is a very quick trip (30–40 minutes). Regular flights also connect Galway and the Aran Islands (15–25 minutes), operated by Aer Arann, weather permitting. Business travel and tourism have opened up a number of provincial airports with regular internal services and flights to the UK run by Aer Lingus and Ryanair.

Train The rail network in the Republic is controlled by the state-owned Irish Rail (Iarnrod Éireann), the rail division of CIE (Coras Iompair Éireann). Trains are fairly slow and infrequent, but generally reliable and comfortable. Most routes radiate from Dublin. The only service connecting the Republic and the North is the Dublin–Belfast Express (about six trains each way a day). Large parts of the country are not covered by the rail network at all, such as Donegal and the border counties, Clare, Connemara and southwest Cork. Fares are complex and not especially cheap—consider a discount pass if you plan to do much rail travel (see Passes, opposite). The Dublin area has its own transportation system, DART (Dublin Area Rapid Transit), a suburban electric train service operating between Howth and Greystones. The new Luas electric trams run from the city centre to suburban areas.

In Northern Ireland there are three routes run by Northern Ireland Rail. You can take a bicycle on mainline trains if there is room, for a charge.

Bus Bus Éireann and Ulsterbus respectively provide the Republic's and Northern Ireland's national express bus systems, supplemented by Dublin Bus in the Dublin area, and by many private bus lines (sometimes cheaper and faster than the national buses, though insurance cover may be dubious). Various bus operators offer sightseeing tours (such as Gray Line).

Bus travel in the Republic is often very slow, but is much cheaper than by train. Off-season services may be very infrequent, but conversely weekend services may be over-subscribed. Small villages are sometimes served by only a couple of buses a week. Many bus indicators are in Gaelic, so check your destination.

Midweek 'single' (one-way) tickets can be used for a free return trip and remain valid for a month. Bicycles can be carried (for a charge) at the driver's discretion, if there is room.

Post boxes are green south of the border, and red to the north

The DART at Dun Laoghaire station

Bus travel in the North is generally reliable and serves most areas not reached by train.

Ferry or boat Three useful car ferries across estuaries cut down long detours inland. One is at Waterford (between Ballyhack and Passage East), linking counties Waterford and Wexford. The second is across the Shannon estuary between Killimer and Tarbert, linking Kerry and Clare and cutting out the bottleneck journey through Limerick. The third is between Strangford and Portaferry in County Down.

Most of Ireland's islands can be reached by ferry, too. There are regular services to the Aran Islands from Galway City, Rossaveal (farther west along the south Galway coast) and Doolin in County Clare. The islands off Donegal (Inishbofin, Aran Island) and those off Cork (Bear, Sherkin and Clear Island) are also linked with regular ferries. Others can be reached by private charter services (such as the Blaskets, Skelligs and Tory Island), usually in the summer only. Get the tourist office leaflet *Island Boat/Air Services* (No. IS50C) for further details. Rathlin is reached from Ballycastle.

Passes Many different discount schemes operate, but you need to assess your probable usage carefully before investing in a pass. Ask the tourist office which would be most appropriate for you.

Emerald Cards cover unlimited bus and rail travel throughout Ireland for 8 or 15 days.

Rambler or Rover Tickets buy you unlimited travel on Bus Éireann or Irish Rail for a certain number of days within a given period.

Runaround tickets are valid on Northern Irish trains. Check at tourist offices for the most up-to-date information.

More information Irish Rail (Iarnrod Éireann, tel: 01 836 6222); Bus Éireann (tel: 01 836 6111); Ulsterbus (tel: 028 9033 3000); Northern Ireland Railways (tel: 028 9089 9411). For guided tour information, contact CIE. Tours International, 35 Lower Abbey Street, Dublin (tel: 01 873 1100) or, in Northern Ireland, the Ulsterbus Travel Centre, Glengall Street, Belfast (tel: 028 9033 3000).

Restrooms (toilets)
Public conveniences (restrooms) are generally available in towns and visitor sites throughout Ireland. You may see the Gaelic signs *Mná* (women) or *Fir* (men) on some, but ideograms usually leave you in no doubt which is which. Toilets in traditional spit-and-sawdust bars may not be particularly well kept.

Security

Most of Ireland is extremely relaxed; even in the tension zones of the North security measures are less stringent than before. Nonetheless, be vigilant. Leave no baggage unattended and always park in authorized places (some central areas are controlled zones where any unattended vehicles will be removed or possibly detonated by security forces). If there is an alert, you may have to move very fast. Be prepared to show identification (a passport or driver's licence). Always stop at road checks. There are no public places to store luggage in the North, but lockers are usually available at bus and train stations in the Republic. It is generally illegal to take photographs of police or military barracks in the North and if you are noticed you may be suspected of terrorism. Security forces on both sides of the border are usually extremely polite to bona fide travellers, and if you have nothing to hide, you have nothing to fear.

Student and youth travel

Discounts are available for young people and students. Check fares through specialist agencies such as British-based STA Travel or Campus Travel, or ask ferry and airline companies direct. Tickets may be subject to availability (only bookable the day before you travel, for example), so you need to be more flexible than you might like during busy periods. Check youth fares against other types of discount tickets—there are many cheap fares available. You may need an international student identity card (ISIC), Youthcard or Travelsave Stamp to obtain these low fares; in some cases a passport or driving licence will do. Eurail passes (for under-26-year-olds) are valid in Ireland.

Cheap travel concessions (such as combined accommodation and rail or bus tickets) are also available from The Irish Youth Hostel Association, An Óige, based at 61 Mountjoy Street, Dublin 7 (tel: 01 830 4555). It has about 50 hostels all over the Republic, some in attractive old buildings and beautiful settings. The

Hostelling International Northern Ireland runs six hostels (HINI, 22 Donegall Road, Belfast BT12 5JN, tel: 028 9032 4733). The 93 hostels of the Independent Hostel Owners group (IHO Information Office, tel: 073 30130) are run along rather more relaxed lines, with private double, single and family rooms as well as traditional dormitory accommodation. Fáilte Ireland runs an inspection scheme for independent hostels. Budget accommodation can become overcrowded during peak season.

Taxis (cabs)

Taxis are available in major towns and cities, at taxi stands or outside hotels, and at main rail stations, ports and airports. In Dublin taxis are in short supply, especially at night. Taxis stands are found outside hotels, train and bus stations. In Belfast black cabs may be shared by customers and operate rather like buses, shuttling their passengers between the city and the suburbs.

Telephones

Mobile phone use has seen a reduction in public payphones but you

The older style of Irish phone booth

can still find them in street booths and bars or shops (some with a sign saying 'you can phone from here'). Older-style call boxes in the Republic are blue and cream and marked in Gaelic *'Telefón.'* Some are quite old; follow the instructions carefully. Northern Irish phone booths are red. Newer automatic glass and metal boxes are replacing both types. Calls connected by the operator—dial 190 (100 in the North)—are much more expensive than direct-dial calls (cheaper after 6pm and on weekends); so are those made from hotels. Calls to Britain and parts of Europe (including EU countries) are cheaper after 6pm; to the US or Canada after 10pm; both are cheaper

The greener form of transportation

267

❏ **International Dialling**
Omit the initial zero of the local code when dialling internationally.
Access codes to Ireland from:
● United States 011
● Canada 011
● Britain 00353 (for the Republic)
● Australia 0011
● New Zealand 00
followed by 353 for the Republic or 44 for Northern Ireland.

Access codes from the Republic:
● United States 001
● Canada 001
● Britain 0044
● Australia 0061
● New Zealand 0064.

● To dial the North from the Republic, replace the 028 code with 048. Check in the phonebook or dial 11811 for local codes.
● To dial the Republic from the North dial 00, followed by 353, then the local code, omitting the initial zero. ❏

(buy cards at newsdealers or post offices). Internet cafés usually double as cheap call shops. A useful booklet summarizing telephone information and listing international codes is available at airports, and post or tourist offices.

Time
Ireland is on Greenwich Mean Time (GMT) in winter; GMT plus one hour in summer (British Summer Time or Central European Time). 'Summer' runs from March to October. When GMT is in effect, it is five hours later in Ireland than in New York, eight hours later than in California.

Tipping
If service is not included (it often is, at 12 or 15 per cent), leave a 10–15 per cent tip on restaurant bills. Taxi drivers, hotel porters, lounge bar waiters and so forth like receiving tips as much as anyone, but in general help and advice to strangers is proffered as a natural courtesy in Ireland, without expectation of reward. Tipping is not customary in pubs.

Tourist information
A list of Ireland's tourist information offices can be picked up in any tourist office, North or South. These can supply maps, town plans, timetables, brochures and information on local

at weekends. Lower rates operate between the Republic and Britain than elsewhere (cheapest of all between midnight and 8am—direct-dial from an ordinary phone only). Other countries have no reduced-rate call times. Cardphones are a convenient way of making long-distance calls sights, events, sports facilities, and so on, though for many items a charge is made. Fáilte Ireland's information sheets give summaries on many topics (such as fishing, car rental, horse-drawn caravans, Irish folklore). Maps of Ireland are often out of date and inaccurate, fine for general motoring, but not ideal for exploring in detail. Local maps, such as those produced by Tim Robinson, of Connemara, the Aran Islands and the Burren, are the best bet for walking.

Northern Ireland has useful (free) information. Most tourist offices will book accommodation for you, though you have to pay a fee for the telephone calls; it is often better to get the lists and do your own phoning. A 10 per cent deposit is taken at the time of booking, later deducted from your final bill. Accommodation unlisted by Fáilte Ireland is not necessarily substandard. Outside of Ireland Fáilte Ireland and the Northern Irish Tourist Board until under the banner Tourism Ireland (www.tourismireland.com).

Fáilte Ireland (Irish Tourist Board)
● Britain: Nations House, 103 Wigmore Street, London W1U 1QS (tel: 0800 039 7000).
● Australia: 5th Level, 36 Carrington Street, Sydney, NSW 2000 (tel: 02 299 6177)
● Canada: 2 Bloor Street West , Suite 1501, Toronto, Ontario M4W 3E2 (tel: 1800 223 6470)
● United States: 345 Park Avenue, New York, NY 10154 (tel: 212/418-0800)
● Northern Ireland: 53 Castle Street, Belfast BT1 1GH (tel: 028 9032 7888).

Northern Ireland Tourist Board
● Republic of Ireland: 16 Nassau Street, Dublin 2 (tel: 01 679 1977)

Within the Republic there are about 100 tourist offices marked with the information symbol 'i' on a green background. Those in major towns usually stay open all year, Mon–Sat.

Dublin Tourism's main office is on Suffolk Street (tel: 01 605 7700; www.visitdublin.com).
Fáilte Ireland is at Baggott Street Bridge, Dublin 2 (tel: 01 602 4000; www.failteireland.ie).

A Kinsale character

Northern Ireland has about 30 tourist information centres; NITB head office is at Donegal Square, Belfast (tel: 028 9024 6609; www.discovernorthernireland.com).

Useful things to bring
Warm clothes, comfortable footwear and wet-weather gear are essential. Bring waterproof boots if you are planning to explore the boglands; sensible walking shoes and a compass if you are planning to do any serious walking. A flashlight can be handy for dark churches, caves or castle ruins, or simply for finding your way home from the pub late at night.

Take a sleeping bag for staying in hostels. A good flower or bird identification guide and binoculars are musts for keen naturalists.

Camera film is quite expensive in the Republic.

Bring any prescribed medicines or contraceptives you need; they may not be available locally.

Non-British visitors with electrical appliances will need to bring an adaptor and possibly a transformer.

Take your driver's licence if you want to rent a car. A passport provides useful identification. Leave room in your suitcase, though, for an Irish sweater or some tweed clothing. You will certainly want to take home something from the Emerald Isle.

Hotels and Restaurants

HOTELS

Accommodation registered with Fáilte Ireland (in the Republic) has a shamrock sign outside. All hotels in the North are inspected and graded by the NITB. This isn't always a guarantee of excellence, but it does indicate that some basic standards have been met. Standards of accommodation have risen dramatically. Many establishments have been totally renovated in the last few years, with modern bathrooms and all conveniences. Some visitors may feel that some of the old-style charm and period interest has consequently been lost.

There are many splendid country-house hotels in Ireland and lots of good-value, friendly B& Bs. Middle-range places offering character and value are harder to find—there are many dull and shabby commercial hotels and seedy guesthouses with few attractions for the visitor. In high season all available accommodation can be very busy and it is advisable to book ahead, especially if some popular event or festival is taking place (the Kinsale Food Festival or the Cork Jazz Festival, for example). All the Fáilte Ireland and Northern Ireland Tourist Board offices will call around to book a room for you for a small fee.

Three leaflets are well worth looking for: *The Blue Book (www.irelands-blue-book.ie), The Hidden Ireland (tel: 662 7166)* and *Friendly Homes of Ireland (tel: 01 668 6463)*. The Tourist Office publications *Town and Country Homes, Farm Holidays in Ireland*, and *Be Our Guest* also have useful if less discriminating selections. It is also worth getting hold of a copy of *Where to Stay in Northern Ireland*, published by the:
NITB, which lists all the recommended accommodation in the province. To stay really cheaply, look for the leaflet *Irish Hostel Guide*, a list of approved independent hostels, or contact An Óige, the Irish Youth Hostel Association (61 Mountjoy Street, Dublin 7, tel: 01 830 4555) in the Republic the Hostelling International (22 Donegall Road, Belfast BT12 5JN, tel: 01232 324733) in the North. You need an international youth hostel membership card to stay in these hostels. *Self-catering*, listing cottage rentals, is also available. Self Catering Ireland (Kilrane, Rosslare, Co. Wexford, tel: 053 33999) offers inclusive self-catering vacations.

The list of accommodation that follows has been divided into three price categories, based on rates in high season (including tax):

● budget (€): you are likely to find a double bedroom for less than €100, including breakfast for two;
● moderate (€€): you are likely to find a double bedroom for between €100 and €175, including breakfast for two;
● expensive (€€€): you are likely to pay more than €175 for a double bedroom, including breakfast for two.

DUBLIN
(the code for Dublin is 01)

Butlers Town House (€€)
44 Lansdowne Road, Ballsbridge, 4
tel: 667 4022 fax: 667 3960
www.butlers-hotel.com
This restored Georgian townhouse near the rugby ground has all the modern comforts: air conditioning, modem points and good breakfasts.
Burlington Hotel (€€€)
Upper Leeson Street, Ballsbridge 4 tel: 660 5152 fax: 660 8496 www.jurysdoyle.com
A genuine institution, this rather impersonal looking glass-and-concrete building is home to Ireland's largest hotel, famous for its friendly and attentive staff.
The Clarence (€€€)
6-8 Wellington Quay, 2 tel: 407 0800
fax: 407 0820 www.theclarence.ie
The Clarence is one of the chicest, most expensive hotels in the city—it's owned by Bono and The Edge of U2 and Harry Crosbie, who refurbished it with superb contemporary design.
Herbert Park Hotel (€€€)
Ballsbridge, 4 tel: 667 2200
fax: 667 2595 www.herbertparkhotel.ie
The attractive and original décor and relaxing, informal atmosphere make this a popular choice. Excellent location beside the Royal Dublin Showroom and overlooking Herbert Park.
Jury's Custom House Inn (€)
Custom House Quay, 1 tel: 607 5000
fax: 829 0400 www.jurysdoyle.com
This is the best of these good value hotels, close to the Financial Centre overlooking the Liffey. The tasteful accommodation includes all the latest facilities for both the business and tourist market. (Jury's Christchurch Inn, tel: 454 0000, on Christchurch Place is run on the same formula.)
Longfield's Hotel (€€–€€€)
Fitzwilliam Street, 2 tel: 676 1367
fax: 676 1542 www.longfields.ie
Attractively furnished Georgian townhouse with intimate basement restaurant, No. 10; near the city centre. Personalized service, a relaxed atmosphere and good food.
Merrion Hall (€€–€€€)
55–56 Merrion Road, Ballsbridge, 4
tel: 668 1426 fax: 668 4280
www.haplinsprivatehotels.com
Four-poster beds, stand alone baths and whirlpool spas are some of the luxuries showered upon you at this elegant Edwardian townhouse hotel.
Merrion Hotel (€€€)
Upper Merrion Street, 2 tel: 603 0600
fax: 603 0700 www.merrionhotel.com
Arguably Dublin's most luxurious hotel, this meticulously renovated terrace of Georgian townhouses lies opposite the Irish Parliament and is connected to the French Restaurant Patrick Guilbaud.
Mount Herbert Hotel (€)
7 Herbert Road, 4 tel: 668 4321
fax: 660 7077 www.mountherberthotel.ie
You can expect welcoming service and pleasantly-

comfortable, well-stocked rooms at the Loughran family's guesthouse. Facilities include a pleasant garden-level restaurant, children's outdoor play area, badminton courts and lots of parking space.

Number 31 (€€–€€€)
31 Leeson Close, 2 tel: 676 5011 fax: 676 2929; www.number31.ie
These two Georgian mews have been strikingly renovated in contrasting modern and traditional styles. The guesthouse atmosphere is cosy and the made-to-order breakfast is one of the best in town.

Raglan Lodge (€€)
10 Raglan Road, Ballsbridge, 4 tel: 660 6697 fax: 660 6781
This attractive Victorian guesthouse is in a quiet residential area. All the bedrooms have private bathrooms.

Temple Bar Hotel (€€)
Fleet Street, Temple Bar, 2 tel: 667 3333 fax: 677 3088 www.towerhotelgroup.ie
A classy, contemporary place in the heart of old Dublin, this hotel provides comfortable rooms and good service; food available all day.

EASTERN COUNTIES

County Kildare
Coursetown Country House (€)
Stradbally Road, Athy tel: 059 86 31101 fax: 0507 32740
A charming Victorian country house set on a farm and bird sanctuary near Athy.

The Kildare Hotel & Country Club (€€€)
Straffan tel: 01 601 7200 fax: 01 601 7299 www.kclub.ie
Better known as The K Club, this is one of the most luxurious hotels in the country. It has fine grounds, including two championship golf courses.

Moyglare Manor (€€€)
Moyglare, Maynooth tel: 01 628 6351 fax: 01 628 5405 www.moyglaremanor.ie
Luxuriously furnished Georgian house set in extensive parkland; an easy run from Dublin (see also *restaurants* section, page 280).

County Louth
Ballymascanlon House Hotel (€€€)
Dundalk tel: 042 935 8200 fax: 042 937 1598 www.ballymascanlon.com
A warm, comfortable hotel in its own grounds, which include an 18-hole golf course and health centre with gym, sauna and Jacuzzi. Most rooms have excellent views. Woodland grounds covering 320ha (130 acres), screened from traffic noise and the road. Restaurant.

Boyne Valley Hotel & Country Club (€€)
Dublin Road, Drogheda Tel: 041 983 7737 fax: 041 983 9188 www.boyne-valley-hotel.ie
This rambling Victorian mansion, set in extensive grounds, has a traditionally comfortable interior. Conservatory bar and basement restaurant.

County Meath
Ardboyne Hotel (€€)
Dublin Road, Navan tel: 046 23119 fax: 046 22355 www.quinnhotels.com
Low-rise modern hotel on the outskirts of the town, overlooking pretty gardens. Simple accommodation and above-average food.

Conyngham Arms Hotel (€€)
Slane tel: 041 988 4444 fax: 041 982 4205
This unpretentious but comfortable stone-built village hotel has been renovated in Edwardian style with modern facilities. Good bar snacks.

Killyon (€)
Dublin Road, Navan tel: 046 71224 fax: 046 72766
Very comfortable, hospitable B&B opposite the Ardboyne Hotel, on the river side of the road.

Neptune Beach Hotel & Leisure Club (€€–€€€)
Bettystown tel: 041 982 7107 fax: 041 982 7412 www.neptunebeach.ie
This dashing new beachside hotel with old-world bar provides excellent leisure facilities and an interesting restaurant. Golf nearby.

County Wicklow
Ballyknocken House (€–€€)
Glenealy tel: 0404 44627 fax: 0404 44696 www.ballyknocken.com
A simple 80ha (200-acre) working farm in the foothills of the Wicklow Mountains, with peaceful gardens. It is transformed by its welcoming hostess into a charming guesthouse. Tennis courts available. Walking holidays can be arranged.

Barraderry House (€)
Kiltegan tel: 059 64 73209 fax: 0508 73209
A charming Georgian farmhouse, which has been refurbished to a high standard. Six golf courses and three race tracks within easy reach.

Brooklodge (€€€)
Macreddin Village tel: 0402 36444 fax: 0402 36580 www.brooklodge.com
Where the ruins of an old village lay, imaginative developers have built a delightful country-house hotel with excellent food and adjacent "village," including a traditional pub and specialist shops.

Tinakilly (€€€)
Rathnew tel: 0404 69274 fax: 0404 67806 www.tinakilly.ie
Once the house of Captain Halpin, the Victorian seafarer who commanded the Great Eastern. Though now somewhat businesslike, the house retains the imposing dimensions specified by its creator, and overlooks lovely gardens to the sea. (See also *restaurants* section, page 280.)

Tynte House (€)
Dunlavin tel: 045 401561 fax: 045 401586 www.tyntehouse.com
A 19th-century farmhouse in the main street of this quiet country village, with farmland reaching up to the back door. Large, comfortable rooms overlook the Market House to the front and the farm at the back. This hotel is excellently situated for all the main tourist attractions in County Wicklow.

Woodenbridge Hotel (€€)
Wooden Bridge, Vale of Avoca tel: 0402 35146 fax: 0402 35573 www.woodenbridgehotel.com
Dating from 1608, this is probably the oldest inn in Ireland. Two rooms have four-poster beds; some balconied rooms overlook an 18-hole golf course and there is fishing nearby.

Hotels and Restaurants

SOUTHEASTERN COUNTIES

County Kilkenny
Abbey House (€)
Jerpoint Abbey, Thomastown tel: 056 77 24166 fax: 056 77 24192
www.abbeyhousejerpoint.com
Strikingly modernized guesthouse that was once part of, and located very close to, the abbey.
Berryhill (€)
Inistioge tel: 056 77 56434 fax: 056 77 58434 www.berryhillhouse.com
This welcoming country house with open fires and antiques can be rented by the week or month.
Butler House (€€)
16 Patrick Street, Kilkenny tel: 056 77 22828 fax: 056 77 65626 www.butler.ie
This 1970s restoration of the former Dower House of Kilkenny Castle, combines stylish modern conveniences with gracious 1770 proportions.
Mount Juliet (€€€€)
Thomastown tel: 056 77 73000 fax: 056 77 73019 www.mountjuliet.ie
A luxurious and beautifully furnished 18th-century house. The 600ha (1,500-acre) estate includes a golf course and equestrian and health centres.
Newpark Hotel (€€)
Kilkenny tel: 056 77 60500 fax: 056 77 60555 www.newparkhotel.com
Set in grounds on the edge of town, this friendly hotel has been made over in dashing, contemporary style. Facilities include a well-equipped leisure centre, a good restaurant, comfortable residents' lounge and plenty of parking.

County Tipperary
Aherlow House (€€)
Glen of Aherlow, Bansha tel: 062 56153 fax: 062 56212 www.aherlowhouse.ie
This chintzy interpretation of an old hunting lodge is fitted with antiques and modern furnishings. This hotel is in the shadow of the Galtee Mountains and surrounded by coniferous forest.
Ashley Park House (€–€€)
Nenagh tel: 067 38223 fax: 067 38013 www.ashleypark.com
This graciously proportioned 18th-century farm house is set in wooded grounds, overlooking a private lake; close to Lough Derg. Fishing, horseback-riding and golf can all be found nearby.
Bansha House (€)
Bansha tel: 062 54194 fax: 062 54215 www.tipp.ie/banshas.htm
A pleasant Georgian guesthouse set in 40ha (100 acres) of farmland where brood mares and foals roam. Modest modern furnishings.
Cashel Palace (€€€)
Cashel tel: 062 62707 fax: 062 61521 www.cashel-palace.ie
Architecturally imposing former bishop's residence in quiet setting below the Rock of Cashel, somewhat staid inside.
Inch House Country House & Restaurant (€)
Thurles tel: 0504 51348 fax: 0504 51754 www.tipp.ie/inch-house/htm
The 18th-century country house (on a 130ha/330-acre farm) is furnished carefully in period style with antiques and log fires; excellent breakfasts.

Legend's Townhouse & Restaurant (€)
The Kiln, Cashel tel: 062 61292
www.legendsguesthouse.com
This comfortable, brightly furnished guesthouse and small restaurant lies adjacent to the Rock of Cashel. Back bedrooms overlook the Rock.
Minella Hotel (€€–€€€)
Clonmel tel: 052 22388 fax: 052 24381 www.hotelminella.ie
Public rooms at Minella Hotel, an owner-managed mansion in extensive grounds on the banks of the River Suir, are in the main building and the comfortable, well-equipped bedrooms in the east wing extension. Some have Jacuzzis; all have good views. Sauna, Indoor pool.

County Waterford
Annestown (€€)
Annestown tel: 051 396160 fax: 051 396474 www.annestown.com
This comfortable Victorian house, complete with wood fires and excellent food, is in a superb location on the Waterford coast. Private access to beach.
Diamond Hill Guest House (€)
Slieverue, Waterford tel: 051 832855 fax: 051 832254 www.diamondhillhouse.com
Though the rooms at this competently run town-centre guesthouse are somewhat impersonal, the Irish welcome and lovely gardens more than compensate.
Foxmount Country House (€)
Passage East Road, Waterford tel: 051 874308 fax: 051 854906 www.iol.ie/tipp/foxmount.htm
This 17th-century house, set in mature gardens on a working farm, provides good value and is convenient for exploring Waterford City or the attractive harbour scenery. Delicious home cooking uses produce from the dairy farm and garden.
Granville Hotel (€€€)
The Quay tel: 051 305555 fax: 051 305566 www.granville-hotel.ie
This historic, centrally located hotel has been totally renovated and now matches modern comforts with real character.
Richmond House (€€–€€€)
Cappoquin tel: 058 54278 fax: 058 54988 www.richmondhouse.net
This interesting Georgian house was once part of the Earl of Cork's estate. A lovely setting, antiques, warm hospitality and great food.

County Wexford
Ballinkeele House (€€)
Ballymurn, Enniscorthy tel: 053 38105 fax: 053 38468 www.ballinkeele.com
Delightful, welcoming house on a 140ha (350-acre) working farm built (imposingly) in 1840, with early Victorian feel and many interesting features. Fine country-house cooking. Private fishing available.
Clonard House (€)
Clonard Great, Wexford tel: 053 43141 or 053 47337 fax: 053 43141
An above-average B&B in a Georgian farmhouse in a peaceful location just outside Wexford. Some four-poster beds. Unassuming hospitality. Serves informal dinners—good value.

Hotels

Dunbrody Country House & Restaurant (€€–€€€)
*Arthurstown tel: 051 389600
fax: 051 389601 www.dunbrodyhouse.com*
An impressive, luxuriously furnished Georgian manor set in parkland. Croquet lawn, clay pigeon shooting and horseback-riding available. Owner-run with warmth and professionalism. Outstanding food.

Kelly's Resort Hotel (€€€)
*Rosslare tel: 053 32114 fax: 053 32222
www.kellys.ie*
This rambling, well-run, seafront family hotel has a striking modern art collection. The rooms are very comfortable (some with balconies) and leisure facilities include sauna, gym, tennis and croquet. Exceptional service and food.

Lemongrove House (€)
Blackstoops, Enniscorthy tel/fax: 054 36115
A large house in its own grounds surrounded by gardens and plenty of parking space. Comfortable ensuite bedrooms and public rooms. Near Rosslare Ferry.

McMenamin's Townhouse (€)
*3 Auburn Terrace, Redmond Road, Wexford tel: 053 46442 fax: 053 46442
www.wexford-bedandbreakfast.com*
This popular, hospitable B&B, near Wexford and Rosslare, serves good breakfasts. Golf nearby.

Marlfield House (€€€)
*Gorey tel: 055 21124 fax: 055 21572
www.marlfieldhouse.com*
Opulently furnished with flair. Both bedrooms and public areas of this aristocratic country house, once the residence of the Earl of Courtown, are a memorable experience (see also *restaurants* section, page 281).

Talbot Hotel Conference & Leisure Centre (€€€)
*Trinity Street, Wexford tel: 053 22566
fax: 053 23377 www.talbothotel.ie*
In a central quayside location. Extensive refurbishment has given all bedrooms attractive decor and new bathrooms. Day rooms include a spacious foyer, lounge and bar with an open fireplace. Informal cuisine in country-style kitchen. Children's room and beauty salon.

SOUTHWESTERN COUNTIES

County Cork
Assolas Country House (€€€)
*Kanturk tel: 029 50015 fax: 029 50795
www.assolas.com*
This is one of Ireland's most charming country houses—and one of the oldest (17th century in parts)—on a tributary of the River Blackwater (fishing available). Expect serene surroundings, period features, log fires and antiques throughout. Welcoming atmosphere and lovely gardens with croquet lawn and tennis. Excellent food (available to residents only).

Ballymaloe House (€€€)
*Shanagarry, Midleton tel: 021 465 2531
fax: 021 465 2021 www.ballymaloe.com*
A well-loved hotel, offering peace and some of the best food in Ireland (see also *restaurant* section, page 281). Part of the old Geraldine castle estate, the keep of which stands by the

mellow, creeper-covered farmhouse. Several outbuildings now house extra rooms.
Modern paintings include many works by Jack Yeats. Superbly relaxing bedrooms. Family-run with enthusiasm and enterprise. Golf course nearby, outdoor heated swimming pool, tennis courts.

Ballyvolane House (€€–€€€)
*Castlelyons, Fermoy tel: 025 36349
fax: 025 36781 www.ballyvolanehouse.ie*
An Italianate country house offering classy but completely unpretentious hospitality in a fine parkland setting. Beautiful park and gardens and country-house cooking. House-party style dining at one table. Fishing is available in the three lakes, one of which is stocked with brown trout. Croquet lawn.

Bay View Hotel (€€€)
*Ballycotton, Cork tel: 021 464 6746
fax: 021 464 6075 www.bayviewhotel.net*
Rebuilt to very high standards, reflecting the owner's wish to retain the character of the original building while providing modern comforts and facilities. Comfortable bedrooms, some with superb views over Ballycotton Bay. Friendly and efficient staff. Horseback-riding, fishing and golf can all be enjoyed nearby.

Castle Hotel (€€)
*Macroom, Cork tel: 026 41074
fax: 026 41505 www.castlehotel.ie*
This classy stone-built hotel provides comfortable rooms with en-suite bedrooms (some rather small). The restaurant serves good food, and a range of bar meals is also available. Facilities include a relaxing lounge, private dining/meeting room and leisure centre which includes heated indoor swimming pool, gym, steam room, pool table and solarium. Golf nearby.

Desert House (€)
*Coast Road, Clonakilty
tel: 023 33331 fax: 023 33048
deserthouse@eircom.net*
Desert House, a Georgian farmhouse overlooking Clonakilty Bay, makes an ideal base for touring West Cork and Kerry. Dogs accepted.

Glebe Country House (€)
*Ballinadee, Bandon
tel: 021 477 8294 fax: 021 477 8456
www.glebecountryhouse.com*
Accommodation in this beautiful Georgian rectory, with predominantly antique furnishings, is both elegant and good value. The hosts are very welcoming. Dogs accepted.

Hayfield Manor Hotel (€€€)
*Perrott Avenue College Road, Cork
tel: 021 484 5900 or 021 431 6839
www.hayfieldmanor.ie*
Cork city's premier hotel is set in its own gardens in the university area and provides old-style comfort and service with modern convenience and good food. Exclusive health club including indoor swimming pool and gym.

The Heron's Cove (€)
*The Harbour, Goleen tel: 028 35225
fax: 028 35422 www.heronscove.com*
Beautifully located in a quiet position; rooms with balconies overlook a small tidal harbour. Good food (also open to non-residents).

273

Hotels and Restaurants

Innishannon House (€€€)
Innishannon tel: 021 477 5121
fax: 021 477 5609 www.innishannon-hotel.ie
This romantic 1720 'petit chateau' style house
(tastefully furnished, with an original art collection
and some unusual bedrooms, including two with
four-poster beds) lies in peaceful riverside setting.
Hospitable and comfortable, with good cooking by
the son of the house. Private fishing available.

Lancaster Lodge (€—€€)
Western Road, Cork tel: 021 425 1125
fax: 021 425 1126 www.lancasterlodge.com
A large, owner-run guesthouse convenient to city
centre. Overlooks the River Lee. Purpose-built to
a high standard; good breakfasts. Exceptional
value. Two ground-floor rooms available for
visitors with disabilities.

The Lodge & Spa at Inchydoney Island (€€€)
Clonakilty tel: 023 33143 fax: 023 35229
www.inchydoneyisland.com
Former winner of the Hotel of the Year for Ireland.
The bedrooms and public areas at this fashionable new hotel overlooking a sandy beach are
finished to a high standard. Most rooms have
sea views. The restaurant—built on the second
floor, with a view from some tables—is
quite ambitious. The health centre has a
thalassotherapy spa, indoor heated swimming
pool, gym and sauna.

Longueville House (€€€)
Mallow tel: 022 47156 fax: 022 47459
www.longuevillehouse.ie
This is one of Ireland's most renowned country
manors, a grand building overlooking many acres
of parkland. The period features include an original Victorian conservatory, and the house has a
welcoming feel. Formal dining room with portraits
of all Ireland's presidents; superb food and hospitality (see also *restaurants* section, page 281).

Midleton Park (€€)
Midleton tel: 021 463 1767 fax: 463 1605
www.midletonpark.com
This well-appointed modern hotel lies 16km (10
miles) from Cork, off the N25 Cork–Rosslare route.
Spacious bedrooms, two with four-poster beds and
comfortable public areas.

Old Bank House (€€)
11 Pearse Street, Kinsale
tel: 021 477 4075 fax: 021 477 4296
www.oldbankhousekinsale.com
Old Bank House, a discreetly elegant, well-run B&B
in tastefully furnished Georgian buildings near the
quayside, is stylish and comfortable.

Old Presbytery (€)
43 Cork Street, Kinsale tel: 021 477 2027
fax: 021 477 2166 www.oldpres.com
This welcoming B&B in a quiet (but central) location is personally and interestingly furnished. The
breakfasts are especially good here. Sailing and
sea fishing available.

Sea View Hotel (€€—€€€)
Ballylickey, Bantry tel: 027 50073 fax: 027
51555 www.cmvhotels.com
A large old house in lovely gardens, hospitable and
well furnished in traditional style. The rooms are
large and light, some with views. Good food is
served in the restaurant where diners can enjoy
wonderful sea views. Dogs accepted.

Trident Hotel (€€—€€€)
Kinsale, Cork tel: 021 477 2301
fax: 021 477 4173 www.tridenthotel.com
This blocky modern hotel at the harbour's edge
has its own marina with boats for rental. Many
bedrooms have superb views; two have
balconies. The restaurant and lounge overlook
the harbour; the food is above-average. Sauna
and gym.

County Kerry

Butler Arms Hotel (€€)
Waterville, Kerry tel: 066 947 4144
fax: 066 947 4520 www.butlerarms.com
This famous owner-run hotel on the Ring of Kerry
was once a favourite haunt of Charlie Chaplin and
still offers the same high standards of comfort and
service. Most bedrooms have sea views; public
areas include sun lounges and a billiards room.
Championship golf opposite. Tennis court, private
fishing available.

Cleevaun Country Guest House (€)
Lady's Cross, Milltown, Dingle tel: 066 915
1108 fax: 066 915 2228 www.cleevaun.com
A simple but welcoming B&B in modern bungalow.
Rural setting overlooking Dingle Bay.

Dingle Skellig Hotel (€€—€€)
Dingle tel: 066 915 0200 fax: 066 915 1501
www.dingleskellig.com
Well-located modern hotel with good facilities,
including massage, aromatherapy and reflexology.
You will find this hotel on the sea side of the road
entering Dingle.

Greenmount House (€—€€)
Dingle tel: 066 915 1414 fax: 066 915 1974
www.greenmounthouse.com
This exceptionally well-appointed, comfortable
and hospitable B&B, just a five minute walk
from the town centre. An extension contains
six mini-suites, all overlooking Dingle harbour.
The breakfasts are outstanding.

Kathleen's Country House (€—€€)
Madam's Height, Tralee Road, Killarney
tel: 064 32810 fax: 064 32340 www.kath-
leens.net
An exclusive, modern, purpose-built guesthouse,
set in its own lovely gardens. Pleasantly furnished.
Kathleen's brand of hospitality engulfs you as
soon as you step inside.

Killarney Park Hotel (€€€)
Kenmare Place Killarney tel: 064 35555
fax: 064 35266 www.killarneyparkhotel.ie
If you have to stay in the centre of Killarney, this
attractive, well-run contemporary hotel is a safe
choice and has good facilities, including indoor
swimming pool and gym.

Park Hotel (€€€)
Kenmare tel: 064 41200 fax: 064 41402
www.parkkenmare.com
All the trimmings of this fine hotel, in lovely
grounds overlooking the Kenmare River estuary,
make it expensive, but its particular brand of
luxury is more than merely professional. It is also
remarkably friendly. Excellent food (see also
restaurants section, page 281).

Sallyport House (€€)
Glengarriff Road Kenmare tel: 064 42066
fax: 064 42067 www.sallyporthouse.com

This well-run, comfortable guesthouse lies on the edge of town within walking distance of restaurants and shops. One room has a four-poster bed.

Sheen Falls Lodge (€€€)
Kenmare tel: 064 41600 fax: 064 41386
www.sheenfallslodge.ie
Sheen Falls, a very expensive but extremely luxurious and friendly place, has views over the waterfalls. Excellent food and service. Indoor heated swimming pool.

Tahilla Cove (€€)
Tahilla, near Sneem tel: 064 45204
fax: 064 45104 www.tahillacove.com
This charming, relaxed waterside guesthouse, set in 5ha (13 acres) and overlooking Kenmare Bay, has pretty gardens and an exceptionally quiet location. Delicious home cooking. Dogs allowed.

County Limerick

Castle Oaks House Hotel (€€)
Castleconnell, Limerick tel: 061 377666
fax: 061 377717 www.castle-oaks.com
Castle Oaks, a fine old Georgian house with grounds reaching down to the River Shannon, is set in a tiny island. Features include river walks, fishing and free use of a health centre.

Castletroy Park Hotel (€€€)
Dublin Road, Limerick tel: 061 335566
fax: 061 331117 www.castletroy-park.ie
Limerick city's leading hotel is just a short distance from the centre. Rooms are spacious, and leisure and business facilities good.

Dunraven Arms (€€€)
Adare tel: 061 396633 fax: 061 396541
www.dunravenhotel.com
This well-known village inn remains unspoiled despite the hordes from bus tours. Tasteful decor, some antiques and comfortable public rooms. Refurbished bedrooms, some with four-poster beds. Good food, formal and informal (see also restaurant section, page 281). Beauty salon, gym and sauna.

WESTERN COUNTIES

County Clare

Dromoland Castle (€€€)
Newmarket-on-Fergus tel: 061 368144
fax: 061 363355 www.dromoland.ie
A luxuriously appointed castle hotel in large estate, favoured by the wealthy. The hotel has a private golf course and heated indoor swimming pool.

Fergus View (€)
Kilnaboy, Corofin tel: 065 683 7606
fax: 065 683 7192 dechell@indigo.ie
Expect exceptionally wholesome cooking and pleasant, simple decor at this reasonably priced guesthouse quietly set above the lakes.

Fitzpatrick Bunratty Hotel (€€€)
Bunratty, Clare tel: 061 361177
fax: 061 471252 www.fitzpatrickhotels.com
In a picturesque village famous for its medieval castle, this modern, ranch-style building is surrounded by lawns and flower beds. Bedrooms and public rooms are timbered, and there is a helipad in the grounds. Indoor heated swimming pool, gym, sauna and solarium.

Halpin's Hotel (€–€€)
Erin Street, Kilkee tel: 065 905 6032
fax: 065 905 6317
www.halpinsprivatehotels.com
Personal service at a family-run hotel with a commanding view of the town. Attractive, comfortable bedrooms.

Rusheen Lodge (€)
Knocknagrough, Ballyvaughan
tel: 065 707 7092 fax: 065 707 7152
www.rusheenlodge.com
This highly thought-of guesthouse in a bungalow on the edge of the village, nestling in the valley of the Burren Mountains, makes an inexpensive, comfortable base for exploring the north of the Burren.

Sheedy's Hotel (€€)
Lisdoonvarna tel: 065 707 4026
fax: 065 707 4555
www.sheedyscountryhouse.com
Close to Lahinch Golf Course and the Cliffs of Moher. A friendly, family-run hotel, Sheedy's offers unexceptional accommodation but is renowned for its food (see also restaurant section, page 282).

275

County Galway

Abbeyglen Castle Hotel (€€–€€€)
Sky Road, Clifden tel: 095 21201
fax: 095 21797 www.abbeyglen.ie
Set in its own grounds with views over Clifden Bay, this friendly, family-run hotel gives high priority to hospitality and good food. Regular musical evenings in the bar, which has log fires. Heated outdoor swimming pool and sauna. Golf tours can be arranged.

Ardagh Hotel (€€€)
Ballconneely Road, Clifden, Connemara
tel: 095 21384 fax: 095 21314
ardagh@irishcountryhotels.com
A modern hotel, overlooking a splendid chunk of Connemara's coastal scenery, the Ardagh has pleasing decor (lots of plants) and extensive public rooms. Spacious, comfortable bedrooms, many with sea views.

Ardilaun Conference & Leisure Centre (€€€)
Taylors Hill, Galway tel: 091 521433
fax: 091 521546 www.ardilaunhousehotel.ie
A tastefully furnished hotel with good facilities in a pleasant suburb near the resort of Salthill. Facilities include a gym and heated indoor swimming pool.

Ballynahinch Castle (€€€)
Recess, Connemara tel: 095 31006
fax: 095 31085 www.ballynahinch-castle.com
On the bus tour circuit, but set in beautiful scenery, this large estate house is very comfortable. Tennis courts and private fishing available in salmon river. (See restaurant section, page 282.)

The Boat Inn (€)
The Square, Oughterard, Connemara
tel: 091 552196 fax: 091 552694
www.theboatinn.com
This is a popular guesthouse, bar and bistro in the centre of the village near Loch Corrib. Excellent fishing and a choice of golf courses in the area. In summer, live Irish music is provided most evenings.

Hotels and Restaurants

Cashel House (€€€)
*Cashel Bay, Connemara tel: 095 31001
fax: 095 31077 www.cashel-house-hotel.com*
Cashel House, a peaceful, luxuriously furnished
small hotel in a white-painted Victorian house
by the coast, has lush, subtropical gardens.
Many antiques and excellent food and wines.

Galway Ryan Hotel (€€–€€€)
*Dublin Road, Galway tel: 091 753181
fax: 091 753187 www.ryan-hotels.com*
A modern comfortable hotel with refurbished public
areas, including a spacious, well-decorated lounge
and health club.

Killary Lodge (€–€€)
*Leenane tel: 095 42276 fax: 095 42314
www.killary.com*
In common ownership with a nearby adventure
centre, this guesthouse provides informal comfort
and good food in a spectacular lake setting.
Adventure sports such as mountain biking, rock
climbing and kayaking are available.

Lochlurgain Hotel (€)
*22 Monksfield, Upper Salthill, Galway
tel: 019 529595 fax: 091 522399
www.lochlurgain.com*
A family-run hotel near the promenade and beach.

Rock Glen Country House Hotel (€€€)
*Clifden, Connemara tel: 095 21035 or 095
21393 fax: 095 21737 rockglen@
manorhousehotels.ie*
This traditional hotel occupies a lovely setting
above the bay. Inside it is solidly comfortable
and has a relaxing and friendly air—and
good food.

Ross Lake House Hotel (€€)
*Rosscahill, Oughterard, Connemara
tel: 091 550109 fax: 091 550184
www.rosslakehotel.com*
This modern, Georgian-style house is at the end
of a winding country road in a panoramic garden
setting. Family-run, with well-furnished rooms and
a comfortable, relaxed atmosphere. Four-poster
bed available. Golf, lake fishing and boating can
all be enjoyed in the area.

Waterfall Lodge (€)
*Oughterard, Connemara tel: 091 552168
www.waterfalllodge.net*
An elegant period residence beside a river and
waterfall, with private fishing. Antique furnishings, wooden floors, log fires. Nearby activities
include pony trekking, climbing, golf and fishing.

Zetland Country House Hotel (€€€)
*Cashel Bay tel: 095 31111 fax: 095 31117
www.zetland.com*
Sophisticated, comfortable country house hotel,
with spacious public rooms and large bedrooms
furnished with antiques. Wonderful views and
good food served in the restaurant.

County Mayo
Gray's Guest House (€)
*Dugort Achill Island tel: 098 43244 or
098 43315*
Family-run guesthouse with numerous sitting
rooms and sun lounges for quiet relaxation;
open fires, genuine hospitality and garden.
No-smoking dining room. Self-contained family
villa also available.

Hotel Westport (€€).
*Newport Road, Westport, Mayo
tel: 098 25122 fax: 098 26739 www.hotel-
westport.ie*
Set in parkland next to Westport House.
Spacious restaurant and comfortable rooms,
including six suites and one room with a four-
poster bed. Swimming pool, sauna and gym.

Olde Railway Hotel (€€)
*The Mall, Westport tel: 098 25166
fax: 098 25090 www.anu.ie/railwayhotel*
Characterful old coaching inn with open turf
fires, set on a tree-lined mall overlooking the
river. Comfortably refurbished in traditional style.
En-suite bedrooms in varying sizes, some with
four-poster beds.

Welcome Inn Hotel (€–€€)
*Castlebar, Mayo tel: 094 22288 or
094 22054 fax: 094 21766
www.welcomeinnhotel.com*
This central hotel with a Tudor façade has
modern facilities. Rooms are well equipped;
disco on some evenings, also traditional Irish
music in summer.

NORTHWESTERN COUNTIES

County Donegal
Abbey Hotel (€€)
*The Diamond, Donegal tel: 074 97 21014 fax:
074 97 21014 www.whites-hotelsireland.com*
An owner-managed hotel in the centre of the town.
Four-poster beds. Heated indoor pool. Golf nearby.

Castle Grove Country House & Restaurant
(€–€€)
*Castlegrove, Ballymaleel tel: 074 91 51118
fax: 074 91 51384 www.castlegrove.com*
Elegant country house just outside Letterkenny,
set in well-maintained gardens and parkland
and furnished with antiques. Spacious, comfortable bedrooms; good food—restaurant open to
non-residents.

Fort Royal Hotel (€€–€€€)
*Rathmullan tel: 074 91 58100 fax: 074 91
58103 www.fortroyalhotel.com*
Period house overlooking Lough Swilly.
Comfortable and restful, with attractively deco-
rated bedrooms and pleasant public areas.
Croquet, tennis and golf are all available.

Harvey's Point Country Hotel (€€€)
*Lough Eske, Donegal tel: 074 97 22208
fax: 074 97 22352 www.harveyspoint.com*
Swiss-owned modern hotel with alpine
atmosphere, scenically located on the shores
of the lough. Eighteen rooms have four-poster
beds. Good facilities and fine food (see also
restaurants section, page 282).

Rossaor House (€)
*Ballyliffin tel: 074 93 76498 fax: 074 93
76498 www.ballyliffin.com/rossaor*
Hospitable and very comfortable modern house
which has spectacular views. The hotel stands
among mature gardens in a peaceful setting on
the Inishowen peninsula.

Sand House (€€–€€€)
*Rossnowlagh tel: 071 98 51777
fax: 071 98 52100 www.sandhouse-hotel.ie*
Long-established, family-run, castellated resort

otel on one of Donegal's best beaches. Many of the rooms have sea views. Inside it is lively but relaxing, with open fires and traditional furnishings.

Smuggler's Creek (€)
Rossnowlagh tel: 071 98 52366
fax: 071 98 22000
Cheerful and popular bistro-style bar overlooking the bay. Bedrooms are fresh and clean with floral wallpapers and modern pine. Breakfast served in conservatory extension with lovely views (see also restaurants section, page 283).

County Sligo
Cruckawn House (€)
Ballymote/Boyle Road Tobercurry
tel/fax: 071 91 85188
www.sligotourism.com/cruckawn
This attractively decorated guesthouse is family-run and offers comfortable accommodation. It has good facilities, including a gym and golf and salmon and coarse fishing are available nearby.

Sligo Park Hotel (€€–€€€)
Pearse Road, Sligo tel: 071 91 60291
fax: 071 91 69556 www.leehotels.ie
Set in parkland on the southern edge of Sligo, this hotel is an ideal touring base for the attractions of Yeats Country, and is also near Rosses Point Golf Club. All rooms have modern facilities, in particular the excellent 'executive' rooms. Health centre with heated indoor pool; good beaches nearby.

Southern Hotel (€€)
Strandhill Road, Sligo tel: 071 91 2101 fax: 071 91 0328 www.sligosouthernhotel.com
An oasis in the middle of Sligo town, this period-fronted hotel and leisure centre has a swimming pool and gym. The garden restaurant is perfect for breakfast in summer.

NORTHERN IRELAND

County Antrim
Dobbins Inn (€€)
6–8 High Street, Carrickfergus BT38 7AP
tel: 028 9335 1905 fax: 028 9335 1905
www.dobbinsinnhotel.co.uk
Historic family-run inn in town centre, offering plain accommodation with private baths. Popular, lively bar; good snacks and morning coffee.

Londonderry Arms (€€)
20 Harbour Road, Carnlough BT44 0EU
tel: 028 2888 5255 fax: 028 2888 5263
www.glensofantrim.com
Creeper-covered coaching inn with seaside garden. Some rooms are furnished with antiques, while others are modern and functional. Hearty Irish food is served in the dining room, accompanied by traditional music in summer. Private fishing. Golf available by arrangement.

County Down
The Narrows (€–€€)
8 Shore Road, Portaferry BT22 1JY
tel: 028 4272 8148 fax: 028 4272 8105
www.narrows.co.uk
Built around an 18th-century courtyard, the Narrows has spacious guestrooms and a restaurant with a reputation for imaginative, skilfully prepared food.

Portaferry (€€)
10 The Strand, Portaferry BT22 1PE
tel: 028 4272 8231 fax: 028 4272 8999
www.portaferryhotel.com
Traditional inn overlooking Strangford Lough, a stone's throw from the ferry. Well-kept modern rooms. Serves predictable, but enjoyable, seafood.

Slieve Donard Hotel (€€–€€€)
Downs Road Newcastle BT33 0AH
tel: 028 4372 3681 fax: 028 4372 4830
www.hastingshotels.com
This large Victorian redbrick hotel adjoining the Royal County Down Golf Links and the beach is at the foot of the Mountains of Mourne, in 2ha (6 acres) of gardens. Comfortable, well-furnished bedrooms, spacious public areas and excellent facilities, including a heated indoor pool.

County Fermanagh
Dromard House (€)
Tamlaght, Enniskillen BT74 4HR tel: 028 6638 7250 dromardhouse@yahoo.co.uk
Stately, 19th-century Dromard House is set on a conservation farm with its own woodland trail down to the shores of Lough Erne. Modern accommodation in a converted stable block; breakfast in the Victorian-style dining room in the main house. Private fishing available.

Mahons Hotel (€€)
Mill Street, Irvinestown BT74 1GS
tel: 028 6862 1656 or 028 6862 8344
www.mahonshotel.co.uk
For over 100 years the Mahon family have been welcoming guests to this popular hotel. Characterful but with modern comforts and amenities. Bar, lounges, coffee shop, restaurant. Horseback-riding and golf available.

County Londonderry
Beech Hill Country House Hotel (€€–€€€)
32 Ardmore Road, Londonderry BT47 3QP
tel: 028 7134 9279 fax: 028 7134 5366
www.beech-hill.com
Comfortable country house with antiques, set in 13ha (32 acres) of woodlands and gardens, close to the city. Public areas include a bar and airy restaurant overlooking the garden. Genuine hospitality and good food. Facilities include a gym and sauna.

Everglades Hotel (€€)
Prehen Road, Londonderry BT47 2NH
tel: 028 7134 6722 fax: 028 7134 9200
www.hastingshotels.com
Modern hotel alongside the A5 and the River Foyle. Cheerfully decorated bedrooms, including one with a four-poster bed. Enthusiastic staff.

Greenhill House (€)
24 Greenhill Road, Aghadowey, Coleraine BT51 4EU tel: 028 7086 8241 fax: 028 7086 8365 www.greenhill.house.btinternet.co.uk
Georgian farmhouse in secluded countryside. Relaxed and welcoming atmosphere with substantial country cooking.

Radisson Roe Park Hotel and Golf Resort (€€€)
Roe Park, Limavady, Derry BT49 9LB
tel: 028 7772 2222 fax: 028 7772 2313
www.radissonroepark.com
Relaxation and elegance are on offer at this hotel, with a golf course, health club and beauty salon.

LAKELAND COUNTIES

County Laois
O'Sullivan Guesthouse (€)
8 Kelly Villa Park, Portlaoise tel: 0502 22774
Welcoming, family-run guesthouse with a friendly atmosphere, offering pleasant rooms and good value.

County Monaghan
Nuremore Hotel (€€–€€€)
Carrickmacross tel: 042 966 1438
fax: 042 966 1853 www.nuremore-hotel.ie
With impressive grounds, well-maintained gardens and its own golf course, this is the leading hotel in a wide area and offers spacious accommodation and excellent facilities, including indoor heated pool, tennis and fishing.

County Roscommon
Abbey Hotel (€€)
Galway Road, Roscommon tel: 0903 26240
fax: 0903 26021 www.abbeyhotel.ie
Fine, carefully restored 19th-century manor house. Rooms decorated in traditional period style, with modern facilities. Some four-poster beds. Comfortable foyer, lounge, bar, restaurant and gardens. Indoor heated pool; golf available by arrangement.

County Westmeath
Hodson Bay Hotel (€€€)
Hodson Bay Athlone tel: 090 644 2000
fax: 090 644 2020 www.hodsonbayhotel.com
A lovely lakeside position, high standards of accommodation and excellent facilities make this the leading hotel in the area. Good food, golf and water activities. Indoor heated pool.

Royal Hoey Hotel (€)
Mardyke Street, Athlone tel: 090 64 72924
fax: 090 64 75194
Family-run hotel in the centre of town, proud of its tradition of warm hospitality. Rooms are carefully maintained and well appointed, with an elevator to all floors; snacks are available all day in the coffee shop.

Woodlands Farmhouse (€)
Horseleap, Streamstown tel: 044 26414
Large, attractive house in 48ha (120 acres) of sylvan woodland off the Mullingar–Athlone road.

RESTAURANTS

The following restaurants have also been divided into three price categories: budget (€), moderate (€€) and expensive (more than €€€).

DUBLIN

(the code for Dublin is 01)

Bad Ass Café (€)
9–11 Crown Alley, Temple Bar, 2
tel: 671 2596
Lively pizza place in converted warehouse where Sinéad O'Connor (Irish songstress) was once a waitress. Popular with all age groups.

Bewley's Oriental Café (€)
78–79 Grafton Street tel: 672 7719
Coffee shop *par excellence*, embellished with mahogany and stained glass. Bewley's new Café Theatre is located in the former Oriental room hosting lunchtime drama and evening cabaret, jazz and comedy. Flashy fish restaurant Mackerel upstairs.

Burdock's (€)
2 Werburgh Street, 2 tel: 454 0306
A legend in fish and chips. Closed Sunday.

Chapter One (€€€)
The Dublin Writers' Museum, 18–19 Parnell Square, 1 tel: 873 2266
Cellar restaurant below the Writers' Museum; great atmosphere and reliably good food.

Cookes Café (€€€)
14 South William Street, 2 tel: 679 0536
Fashionable café-style restaurant. Cool, airy rooms and an appetizing mixture of modern and classical dishes are served.

Diep Le Shaker (€€–€€€)
55 Pembroke Lane off Pembroke Street, 2
tel: 661 1829
Chic, contemporary restaurant on two floors in a laneway near Fitzwilliam Square, featuring Chinese dishes (marked in blue on the menu) and Thai (marked in red). Hospitable service.

L'Écrivain (€€€)
109a Lower Baggot Street, 2 tel: 661 1919
One of the best restaurants in town. You will find delicious contemporary food served in a smart yet informal setting.

Elephant and Castle (€€)
18 Temple Bar, 2 tel: 679 3121
Bustling, youthful venue for drinks or dinner. Eclectic, Californian-style cuisine—burgers, guacamole and tortilla chips, pasta, omelets.

Fitzers, National Gallery Restaurant (€)
Merrion Square, 2 tel: 661 4496
Good self-service restaurant to stave off hunger brought on by cultural overdose. Reasonably priced wine. Open daytime only. Fitzers also has outlets in Temple Bar (tel: 679 0440) and Dawson Street (tel: 667 1155), all open evenings.

Les Frères Jacques (€€–€€€)
74 Dame Street, 2 tel: 679 4555
Very popular, very French restaurant. Delicious, if pricey, food and good atmosphere.

Gallagher's Boxty House (€–€€)
20 Temple Bar, 2 tel: 677 2762
A formula based on griddled Irish potato cakes (boxties) wrapping up all kinds of savory fillings. Bacon and cabbage, champ, smoked fish and other Irish fare. Always popular. Modern country decor of pine and pottery.

L'Gueuleton (€€)
2 Fade Street, 2 tel: 675 3708
This authentic French eatery might be small but the hearty peasant dishes and quality wine list make it stand out among the city's newer restaurants. Interesting dessert menu includes chocolate beetroot brownie.

Imperial (€€)
12a Wicklow Street, 2 tel: 677 2580
Superior Chinese, specializing in dim sum. Popular at Sunday lunchtime. Good value if you stick to tea rather than wine.

278

Jacob's Ladder (€€€)
4 Nassau Street, 2 tel: 670 3865
Minimalist, upstairs restaurant overlooking the
playing fields of Trinity College. Owner-chef Adrian
Roche cooks in the new Irish style with international
influences.

Kilkenny Restaurant & Café (€)
Nassau Street, 2 tel: 677 7066
At the Kilkenny shop. Excellent self-service coffee
shop and restaurant, capitalizing on the success of
the original in Kilkenny. Always busy at lunchtime.

Locks (€€€)
1 Windsor Terrace, 2 tel: 454 3391
Situated near poet Patrick Kavanagh's favourite
spot on the Grand Canal, a genuinely warm welcome awaits you at this adorably Soigné country-
house style restaurant.

Mermaid Café (€€)
69–70 Dame Street, 2 tel: 670 8236
Imaginative American-inspired cooking and
interesting decor in a small restaurant on the
edge of Temple Bar.

No. 10 (€€€)
*Longfield's Hotel, Fitzwilliam Street, 2
tel: 676 1367*
This intimate restaurant, in the basement of a city
centre hotel, serves a successful blend of French
and Irish cooking. (See also restaurants section,
page 270.)

One Pico (€€–€€€)
5–6 Molesworth Place, 2 tel: 676 0300
This elegant restaurant seems traditional, but the
cooking is contemporary. Ranks among Dublin's
best restaurants.

101 Talbot (€€)
101 Talbot Street, 1 tel: 874 5011
Relaxed and informal restaurant on the upper
floor, on a popular shopping street north of the
river. Healthy mixture of European and Eastern
dishes. Near the Abbey Theatre.

Pasta Fresca (€)
3–4 Chatham Street, 2 tel: 679 2402
Stylish Italian cuisine, including good versions of
well-known favourites and more unusual things.
The pasta, of course, is *fresca* (fresh).

Patrick Guilbaud (€€€)
21 Upper Merrion Street, 2 tel: 676 4192
Adjacent to the Merrion Hotel, the hushed, reveren-
tial atmosphere has modified somewhat but this
remains *cuisine sérieuse*: mostly classic French,
with an occasional pig's trotter thrown in for regional
interest. Business clients dine in discretion here.

Queen of Tarts (€)
4 Cork Hill, Dame Street, 2 tel: 670 7499
Gorgeous display of scrumptious homemade
cakes, tarts, cookies and savoury treats await you
in this tiny traditional teashop. Nice for coffee,
light lunch or afternoon tea, seven days a week.

Rajdoot Tandoori (€€)
*26–28 Clarendon Street, Westbury Centre, 2
tel: 679 4274*
High-quality Moghul dishes are on the menu here,
served in an elegant, discreetly formal setting.

Roly's Bistro (€€€)
7 Ballsbridge Terrace, 4 tel: 668 2611
One of the most popular restaurants in town. A
great atmosphere with delicious, reasonably priced
dishes and excellent service.

Shalimar (€€–€€€)
*17 South Great George's Street, 2
tel: 671 0738*
Yet another of Dublin's surprising ethnic winners.
North Indian and Pakistani cooking.

La Stampa (€€–€€€)
35 Dawson Street, 2 tel: 677 8611
Elegant, mirrored surroundings reflect a serious
but unstuffy interest in food. Despite the name,
the style is French.

The Tea Rooms (€€€)
*The Clarence, 6–8 Wellington Quay, 2
tel: 670 9000*
A stunning room sets off a varied menu of modern
European dishes. Excellent service.

Thornton's (€€€)
1 Portobello Road, 8 tel: 454 9067
In an off-the-beaten-track, canalside location
Kevin Thornton—widely regarded as Ireland's
finest chef—runs this small but perfectly
formed two-story restaurant with his wife,
Muriel and a very professional, mostly
French, staff. Seriously good cooking and
excellent service.

EASTERN COUNTIES

279

County Dublin
Abbey Tavern (€€–€€€)
Abbey Street, Howth tel: 01 839 0307
Old-world tavern (parts of the building can
be dated back to the 13th century) specializing
in fish. Traditional Irish music most nights
(separate annex). Bar meals available at
lunchtime.

Blue Orchid (€€)
*Newpark Centre, Newtownpark Avenue,
Blackrock tel: 01 283 1767*
Acclaimed traditional Thai menu with extensive
wine list.

Brasserie Na Mara (€€€)
*Railway Station, Harbour Road, Dun Laoghaire
tel: 01 280 0509*
Contemporary style and cooking in one of Ireland's
earliest railroad stations. Fresh seafood dishes
are a house special.

Guinea Pig (€€)
*17 Railway Road, Dalkey
tel: 01 285 9055*
Seafood dishes are served up by a former local
mayor. There is also a good-value early bird dinner
menu.

King Sitric (€€€)
East Pier, Howth tel: 01 832 5235
Celebrated seafood in delightful harbourside
setting. Completely rebuilt in 1999—the
restaurant is now on the upper floor and there
are eight guest bedrooms.

Red Bank (€€)
7 Church Street, Skerries tel: 01 849 1005
Relaxing family-run seafood restaurant in
converted bank. Lunch Sundays only.

County Kildare
Barberstown Castle (€€€)
Straffan tel: 01 628 8157
Imaginative dishes served in the impressive
16th-century stone banqueting hall.

Hotels and Restaurants

Moyglare Manor (€€€)
Moyglare, Maynooth tel: 01 628 6351
Elaborate French menu complements the
sumptuous decor (see also *hotels* section, page
271). Outstanding wine list.

County Louth
Black Bull Inn (€€)
*Dublin Road, Drogheda
tel: 041 983 7139*
Interesting, friendly roadside pub/restaurant and
delicatessen. Good value all-day food.
Forge Gallery (€€)
Church Street, Collon tel: 041 982 6272
Well-established restaurant, decorated with the
work of local artists. Generous portions of French
provincial and traditional Irish cooking.
Jordans (€€)
Carlingford tel: 042 937 3223
Village centre restaurant with rooms. Good fish
and baking, with some surprises.

County Meath
Station House (€€)
Kilmessan tel: 046 25239
Local fresh produce served in calm, unflashy setting.

County Wicklow
Avoca Handweavers (€)
Kilmacanogue tel: 01 286 7466
Stylish home cooking that's as healthy as it is
delicious. There is also delicatessen.
The Hungry Monk (€€)
*Southview Church Road, Greystones
tel: 01 287 5759*
This unusual restaurant situated on an upper
floor is run with style and flair. Particularly
good for Sunday lunch. There is also a great
wine list.
Rathsallagh House (€€€)
Dunlavin tel: 045 403112
This classy dining room serves interesting
country game cooking, and the menu also
includes some more sophisticated fare.
Tinakilly (€€€)
Rathnew tel: 0404 69274
Elegant Irish/French cooking in formal surroundings
(see also *hotels* section, page 271).
Tree of Idleness (€€)
Seafront, Bray tel: 01 286 3498
Unusually excellent Greek-Cypriot cooking in a
restaurant situated in a Victorian house. Open for
dinner only.

SOUTHEASTERN COUNTIES

County Carlow
Lord Bagenal Inn (€€–€€€)
Leighlinbridge tel: 059 97 21668
Famous old riverside inn serving a good range
of undemanding food in the bar, with more
sophisticated French cuisine served up in the
restaurant. Open fires and rustic decor. Guest
accommodation available.

County Kilkenny
Café Sol (€–€€)
William Street, Kilkenny tel: 056 77 64987

Fun café-restaurant serving inexpensive home-style
daytime fare changing to more ambitious menus
for evening diners.
Kilkenny Design Centre (€)
Castle Yard, Kilkenny tel: 056 77 22118
This sparkling self-service restaurant can be
found in attractive upper floors of the castle
stable building. It houses a fine selection of Irish
craft products.

County Tipperary
Angela's Wholefood Restaurant (€)
*14 Abbey Street, Clonmel
tel: 052 26899*
A good organic café which serves healthy
daytime snacks.
Chez Hans (€€)
Rockside, Cashel tel: 062 61177
Parisian bistro style in the setting of an old Baptist
church. Generous portions. Local Cashel blue
cheese figures on the menu.
Spearman Restaurant (€€)
97 Main Street, Cashel tel: 062 61143
Down-to-earth, family-run restaurant offering
efficiently served, good value lunches and more
adventurous evening meals.

County Waterford
Dwyers (€€)
*8 Mary Street, Waterford
tel: 051 877478*
Pleasantly intimate restaurant a block or two back
from the waterside. Small, interesting menu. Open
evenings only.
Ship Inn (€€–€€€)
Dock Road, Dunmore East tel: 051 383144
Nautically decorated bar/restaurant serving
interesting fish dishes.
Waterford Castle (€€€)
*The Island, Ballinakill, Waterford
tel: 051 879316*
The restaurant serves classily presented
gourmet food (lobster, asparagus, poached
salmon) and home-style classics like bread-and-
butter pudding.

County Wexford
Cellar Restaurant (€€)
Horetown House, Foulksmills tel: 051 565771
Country cooking in the characterful basement of a
300-year-old Georgian country house.
Dunbrody Country House (€€)
Arthurstown, New Ross tel: 051 389 600
The oak-floored dining room in this historic
country house overlooks a sunken garden.
Continental cuisine.
La Marine (€€)
*Kelly's Resort Hotel, Rosslare
tel: 053 32114*
This contemporary bistro/restaurant can be found
at Kelly's Resort Hotel. It serves Irish produce in
Mediterranean style.
Marlfield House (€€€)
Courtown Road, Gorey tel: 055 21124
The style of the food, served in a luscious
conservatory dining room, matches the rest of the
house—rich, opulent, complicated. (See also
hotels section, page 273.)

SOUTHWESTERN COUNTIES

County Cork
Aherne's (€€)
63 North Main Street, Youghal
tel: 024 92424
Excellent range of seafood produced in various
levels of elaboration in this thriving enterprise.

Ballymaloe House (€€€)
Shanagarry tel: 021 465 2531
An Irish legend that now dispenses the talent
and experience of the Allen dynasty through its
cookery school. Superbly accomplished and
reasonably priced food, using local produce to
full advantage (see also hotels section,
page 273).

Blairs Cove (€€–€€€)
Durrus tel: 027 61127
Buffet-style seafood appetizers, local fish and meat,
and splendid desserts served on the grand piano. A
lovely Georgian house overlooking the sea.

Bosun (€–€€)
The Pier Monkstown, Cork tel: 021 484 2172
Thriving pub and restaurant (with rooms) beside
the Cobh car ferry.

Chez Youen (€€–€€€)
Baltimore tel: 028 20136
This popular Breton seafood restaurant
overlooks the harbour. The informal (and less
expensive) Jolie Brise, nearby on the square, is a
sister restaurant.

Crackpots (€–€€)
3 Cork Street, Kinsale tel: 021 477 2847
Unusual, stylish little restaurant, wine bar and pottery in the town centre.

Crawford Gallery Café (€–€€)
Emmet Place, Cork tel: 021 427 4415
A scion of the Allen family of Ballymaloe House
(see above) masterminds this attractive gallery
restaurant. Whether you call in for a cake or a full
meal, excellence is assured.

Finins (€€)
75 Main Street, Midleton tel: 021 463 1878
Simple meat and seafood dishes and soups are
served in this traditional pub and restaurant.

Isaacs (€–€€)
48 MacCurtain Street, Cork
tel: 021 450 3805
Good-value and stylish contemporary cooking
are the secrets of this city centre restaurant's
enduring popularity.

Larchwood House (€€)
Pearsons Bridge, Bantry tel: 027 66181
Imaginative and satisfying Irish country cooking in a
modest guesthouse (see hotels section).

Longueville House (€€€)
Mallow tel: 022 47156
Home produced and local ingredients prepared by
a talented young chef for serious eaters. (See also
hotels section, page 274.)

O'Callaghan-Walshe (€€)
The Square Rosscarbery tel: 023 48125
Skillfully cooked local seafood is among the
specials at this simple restaurant.

Quay Coop (€–€€)
24 Sullivans Quay, Cork tel: 021 431 7026
A selection of thoroughly imaginative wholefood
and vegetarian dishes.

Shiro (€€€)
Ahakista, near Bantry tel: 027 67030
Remarkably located restaurant serving exquisitely
presented authentic Japanese food. Good,
attentive service. Advance reservations are
always essential.

County Kerry
Gaby's (€€–€€€)
27 High Street, Killarney
tel: 064 32519
A long-established, good seafood restaurant.

Lime Tree (€€)
Shelbourne Street, Kenmare
tel: 064 41225
Intimate setting for contemporary fish and
meat dishes.

Nick's (€€–€€€)
Killorglin tel: 066 976 1219
Relaxed, beamed dining room where excellent fish
dishes are prepared.

Park (€€€)
Kenmare tel: 064 41200
Gourmet food in serene surroundings on the outskirts of this lovely small town. Outstanding service
(see hotels section, page 274).

281

County Limerick
Dunraven Arms (€€€)
Adare tel: 061 396633
Reliable Irish cooking, whether a sandwich in the
bar or a full meal in the restaurant (see also hotels
section, page 275).

Mustard Seed at Echo Lodge (€€€)
Ballingarry tel: 069 68508
Inventive food in charming country-house
restaurant. Organic produce from their garden
is served.

WESTERN COUNTIES

County Clare
Bunratty Castle (€€–€€€)
Bunratty tel: 061 360788
Classic medieval banquets and entertainment in
this well-known genuine 15th-century castle. There
are two sittings; book at any tourist office.

The Cloister (€€)
Abbey Street, Ennis tel: 065 682 9521
Simple seafood and snacks are available in
the bar from lunchtime onwards. For more complex fish dishes, try the dining room. Delicious
treacle bread and Inagh goat's cheese salad are
specials at this restaurant.

Kelly's Bar & Restaurant (€–€€)
26 Henry Street, Kilrush tel: 065 905 1133
Hearty pastas and Irish stews make this
atmospheric pub/restaurant popular with the locals.

Knappogue Castle (€€€)
near Quin tel: 061 360788
Medieval feasting in well-restored castle,
accompanied by entertainers recounting stories
of Celtic Ireland; book at any tourist office.

Sheedy's (€€)
Lisdoonvarna tel: 065 707 4026
French and Irish cuisine is prepared by the
proprietor in this friendly hotel restaurant (see
hotels section, page 275).

Hotels and Restaurants

County Galway

Ballynahinch Castle (€€€)
Recess, Connemara tel: 095 31006
Formal food is served in a wonderful dining room overlooking the river. If you want something simpler, there is an excellent range of bar food available in the Fisherman's pub. (See also *hotels* section, page 275.)

Dunguaire Castle (€€)
Kinvara tel: 091 637108
Banquet fare accompanied by literary gleanings from Synge, Shaw and O'Casey; book at any tourist office.

Erriseask House (€€)
Ballyconneely tel: 095 23553
Exquisite contemporary food in a magnificent setting on Mannin Bay. Cool, modern restaurant with rooms.

Fat Freddy's (€)
Quay Street, Galway tel: 091 567279
One of the best places for pizza; a cheerful, youthful and informal atmosphere.

Hotel Inisheer (€)
Lurgan Village, Inisheer, Aran Islands tel: 099 75020
Simple Irish fare at a good price.

McDonagh's Seafood Bar (€€)
22 Quay Street, Galway tel: 091 565001
A great place for seafood, relaxed and informal, with long opening hours.

Moran's Oyster Cottage (€€–€€€)
Kilcolgan, Clarinbridge tel: 091 796113
Oysters are what they do best here, brought in from their own beds just outside. But you can get a great chowder and lots of other seafood besides, accompanied by delicious soda bread and chilled white wine—or the customary Guinness.

Moycullen House (€€)
Moycullen tel: 091 555621
Surprisingly contemporary restaurant with accommodation in an unusual (and otherwise traditional) arts and crafts style sporting lodge in the hills above Moycullen.

O'Dowds (€–€€)
Roundstone tel: 095 35809
This popular pub and restaurant specializes in seafood: The O'Dowds' seafood chowder is renowned countrywide.

O'Grady's Seafood (€€)
Clifden tel: 095 21450
It was all change at this traditional seafood restaurant when the next generation of O'Gradys took over a while back—now it's a cool and contemporary space offering interna- tional cuisine.

Paddy Burke's (€€)
Clarinbridge tel: 091 796226
This is a great place for oyster-sampling, but you can find plenty of other seafood and hearty Irish cooking here. The place is always popular and bustling.

Rosleague Manor (€€)
Letterfrack, Connemara tel: 095 41101
Country-house restaurant serving seafood and home-grown vegetables.

County Mayo

Beehive (€)
Keel, Achill Island tel: 098 43134
Craft shop and informal daytime restaurant serving local produce, simply and pleasingly cooked. Baking is a specialty.

Durkans Weir House & Restaurant (€€)
Louisburgh tel: 098 66140
Traditional pub, with open fire and home-cooked bar food and adjacent restaurant for more formal dining.

Lemon Peel (€€)
The Octagon, Westport tel: 098 26929
Popular, buzzy restaurant offering a pleasing mixture of style and good home-style cooking.

Quay Cottage (€€)
The Quay, Westport (near entrance to Westport House) tel: 098 26412
Atmospheric high-ceilinged wine bar and shellfish restaurant converted from a waterside cottage. Wood fires and nautical knickknacks on the rafters.

NORTHWESTERN COUNTIES

County Donegal

Le Châteaubrienne (€€)
Sligo Road, Bundoran tel: 071 98 42160
This professional but welcoming family-run place has had a dynamic impact on Donegal's food scene. The emphasis is on quality without pomposity. Imaginative use is made of fresh local ingredients.

Harvey's Point (€€)
Lough Eske, Donegal tel: 074 97 22208
Good French/Swiss cuisine served here in nouvelle style. The atmosphere is fairly formal. (See *hotels* section, page 276.)

Rathmullan House (€€€)
Rathmullan tel: 074 91 58188
Country-house restaurant with lovely views of the gardens; fixed price menus available to residents in the evenings. Local seafood and farmhouse cheeses offered.

St. Ernan's House (€€€)
St. Ernan's Island, Donegal tel: 074 97 21065
Attractively presented five-course dinners served in true Irish country-house style.

St. John's (€€)
Fahan tel: 074 93 60289
Well-cooked local produce is accompanied by well-priced wine and great hospitality on the shores of Lough Swilly.

Smuggler's Creek (€)
Rossnowlagh tel: 071 98 52366
Imaginative range of bistro fare is on offer at this simple stone-built inn. Ingredients used include fresh seafood and organically grown vegetables. (See *hotels* section, page 277).

County Sligo

Cromleach Lodge (€€€)
Castlebaldwin, near Boyle tel: 071 91 65155
Accomplished food is served in this renowned restaurant with rooms, in a scenic location overlooking Lough Arrow.

Glebe House (€€)
Collooney tel: 071 91 67787
This is a respected family-run restaurant that also has some accommodation, and is located just outside Collooney village.
Markree Castle (€€)
Collooney tel: 071 91 67800
The food is assured at Knockmuldowney restaurant, in the medieval-looking setting of this castle. (See *hotels* section, page 276.)
The Moorings (€€–€€€)
Rosses Point tel: 071 91 77112
There is a relaxed atmosphere at this seafood restaurant serving fresh-cooked, popular dishes at reasonable prices. Close to the waterfront. Good for Sunday lunch.

NORTHERN IRELAND

County Antrim
Aldens (€€–€€€)
*229 Upper Newtownards Road, Belfast
tel: 028 9065 0079*
Warmth, elegance and good contemporary cooking, can all be found at this restaurant in an unlikely area of the city.
Cayenne (€€–€€€)
*Shaftesbury Square, Belfast
tel: 028 9033 1532*
Chic, vibrant, informal re-invention of Roscoff, TV chefs Paul and Jeanne Rankins' original ground-breaking Belfast restaurant.
Crown Liquor Saloon (€)
*46 Great Victoria Street, Belfast
tel: 028 9024 9476*
The National Trust's superbly restored Victorian pub is a must for any visitor; good lunchtime food, including oysters throughout the year. Irish dishes also available.
Europa Hotel (€€–€€€)
*Great Victoria Street, Belfast
tel: 028 9033 3366*
A plethora of eating options on offer in this city-centre hotel, from Irish stew in the stylish Lobby Bar to the more elaborate cuisine of the Gallery Restaurant.
Giant's Causeway (€)
*44a Causeway Road, Bushmills
tel: 028 2073 1159*
After visiting the Causeway, the National Trust tea-room is an ideal place for lunch or afternoon tea.
Nick's Warehouse (€€)
*35–39 Hill Street, Belfast
tel: 028 9043 9690*
Morning coffee, lunchtime or evening snacks, or full meals are all available here either in wine bar or in the more formal restaurant setting.
Ramore (€€€)
The Harbour, Portrush tel: 028 7082 4313
Classy contemporary waterside restaurant overlooking the harbour, with informal sister establishments nearby—wine bar below and traditional pub along the quay. Cooking was way ahead of its time and there is a good-value wine list.
Rayanne Country House and Restaurant (€€)
*60 Desmesne Road, Belfast
tel: 028 9042 5859*

A range of varied and interesting fresh dishes offered in the dining room of this elegant Victorian house, set well back from the road and overlooking its own lawns.

County Down
Castle Ward (€)
*Strangford, Downpatrick
tel: 028 4488 1204*
The tearoom at this National Trust property is a good place for light lunches or afternoon teas.
Shanks (€€€)
*150 Crawfordsburn Road, Clandeboye, Bangor
tel: 028 9185 3313*
Classic, deceptively simple dishes with imaginative variations. Excellent service.

County Fermanagh
Blake's of the Hollow (€)
Enniskillen tel: 028 6632 2143
Good sandwiches in characterful Victorian pub.
Florence Court (€)
Enniskillen tel: 028 6634 8249
National Trust tea-rooms; wholesome lunches and snacks.
The Sheelin (€–€€)
Bellanaleck tel: 028 6634 8232
Thatched-cottage bakery serving teas, snacks and gourmet dinner.

County Londonderry
Ardtara House (€€€)
*8 Gorteade Road, Upperlands
tel: 028 7964 4490*
Elegantly prepared local produce served in classy decorated setting.
Beech Hill Country House (€€€)
32 Ardmore Road, Derry tel: 028 7134 9279
Carefully prepared food using mostly organic produce.
Brown's (€–€€)
Bonds Hill, Derry tel: 028 7134 5180
Popular long-established restaurant, valued for its reliability.
The Lime Tree (€€–€€€)
*60 Catherine Street, Limavady
tel: 028 7776 4300*
Creative Mediteranean cuisine, served in a relaxed setting. Advance booking recommended.

LAKELAND COUNTIES

County Laois
Roundwood House (€€)
Mountrath tel: 0502 32120
Accomplished cooking by a natural hostess in gently time-worn Palladian surroundings.
The Stables (€€)
6 Oxmantown Mall tel: 0509 20263
Simple but comfortable surroundings of plain white walls and oakwood chairs make a perfect foil for competently prepared local produce.

County Westmeath
Crookedwood House (€€)
Crookedwood, Mullingar tel: 044 72165
Copious and good, interesting food served in a relaxing setting of a whitewashed cellar restaurant.

283

Index

285

Index

Index and Acknowledgements

Picture credits

The Automobile Association would like to thank the following photographers, libraries, and associations for their assistance in the preparation of this book.
FÁILTE IRELAND 22a horse-racing, 22b hurling, 23 football, 30a Muiredach's Cross, 102–103 Punchestown races, 105 Malahide Castle, 112b Slane Abbey, 122 Ardmore Round Tower, 127b Rock of Cashel Museum, 141 cannon, Rosslare, 142 Georges St., Waterford, 164b Ashford Castle Hotel, 165 Adare Manor Hotel, 175 banquet, Knappogue Castle, 179a flora, 190a Thoor Ballylee, 202a Glebe House, 202b Glencolumbkille standing stone, 20 St. Eunan's, 249 Old Gaol. BRIDGEMAN ART LIBRARY 73 Chirho (initials of Christ's name) Gospel of St. Matthew, chapter 1 verse 18,/© The Board of Trinity College, Dublin, Ireland. H. CHEVALLIER 177b Aran Island gate. GETTY IMAGES 35 Oliver Cromwell, 38b Emmett, 40a O'Connell Street, 1900, 41 Signing the Treaty, 43a Charles Stewart Parnell, 43b Liberation of Daniel O'Connell, 54/5a Easter Rising, 54b GPO 1916, 62 Oscar Wilde; G. GOSSIP 164 Bantry House, 242a Hilton Park Hotel, 242b, 243b Tullanisk. CHRISTOPHER HILL PHOTOGRAPHIC 7a lobster fishing, 10b Dunluce Castle, 15 Irish dancing, 16a W. B. Yeats, 18a Irish fry, 18–19 seafood, 20b farming, 24b Roundstone Bog, 32a Boa Island Figure, 79a seafood, 155b Rowallane Gardens, 182–183 Clifden, 186 Oyster Festival, 190b Westport, 199 Donegal, 200–201 Atlantic Drive, 206 Grianán of Aileach, 208 Parke's Castle, 209a Lough Gill, 210a Sligo Abbey, 210b W. B. Yeats, 212 Crown Liquor Saloon, 214 Relief of Derry, 217a Belfast, 217 Larry's Bar, 218, 219a City Hall, 219b Palm House, 220 Opera House, 221a Queen's University, 222a Belfast Castle, 222b Belfast Zoo, 223 Navan Fort, 224 Derry, 225b St. Patrick's window, 226a Stone, 230b Wellbrook Mi 232 Mourne Mountains, 235b Transport Museum, 238 Lough Key, 247b Lough Key, 251 Giant's Causeway, 256 cycles. KOBAL COLLECTION 204a *The Quiet Man*, 204b *The Field*, 205 *Ryan's Daughter*. MARY EVANS PICTURE LIBRARY 17a Samuel Beckett, 17b G. B. Shaw, 26a creatures, 27 Cuchulainn, 36b William III, 37 James II, 39 Lor Kilwarden, 40b de Valera and Lloyd George, 42b Sir Edward Carson, 63a G. B. Shaw, 63b W. B. Yeats © The Esta of Jack B. Yeats 2005. All Rights Reserved, DACS, 114 St. Columba, 138 James Joyce. NATIONAL MUSEUM OF IRELAND 66 Tara Brooch. NATURE PHOTOGRAPHERS LTD 180a mountain avens (R. Bush), 180b fly orchid (P. Sterry), 181a pine marten (W. S. Paton), 181b corncrake (P. Sterry). NORTHERN IRELAND TOURIST BOARD 227b Marble Arch Caves. OFFICE OF PUBLIC WORKS, DUBLIN 34a Silken Thomas. REX FEATURES 12b Mary Robinson. ROYAL GEOGRAPHICAL SOCIETY 28a map. STROKESTOWN PARK 250 Strokestown Park. THE SLIDE FILE 24–25 turf cutting, 245 Clonmacnois, WATERFORD CRYSTAL 143a Copper Wheel Engraver, 143b Master Cutter.
All remaining pictures are held in the Association's own library (A.A. PHOTO LIBRARY) with contributions from: P. BAKER 12t. L. BLAKE 11, 110, 115a, 145, 184, 185, 187, 188, 191, 226b, 240a, 241, 244, 246a, 260. J. BLANDFORD 9b, 21, 25, 121, 136, 146, 148, 149b, 152, 154, 155a, 159, 161, 163a, 163b. S. DAY 4, 144. M. DIGGIN 9b, 87b, 195, 237. S. Day 5, 6, 243; D. FORSS 33, 51, 149a, 152–153, 162. C. HILL 3, 198. S. HILL 10 14b, 30b, 123a, 147b, 150a, 150b, 151, 156, 157, 158, 167a, 167b, 168, 169, 170, 171, 172, 173, 174, 17 177a, 189, 192a, 193a, 194bl, 251b, 266, 268. J. JENNINGS 19b, 38a, 192b, 193b, 196, 213, 225a, 235a, 246b. C. JONES 13t. T. KING 29b, 46, 55b, 83a, 98. S. MCBRIDE 126, 179b. G. MUNDAY 6, 26b, 29, 49a, 52, 53, 57a, 57b, 61a, 68a, 68b, 69a, 69b,70a, 70b, 72b, 76, 96, 104, 112a, 116, 213, 215, 216, 219b, 221b, 227a, 228, 230a, 231, 233, 234, 269. M. SHORT 7b, 8a, 9a, 12b, 13b, 16b, 20a, 28b, 32b, 44–45, 45b, 47, 48a, 48b, 49b, 50, 56, 58b, 59, 60, 64, 65b, 67, 71, 72a, 74a, 74b, 75, 78, 79b, 80, 81a, 81b, 82, 83b, 84a, 84b, 85, 87, 88, 89a, 89b, 91b, 92, 94, 95, 97a, 97b, 99a, 99b, 100b, 101, 102a, 103, 106a, 109, 111, 113, 115b, 117, 119, 124a, 124b, 128, 130a, 130b, 131, 132, 133, 135, 137, 139a, 140, 236, 239, 247t, 248, 253, 258, 259, 262, 263, 264, 265, 269b. W. VOYSEY 42a, 58a, 61b, 65a, 77a, 77b. S. WHITEHORN 44a. P. ZOELLER 91a, 107, 108a, 108b, 118, 120, 123b,125, 127a, 129, 166, 267.

Acknowledgements

The author would like to thank the following for their help in the production of this book: Fáilte Ireland; Aer Lingus; Avis/Johnson & Perrott; and British Midland Airways Ltd.

Contributors

Original copy editor: Hugh Chevallier
Revision verifier: Anto Howard
Editorial management: Apostrophe S Limited

or back to the ranch house.

Diana looked at him. Part of her was frankly terrified at the prospect of being alone with him for days on end. Part of her was not—and in some ways that was the most terrifying of all.

Shutting out everything, she closed her eyes. *What am I going to do?*

The ingrained habit of years made her mind veer away from the bleak night when she had learned once and forever to distrust men, and her own judgment.

Unbidden came thoughts that made her tremble with a tangle of emotions she refused to name and questions she knew she shouldn't ask, even in the silence of her own mind....

"I'll buy any book with Elizabeth Lowell's name on it."

—Jayne Ann Krentz

ELIZABETH LOWELL

OUTLAW

MIRA®

ISBN 1-55166-619-7

OUTLAW

Copyright © 1991 by Two Of A Kind Inc.

Visit us at www.mirabooks.com

Printed in U.S.A.

For Isabel Swift,
who permits a variety of romance stories

1

Diana Saxton drove into the Rocking M's dusty ranch yard and shut off the car's engine. The first thing she saw was a cowboy as big as a barn door standing on the front porch. Unconsciously her hands clenched on the wheel, betraying her instant unease in the presence of men in general and big, well-built men in particular.

The ranch house's front door opened and closed. When another equally big, hard-looking man in boots and jeans came out of the house and began walking toward Diana, carrying a geologist's hammer. Over toward the corral, a third cowboy was climbing onto a horse. The man was so big that he made the horse look like a kid's pony.

My God, Diana thought, *don't they have any normal-size men out here?* Crowding that thought came another. *I can't spend a summer close to these men!*

But then, I won't have to. I'll be at the September Canyon site.

Someone called out from the house. Diana recognized Carla MacKenzie's voice and let out a soundless sigh of relief as the first big man turned immediately and went back inside at the sound of his name. Luke MacKenzie, Carla's husband.

As a bit of Diana's uneasiness faded, she recognized the second man. Cash McQueen, Carla's half brother. He was coming toward Diana, slipping the hammer into a loop on his leather belt as he walked. Hastily she got out of her car. She had learned in the past few years not to show her distrust of men—especially big men—yet she still couldn't force herself to be close to any man in a confined space, particularly a car.

Before Cash got to Diana, another call from the house stopped him. He waved to her, said something she couldn't understand and went back into the ranch house.

A sudden burst of activity outside the corral caught Diana's attention. A horse had its head down between its forelegs, its back was steeply arched and its body was uncoiling like a released spring. A few spectacular bucks later, the horse's beefy rider lost his grip on the saddle. He hit the ground, rolled to his hands and knees and came up onto his feet with a lunge. He grabbed the bridle close to the bit and began beating the horse with a heavy quirt. The horse screamed and tried to escape but was helpless against the cruel grip on the bridle.

Without stopping to think, Diana started toward the terrified horse, yelling at the man to stop. Before she had taken three steps, a man in a light blue shirt vaulted the corral fence and landed like a cat, running toward the brutal cowboy, gaining speed with every stride. The running man was smaller and unarmed, hardly a fair match against the huge, beefy man wielding a whip.

Behind Diana, the ranch house door slammed and men came running. Another man ran out of the barn, saw what was happening and yelled, "Careful, ramrod! Baker's quirt has lead shot in it!"

Baker wheeled to face Tennessee Blackthorn, the Rocking M's ramrod. Baker flipped the quirt over in his hand, wielding the thick leather stock as a club rather than using the whip end against Ten. When his thick arm lifted, Diana screamed and men shouted. Only Ten was silent. He closed the last few feet between himself and Baker as the lead-weighted quirt came smashing down.

Ten didn't flail with his fists or duck away from the blow. The edge of his left hand connected with Baker's wrist. The quirt went spinning up and away, flying end over end through the air. Simultaneously the ramrod's right fist delivered a short, chopping blow to Baker's heart. Ten pivoted, slammed an elbow into Baker's diaphragm and sent another chopping blow to his neck as the big man bent over, folding up, all fight gone. Before the quirt even hit the ground, Baker was stretched out full length facedown in the dirt, unmoving.

Torn between disbelief and shock, Diana came to a stop, staring at the Rocking M's ramrod. She shook her head, trying to understand how a man who was six inches shorter and sixty pounds lighter than his adversary had begun and ended a fight before the bigger man could land a blow. As though at a distance she heard Cash and Luke go by her, moving more slowly now.

"Nice work, Ten," Luke said.

"Amen," said Cash. Then, to Luke, "Remind me never to pick a fight with your ramrod. Somebody taught that boy how to play hardball."

Ten said nothing, for he was more interested in calming the frightened horse than in talking about the brief fight. "Easy, girl. Easy now. No one's going to hurt you. Easy...easy."

As he spoke, he approached the sweating, trembling mare. When he saw streaks of blood mixed with the horse's lather, he swore, but the soothing tone of his voice never changed despite the scalding nature of his words. Slowly he closed his hands around the reins and began checking over the mare.

As Ten's hands moved over the animal, it began to calm down. Not once did the ramrod look toward the motionless Baker. Ten knew precisely how much damage he had done to the brutal cowboy; what Ten wanted to know was how badly the horse had been hurt.

Cash sat on his heels next to Baker and checked for a visible injuries. There was nothing obvious. After a few moments Cash stood and said, "Out cold, but still breathing."

Luke grunted. "Any permanent damage?"

"Not that I can see."

"He won't be swinging a quirt for a while," Ten said without looking up from the mare. "Not with his right hand, anyway. I broke his wrist."

"Too bad it wasn't his neck," Luke said. "You warned him last week about beating a horse." Luke turned to Cosy, who had yelled the warning about the quirt to Ten. "Bring the truck around. You're on garbage detail tonight."

"Where to?" asked Cosy.

"West Fork."

"Forty miles out and forty miles back, damn near all of it on dirt roads," Cosy grumbled. "In the old days we'd have dumped his carcass on the ranch boundary and let him walk to town."

"Not on the Rocking M," Luke said, stretching lazily. "My great-granddaddy Case MacKenzie once killed a man for beating a horse."

Slowly Diana retreated, walking backward for a few steps before turning and moving quickly toward her car. Though she was a student of human history—

Anasazi history, to be precise—she wasn't accustomed to having her history lessons served to her raw. She didn't like having it pointed out that the veneer of civilization was quite thin, even in modern times, and it was especially thin in men.

I shouldn't be shocked. I know better than most women what men are like underneath their shirts and ties, shaving lotions and smiles. Savages and outlaws. All of them. Outlaws who use their strength against those who are weaker.

A vivid picture came to Diana's mind—the man called Ten coming over the fence, attacking the big cowboy, reducing the larger man to unconsciousness with a few violent blows. She shuddered.

"Diana? What happened?"

She looked up and saw Carla standing on the front porch, holding a tiny baby in her arms.

"One of the men was beating a horse," Diana said.

"Baker." Carla's mouth flattened from its usual generous curve. "Ten warned him."

"He did more than that. He beat him unconscious."

"Ten? That doesn't sound like him. I've never seen him lose his temper."

"Is he your ramrod?"

Carla nodded. "Yes, he's the Rocking M's foreman."

"Light blue shirt, black hair, small?"

"Small?" she asked, surprised. "I don't think of Ten as small."

"He's a lot smaller than Baker."

"Oh, well, even Luke and Cash are smaller than Baker. But Ten's at least six feet tall. A bit more, I think." Carla stood on tiptoe and looked out toward the corral. "Is he all right?"

"His wrist is broken."

"Ten's hurt? Oh my God, I've got to—"

"Not Ten," Diana interrupted quickly. "Baker is the one with a broken wrist."

"Oh." Relief changed Carla's face from strained to pretty. "Then Ten will take care of it. He's had medic training." She looked closely at Diana. "You're pale. Are you all right?"

Diana closed her eyes. "I'm fine. It was a long drive out and the road was rough. Now I know why. I was going back in time as well as miles."

Laughing, shaking her head, Carla shifted the sleeping baby and held out her hand to Diana. "Come in and have some coffee. French roast, Colombian beans, with just enough Java beans blended in to give the coffee finesse as well as strength."

Diana's eyelids snapped open. The dark blue of her eyes was vivid against her still-pale face. "I'm hallucinating. They didn't have French roast in the Old West, did they?"

"I don't know, but this isn't the Old West."

"You could have fooled me," Diana said, thinking

about outlaws and brawls and a man with the lethal quickness of a cat. But despite her thoughts, she allowed Carla to lead her across the porch and into the cool ranch house. "Your ramrod would have made one hell of an outlaw."

"In the old days, a lot of good men were outlaws. They had no choice. There wasn't any law to be *in*side of." Carla laughed at the expression on Diana's face. "But don't worry. The bad old days are gone. Look in our side yard. There's a satellite dish out there sucking up all kinds of exotic signals from space. We have television, a VCR, radios, CD players, personal computers, a dishwasher, microwave, washer-dryer—the whole tortilla."

"And cowboys swinging quirts full of lead shot," Diana muttered.

"Is that what Baker did?"

Diana nodded.

"My God. No wonder Ten lost his temper."

"What temper? He looked about as angry as a man chopping wood."

Carla shook her head unhappily. "Poor Ten. He's had a tough time ramrodding this crew in the past year."

"'Poor Ten' looked like he could handle it," Diana said beneath her breath.

"The ranch is so remote it's hard to get good men to stay. I don't know how we'd manage without Ten. And now that we've found museum-quality Anasazi artifacts in September Canyon, the pothunters are descending in hordes. Someone has to stay at the site all the time. Cash has been doing it, but he has to leave tomorrow for the Andes. We're going to be more shorthanded than ever.''

"The Andes, huh? Great. Everybody deserves a vacation,'' Diana said, cheered by the thought that there would be one less big man on the Rocking M.

"Cash isn't exactly going on a vacation. One of his colleagues thinks there's a mother lode back up on the flanks of one of those nameless granite peaks. That's the one thing Cash can't resist.''

"Nameless peaks?''

"Hard rock and gold. Ten calls Cash the Granite Man but swears it's because of Cash's hard head, not his love of hard-rock mining.''

Carla tucked the baby into an old-fashioned cradle that was next to the kitchen table. The baby stirred, opened sleepy turquoise eyes and slid back into sleep once more as Carla slowly rocked the cradle.

"How's the little man doing?'' Diana asked softly, bending over the baby until her short, golden brown hair blended with the honey finish of the cradle.

"Growing like a weed in the sun. Logan's going to be at least as big as his daddy.''

Diana looked at the soft-cheeked, six-week-old baby and tried to imagine it fully grown, as big as Luke, beard stubbled and powerful. "You'd better start domesticating this little outlaw real soon or you'll never have a chance.''

Carla laughed in the instant before she realized that Diana was serious. She looked at the older woman for a moment, remembering the class she had taken from Dr. Diana Saxton, artist and archaeologist, a woman who was reputed not to think much of men. At the time Carla had dismissed the comments as gossip; now she wasn't sure.

''You make it sound like I'm going to need a whip and a chair,'' Carla said.

''Those are the customary tools for dealing with wild animals, and men are definitely in that category. What a pity that it takes one to make a baby.''

''Not all men are like Baker.''

Diana made a sound that could have been agreement or disbelief as she began stroking the baby's cheek with a gentle fingertip, careful not to awaken him. She admired the perfect, tiny eyelashes, the snub nose, the flushed lips, the miniature fingers curled in relaxation on the pale cradle blanket. Gradually she noticed more of the cradle itself, how the grain of the wood had been perfectly matched to the curves of the cradle, how the pieces had been fitted without nails, how the wood itself had been polished to a gentle satin luster.

''What a beautiful cradle,'' Diana said softly, running her fingertips over the wood. ''It's a work of art. Where did you get it?''

"Luke made it. He has wonderful hands, strong and gentle."

Diana looked at the cradle once more and the baby lying securely within. She tried not to think how much she would like to have a child of her own. Sex was a necessary step toward conception. For sex, a woman had to trust a man not to hurt her—a man who was bigger, stronger and basically more savage than a woman. Years ago, Diana had abandoned the idea of sex. The thought of a baby, however, still haunted her.

"If Luke is gentle with you and little Logan," Diana said quietly, touching the pale blanket with her fingertips, "you're a lucky woman. You have one man in a million."

Before Carla could say anything more, Diana stood and turned away from the cradle.

"I think I'll take a rain check on that coffee. I want to get my stuff unloaded before dinner."

"Of course. We're putting you in the old ranch house where all the artifacts from the site are being kept. Just follow the road out beyond the barn. When the road forks, go to the right. The old house is only about a hundred yards from the barn. Dinner is at six. Don't bother to knock. Just come in the back way. The dining room is just off the kitchen and both rooms have outside doors. We all eat together during the week. Sundays the hands fend for themselves. You'll eat with us."

Diana looked at the long, narrow room just off the kitchen. Two rectangular tables pushed together all but filled the room. She tried to imagine what it would be like to eat surrounded by big male bodies. The thought was daunting. She took a slow breath, told herself that she would be spending nearly all of her time at the site in September Canyon, and turned back to Carla.

"Thanks," Diana said. "I'll be back at six, whip in one hand and chair in the other."

2

The alarm on Diana's digital watch cheeped annoyingly, breaking her concentration. She set aside the stack of numbered site photos, reset her watch for a short time later, stretched and heard her stomach rumble in anticipation of dinner. Despite her hunger, she was reluctant to leave the hushed solitude of the old house and the silent companionship of the ancient artifacts lining the shelves of the workroom.

Slanting yellow light came through the north window, deepening the textures of stone and sandal fragments, potshards and glue pots, making everything appear to be infused with a mystic glow. Diana couldn't wait until tomorrow, when she would drive to September Canyon. Photos, artifacts and essays, no matter how precise and scholarly, couldn't convey the complexity of the interlocking mystery of the Anasazi, the land and time.

Her mind more on the past than the present, Diana

walked slowly into the bathroom. The slanting light coming through the small, high window made the gold in her hair incandescent and gave the darker strands a rich satin luster. Her eyes became indigo in shadow, vivid sapphire in direct light. The natural pink in her smooth cheeks and lips contrasted with the dark brown of her eyebrows and the dense fringe of her eyelashes.

Once Diana would have noticed her own understated beauty and heightened it with mascara and blusher, lipstick and haunting perfumes. Once, but no longer. Never again would she be accused by a man of using snares and lures to attract members of the opposite sex, then teasing and maddening them with what she had no intention of giving. Never again would she put herself in a position where a man felt entitled to take what he wanted in the belief that it had been offered—and if it hadn't, it should have been.

Soap, water, unscented lotion and a few strokes with a hairbrush through her short, gamine hairstyle and Diana was ready for dinner. She thought longingly of the four-inch heels she wore when she was teaching to add to her own five feet three inches of frankly curved female body, but wearing a cotton pullover sweater big enough for a man and faded jeans with four-inch heels would be ludicrous. Besides, the scarred, rough-country hiking boots she wore most of the time added at least two inches to her height.

And she was going to need every inch of confidence she could get.

"Mmmrreooow."

Diana's head snapped toward the window at the unexpected sound. A lean, tiger-striped cat with one chewed ear was standing outside on the tree limb that brushed against the bathroom window. The cat's forepaw was batting hopefully at the bottom of the window, which was open a crack.

"Hello," Diana said, smiling. "Do you live here?"

The paw, claws politely sheathed, patted again beneath the length of the opening.

"I get the message."

She pushed up the window enough for the cat to come in. It leaped from windowsill to the edge of the sink with an effortless grace that reminded her of the Rocking M's ramrod vaulting the corral fence and landing running.

The cat sniffed Diana's meager toiletries, nosed the peppermint toothpaste, sneezed, *yeowed* softly and stropped itself against her midriff. She ran her palm down the cat's spine, enjoying the supple arch of the animal's body as it rubbed against her in turn. Soon the vibrations of an uninhibited purr were rippling from the cat.

"You're a sweetheart," Diana said. "Would you let me hold you?"

The cat would. In fact, it insisted.

"Goodness, you're heavy! Not fat, though. You must be all muscle."

The purring redoubled.

Laughing softly, Diana smoothed her cheeks and chin against the vibrant bundle of fur. The cat moved sinuously in return, twisting against her in slow motion, relishing the physical contact. And shedding, of course.

Diana looked at the gray and black hairs sticking to the navy cotton sweater she was wearing. She shrugged. Maybe some of the men would be allergic to cats. The thought had a definite appeal.

"C'mon, cat. Let's see if they allow felines in the dining room."

The cat burrowed more tightly into Diana's arms, clinging with just a hint of claws while she closed the bathroom window. Cradling the purring animal, Diana made a quick circuit of the old house, making sure that everything was buttoned up in case the thunderstorm that had been threatening for the past hour actually got down to work. The bedroom was in order—windows shut, clothes put away, sheet turned down on the double bed with its antique headboard and blessedly new mattress set. The window over the kitchen sink was closed. The workroom with its two long tables and countless bins and cubbyholes and shelves was as orderly as it was ever likely to be.

Absently Diana ran her fingertips over the smooth

surface of a cabinet, wondering if Luke had made this furniture as well as the cradle. She suspected he had. There was a quality of craftsmanship and care that was rare in modern furniture.

Her stomach growled. She eased her wrist out from under the cat and looked at her watch. Twenty minutes to six. Her alarm would be going off again soon, telling her she had to be where she very much didn't want to be—in a room full of strange men.

Maybe if I get there early, I can grab a plate of food and a seat at the corner of the table. That way I won't be completely surrounded by savages.

Men, not savages, she reminded herself automatically, trying to be fair.

The part of herself that didn't care about fair shot back: *Men or savages. Same difference.*

Diana remembered the fine-grained, carefully wrought cradle and mentally placed a question mark beside Luke's name. It was just possible that he wasn't a savage or an outlaw beyond the pale of gentle society. For Carla's sake, Diana hoped so. Carla had been one of her favorite students—bright, quick, eager, fascinated by the Anasazi's complex, enigmatic past.

The watch alarm cheeped again. The cat's tail whipped in annoyance.

"I agree, cat, but it's the only way I remember to be anywhere. Once I start working over potshards or sketchbooks, everything else just goes away."

The cat made a disgruntled sound and resettled itself more comfortably in her arms.

Diana shut the front door and looked down the narrow path that led from the old ranch house to the bigger, more modern one. Reluctant to confront the Rocking M's oversize men, she lingered for a moment on the front step of the old house. The grove of dark evergreens that surrounded the original ranch house was alive with rain-scented wind. Clouds were seething overhead, their billows set off by spears of brassy gold light that made the wild bowl of the sky appear to be supported by shafts of pure light. Distant thunder rumbled, telling tales of invisible lightning.

She took a deep breath and felt excitement uncurl along her nerves as the taste of the storm wind swept through her. She had been cooped up in classrooms too long, earning money so that she could explore the Anasazi homeland during the long summer break. The boundless, ancient land of the Four Corners called to her, singing of people and cultures long vanished, mysteries whispering among shadow, shattered artifacts waiting to be made whole. That was what she had come to the Rocking M for—the undiscovered past.

Caressing the cat absently with her chin, Diana walked the short distance to the big house. When the wind shifted, the smell of food beckoned to her, making her aware of the fact that she had missed lunch.

The outside door into the dining room was open.

Diana looked in, but nobody was inside yet. From the bunkhouse beyond the corral came the sound of men calling to one another, talking about the day's work or the pending storm or the savory smell of dinner on the wind. Quietly Diana walked the length of the dining room toward the door leading into the kitchen. She had just begun to hope that she would be able to grab a plate and eat alone when she stepped into the kitchen and stopped as though her feet had been nailed to the floor.

There was a man standing with his back to her, a stranger with wide shoulders stretching against the black fabric of his shirt. The suggestion of male power was emphasized by the line of his back tapering down to lean hips, the muscular ease of his stance and the utter confidence of his posture as he stood motionless in black jeans and black boots that were polished by use.

My God, he's as tall and straight and hard as a stone cliff. No wonder he's confident. All he has to do is stand there and he dominates everything.

Reflexively Diana backed up but succeeded only in giving away her presence by bumping into a counter.

"Carla?" the man said, turning around slowly. His voice was deep, slightly rough, a ragged kind of velvet that was as dark as his clothes. His head was bent over something he was holding. His hair was intensely black, subtly curly, thick. "Can you give me a hand?"

Diana opened her mouth to say that she wasn't Carla but was so surprised by what she saw that no words came out.

A tiger-striped kitten lay cupped in the man's lean, callused hands. The contrast between the man's strength and the kitten's soft body was as shocking as the clarity of the man's ice-gray eyes looking at her. Abruptly she realized that she had seen him once before, under very different circumstances.

"Y-you're the ramrod," she said without thinking.

"Most people call me Ten. Short for Tennessee."

"You—Baker—the horse—"

Ten looked more closely at the woman who stood before him, her unease as badly concealed as the alluring curves of her body beneath her loose cotton sweater.

"Don't worry," Ten said. "He won't be back. Have you seen Carla?"

Diana shook her head, making light twist through her short, silky hair. Ten's nostrils flared slightly as he smelled the freshness of soap and sunshine and female skin.

"Think you could put Pounce down long enough to help me with Nosy?"

"Pounce?" Diana asked, wondering if she had lost her mind.

"That sly renegade who's grinning and purring in your arms."

"Oh...the cat." Diana looked down. "Pounce, huh?"

Ten made a sound of agreement that was suspiciously like a purr. "Best mouser on the Rocking M. Usually he's standoffish, but he can sense a particular kind of soft touch three miles away. From the smug look on his face, he was right about you."

The kitten stirred as though it wanted to be free. Long fingers closed gently, restraining the tiny animal without hurting or frightening it.

"Easy there, Nosy. That wound has to be cleaned up or you're going to be dead or three-legged, which amounts to the same thing out here. And that would be a shame. You're the best-looking kitten that ugly old mouser has sired."

Bemused by the picture man and kitten made, Diana opened her arms. Pounce took the hint, leaped gracefully to the floor and vanished into the house. Drawn against her will by the kitten's need, Diana bent over Ten's hands.

"What's wrong with it?" she asked.

"She was just living up to her name. Nosy. Either one of the chickens pecked her, or a hawk made a pass at her and she got free, or one of the bunkhouse dogs bit her, or..." Ten shrugged. "Lots of things can happen to a newly weaned kitten on a ranch."

"Poor little thing," Diana murmured, stroking the kitten with a fingertip, noticing for the first time that the fur on the animal's left haunch was rucked up over a knot of swollen flesh. "What do you want me to do?"

"Hold her while I clean her up. Normally her mother would take care of it, but she went hunting a week ago and didn't come back."

Diana looked up for an instant and received a vivid impression of diamond-clear eyes framed by thick black eyelashes that any woman would have envied. The eyelashes were the only suggestion of softness about Ten, but it reassured Diana in an odd way.

"Show me what to do."

The left corner of Ten's mouth tipped upward approvingly. "Hold your hands out. That's it. Now hold Nosy here, and here, so I can get to the haunch. Hold on a little harder. You won't hurt her. She's still at the age where she's all rubber bands and curiosity."

The description made Diana smile at the same instant that warm, hard fingers pressed over her own, showing her how much restraint to use on the kitten.

"That's good. Now hold tight."

In the silence that came while Ten gently examined the kitten, Diana could hear her own heartbeat and feel the subtle warmth of Ten's breath as he bent over the furry scrap of life she held in her hands.

"Damn. I was afraid of that."

"What?" she asked.

"I'll have to open it up."

Ten reached toward the counter with a long arm. For the first time Diana noticed the open first aid kit.

The sound of the wrapper being removed from the sterile, disposable scalpel seemed as loud to her as thunder.

Gray eyes assessed Diana, missing nothing of her distress.

"I'll get Carla," he said.

"No," Diana said quickly. "I'm not squeamish. Well, not horribly squeamish. Everyone who works at remote sites has to go through first aid training. It's just…the kitten is so small."

"Close your eyes. It will make it easier on all of us."

Diana closed her eyes and held her breath, expecting to hear a cry of distress from the kitten when Ten went to work. Other than a slight twitch, the animal showed no reaction. Diana was equally still, so still that she sensed the tiny currents of air made when Ten's hands moved over the small patient. The words he spoke to Nosy were like the purring of a mama cat, sound without meaning except the most basic meaning of all—reassurance.

There was the sharp smell of disinfectant, the thin rasp of paper wrappings being torn away and a sense of light pressure as Ten swabbed the wound clean.

"Okay. You can open your eyes now."

Diana looked down. The kitten's haunch was wet, marred only by a tiny cut. Most of the swelling was gone, removed when Ten lanced the boil that had formed over the wound.

"Thorn," Ten said, holding up a wicked, vaguely curved fragment. "Wild rose from the looks of it."

"Will Nosy be all right now?"

"Should be."

Long fingers slid beneath the kitten, moving over Diana's skin almost caressingly as Ten lifted the animal from her hands. Her breath froze, but Ten never so much as glanced at her.

"C'mon, Nosy," he said, cradling the kitten against his neck with his left hand. "You've taken up enough of the lady's time. What you need now is a little sleep and TLC."

"TLC? Is that a medicine?"

The corner of Ten's mouth curved up again. "Best one in the world. Tender Loving Care."

As he spoke, Ten stroked Nosy's face with a fingertip that was as gentle as a whisper. After a few strokes the kitten looked bemused and altogether content. Within moments Nosy's eyelids lowered over round amber eyes. There was a little yawn, the delicate curl of a tiny pink tongue, and the kitten was asleep.

With a feeling of unreality, Diana looked at the ramrod's hard hand curled protectively around the sleeping kitten and remembered that same hand breaking a man's wrist and then slamming him into unconsciousness before he could even cry out in pain.

Ramrod. The name suits him.

But so did the sleeping kitten.

3

Dinner was on the table at six o'clock, straight up. By long-standing custom, no one waited for latecomers. That included Luke, who was still on the phone talking to the sheriff. No one took Luke's place at the head of the table, but formality ended there. Cash and Carla sat facing Diana and Ten across the table. Diana had managed to secure a seat just to the left of the head of the table, ensuring that she would have only one person seated next to her. Even so, she felt crowded, because that one person was Ten.

To Diana's eyes, the long dining table was supporting enough food for at least twenty people. Five cowhands sat at the other end of the table. There was room for five more men and seven men in a squeeze, but the Rocking M was shorthanded. Only nine people were seated at the moment. Then the outside door banged and a new cowhand called Jervis rushed in and snagged the platter of pork chops before he had even sat down.

"Where's Cosy?" Jervis asked as he slid into a chair and began forking pork chops onto his plate.

"Garbage run," Ten said.

Jervis hesitated, looked around the table and said to Ten, "Baker, huh?"

Ten grunted.

"Who gave him the good word?"

"I did."

"How'd he take it?"

"I didn't hear any complaints."

Cash half strangled on laughter and coffee.

"Something funny?" asked Jervis.

"Ten had Baker laid out cold in six seconds flat," Cash said casually, reaching for the gravy. "He's probably still wondering what hit him."

"Can't say as I'm sorry," Jervis said. He dished a mountain of potatoes onto his plate before he turned and looked Ten over. "Not a mark on you. You must be as much an outlaw as Cosy said you were. That Baker did a lot of bragging about what a fighter he was. Talked about men he'd busted up so bad they pi—er, passed blood for months."

Ten glanced at Diana before he gave the cowhand an icy look. "Jervis, why don't you just shovel food and leave the dinner conversation to Carla. Miss Saxton isn't used to anything less polished than a faculty tea."

"Sorry, ma'am," Jervis said to Diana.

"Don't apologize on my account," she quickly. "Life at remote archaeological sites isn't as polished as Mr., er—"

"Blackthorn," Ten said politely.

"—Blackthorn seems to think," Diana finished. "I don't cringe at a few rough edges."

"Uh, sure," Jervis said, trying and failing not to stare at the noticeable gap that had opened up between Diana's chair and Ten's.

The other cowhands followed Jervis's look. Snickers went around the table like distant lightning, but not one man was going to call down their ramrod's ire by being so rude as to point out that the university woman was politely lying through her pretty white teeth.

Diana didn't notice the looks she received, for she was grimly concentrating on her single pork chop, scant helping of potatoes and no gravy. Despite her usually healthy appetite, her empty stomach and the savory nature of Carla's cooking, Diana was having trouble swallowing. Even though none of the other men at the table were as big as Cash—and Luke wasn't even in the dining room—she felt suffocated by looming, uncivilized, unpredictable males.

"Miss Saxton," Ten continued, "will be here for the summer, working at the September Canyon site." He glanced at the woman, who was at the moment subtly hitching her chair even farther away from him, and drawled, "It *is* Miss, isn't it?"

Carla gave Ten a quick glance, caught by the unusual edge in his normally smooth voice. Then she noticed what the cowhands had already seen—the gap that had slowly opened up between Diana's chair and the ramrod's.

"Actually," Diana said, "my students call me Dr. Saxton and my friends call me Di."

"What does your husband call you?" Ten asked blandly.

"I'm not married."

Ten would have been surprised by any other answer, a fact that he didn't bother to conceal.

"Dr. Diana Saxton," Ten continued, "will be spending most of her time at the September Canyon digs. In between, she'll be living at the old house, which means that you boys better clean up your act. Voices carry real well from the bunkhouse to the old house. Anybody who embarrasses the lady will hear from me."

"And from me," Luke said, pulling out his chair and sitting down. "Pass the pork chops, please." He looked at Diana, saw the gap between her chair and Ten's and gave the ramrod a look that was both amused and questioning. "Didn't you have time to shower before dinner?"

The left corner of Ten's mouth lifted in wry acknowledgment, but he said nothing.

"When are you leaving?" Carla asked quickly, turning toward her brother, Cash. She didn't know why Diana kept edging farther away from Ten but guessed that she would be embarrassed if it were pointed out. By and large the cowhands were kind men, but their humor was both blunt and unrelenting.

"Right after we play poker tonight," Cash said.

"Poker?" Carla groaned.

"Sure. I thought I'd introduce Dr. Saxton to the joys of seven-card stud."

Smiling politely, Diana looked up from her plate. "Thanks, but I'm really tired. Maybe some other time."

The cowhands laughed as though she had made a joke.

"Guess they teach more than stones and bones at that university," Jervis said when the laughter ended. "Must teach some common sense, too."

Diana looked at Carla, who smiled.

"My brother is, er, well…" Carla's voice faded.

"Cash is damned lucky at cards," Ten said succinctly. "He'll clean you down to the lint in your pockets."

"It's true," said Carla. "His real name is Alexander, but anyone who has ever played cards with him calls him Cash."

"In fact," Luke said, pouring gravy over mounds of food, "I'm one of the few men in living memory ever to beat Cash at poker."

Cash smiled slightly and examined his dinner as though he expected it to get up and walk off the plate.

"Of course," Luke continued, "Cash cheated."

Cash's head snapped up.

"He wanted Carla to spend the summer on the Rocking M," Luke said matter-of-factly. "So he suckered her into betting a summer's worth of cooking. Cash won, of course. Then he turned around and carefully lost his sister's whole summer to me." Luke ran his fingertip from Carla's cheekbone to the corner of her smile before he turned to Cash and said quietly, "I never thanked you for giving Carla to me, but not a day goes by that I don't thank God."

Diana looked at the two big men and the woman who sat wholly at ease between them, smiling, her love for her husband and her brother as vivid as the blue-green of her eyes. The men's love for her was equally obvious, almost tangible. An odd aching closed Diana's throat, making an already difficult dinner impossible to swallow.

"I hope you know how lucky you are," she said to Carla. Without warning, Diana pushed back from the table and stood. "I'm afraid I'm too tired to eat. If you'll excuse me, I'll make it an early night."

"Of course," Carla said. "If you're hungry later, just come in the back way and eat whatever looks good. Ten does it all the time."

"Thanks," Diana said, already turning away, eager to be gone from the room full of men.

Nobody said a word until Diana had been gone long enough to be well beyond range of their voices. Then Luke turned, raised his eyebrows questioningly and looked straight at Ten.

"Are you the burr under her saddle?" Luke asked.

There was absolute silence as all the cowhands leaned forward to hear the answer to the question none of them had the nerve to ask their ramrod.

"She saw me take down Baker," Ten said. "Shocked her, I guess. Then I made her hold Nosy while I cut that boil. Now she thinks I'm a cross between Attila the Hun and Jack the Ripper."

Luke grunted. "Nice work, by the way. Baker, I mean. Nosy, too, I suppose. Carla was worried about that fool kitten. Me, I think we have too darn many cats as it is."

Luke caught the light, slow-motion blow Carla aimed at his shoulder. He brushed a kiss over her captive hand and said, "Honey, from now on put Diana next to you at the table. If the pretty professor moves her chair any farther away from Ten, we'll have to serve her food in the kitchen."

The cowhands burst out laughing. For a few minutes more the talk centered around the overly shy professor with the striking blue eyes and very nicely rounded body. Then food began to disappear in earnest and conversation slowed. After dessert vanished as well, so did the cowhands. Cash went upstairs to pack, leaving Ten, Luke and Carla alone to enjoy a final cup of coffee before the evening's work of kitchen cleanup and bookkeeping began.

Ten rubbed his jaw thoughtfully and was rewarded by the rasp of beard stubble. Undoubtedly that, too, had counted against him with the wary professor. Which was too bad—it had been a long time since a woman had interested him quite as much as the one with the frightened eyes and a body that would tempt a saint.

"How do you want to divide up Baker's work?" Luke asked Ten.

"I can take the leased grazing lands over on the divide, but that leaves the Wildfire Canyon springs without a hand."

"I'll take the grazing lands and have Jervis camp over at Wildfire Canyon during the week and weekends at September Canyon."

"That will make for long days for you," Ten said, glancing quickly at Carla. He knew that Luke had been trying to spend as much time as possible with his wife and new son.

"Your days will be even longer," Luke said. "Starting tomorrow, you're ramrodding the dig at September Canyon."

"Jervis can do it. He gets along with the university types real well. You'd never know it to listen to him, but he taught math in Oregon before he took up ranch work."

"You'd never know it to listen to you, either,"

retorted Luke, "but I happen to know a certain ramrod who speaks three languages and who still gets calls in the middle of the night from official types who want advice on how to get sticky jobs unstuck."

Ten said nothing.

"But they're just going to have to wait in line," Luke continued. "I've got all the trouble you can handle right in September Canyon."

Without moving, Ten became fully alert. Luke saw the change and smiled thinly.

"You expecting some kind of trouble at the site?" Ten asked.

Luke looked at Carla. "Don't I hear Logan crying?" he asked.

"Why don't you go and check?" Carla offered.

The look Luke gave Carla plainly said he wished she weren't listening to what he was saying to Ten. She looked right back, plainly telling Luke that she wasn't leaving without a good reason. Reluctantly he smiled, but when he turned to Ten the smile faded.

"The sheriff called," Luke said. "There's a ring of pothunters working the Four Corners. They dig during the week and avoid the weekends when there are more people in the back country. They're professional and they're tough."

"How tough?"

"They roughed up some folks over in Utah. The Park Service isn't making any noise about it, but the back-country rangers are going armed these days. So are the pothunters.''

''Want me to leave now for the site?'' Ten asked.

''No. One of the sheriff's men is camping out that way, unofficially. But he's got to be back on the road early tomorrow.''

Into the dining room came the clear sound of an unhappy baby. Carla put her hand on Luke's shoulder and pressed down, silently telling him not to get up.

''I'll leave before dawn,'' Ten said, watching Carla hurry from the room.

''The professor won't like that.''

''I'll be quiet,'' Ten said dryly.

''Don't bother. She's going with you. That little Japanese rice burner of hers wouldn't get four miles up the pasture road, much less across Picture Wash to September Canyon.''

Ten smiled rather wolfishly. ''She's not going to like being trapped in a truck with me. Or are you sending Carla to ride shotgun?''

''Nope,'' Luke said cheerfully. ''She's got two full-time jobs riding herd on me and the baby.''

''That's the problem. We've all got too damn many full-time jobs and not enough hands.''

''I put the word out at every ranch for three hundred miles,'' Luke said, stretching his long arms over his head. ''All we can do is wait. Jason Ironcloud promised he'd start breaking horses as soon as his sister's husband is out of jail. Until then, he's got to take care of her ranch.''

''What's the husband in for—the usual?'' Ten asked.

''Drunk and disorderly.''

''The usual.''

Luke grunted agreement.

Ten rubbed his raspy chin thoughtfully. ''Nevada called. He's pulling out of Afghanistan. He'll be home in a few weeks.''

Luke glanced sideways at Ten. ''Is he still a renegade?''

''All the Blackthorns are wild. It's the Highland Scots blood.''

''Yeah. Outlaws to the bone. Like you. You don't make any noise about it, but you go your own way and to hell with what the rest of the world thinks.''

Ten said only, ''A few years of guerrilla warfare tends to settle down even the wildest kid.''

''You should know.''

''Yes. I should know.''

Luke nodded and said softly, ''Hire him.''

Ten looked at Luke. ''Thanks. I owe you one.''

''No way, *compadre*. I should have been the man to shake the kinks out of Baker, not you.''

A slight smile crossed the ramrod's face. ''My pleasure.''

Luke looked thoughtful. ''Does Nevada fight the same way you do?''

"Wouldn't surprise me. He was taught by the same people."

"Good. He can trade off guarding September Canyon with you." Luke sighed and rubbed his neck wearily. "You know, there are days I wish Carla had never found those damn ruins. It's costing us thousands of dollars a year in manpower alone just to keep pothunters out."

"We could do what some of the other ranchers have done."

"What's that?"

"Sell some of the artifacts to pay for protecting the ruins."

"The September Canyon ruins are on your part of the ranch," Luke said, his face expressionless. "Is that what you want to do?"

Ten shook his head. "I'll give the land back to you before I sell off artifacts. Or I'll give the land back to the government if neither one of us can afford to protect the ruins. My head knows that ninety-eight percent of those artifacts aren't unique—universities and museums are full of Anasazi stuff as good or better. Once the excavation has been carefully done, there's no good reason not to get back the cost of the digging by selling off some of the stuff."

"But?" Luke asked.

Ten shrugged. "But my gut keeps telling me that those artifacts belong in the place where they were made and used and broken and mended and used again. It's pure foolishness but that's how I feel about it, and as long as I can afford it, I plan on keeping my foolish ways."

Luke looked at Ten and said quietly, "If my drunken daddy had sold pieces of the Rocking M to anybody but you, I would have been in a world of hurt with no place to call home."

Ten stood and clapped Luke on the shoulder. "It was an even trade, *compadre*. Back then, I was in a world of hurt and looking for a home."

"You've got the home. What about the hurt? Still have that?"

"I got over it a long time ago."

"Then why haven't you married again?"

"A smart dog doesn't have to be taught the same lesson twice," Ten said sardonically. "I'm a hell of a lot smarter than a dog."

"She must have been something."

"Who?"

"Your ex-wife."

Ten shrugged. "She was honest. That's better than most. When the sex wore off she wanted out. By then I was more than willing. Next time I was smarter. I didn't marry just because my blood was running hot. After a few weeks the same thing happened, only this time the girl didn't want to admit it. I shipped out the first chance I got."

"That was a long time ago. You were a wild kid

chasing girls who were no better than they had to be. You're different now."

Ten shook his head, "You got lucky, Luke. I didn't. You learned one thing about women and marriage. I learned another."

Without giving Luke a chance to speak, Ten left the room. Behind him, Luke sat motionless, listening to the sound of Ten's fading footsteps and the soft thump of a closing door.

4

As the dirt road zigzagged across national forest lease lands and down the steep side of the high, mountainous plateau where the Rocking M ranch buildings were located, the land became more dry and the earth more intensely colored. Gullies became deeper, rocky cliffs more common, and the creeks and rivers widened into broad, often dry washes winding among spectacular stone-walled canyons. Juniper and piñon mixed with sagebrush, giving the air a clean, pungent smell. In deep, protected clefts where tiny springs welled forth, a handful of true pine trees grew next to cottonwoods. Along the canyon bottoms the brush thinned to clumps. Depending on altitude or exposure, juniper, piñon, cedar and big sage grew.

Diana watched the changing landscape intently, seeking the plants that were the hallmark and foundation of Anasazi culture—yucca and piñon, bee plant and goosefoot. On the higher flatlands she also looked for stands of big sage, which grew where the earth had been disturbed and then abandoned by man. Each time another nameless canyon or gully opened up along the rough dirt road, she looked at the unexplored land with a yearning she couldn't disguise.

"Stop it," Ten said finally. "You're making me feel like the Marquis de Sade."

Startled, Diana turned toward him. "What?"

"Don't worry. I'm not talking about the way you hug the door handle as though it were your last hope of safety," Ten drawled, giving her a sideways glance.

A flush crawled up Diana's cheeks. She looked down and saw that she was all but sitting on the door handle in order to get as much distance as possible between herself and Ten.

"I—it's nothing personal," she said, her voice strained.

"Like hell it isn't," Ten said calmly. "But that's not what made me feel like a sadist. It's the way you look at all those canyons that's getting to me. It's the way a starving man looks at food, or a thirsty man looks at water, or Luke looks at Carla when they all sit in the rocking chair while she nurses Logan. If it will make you feel any better, we can stop and get closer to whatever it is you love so much."

Ten's perceptivity startled Diana. It was unexpected in a man. But then, Ten had been unexpected from the first moment she saw him. The longer she was around him, the more unexpected he became.

"That's—that's very kind of you, Mr. Blackthorn, but I'm afraid looking won't make me feel much better."

Clear, ice-gray eyes glanced briefly at Diana, then resumed watching the rough road.

"What would make you feel better, professor?"

"Being called something else, *ramrod,*" she shot back before she could think better of it.

The corner of Ten's mouth tugged up. "I'm not much on formality. Call me Ten."

Diana started to reciprocate, then stopped, afraid that Ten would mistake politeness for an entirely different sort of offer.

He shot her another quick glance. "Go ahead, I won't take it as a come-on."

"I beg your pardon?"

"Go ahead and ask me to call you Diana. I'll assume you're being polite, not looking for a little action."

"Let me assure you, I'm not looking for a 'little action.'"

"I figured that out the first time I saw you. So uncramp your hand from the door handle and tell me why you're looking at the countryside like you're saying goodbye to your only friend."

"Are you always this direct?"

"Yes. Are you always this nervous around men or is it me in particular?"

"Does it matter?"

"If I'm the one setting you on edge, I'll get out of your hair as soon as possible," Ten said matter-of-factly. "If it's just men in general you don't like, it won't matter who's on site with you."

Diana was silent.

"Well that tells me," Ten said, shrugging. "As soon as Nevada arrives, I'll turn September Canyon over to him."

"It's not you," Diana said, forcing out each word.

"Did anyone ever mention that you don't lie worth a damn? You've been terrified of me ever since I came over the corral fence and taught Baker what his horse already knew—in a fight, smart goes farther than big."

Diana closed her eyes, seeing again the blows landing too quickly to be believed. "Fast, strong and lethal count, too. Baker never had a chance, did he?"

"Only a fool, a horse or a woman would give a man like Baker a chance."

"Are you calling me a fool?"

"No. I'm not calling you a horse, either."

She made a strangled sound that was close to laughter, surprising herself.

A quick, sideways glance told Ten that Diana's grip on the door handle had eased. It also told him that her eyes were an even deeper, more brilliant blue than he had thought, and that the curve of her mouth was made to be traced by a man's tongue.

The shadow of another small canyon opening up off the road caught Diana's attention. The hint of laughter that had curved her mouth faded, leaving behind a yearning line.

"What is it that you see?" Ten asked softly.

The words slid past Diana's reflexive defenses and touched the one thing she permitted herself to love, the Anasazi homeland with its mixture of mountains and mesas and canyons, sandstone and shale, its violent summer storms, and the massive silence that made her feel as though time itself flowed through the ancient canyons.

"That canyon off to the right," Diana said, pointing to a place where a crease opened up at the base of a mesa. "Does it have a name?"

"Not that I know of."

"That's what I thought. There are hundreds of canyons like it on the Colorado Plateau. Thousands. And in each one, it would be unusual to walk more than a mile along the mesa top or the canyon bottom without finding some legacy of the Anasazi, such as broken pots or masonry or ruined stone walls."

Ten made a startled sound and glanced quickly at Diana.

"It's true," she said, turning to face him. "The Colorado Plateau is one of the richest archaeological areas of the world. Some experts say that there are a hundred archaeological sites per square mile. Others say a hundred and twenty sites. Naturally, all of the sites aren't important enough to excavate, but the sheer number of them is amazing. For instance, in Montezuma County alone, there are probably one hundred *thousand* archaeological sites.''

Ten whistled through his teeth. The boyish gesture both startled and intrigued Diana, for it was so much at odds with the fierce man who had fought Baker and the quiet man who had treated a sick kitten with such care.

''How many Anasazi lived around here, anyway?'' Ten asked.

''Here? I don't know. But over in Montezuma Valley there were about thirty thousand people. That's greater than the population today. It's the same for the rest of the Colorado Plateau. At the height of the Anasazi culture, the land supported more people than it does today with twentieth-century technology.

''And up every nameless canyon,'' Diana continued, her voice husky with emotion, ''there's a chance of finding the one extraordinary ruin that will explain why the Anasazi culture thrived in this area for more than ten centuries and then simply vanished without warning, as though the people picked up in the middle of a meal and left, taking nothing with them.''

''That's what you're looking for? The answer to an old mystery?''

She nodded.

"Why?"

The question startled Diana. "What do you mean?"

"What is it you really want?" Ten asked. "Glory? Wealth? A tenured job at an eastern university? Classrooms full of students who think you're smarter than God?"

"Is it academia in general you dislike or me in particular?"

Ten heard the echo of his own previous question and smiled to himself. "I don't know you well enough to dislike you. I'm just curious."

"So am I," Diana said tightly. "That's why I want to know about the Anasazi. Their abrupt disappearance from the cliff houses at the height of their cultural success is as big a mystery as what really caused the extinction of dinosaurs."

She glanced covertly at Ten. Though he was watching the rough, difficult road, she sensed that he was listening closely to her words. Despite her usual reticence on the subject of herself, there was something about Ten that made her want to keep talking, if only to give him a better opinion of her than he obviously had. Not that she could really blame him for being cool toward her; she had done everything but crawl under the table to avoid him at dinner.

The contrasts and contradictions of the man called Tennessee Blackthorn both intrigued and irritated Diana. A man who could fight with such savage effi-

ciency shouldn't also care about sick kittens. A man
who could handle the physical demands of the big
truck and the rotten road with such effortless skill
shouldn't be so interested in something as abstract
and intangible as the vanished Anasazi, yet he had
shown obvious interest every time the subject had
come up.

But most of all, a man who was so abrasively masculine shouldn't have been perceptive enough to notice her silent yearning after unexplored canyons. Nor
should she be noticing right now the clean line of his
profile, the high forehead and thick, faintly curling
pelt of black hair, the luxuriant black eyelashes and
crystal clarity of his eyes, the subdued sensuality of
his mouth.

The direction of Diana's thoughts made her distinctly uneasy. She turned and looked out the window
again, yet it was impossible for her to go back to the
long silences of the previous hours in the truck when
she had tried to shut out the presence of everything
except the land.

"As for prestige or a tenured teaching position,"
Diana continued, looking out the window, "I'm not
a great candidate for any university, especially an
eastern one. I love the Colorado Plateau country too
much to live anywhere else. I stand in front of classrooms full of students—worshipful or otherwise—because teaching gives me the money and time to explore the Anasazi culture in the very places where the

Ancient Ones once lived, and then make what I've seen and learned come alive in drawings.''

''You're an artist?''

Short, golden brown hair rippled and shone in the sun as Diana shook her head in a silent negative. ''At best, I'm an illustrator. I take the site photographer's pictures, read the archaeological summaries of the site and study the artifacts that have been excavated. Then I combine everything with my own knowledge of the Anasazi and make a series of drawings of the site as it probably looked when it was inhabited.''

''Sounds like more than illustration to me.''

''I assure you, it's less than art. My mother is an artist, so I know the difference.''

''Do your parents live in Colorado?''

''My mother lives in Arizona.''

Normally Ten would have let the matter of parents drop, especially since Diana's voice had planted warning flags around the subject, but his curiosity about Diana Saxton wasn't normal. She showed flashes of passion coupled with unusual reserve. And it was reserve rather than shyness. Ten had known more than a few shy cowboys. Not one of them would have been able to get up in front of a room full of people and say a single word, much less teach a whole course.

Diana wasn't shy of people. She was shy of men. Ten had immediately figured out that she didn't much care for the male half of the human race. What he hadn't figured out was why.

"What about your father?" Ten asked.

"What about him?"

Though Diana's voice was casual, Ten noted the subtle tightening of her body.

"Where does he live?" Ten asked.

"I don't know."

"Is he why you don't like men?"

"Frankly, it's none of your business."

"Of course it is. I'm a man."

"Mr. Blackthorn—"

"Ten," he interrupted.

"—whether I hate or love men is irrelevant to you or any other man I meet."

"I'll agree about the other men, but not me."

"Why?"

"I'm the man you're going to spend the next five days alone with."

"What?" Diana asked, staring at Ten.

"One of the grad students broke his ankle climbing up a canyon wall," Ten said. Without pausing in his explanations, he whipped the truck around a washout on one side of the road and then a landslide ten yards farther down. "Another one got a job in Illinois working on Indian mounds. The other three can come out only on the weekends because they work during the week."

"So?"

"So I'm staying at the September Canyon site with you."

"That's not necessary. I've been alone at remote digs before."

"Not on the Rocking M you haven't. There will be an armed guard on the site at all times." Without altering his tone at all he said, "Hang on, this will get greasy."

The relaxed lines on Ten's body didn't change as he held the truck on a slippery segment of road where sandstone gave way to thin layers of shale that were so loosely bonded they washed away in even a gentle rain. During the summer season of cloudbursts, the parts of the road that crossed shale formations became impassable for hours or days. Nor was the sandstone itself any treat for driving. Wet sandstone was surprisingly slick.

"There are professional pothunters in the area," Ten continued. "They've worked over a lot of sites. If someone objects, they work them over, too. Luke and I decided that no one goes to September Canyon without a guard."

"Why wasn't I told this before I was hired?" Diana asked tightly.

"Because the sheriff didn't tell us until last night."

Diana said something beneath her breath.

Ten glanced sideways at her. "If you can't handle it, tell me now. We'll be back at the ranch in time for dinner."

She said nothing, still trying to cope with her seething feelings at the thought of being alone with Ten in a remote canyon for five days.

"If I thought it would do any good," Ten said, "I'd give you my word that I won't touch you. But you don't know me well enough to believe me, so there's not much point in making any promises, is there?"

Diana didn't answer.

Without warning Ten brought the truck to a stop in the center of a wide spot in the road. He set the brake and turned to face his unhappy passenger.

"What will it be?" he asked. "September Canyon or back to the ranch house?"

Almost wildly Diana glanced around the countryside. She had been so excited when Carla had offered employment for the summer. The salary was minimal, but the opportunity to study newly discovered ruins was unparalleled.

And now it was all vanishing like rain in the desert.

She looked at Ten. Part of her was frankly terrified at the prospect of being alone with him for days on end. Part of her was not—and in some ways, that was most terrifying of all.

Shutting out everything, Diana closed her eyes. *What am I going to do?*

The image of Ten's powerful hands holding the kitten with such care condensed in her mind.

Surely Carla wouldn't send me out here alone with

a man she didn't trust. After that thought came another. *My father was never that gentle with anything. Nor was Steve.*

The ingrained habit of years made Diana's mind veer away from the bleak night when she had learned once and forever to distrust men and her own judgment. Yet she had been luckier than many of the women she had talked with since. Her scars were all on the inside.

Unbidden came a thought that made Diana tremble with a tangle of emotions she refused to name and a question she shouldn't ask, even in the silence of her own mind.

Would Ten be as gentle with a woman as he was with that kitten?

5

Ten sat and watched the emotions fighting within Diana—anger, fear, hope, confusion, curiosity, longing. The extent of Diana's reluctance to go on to September Canyon surprised him. He had glimpsed the depth of her passion for the Anasazi; if she were considering turning and walking away from September Canyon, she must be in the grip of a fear that was very real to her, despite the fact that Ten knew of no reason for that fear. While most women might have been initially uneasy at spending time alone with a stranger in a remote place, their instinctive wariness would have been balanced by the knowledge that their unexpected companion was a man who had the respect and trust of the people he lived among.

That fact, however, didn't seem to make much difference to Diana.

"Can you talk about it?" Ten asked finally.

"What?"

"Why you're afraid of men. Is it your father?"

Diana looked at Ten's searching, intent eyes, sensing the intelligence and the strength of will in him reaching out to her, asking her to trust him.

Abruptly she felt hemmed in, required to do something for which she was unprepared.

"Stop hounding me," Diana said through clenched teeth. "You have no right to my secrets any more than any man has a right to my body!"

For an instant there was an electric silence stretching tightly between Ten and Diana; then he turned away from her to look out over the land. The silence lengthened until the idling of the truck's engine was as loud as thunder. When Ten finally turned back toward Diana his face was expressionless, his eyes were hooded, and his voice held none of the mixture of emotions it had before.

"In an hour or less those clouds will get together and rain very hard. Then Picture Wash will become impassable. Anyone who is at the September Canyon site will be forced to stay there. Which will it be, Dr. Saxton? Forward to the dig or back to the ranch?"

Ten's voice was even, uninflected, polite. It was like having a stranger ask her for the time of day.

Bitterly Diana reminded herself that Ten was a stranger. Yet somehow he hadn't seemed like one until just now. From the moment Ten had held out the injured kitten to Diana, he had treated her as though she were an old friend newly discovered. She hadn't even realized the…warmth…of his presence until it had been withdrawn.

Now she had an absurd impulse to reach out and touch Ten, to protest the appearance of the handsome, self-contained stranger who waited for her answer with cool attention, his whole attitude telling her that whether she chose to go forward or back, it made no personal difference to him.

"September Canyon," Diana said after a minute. Although she tried, her voice wasn't as controlled as his had been.

Ten took off the brake and resumed driving.

Eventually the silence, which Diana had welcomed before, began to eat at her nerves. She looked out the window but found herself glancing again and again toward Ten. She told herself that it was only his casual skill with the truck that fascinated her. She had done enough rough-country travel in the past to admire his expertise. And it was his expertise she was admiring, not the subtle flex and play of his muscles beneath the faded black work shirt he wore.

"You're a very good driver," she said.

Ten nodded indifferently.

Silence returned, lengthened, filling the cab until Diana rolled down the window just to hear the whistle of wind. She told herself the lack of conversation didn't bother her. After all, she had been the one to resist talk during the long hours since dawn. When Ten had pointed out something along the road or asked about her work, she had nodded or answered briefly and had no questions of her own to offer.

But now that she thought about it, she had a perfect right to ask a few businesslike questions of Ten and get a few businesslike answers.

"Will it distract you to talk?" she asked finally.

"No."

Brief and to the point. Very businesslike. Irritating, too. Silently Diana asked herself if her earlier, brief, impersonal answers had seemed cool and clipped to Ten.

"I didn't mean to be rude earlier," she said.

"You weren't."

Diana waited.

Ten said nothing more.

"How much farther is it to September Canyon?" she asked after a few minutes.

"An hour."

Diana looked up toward the mesa top where piñon and juniper and cedar grew, punctuated by pointed sprays of yucca plants. The clouds had become a solid mass whose bottom was a blue color so deep it was nearly black.

"Looks like rain," she said.

Ten nodded.

More silence, more bumps, more growling sounds from the laboring four-wheel-drive truck.

"Why is it called Picture Wash?" Diana asked in a combination of irritation and determination.

"There are pictographs on the cliffs."

Six whole words. Incredible.

"Anasazi?" she asked.

Ten shrugged.

"Did other Indians live here when the white man came?" Diana asked, knowing very well that they had.

Ten nodded.

"Mountain Utes?" she asked, again knowing the answer.

"Yes," he said as he swerved around a mass of shale that had extended a slippery tongue onto the roadway.

Diana hardly noticed the evasive maneuver. She was intent on drawing out the suddenly laconic Ten. Obviously that would require a question that couldn't be answered by yes, no or a shrug. Inspiration came.

"Why are you called Tennessee?"

"I was the oldest."

"I don't understand."

"Neither did Dad."

Diana gave up the word game and concentrated on the land.

The truck kicked and twitched and skidded around a series of steep, uphill curves, climbing up a mesa spur and onto the top. There was a long, reasonably straight run across the spur. Piñon and juniper whipped by, interspersed with a handful of big sage and other drought-adapted shrubs.

Abruptly there was an opening in the piñon and juniper. Though the ground looked no different, big sagebrush grew head-high and higher. Their silver-gray, twisting branches were thicker than a strong man's arm.

"Stop!" Diana said urgently.

The truck shuddered to a halt. Before the pebbles scattered by the tires finished rolling, Diana had her seat belt off and was jumping down the cab.

"What's wrong?" Ten asked, climbing out of the truck.

Diana didn't answer. Watching the ground with intent, narrowed eyes, she quartered the stand of big sage, twisting and turning, zigzagging across the open areas in the manner of someone searching for something. She was so involved in her quest that she didn't seem to notice the scrapes and scratches the rough brush delivered to her unprotected arms.

Ten hesitated at the edge of the road, wondering if Diana was looking for a little privacy. It had been a long drive from the ranch, and there were no amenities such as gas stations or public rest rooms along the way. Yet Diana seemed more interested in the open areas between clumps of big sage than in the thicker growths that would have offered more privacy.

Without warning Diana went down on her knees and began digging hurriedly in the rocky ground. Ten started toward her, ignoring the slap and drag of brush over his clothes. When he was within ten feet of her, she gave a cry of triumph and lifted a squarish rock in both hands. Dirt clung to the edges and dappled light fell across the stone's surface, camouflaging its oddly regular shape.

"Look!" she cried, holding up her prize to Ten.

He eased forward until her was close to her, ducked a branch that had been going after his eyes, straightened and looked.

"A stone," Ten said neutrally.

Diana didn't notice his lack of enthusiasm. She had enough for both of them and the truck, as well. Nor did she notice the dirty streaks left on her jeans when she rubbed the rock back and forth, cleaning the part of the stone that had been buried beneath the dirt. After a few moments she held the rock in a patch of sunlight coming through the open branches of the sage.

"Beautiful," she crooned, running her fingertips delicately along the stone, absorbing the subtle variations in the surface, marks that were the result of applied intelligence rather than random weathering. "Just...beautiful."

The throaty timbre of Diana's voice lured Ten as no stone could have. He sat on his heels next to her and looked closely at the rock that she was continuing to stroke as though it were alive.

The contours of the stone were too even, its edges too angular to be the result of chance. When the light touched the rock just right, tiny dimples could be seen, marks left by countless patient blows from a stone ax held in the hands of an Anasazi stone mason. Seeing those tangible marks of a long-dead man made the skin on Ten's skull tighten in a primal reflex that was far older than the civilized artifact Diana was cherishing in her hands.

Without realizing it, Ten stretched out his own hand, feeling a need to confirm the stone's reality through touch. The rock had the texture of medium sandpaper. The dimples were shallow, more a vague pattern than true pockmarks. Cold from the ground on one end, sun warmed on the other, bearing the marks of man all over its surface, the stone was enduring testimony to a culture that was known only by its fragmentary ruins.

"How did you know this was here?" Ten asked.

"No juniper or piñon," Diana said absently as she turned the relic of the past over and over in her hands.

Ten glanced around. She was right. Despite the luxuriant growth of big sage on the ground, there were no junipers or piñons for fifty yards in any direction.

"They don't grow on ground that has been disturbed," Diana continued, measuring the area of the big sage with her eyes. "When you see a place like this, there's a very good chance that Anasazi ruins lie beneath the surface, covered by the debris of time and rain and wind."

Gray eyes narrowed while Ten silently reviewed his knowledge of the surrounding countryside.

"There are a lot of patches of big sage on Wind Mesa," he said after a minute. "My God, there must be hundreds of places like this on both sides of Picture Wash. That and the presence of year-round water is why the MacKenzies bought rights to this land more than a century ago."

"It was the water and the presence of game that attracted the Anasazi a thousand years ago. Human needs never change. All that changes is how we express those needs."

With the care of a mother returning a baby to its cradle, Diana replaced the rock in its hollow and smoothed dirt back in place.

"That's what is so exciting about the whole area of Wind Mesa," she said as she worked. "For a long time we believed that the Durango River was the farthest northern reach of the Anasazi in Colorado. September Canyon proved that we were wrong."

"Not all that wrong," Ten said dryly. "You talk as though we're a hundred miles from the river. We're not. It just seems like it by the time you loop around mountains and canyons on these rough roads."

Absently, Diana nodded. When she stood up, she was quite close to Ten. She didn't even notice. Her attention was on the area defined by the silvery big sage, and she was looking at her surroundings with an almost tangible hunger.

"This could have been a field tended by a family and watered by spreader dams and ditches built by the Anasazi," she said. "Or it could have been a small community built near a source of good water and food. It could have been the Anasazi equivalent of a church or a convent or a men's club. It could have been so many things...and I doubt if we'll ever know exactly what."

"Why not?"

Diana turned and focused on Ten with blue eyes that were as dark and as deep as the storm condensing across the western sky.

"This is Rocking M land," Diana said simply. "Private land. Luke MacKenzie is already bearing the cost of excavating and protecting the September Canyon ruins. I doubt that he can afford to make a habit of that kind of generosity."

"Luke's partner is absorbing the cost, but you're right. Ranching doesn't pay worth a damn as it is. The cost of protecting the whole of Wind Mesa..." Ten lifted his Stetson and resettled it with a jerk. "We'd do it if we could, but we can't. It would bankrupt us."

The sad understanding in Diana's smile said more about regret and acceptance than any words could have.

"Even the government can't afford it," she agreed,

rubbing her hands absently on her jeans. "County, state, federal, it doesn't matter which level of government you appeal to. There just isn't enough money. Even at Mesa Verde, which is designed to be a public showcase of the whole range of Anasazi culture, archaeologists have uncovered ruins, measured them, then backfilled them with dirt. It was the only way to protect them from wind, rain and pothunters."

Ten looked around the rugged mesa top and said quietly, "Maybe that's best. Whatever is beneath the earth has been buried for centuries. A few more centuries won't make any difference."

"Here, probably not," Diana said, gesturing to the big sage. "But on the cliffs or on the edges of the mesa, the ruins that aren't buried are disintegrating or being dismantled by pothunters. That's why the work in September Canyon is so important. What we don't learn from it now probably won't be available to learn later. The ruins will have been picked over, packed up and shipped out to private collections all over the world."

The passion and regret in Diana's voice riveted Ten. He was reaching out to touch her in silent comfort when he caught himself. A touch from a man she feared would hardly be a comfort.

"Don't sell this countryside short when it comes to protecting its own," Ten said. "The big sage may be a giveaway on Wind Mesa, but this is a damned inconvenient place to get to. There's only one road and half the time it's impassable. There's a horse trail through the mountains that drops down to September Mesa, but only a few Rocking M riders even know about it and no one has used it in years.''

Slowly, almost unwillingly, Diana focused on Ten, sensing his desire to comfort her as clearly as the kitten had sensed its safety within Ten's hands.

''As for the scores of little canyons that might hold cliff ruins,'' Ten said, watching Diana, sensing the soft uncurling of her tightly held trust, ''most of those canyons haven't seen a man since the Anasazi left. Any man. The Utes avoided the ruins as spirit places. Cows avoid the small canyons because the going is too rough, so cowhands don't go there, either. What's hidden stays hidden.''

Ten's deep voice with its subtle velvet rasp swirled around Diana, holding her still even as it caressed her. She stared at the clear depths of his eyes and felt a curious mix of hunger and wariness, yearning and…familiarity.

''And if some of those ruins are never found, is that so bad?'' Ten asked softly. He spoke slowly, watching Diana's eyes, trying to explain something he had never put into words. ''Like the Anasazi, the ruins came from time and the land. It's only right that some of them return to their beginnings untouched by any but Anasazi hands.''

A throaty muttering of thunder rode the freshening wind. The sound seeped into Diana's awareness, bringing with it a dizzying feeling of déjà vu; of overlapping realities; of time, like a deck of cards, being reshuffled, and the sound of that shuffling was muted thunder. Her breathing slowed and then stopped as an eerie certainty condensed within her: *she had known Ten before, had stood on a mesa top with him before, had walked with him through piñon and sun and silence, had slept next to his warmth while lightning and rain renewed the land....*

The feeling passed, leaving Diana shaken, disoriented, staring at a man who should have been a stranger and was not. Thunder came again, closer, insistent. She took a deep breath, infusing herself with the elemental, unforgettable pungency of sage and piñon, juniper and storm. And time. That most of all. The scent of time and a storm coming down.

Closing her eyes, Diana breathed deeply, filling herself with the storm wind, feeling it touch parts of her that had been curled tightly shut for too many years. The sensation of freedom and vulnerability that followed was frightening and exhilarating at the same time, like swimming nude in a midnight lake.

"Storm coming," Ten said, looking away from Diana because if he watched her drink the wind any longer he wouldn't be able to stop himself from touching her. "If we're going to cross Picture Wash, we have to hurry. Unless you've changed your mind?"

Diana's eyes opened. She saw a powerful man

standing motionless, silhouetted against sunlight and
thunderheads, his head turned away from her. Then
he looked back at her, and his eyes were like cut
crystal against the darkness of his face.

"Diana?"

The sound of her name on Ten's lips made sensations glitter through her body from breastbone to
knees.

"Yes," she said, trying to sound businesslike and
failing. "I'm coming."

6

There was some water running in Picture Wash, but the big ranch truck crossed without difficulty. Splash marks on the other side of the ford told Ten that he wasn't the only person who had driven toward September Canyon today. Ten glanced quickly around but saw nothing. They had passed no one the entire length of the one-lane dirt road, which meant that the other vehicle was still in front of them.

Frowning, Ten turned right and drove along the edge of the broad wash. There was no real road to follow, simply a suggestion of tire tracks where other vehicles had gone before. Tributary canyons opened up on the left of the wash, and more were visible across the thin ribbon of water, but Ten made no attempt to explore those openings. After three miles he turned left into the mouth of a side canyon.

Diana looked at him questioningly.

"September Canyon," Ten said. "The mesa it's

eaten out of didn't really have a name, but we've started calling it September Mesa since we've been working on the site. Wind Mesa is behind us now, across the wash.''

"What's upstream?''

"More canyons. Smaller. If you follow the wash upstream long enough, it finally narrows into a crack and disappears against a wall of stone, which is the body of the mesa itself. Almost all the canyons are blind. Only one or two have an outlet on top of the mesa. Other than that, the canyons are a maze. Even with a compass, it's hard not to get lost.''

Diana turned around, trying to orient herself. "Where is the Rocking M?''

Ten gestured with his head because he needed both hands for the wheel. "North and east, on top of the big mesa.''

"It is? I thought the ranch was on the edge of a broad valley.''

He smiled slightly. "So do most people who come on the Rocking M from the north. You don't know the valley is really a mesa until you drive off the edge. The mountains confuse you. All of the Colorado Plateau is like that.''

Diana reached into her back jeans pocket, pulled out a United States Geological Survey map and began searching for the vague line that represented the ranch road they were on. The bouncing of the truck made map reading impossible.

"Perspective is a funny thing," Ten said, glancing at the map for an instant. "Coming in from the south and east, you see the wall of the mesa, the cliffs and gorges and canyons. That's where the explorers were when they started naming things—at the bottom looking up. You can't see the Fire Mountains from that angle, and everything looks dark and jumbled at a distance, so the whole area was once called Black Plateau or Fire Mountain Plateau, depending on which old-timer you talk to."

Diana folded up the map and put it away.

"On the other hand," Ten continued, "if you're coming in from the mountain end of the territory, you see a mesa top as more of a broad valley, and you name it accordingly."

"Is that what happened on the Rocking M?"

Ten nodded. "Case MacKenzie started out with a ranch at the base of what became known as MacKenzie Ridge, which is a foothill of the Fire Mountains. From his perspective, the mesa top is a broad, winding valley. But history named the hunk of land for a hundred miles in all directions Black Plateau, even though it's more like a mesa than a plateau. Then you add a hundred years of Spanish and American cowboys translating Indian names and adding their own to the mix, and you have a mapmaker's nightmare."

"You also have a lot of lost tourists."

The left corner of Ten's mouth lifted slightly. "Just

remember that September Mesa and Wind Mesa and all the nameless mesas are nothing but narrow fingers stretching out from the huge hand known as Black Plateau or MacKenzie Valley, depending on which direction your mapmaker came from.''

"I'm beginning to understand why men invented satellite photos. It's the only way to see how the pieces all fit together.''

Ten shot Diana an amused, approving glance, but only for an instant. The truck, moving at barely five miles an hour, bumped and thumped over the rock-strewn, narrowing canyon bottom. To Diana's eyes there was nothing to distinguish the cliff-rimmed canyon they had entered from the many other tributary canyons that emptied into Picture Wash. The mouth of September Canyon was perhaps eighty yards across, marked by nothing but a faint suggestion of tire tracks in the sand. The cliffs were of a vaguely ruddy, vaguely gold sandstone that overlay narrower beds of shale. The shale crumbled readily, forming steep, slippery talus slopes at the base of the sandstone cliffs.

Scattered on the surface of the gray-brown shale debris were huge, erratic piles of sandstone rubble that were formed when the shale crumbled and washed away faster than the more durable cliffs above, leaving the sandstone cliffs without support at their base. Then great sheets of sandstone peeled away from the overhanging cliffs and fell to the earth below, shattering into rubble and leaving behind arches and alcoves and deeper overhangs—and, sometimes, filling pre-existing alcoves.

In many cases the shale had been eroded by the seeping of groundwater between layers of sandstone and shale. When the water eventually reached the edge of a cliff or a ravine, it became a spring, a source of clean, year-round water for the people who eventually sought shelter in the arching overhangs that the springs had helped to create. Without the water there would have been no cliff-hanging alcoves for men to take shelter within, no easily defended villages set into sheer stone. Without the very special circumstances of sandstone, shale and water, the Anasazi civilization would have developed very differently, if it developed at all.

That interlocking of Anasazi and the land had always fascinated Diana. The fact that their cliff houses were found in some of the most remote, starkly beautiful landscapes in America simply added to her fascination.

"Does the Rocking M run cattle here?" Diana asked.

"Not for several years."

"Then how were the ruins discovered?"

"Carla was returning a potshard that Luke had found years ago in the mouth of September Canyon and given to her. She drove out from Boulder alone and spent several hours walking the canyon floor.

There had been a storm recently and a tree had fallen. She came around a bend and there the ruins were.''

"That must have been incredible," Diana said, her voice throaty with longing.

"I doubt that Carla was in a mood to appreciate it. She had come here to say goodbye to everything she had ever wanted—the land, the ranch, and most of all the man."

"Luke?"

Ten nodded.

"What changed her mind?"

"Luke. He finally got it through his hard head that Carla was the one woman in a million who could live on an isolated ranch and not go sour."

Diana's mouth turned down in a sad curve. "I was ranch-raised. It's not for everyone, man or woman."

"You didn't like it?"

"I loved it. No matter how bad things at home got, the land was always waiting, always beautiful, always there. I could walk away from the buildings and the land would…" Her voice shivered into silence as she realized what she had almost revealed.

"Heal you?" Ten suggested softly.

Diana's eyes closed and a tiny shudder went through her. Ten was too perceptive. He saw things with dangerous clarity.

"The land was here long before a primate climbed down out of a tree and put a kink in his back trying to see over the grass," Ten said matter-of-factly.

"The land will be here long after we're gone. That frightens some people because it makes them feel small and worthless. But some people are made whole by touching something that's bigger than they are, something enduring, something that lives on a different time scale than man."

The words slid past Diana's defenses, making her realize that Ten was one of those who had come to the land to be healed.

"What hurt you?" she asked before she could stop herself.

The lines of Ten's face shifted, reminding Diana of the cold, deadly fighter who had come over the corral fence and flattened a larger, whip-wielding opponent in a matter of seconds.

"I'm sorry," Diana said quickly. "I had no right to ask."

Ten nodded curtly, either agreeing with her or accepting her apology, she wasn't certain which.

It was silent in the truck for a few moments before Ten said, "We're coming up on the base camp. It's beneath that big overhang on the left."

Diana heard more than the words; she heard what wasn't said, as well. Gone was the subtle emotion that had made Ten's voice like black velvet when he talked about the land. His tone was neither reserved nor outgoing, simply neutral. Polite.

Telling herself that Ten's withdrawal didn't matter, Diana looked beyond his handsome, unyielding profile to the smooth cliff wall rising above scattered piñons. The sandstone gleamed against the thunderheads that had consumed the sky. Something bright flickered at the edge of her vision. A few seconds later thunder pealed through the narrow canyon, shaking the ground. Spectral light flickered and danced again, and again thunder reverberated between stone walls.

Diana closed her eyes and breathed in deeply, savoring the pungent, suddenly cool wind. Soon it would begin to rain. She could feel it. She could smell it in the air, the unique blend of heat and dust rising up from the ground and countless water drops reaching down to caress the dry land.

Thunder belled again and then again. A gust of wind came through the open truck window, pouring over Diana. She laughed softly, wishing she were alone so that she could hold out her arms and embrace the wild summer storm.

The subdued music of Diana's laughter drew Ten's attention. He looked at her for only an instant, but it was enough. He knew he would never forget the picture she made with her head thrown back and her hair tousled as though by a lover's hands, her cheeks flushed with excitement and her lips parted as she gave herself to the storm wind.

The persistent male curiosity Ten had felt at his first sight of Diana retreating from the skirmish at the corral became a torrent of desire pouring through him, hardening him with a speed he hadn't known since he was a teenager. Cursing silently, he forced his attention away from his quickened body and onto the demands of the terrain. The last quarter of a mile to the ruins was tricky, because most of it was over greasy shale slopes studded with house-size boulders of sandstone that had fallen from the thick, cliff-forming layer of rock. The truck bucked and tires spun in protest at the slippery going as the vehicle groaned up the final hill.

"Wouldn't it have been better to walk from the base camp?" Diana asked, bracing herself against the dashboard.

"I was in a hurry."

"Why?" she asked, looking toward him as the truck bucked over the ridge and stopped abruptly.

"That's why."

The flat, predatory quality of Ten's voice froze Diana's breath. Slowly she followed his glance.

A dirty Range Rover was parked among the rubble at the base of the cliff. Beyond the vehicle, lightweight aluminum ladders extended up the twenty feet of massive sandstone that separated the ruins from the rubble below.

Ten reached over, unlocked the gun rack that hung over the rear window and chose the shotgun, leaving the rifle in place. He checked the shotgun's load, racked a shell into the chamber, then got out of the truck and closed the door before he turned to look at Diana through the open window.

"Stay here."

Thunder belled harshly, followed by a cannonade of rain sweeping in shining veils over the ground. Holding the shotgun muzzle down, Ten ignored the rain that quickly soaked through his clothing. There was a muffled shout from the ruins. He ignored that, too. The Range Rover was unlocked. He went through the vehicle quickly, finding and unloading a pistol and a rifle. A quick motion of his wrist sent bullets arcing out into the rain. The weapons he put way in the back of the Rover, next to a big carton. With one eye on the pothunters who were scrambling down the rain-slick ladders, Ten ripped open the box.

It was filled with Anasazi pots, their bold geometries and corrugated finish unmistakable in the watery light. Bits of turquoise and shell gleamed in the bottom of one bowl. Ten lifted the carton out, set it on the ground and returned to the interior of the Rover. It stank of cigarette smoke and gasoline that was evaporating from a five-gallon container with a faulty seal.

As the pothunters hit the bottom of the ladder and started running toward him, Ten opened the container and pushed it over inside the car. The stench of raw gas swirled up, overpowering.

"Hey!" hollered the first man. "Get the hell out of there! That car's private property!"

The Rover was between Ten and the pothunters. When he stepped out around the rear of the Rover, the men could see the shotgun held with professional ease in Ten's hands, muzzle slanted down, neither pointing toward nor away from the men.

The first man slowed his reckless pace to a wary walk. He was in his mid-twenties and carried himself as though he had spent time in the military. He was big, hard-shouldered, used to intimidating people with his sheer size.

"You're trespassing on Rocking M land," Ten said.

"I didn't see any signs."

The line of Ten's mouth lifted in a sardonic curl. "Too bad. Get in your Rover and drive out of here."

The other two men caught up with the first just as he shouted, "You'll be hearing from me, cowboy. You're threatening private citizens. We were just traveling around in the back country and made a wrong turn somewhere. It could have happened to anyone—and that's what I'll tell the sheriff when I file a complaint!"

"The only wrong turn you made was in thinking all you'd find out here were pots and a few grad students even younger than you."

"Think you're a big man with that shotgun, don't you?"

"You sure didn't learn much in the marines before they threw you out."

"How did you know I was..." The man's voice faded even as angry color rose in his face. He jerked his head toward the Rover. The other two men reached for the door handles.

Ten watched with an air of shuttered expectancy. He wasn't disappointed. No sooner did the two men open the Rover's doors than there were simultaneous shouts of outrage.

"He poured gas all over the damn car!"

"Milt, the pots are gone!"

Then one of the men noticed the guns. He slammed the door and said in disgust, "Pack it in, Milt. He got to the guns."

Milt's face flattened into mean lines as he measured the cowboy standing at ease in front of him.

"You heard them," Ten said. "Pack it in." He raised his voice slightly and said to the other two men, "Get in the Rover and shut the doors."

The younger man colored with frustration and anger when his two companions obediently climbed into the Rover, slamming both doors hard behind them.

"Those are my pots," Milt said angrily. "If they're not in the Rover when I leave, I'll sue your smart ass for theft."

"Go home, kid. School's out."

As Ten spoke, he casually broke open the shotgun and removed the shell from the firing chamber.

Milt was as foolish as Ten had hoped. The younger man began weaving and feinting, his body held in the stance of someone who had been trained in unarmed combat.

Ten closed the shotgun with a fast snap of his wrist and set the weapon on the Rover's hood before he turned and walked toward the younger man. As though Ten's calm approach unnerved Milt, he attacked. Ten deflected the charge with a deceptively casual motion of his shoulders that sent Milt staggering off balance over the slippery rubble. He went to his hands and knees, then scrambled to his feet and came after Ten again.

One of the Rover's doors opened just behind Ten. He spun around and lashed out with his booted foot, connecting with metal. There was a startled curse, a cry of pain and the sound of the door slamming closed beneath Ten's foot. Before the echo could return from the stone walls, Ten had turned around again.

Milt was more careful in his tactics this time, but the result was still the same. When he lunged for Ten, Milt got nothing but a handful of mud. It happened again, then a fourth time, and each time Milt ended up on his hands and knees.

"Hurry up, kid," Ten said, watching Milt push to his feet for the fifth time. "I'm getting tired of standing around in the rain waiting for you to get smart."

With an inarticulate cry of rage, Milt came to his feet, clawing beneath his windbreaker with his right hand, tearing a hunting knife free of its sheath. This time when Milt charged, Ten made a single swift movement that sent the other man head over heels to land hard and flat on his back, gasping for air. Ten's boot descended on Milt's right wrist. Bending over, Ten took the knife from Milt's hand, tested the edge of the blade and made a disdainful sound.

"You'd be lucky to cut butter with this, boy."

Milt's glazed eyes focused on Ten, who was throwing the knife from hand to hand, flipping it end over end, testing the knife's balance with the expertise of someone thoroughly accustomed to using a knife as a weapon.

"Other than the edge, it's a nice knife," Ten said after a few moments. "Really fine."

There was a brief blur of movement followed by the sound of steel grating through earth. Buried half the length of its blade, the knife gleamed only inches from Milt's shocked face. Ten removed his boot from Milt's wrist.

"Pull the knife out and put it back in your belt."

Milt reached slowly for the knife. For an instant as his fingers closed around the hilt, he thought of throwing the knife at the smaller, rain-soaked man who had humiliated him with such offhanded ease.

Watching with the clear-eyed patience of a predator, Ten waited to see how smart Milt was.

Slowly, reluctantly, Milt returned the knife to its sheath.

"You're learning, kid. Too bad. I was looking forward to watching you eat that knife." Ten bent down and dragged the younger man to his feet with a single powerful motion. "Now here's something else for you to learn. I've been hearing things about a busted-out gyrene pothunter who gets his kicks slapping around teachers whose only crime is wanting to camp in a national park."

For the first time since the fight had started, Milt was close enough to see Ten's eyes beneath the dripping brim of his cowboy hat. The younger man's face paled visibly.

"Hearing things like that makes me real impatient," Ten said matter-of-factly. "When I get impatient, I get clumsy, and when I get clumsy, I break things. My friends are the same way, and I've got friends all over the Four Corners. So if you know any other pothunting cowards, pass the word. Starting now, my friends and I will be damned clumsy. Understand?"

Slowly Milt nodded.

Ten opened his hands and stepped back, his body both relaxed and perfectly balanced. "You're going to start thinking about this, and drinking, and pretty soon you'll be sure you can take me. So think on this. Next time you come after me, I'll strip you, pin a diaper on you, and walk you through town wearing a pink bonnet. Know something else? You won't have a mark on you, but you'll be marching double time just the same." Ten jerked his head toward the Rover. "Make sure I don't hear about you again, kid. I purely despise bullies."

Milt backed away from Ten and reached for the

Rover's front door with more eagerness than grace. Ten watched. He was about to congratulate the two men in the Rover on their good sense in staying out of his way when he saw that the reason they had sidelined themselves wasn't good sense.

Diana had stepped down from the truck and was standing in the rain, sighting down a rifle she had braced across the hood of the truck.

7

With outward calm Diana watched the Range Rover slither and slide down the shale, retreating from September Canyon as quickly as the rain and rough terrain allowed.

"You can put it away now. They won't be back."

Ten's voice made Diana realize that she was still crouched over the rifle, sighting down its blue-steel barrel, her hands holding the weapon too tightly. She forced herself to take a deep breath and stand upright.

"May I?" Ten asked, holding out a hand for the rifle.

Diana gave the rifle to him and said faintly, "It will need cleaning. The rain is very...wet."

Ten didn't smile, simply nodded his head in agreement. "I'll take care of it."

"Thank you. It's been years since I cleaned a rifle. I've probably forgotten how."

"You sure didn't forget how to use one," Ten said

as he checked the rifle over with a few swift movements. He noted approvingly that there was a round in the chamber. He removed the bullet and pocketed it. "Thanks."

Diana looked at him and blinked, trying to focus her thoughts.

"For aiming the rifle at them rather than at me," Ten explained, smiling slightly. "It's nice to know you think I'm one of the good guys."

"I—they—you didn't need me," she said, rubbing her hands together.

"Three against one? I needed all the help I could get."

Diana shook her head. "You could have made veal cutlets out of that pothunter before his friends could have taken a single step to stop you. Why didn't you?"

"Never did like veal cutlets," Ten said matter-of-factly, opening the truck door. "Get in, honey. It's wet out here."

"I'm serious," she said, climbing up into the dry cab. "Why did you hold back? You certainly didn't with Baker...did you?"

Ten went around the truck and got in behind the wheel. He sensed Diana's intent, watchful, rather wary eyes. Wondering if Diana were still afraid of him, Ten watched her from the corner of his eye as he began wiping down the rifle and shotgun. Despite the vague trembling of her hands and the paleness of her skin, he began to realize that she wasn't afraid of him; she was simply caught in the backlash of the adrenaline storm that had come from her brush with pothunters.

"Why?" Diana persisted, rubbing her arms as though she were cold.

"Baker is a brute who only understands brute force," Ten said finally. "If I had pulled my punches with him, he would have been back for more. That kid Milt was different. He's a swaggering bully. A coward. So I showed him what a candy ass he really is when it comes to fighting. He'll be a long time forgetting."

"Will he be back?"

"Doubt it." Ten turned around and locked the weapons back into the rack. "But if he does come back, he better pray Nevada isn't on guard."

"Nevada?"

"My kid brother. He would have gutted Milt and never looked back. Hard man, Nevada."

"And you aren't?"

Turning, looking at Diana over his shoulder, Ten smiled slowly. "Honey, haven't you figured it out yet? I'm so tenderhearted a butterfly can walk rough-shod all over me."

It was the second time in as many minutes that Ten had called Diana "honey." She knew she should object to the implied intimacy. At the very least she shouldn't encourage him by laughing at the ludicrous image of a butterfly stomping all over Ten's muscular body. So she tried very hard not to laugh, failed, and finally gave into the need, knowing that it was a release for all the emotions seething just beneath her control.

Ten listened, sensing the complex currents of Diana's emotions. He reached for the door before he looked over at her and nodded once, as though agreeing with himself.

"You'll do, Diana Saxton. You'll do just fine."

"For what?" she asked, startled.

"For whatever you want. You've got guts, lady. You'd go to war over a carton of Anasazi artifacts. You stand up for what you believe in. That's too damned rare these days."

Ten was out of the truck and closing the door behind him before Diana could put into words her first thought: she hadn't stood in the rain with an unfamiliar rifle in her hands to save a few artifacts from pothunters. It had been Ten she was worried about, one man against three.

I didn't need to worry. Ten is a one-man army. Cash was right. Someone taught Ten to play hardball. I wonder who, and where, and what it cost....

The truck's door opened. Ten set the closed carton of artifacts on the seat next to Diana, then swung into the cab with a lithe motion. His masculine grace fascinated her, as did the fact that his rain-soaked shirt clung to every ridge and swell of muscle, emphasizing the width of his shoulders and the strength of his back. If he had wanted to, he could have overpowered her with terrible ease, for he was far stronger than Steve had been; and in the end Steve had been too strong for her.

Grimly Diana turned her thoughts away from a past that was beyond her ability to change or forget. She could only accept what had happened and renew her vow that she would never again put herself in a position where a man thought he had the right to take from her what she was unwilling to give.

"Don't worry," Ten said.

"What?" Diana gave him a startled look, wondering if he had read her mind.

"The artifacts are fine. Milt was an amateur when it came to fighting, but he knew how to pack pots. Nothing was lost."

"Just the history."

His hand on the key, Ten turned to look at Diana, not understanding what she meant.

"The real value of the artifacts for an archaeologist comes from seeing how they relate to each other in situ," she explained. "Unless these artifacts were photographed where they were found, they don't have much to tell us now."

"To a scholar, maybe. But to me, just seeing the artifacts, seeing their shapes and designs, knowing they were made by a people and a culture that lived and died and will never be born again..." Ten shrugged. "I'd go to war to save a piece of that. Hell, I have more than once."

Again, Ten had surprised Diana. She hadn't expected a nonprofessional to understand the intellectual and emotional fascination of fragments from the past. His response threw her off balance, leaving her teetering between her ingrained fear of men and her equally deep desire to be close to the contradictory, complex man called Tennessee Blackthorn.

Ten eased the big truck down the slippery shoulder of shale and headed back for the big overhang that served as a base camp for the dig. By the time they had unloaded their gear, set up sleeping bags at the opposite ends of the overhang's broad base and changed into dry clothes behind the canvas privacy screen that had been erected for just such emergencies, the rain was becoming less a torrent.

Neither Diana nor Ten noticed the improving weather at first. They had gravitated toward the shard-sorting area that the graduate students had set up. Numbered cartons held remnants of pottery that had been taken from specific areas of the site. The shards themselves were also numbered according to the place where they had been unearthed. Whoever had the time or the desire was invited to try piecing together the three-dimensional puzzles before they were removed to the old ranch house.

Ten showed a marked flair for resurrecting whole artifacts from scattered, broken fragments. In fact, more than once Diana was astonished at the ease with which he reached into one carton, then another, and came out with interlocking shards. There was something uncanny about how pieces of history became whole in his hands. His concentration on the task made casual conversation unnecessary, which relieved Diana. Soon she was sorting shards, trying out pieces together, bending over Ten to reach into cartons, muttering phrases about gray ware with three black lines and an acute angle versus corrugated ware with a curve and a bite out of one side. Ten answered with similar phrases, handing her whatever he had that matched her description of missing shards.

After the first half hour Diana forgot that she was alone with a man in an isolated canyon. She forgot to be afraid that something she might say or do would trigger in Ten the certainty that she wanted him sexually despite whatever objections she might make to his advances. For the first time in years she enjoyed the company of a man as a person, another adult with whom she could be at ease.

When the rain finally stopped completely, Diana stood, stretched cramped leg muscles and went to the edge of the overhang to look out across the newly washed land. Although no ruins were visible from the overhang itself, excitement simmered suddenly in her blood. Hundreds of years ago the Anasazi had looked out on the same land, smelled the same scent of wet **earth** and piñon, seen the glittering beauty of sunlight captured in a billion drops of water clinging to needles and boughs and the sheer face of the cliff itself. For this instant she and the Anasazi were one.

That was what she wanted to capture in her illustrations—the continuity of life, of human experience, a continuity that existed through time regardless of the outward diversity of human cultures.

"I'm going to the site," Diana said, picking up her backpack.

Ten looked up from the potshards he was assembling. "I'll be along as soon as I get these numbered. Don't go up those ladders until they're dry. And stick to the part of the ruins that has a grid. Some of that rubble isn't stable, and some of the walls are worse."

"Don't worry. I'm not exploring anything alone. Too many of those ruins are traps waiting to be sprung. With the Anasazi, you never know when the ground is a ceiling covering a sunken kiva. I'll stay on the well-beaten paths until there are more people on site."

A long look assured Ten that Diana meant what she said. He nodded. "Thanks."

"For what?" she asked.

"Not getting your back up at my suggestions."

"I have nothing against common sense. Besides, you're the ramrod on this site. If I don't like your, er, 'suggestions,' that's my hard luck, right? You'll enforce your orders any way you have to."

Ten thought of putting it less bluntly, then

shrugged. Diana was right, and it would save a lot of grief if she knew it.

"That's my job."

"I'll remember it."

What Diana said was the simple truth. She would remember. The thought of going against Ten's *suggestions* was frankly intimidating. He had the power to enforce his will and she knew it as well as he did. Better. She had been taught by her father and her fiancé just how little a woman's protests mattered to men whose physical superiority was a fact of life.

"If you hear the truck's horn beep three times, or three shots from the rifle," Ten said, "it means come back here on the double."

Diana nodded, checked her watch and said, "I'll be back before sundown."

"Damn straight you will be." He held two pieces of pottery up against the sunlight streaming into the overhang, frowned and set one piece aside before he said, "Only a fool or a pothunter would go feeling around in the ruins after dark."

Diana didn't bother to answer. Ten wasn't really listening anyway. He was holding another piece of pottery against the sunlight, visually comparing edges. They must have fit, because he grunted and wrote on the inside of both pieces. After they were cleaned they would be glued together, but the equipment for that operation was back at the old ranch house.

Beyond the overhang the land was damp and glistening from the recent rain. The short-lived waterfalls that had made lacy veils over the cliff faces were already diminishing to silver tendrils. Before she left the overhang, Diana glanced back at Ten, only to find him engrossed in his three-dimensional puzzle. She should have been relieved at the silent evidence that she didn't have to worry about fielding any unwanted advances from Ten. Quite obviously she wasn't the focus of his masculine attention.

But Diana wasn't relieved. She was a bit irked that he found it so easy to ignore her.

The realization disconcerted her, so she shoved the thought aside and concentrated on the increasingly rugged terrain as she began to climb from September Canyon's floor up to the base of the steep cliffs, following whatever truck tracks the rain hadn't washed away.

Summer thunder muttered through September Canyon, followed by a gust of rain-scented wind that made piñons moan. From the vantage point where the Rover had been parked, the ruins beckoned. Partial walls were scalloped raggedly by time and falling masonry. Some of the walls were barely ankle-high, others reached nearly twenty-five feet in height, broken only by the protruding cedar beams that had once supported floors. Cedar that was still protected by stone remained strong and hard. Exposed beams weathered with the excruciating slowness of rock itself.

Using a trick that an old archaeologist had taught her, Diana let her eyes become unfocused while she was looking at the ruins. Details blurred and faded, leaving only larger relationships visible, weights and masses, symmetry and balance, subtle uses of force and counterforce that had to be conceived in the human mind before they were built because they did not occur in nature. The multistoried wall with its T-shaped doors no longer looked like a chimney with bricks fallen out, nor did the roofless kivas look like too-wide wells. The relationship of roof to floor to ceiling, the geometries of shared-wall apartment living, became clearer to unfocused modern eyes.

The archaeologist who first examined September Canyon estimated that the canyon's alcove had held between nineteen and twenty-six rooms, including the ubiquitous circular kivas. The height of the building varied from less than four feet to three stories, depending on the height of the overhang itself.

The kivas were rather like basements set off from the larger grouping of rooms. The kivas' flat roofs were actually the floor of the town meeting area where children played and women ground corn, where dogs barked and chased foolish turkeys. The balcony of a third-story room was the ceiling of an adjacent two-story apartment. Cedar ladders reached to cistlike granaries built into lateral cracks too small to accommodate even a tiny room. And the Anasazi used rooms so tiny they were unthinkable to modern people, even taking into account the Anasazi's smaller stature.

Diana opened the outer pocket of her backpack and pulled out a lightweight, powerful pair of binoculars. As always, the patience of the Anasazi stonemasons fascinated her. Lacking metal of any kind, they shaped stone by using stone itself. Hand axes weighing several pounds were used to hammer rough squares or rectangles from shapeless slabs of rock. Then the imagined geometry was carefully tap-tap-tapped onto the rough block, thousands upon thousands of strokes, stone pecking at stone until the rock was of the proper shape and size.

The alcove's left side ended in sheer rock wall. A crack angled up the face of the cliff. At no point was the crack wider than a few inches, yet Diana could see places where natural foot-or handholds had been added. Every Anasazi who went up on the mesa to tend crops had to climb up the cliff with no more help than they could get out of the crack. The thought of making such a climb herself didn't appeal. The thought of children or old people making the climb in all kinds of weather was appalling, as was the thought of toddlers playing along the alcove's sheer drop.

Inevitably, people must have slipped and fallen. Even for an alcove that had a southern exposure protected from all but the worst storms, the kind of daily risking of life and limb represented by that trail seemed a terrible price to pay.

Diana lowered the glasses, looked at the ruins with her unaided eyes and frowned. The angle wasn't quite right for what she wanted to accomplish. Farther up the canyon, where the rubble slopes rose to the point that an agile climber could reach the ruins without a ladder, the angle would be no better. What she needed was a good spot from which to sketch an overview of the countryside with an inset detailing the structure and placement of the ruins themselves. The surrounding country could be sketched almost anytime. The ruins, however, were best sketched in slanting, late-afternoon light, when all the irregularities and angles of masonry leaped into high relief. That ''sweet light'' was rapidly developing as the day advanced.

With measuring eyes, Diana scanned her surroundings before she decided to sketch from the opposite side of the canyon. She shrugged her backpack into a more comfortable position and set off. The rains had been light enough that September Creek was a ribbon she could jump over without much danger of getting her feet wet. She worked her way up the canyon until she was half a mile above the ruins on the opposite side. Only then did she climb up the talus slope at the base of the canyon's stone walls.

When Diana could climb no higher without encountering solid rock, she began scrambling parallel to the base of the cliff that formed the canyon wall. Every few minutes she paused to look at the ruins across the canyon, checking the changing angles until she found one she liked. Her strategy meant a hard scramble across the debris slope at the base of the canyon's wall, but she had made similar scrambles at other sites in order to find just the right place to sit and sketch.

Finally Diana stopped at the top of a particularly steep scramble where a section of the sandstone cliff had sloughed away, burying everything beneath in chunks of stone as big as a truck. She wiped her forehead, checked the angle of the ruins and sighed.

"Close, but not good enough." She looked at the debris slope ahead, then at the ruins again. "Just a bit farther. I hope."

Climbing carefully, scrambling much of the time, her hands and clothes redolent of the evergreens she had grabbed to pull herself along the steepest parts, Diana moved along the cliff base. Suddenly she saw a curving something on the ground that was the wrong color and shape to be a stone. She walked eagerly forward, bending to pick up the potshard, which glowed an unusual red in the slanting sunlight. No sooner had her fingers curled around the shard than the ground gave way beneath her feet, sending her down in a torrent of dirt and stone.

Clutching at air, screaming, she plunged into darkness, and the name she screamed was Ten's.

8

Ten was running before Diana's scream ended abruptly, leaving silence and echoes in its wake. He raced away from the ruins at full speed, not needing to follow Diana's tracks in order to find her. In the first instant of her scream he had seen her red windbreaker vividly against the creamy wall of stone on the opposite side of the canyon.

And then the red had vanished.

"Diana! *Diana!*"

No one answered Ten's shout. He saved his breath for running across the canyon bottom and scrambling up the steep slope. As soon as he saw the black shadow of the new hole in the ground he realized what had happened. Diana had stepped onto the concealed roof of a kiva and it had given way beneath her weight. Some of the kivas were only a few feet deep. Others were deeper than a man was tall. He was afraid that Diana had found one of the deep ones.

Moving slowly, ready to throw himself aside at the first hint of uncertain footing, Ten crept close to the hole that had appeared in the rubble slope.

"Diana, can you hear me?"

A sound that might have been his name came from the hole.

"Don't move," he said. "If you've hurt your spine, you could make it worse by thrashing around. I'll get to you as soon as I can."

This time Ten was certain that the sound Diana made was his name.

"Just lie still and close your eyes in case I knock some more dirt loose."

On his stomach, Ten inched closer to the hole. At the far side he saw stubs of the cedar poles that had once supported a segment of the ceiling. In front of him was an open slot where Diana had gone through about a third of the way across the circular ceiling. Parallel, intact cedar poles crossed the opening Diana had accidentally made.

Ten pulled himself to the edge of the hole and peered over. Eight feet down Diana lay half-buried in rubble, surrounded by a circle of carefully fitted masonry wall.

"I'm coming down now. Just lie still."

Ten tested the cedar poles as best he could. They held. Bracing himself between two poles, praying that the tough cedar would hold under his weight, he slipped through the ceiling and landed lightly on his feet next to Diana. Instinctively she tried to sit up.

"Don't move!"

"Can't—breathe."

The ragged gasps told Ten that she was breathing more effectively than she knew.

"It's all right. You had the wind knocked out by the fall, but you're getting it back now. Does any place in particular hurt?"

"No—"

Ten went down on his knees next to Diana's head. Her eyes went wide and she dragged raggedly at air when he reached for her.

"Easy now, honey," he murmured. "I've got to check you for injuries. Just lie still. I won't hurt you. Be still now. It's all right."

Dazed, helpless, Diana fought her fear and held on to the black velvet of Ten's voice, remembering the moments when he had soothed the panicked horse and held the injured kitten so gently. It was the same now, hands both strong and gentle probing her scalp, her neck, her shoulders, his voice soothing, directing, explaining; and all the while debris was being pushed away, revealing more of her body to Ten's thorough touch, his hands moving over her with an intimacy that she had never willingly allowed any man. All that kept her from panicking was the realization that his hands were as impersonal as they were careful.

"I can't feel anything broken and you didn't flinch

anywhere when I touched you," Ten said finally. "Any numb spots?"

"No—I felt—" Diana sucked in air as much from the emotional shock of being touched as from the force of her recent fall. "Everywhere—you touched—I felt."

"Good. Wiggle your fingers and toes for me."

Diana did.

"Hurt?"

"No."

"I'm going to check your neck again. If it hurts, even a little, you tell me quick."

Long fingers eased once more around Diana's neck, working their way through her hair, taking the weight of her head so slowly that she hardly realized when she was no longer supporting it herself.

"Hurt?"

"N-no."

Ten's fingers spread, surrounding the back of her head, and his thumbs glided gently over the line of her jaw. Diana's breath came in and stayed, trapped by the sensations shivering through her. So slowly that she realized it only after the fact, Ten began to turn her head to the right.

"Hurt?"

She tried to speak, couldn't, and shook her head instead. His smile flashed for an instant in the gloom.

"If shaking your head didn't hurt, you're okay.

Let's see how you do sitting up. We'll take it slow. If your back hurts at any time, tell me. Ready?''

Diana didn't need Ten's assistance to sit up, but she got it anyway. His left arm was a hard, warm, resilient bar supporting her shoulders and his right arm rested across her chest, preventing her from pitching forward if she fainted, which she nearly did at the pressure of his forearm across her suddenly sensitive breasts.

"I'm fine," Diana said in a breathless rush.

"So far so good," agreed Ten. "Dizzy?"

She was, but it had nothing to do with her recent fall and everything to do with the powerful man kneeling next to her in the shadows of an ancient kiva, his arms supporting her, his face so close to hers that she tasted his very breath.

"I'm not—dizzy."

"Good. We'll just sit here for a minute and make sure."

While Ten studied the broken ceiling overhead, Diana studied him. For the first time she was struck by how truly handsome he was with his black, slightly curling hair, broad forehead, widely spaced gray eyes, thick lashes, straight nose, high cheekbones and a beard shadow that heightened the intensely male line of his jaw.

It was more than the regularity of Ten's features that appealed to Diana so vividly at the moment; it was the certainty that his abundant masculine strength wasn't going to be used against her. The relief was dizzying, telling her how much of her energy had been locked up in controlling her fear of men.

Then Diana realized that Ten was looking at her. The clarity of his gray eyes was extraordinary. The clean curves and angles of his mouth made her think of touching him, of finding out if his lips tasted as good as his breath.

"Are you all right?" he asked. "You look a little dazed."

"I am." Diana took a ragged breath, then another. "Having the world jerked out from under your feet does that."

Ten's smile flashed again. "Yeah, I guess so. Ready to try standing up?"

"Um."

"We'll take it nice and easy. Just onto your knees at first. Here we go."

With an ease that would have terrified Diana only yesterday, Ten lifted her into a kneeling position. His eyes measured her response, his hands felt the continued coordination of her body as she took her own weight on her knees, and he nodded.

"Ready to try standing? I don't want to rush you, but I'll feel a lot better once we're out of this kiva."

For the first time the nature of her surroundings sank into Diana.

"A kiva! I fell through the ceiling of a kiva?"

"You sure did, honey."

"We have to mark the site and be careful not to do any more damage and—"

"First," Ten interrupted smoothly, "we have to get the hell out of here. It's dangerous."

The voice was still black velvet, but there was the cool reality of steel beneath.

"Ramrod," she breathed.

"Ready?" was all Ten said.

Ready or not, Diana was on her feet a few seconds later, put there by Ten's easy strength. She braced herself momentarily on his hard forearms, feeling the vital heat of his body radiating through cloth. She snatched back her hands as though she had been burned.

"I'm fine," she said quickly. "Really. I can stand alone."

Ten heard Diana's uneasiness in the sudden tumble of words and released her. He didn't step back, for he wanted to be able to catch her if her knees gave way.

"No dizziness?" he asked.

There was, but it came from Ten's closeness rather than from any injury she might have received in the fall. Diana had no intention of saying anything about that fact, however.

"No," she said firmly. "I'm not dizzy."

"Sure?"

"Where have I heard that question before?"

A smile flashed in the gloom, Ten's smile, warm against the hard lines of his face.

"Feeling feisty, are you?" he asked.

Diana looked away from Ten, afraid her approval of him would be much too clear. She didn't want that. She didn't want to give him any reason to expect anything from her as a woman. With narrowed eyes, she examined the hole in the ceiling that was their only exit from the kiva. If she stretched up all the way on her tiptoes she might be able to brush her fingertips close to a cedar beam. And then again, she might not.

"Actually, I'm feeling rather intimidated," she admitted. "Some women would be able to get out of this hole alone, but not me. In gym classes I was a total disaster at chinning myself on the high bar."

Ten measured the distance to the ceiling and the cedar beams. "No problem. God made men with that in mind."

"He did?"

Ten nodded and kicked aside a bit of loose rubble, giving himself stable footing beneath the hole. He braced his legs and held out his arms to Diana.

"Okay, honey. Up you go."

She looked at him as though he had just suggested that she teleport herself out of the hole.

"Don't worry, I won't drop you," Ten said. "I handle heavier things every day. I'll lift you up. You balance yourself on the cedar poles until you can scramble from my shoulders to the ground.''

''What about you?''

''That's where God's design comes in. He made men stronger than women.'' The smile faded, leaving only the hard male lines of Ten's face. ''It's all right, Diana. I won't hurt you. Trust me.''

''I—'' Her voice broke. She swallowed and forced herself to take the two steps toward Ten. ''I'll—try. What do I have to do?''

''First, put your hands on my shoulders.''

For a few moments Diana was afraid she wouldn't be able to force herself to do it. Silently, fiercely, she closed her eyes and fought old fears.

Ten watched with narrowed eyes, feeling Diana's fear as clearly as he had the soft feminine curves of her body while he checked her for injury.

''Diana. Put your hands on my shoulders.''

Her eyelids snapped open. Gone was the velvet reassurance of Ten's voice. In its place was a steel reality: she could help Ten get her out of the kiva or she could fight him; either way, she was going up through that hole in the ceiling. Diana didn't know how he would manage the feat without her cooperation, but she had no doubt that he would.

Diana lifted her hands to Ten's shoulders. She knew he felt her trembling but was unable to stop it.

''Are you afraid of falling again?'' he asked.

''I—''

Her hands clenched around the hard resilience of Ten's shoulder muscles. He was so strong. Much too strong. She was as helpless as a kitten against his power.

Remember that tiger-striped kitten cuddled in Ten's hands. The kitten was relaxed, purring, trusting. Ten didn't hurt that sick kitten. He won't hurt me.

"What d-do you want me to do?" Diana asked, forgetting everything except the need to hold on to her belief that Ten wouldn't hurt her.

"Brace yourself on my shoulders. I'm going to lift you until you can grab a cedar pole. Use it to help you kneel on my shoulders, then stand on them. From there you should be able to get out of the kiva without much problem. Okay?"

She nodded, gripped his shoulders more tightly and braced herself for whatever might come.

"Not yet," Ten said, stroking Diana's back slowly. "You're shaking too much. Slow down, honey. You're all right."

"Being p-petted is just going to make me m-more nervous."

One black eyebrow lifted, but Ten said nothing except "Hang on. Here we go. And keep your back straight."

Diana didn't understand the last instruction until she felt the brush of Ten's body over hers as he bent his knees, wrapped his arms around her thighs and straightened, lifting her within reach of the cedar poles. He need not have worried about her back being straight—her whole body went rigid at the intimacy of his powerful arms locked around her thighs and his head pressed against her abdomen.

"Ten!"

"It's okay, honey. I've got you."

That's the whole problem! But Diana had just enough control left not to blurt out her thought.

"Can you grab one of the poles yet?" Ten asked.

Diana pulled her scattering thoughts together, lifted one hand from the corded muscle of Ten's shoulder and grabbed a cedar pole. It was as hard as Ten but not nearly so warm.

"Got it," she said breathlessly.

"Good. Now grab the other pole."

A few seconds, then, "Okay. I've got that one, too."

"Hang on."

Ten moved so quickly that Diana was never sure how he had managed it, but within seconds she was kneeling on his shoulders, using her grip on the poles for balance. His hands on her hips were holding her firmly and his face was—

Don't think about it or you'll fall.

"Steady, honey," Ten said in a muffled voice.

"Easy for you to say," Diana muttered through clenched teeth.

He laughed softly.

She felt the intimate heat of his breath.

"Oh, God."

"What's wrong?" Ten asked. "Is one of the beams rotten?"

Diana didn't answer. She pulled herself up and out of the kiva before she had a chance to question the shivering sensations that cascaded throughout her body. She scrambled back from the edge and sat hugging herself, feeling flushed in the most unnerving places.

"Everything okay?" Ten called.

"Yes. No. I—" She clenched her teeth. "Fine. Just fine."

"Get back. I'm coming out."

Diana scooted back away from the hole, wondering how Ten was planning to get out. A few seconds later, two hands closed around a cedar pole. With a grace that startled her, Ten chinned himself, held himself one-handed while he grabbed the second pole with his other hand, swung his legs up and levered himself out of the hole with the ease of a gymnast at work on a set of parallel bars.

"Where did you learn how to do that?" Diana asked.

"Same place I learned to patch up kittens."

"Where was that?"

"Long ago, far away, in another country."

"But where?" she persisted. "Why?"

"Commando training."

Diana opened her mouth but no words came out.

Commando training.

Ten held out his hand to help Diana to her feet. "Let's go, honey. The sun will be setting soon."

A wild glance at the sky told Diana that Ten was right. The sun would soon slip beneath the horizon, leaving her alone in the dark at the ends of the earth with a man who was not only far more powerful than she but who was trained to be a killer, as well.

"You sure you're all right?" Ten asked, sitting on his heels next to Diana. "If you can't walk, I'll carry you."

She flinched away from him before she could grab her unraveling courage in both hands. She gave Ten a searching look but saw no triumph in his expression, no malice, no brute hunger, nothing but polite concern for her welfare.

"I can—" Diana's voice broke. She swallowed. "I can walk."

Ten started to reach for her, saw her flinch away and dropped his hand. He stood and moved a pace back from her.

"Get up. We'll drive back to the ranch after we eat," he said matter-of-factly.

"What? Why?"

"You know why," Ten said, turning away from Diana. "Every time I come close to you, you cringe. You'll feel more at ease with one of the other men."

"No!"

The stark emotion in Diana's voice stopped Ten. He looked back at her.

"Please stay," she said quickly. "I trust you more than I've trusted any man since—since I—since he—Ten, please! It's nothing you've done. It's nothing personal. Please believe me."

"It's hard to," he said bluntly.

"Then believe this. You're the first man who's touched me in any way for years and it scares me to death because I'm not scared and you're so damned *male*."

Ten's eyes narrowed. "You're not making much sense."

"I know. I'll get better. I promise."

For a moment Ten looked at Diana. Then he nodded slowly and held out his hand. If she stretched she could take it and help herself up. She looked at the lean hand and remembered the strength and lethal skill of the man behind it.

Then Diana took Ten's hand in both of hers and pulled herself to her feet.

9

While the night wind blew outside, Diana sat in the old ranch house, staring at a potshard in her palm, remembering the incident two weeks ago when Ten had dropped down into the darkness beside her and lifted her to the solid ground above. The tactile memories had haunted her…his hands searching carefully over her body, his easy strength when he lifted her, his face pressed so intimately against her while she climbed back into sunshine.

Shivering, remembering, Diana saw nothing of the shard in her palm. The memories resonated in her body as much as in her mind, sending sensations rippling through her, heat and cold, uneasiness and curiosity, a strange hunger to touch Ten in return, to know his masculine textures as well as he knew her feminine ones.

I'm going crazy.

Once more Diana tried to concentrate on the shard

lying across her palm, but all she could think about was the instant when she had taken Ten's hand between her own and pulled herself to her feet. She thought she had felt his fingers caressing her in the very act of releasing her, but the touch had stopped before she could be certain.

And since then Ten had been the heart, soul and body of asexual politeness. At the site he treated her with the casual camaraderie of an older brother. It was the same at the ranch. At night they sorted shards together, spoke in broken phrases about missing angles and notched curves, discussed the weather or the ranch or the progress of the dig in slightly more complete sentences—and he never touched her, even when he seated her at the dinner table or passed a box of shards to her or looked over her shoulder to offer advice about a missing piece of a pot. He had every excuse to crowd her personal space from time to time, but he didn't.

For the first few days Ten's distance had reassured Diana. Then it had piqued her interest. By the fourteenth day it outright annoyed her.

You'd think I didn't shower often enough.

"Did you say something?" Ten asked from across the table.

Appalled, Diana realized that she had muttered her thought aloud.

"Nothing," she said quickly.

A few moments later she put the shard aside and

stood up, feeling restless. As it often did, her glance strayed to the man who had shared so many days and evenings and nights with her.

The nights were perfectly proper, of course. Some outlaw. The Rocking M's ramrod is nothing if not proper.

Broodingly Diana watched Ten's long fingers turning potshards over and over, handling the fragile pottery deftly, running his fingertips over the edges as though to learn the tiniest contours by touch alone. She did the same thing when she worked, a kind of tactile exploration that was as much a part of her nature as her expressive eyes and her fear of men.

But she no longer feared men. At least, not all men. Luke still startled her from time to time with his sheer size, yet she had no doubt that Carla was perfectly safe with her chosen man, as was little Logan with his father, a father chosen by fate rather than by the baby. Not all children were that lucky in their parents. Diana hadn't been. Nor were all wives as fortunate in their husbands. Diana's mother certainly had not been safe or cherished with her man.

Restlessly, Diana ran her fingertips over the tabletop, feeling the grit that rubbed off the shards no matter how carefully they were handled. She smoothed her fingers over the table's surface again and again, watching Ten's hands, fascinated by their combination of power and precision.

What would it feel like to be touched with such care?

The glittering sensation that shivered through Diana at her silent question made her feel almost weak. She wanted to be touched by Ten, but it was impossible. He was a man. He would want more than touching, gentleness, cherishing, holding.

With a small sound Diana looked away from Ten. She didn't notice the sudden intensity in his eyes as he watched her over the pot he was assembling from ancient shards.

"Mmrreeow?"

The polite query was followed by another, less polite one. Diana hurried to the window, grateful to have a distraction from her unexpected, unnerving attraction to Ten.

"Hello, you old reprobate," she said, opening the window and holding out her arms.

On a gust of air, the tiger-striped cat flowed into Diana's arms. Pounce's fur smelled cool, fresh, washed by the clean wind. Smiling, rubbing her face against the cat's sleek head, she settled back into her chair. Pounce's rumbling, vibrating approval rippled out, blending with the fitful sound of the wind.

"King of the Rocking M, aren't you?" she asked, smiling. "Think you can trade a few dead mice for some time in my lap, hmm?"

Ten looked up again. Diana was kneading gently down the cat's big back, rubbing her cheek against

Pounce's head while he rubbed his head against her in turn. The old mouser's purring was like continuous, distant thunder, but it was Diana's clear enjoyment of the cat's textures and responses that brought every one of Ten's masculine senses alert. He had kept his distance from her very carefully since the first day at the site; he would never forget the raw terror that he had seen in her eyes the first time he had reached for her in the gloom of the ancient kiva.

No matter how carefully Diana tried to conceal it, Ten sensed that she was still afraid of him. Perhaps it was because the first time she had seen him, he was the victor in a brief, brutal fight. Perhaps it was the way he had handled the pothunters. Perhaps it was his commando training. Perhaps it was simply himself, Tennessee Blackthorn, a man who never had worn well on women—and vice versa. An outlaw, not a lover or a husband.

Pounce purred loudly from Diana's lap, proclaiming his satisfaction with life, himself and the woman who was stroking his sleek body.

"If I thought you'd give me a rubdown like that, I'd go out and catch mice, too."

Diana gave Ten a startled look.

"Don't know that I'd eat them, though," Ten added blandly, measuring a shard against the bright lamplight. "A man has to draw the line somewhere."

Uncertainly Diana laughed. The idea of Ten purring beneath her hands made odd sensations shiver through her. Surely he was joking. But if he weren't…

Shadows of old fear rose in Diana. When she spoke her voice was tight and the words came out in a torrent, for she was afraid of being interrupted before she got everything said that had to be said.

"You'd be better off eating Carla's wonderful chicken than trading dead mice for a pat from me. I'm not the sensual type. Sex is for men, not women. In the jargon, I'm frigid, if frigid defines a woman who can live very well without sex."

Ten looked up sharply, caught as much by the palpable resonances of fear in Diana's voice as he was by her words. He started to speak but she was still talking, words spilling out like water from a river finally freed of its lid of winter ice.

"A man must have thought up the word *frigid*," Diana continued quickly. "A woman would just say she isn't a masochist, that she feels no need of pain, self-inflicted or otherwise. But no matter what label you put on it—and me—the result is the same. Thanks but no thanks."

The words echoed in the quiet room. Their defensiveness made Diana cringe inside, but she wouldn't have taken back a single blunt syllable. Ten had to know.

"I don't recall asking you for sex," Ten said.

For a long minute Diana's hands kneaded through Pounce's fur, soothing the cat and herself at the same time, drawing forth a lifting and falling rumble of purrs.

"No, you haven't," she said finally, sighing, feeling herself relax now that the worst of it was over. Ten knew. He could never accuse her now. "But I've learned the hard way that it's better to be honest than to be quiet and then be accused of being a tease."

"Don't worry, Diana. Like the moon goddess you're named after, you've got No Trespassing signs posted all over you. Any man who doesn't see them would have to be as blind as you are."

"What?"

Ten looked up from the shards he had assembled. "You're stone-blind to your own basic nature. You're not frigid. You have a rare sensuality. You drink storm winds and nuzzle Logan's tiny hands and touch pieces of pottery with fingertips that are so sensitive you don't even have to look to tell what kind of edge there is. You rub that old tomcat until he's a vibrating pudding of pleasure, and you enjoy it just as much as he does. That's all sensuality is—taking pleasure in your own senses. And sex, good sex, is the most pleasure your senses can stand."

Diana sat transfixed, caught within the diamond clarity of Ten's eyes watching her, the black velvet certainty of his voice caressing her. Then he looked back to the shards, releasing her.

"Did a new box come in from the site?" Ten asked in a calm voice, as though they had never discussed anything more personal than potshards. "I've been waiting for one from 10-B. I think part of this red pot might have washed down to that spot on the grid. A long time ago, of course."

Her mind in turmoil, Diana grabbed the question, grateful to have something neutral to talk about. "Yes, it's over there. I'll get it."

If Ten noticed the rapid-fire style of Diana's speech, he didn't comment.

Releasing a reluctant Pounce, Diana went to the corner of the room where recently cleaned, permanently numbered shards were stored in hope of future assembling. The carton collected from 10-B on the site grid was on top of the pile. She brought the box to the long table where Ten worked by the light of a powerful gooseneck lamp.

"Thanks," he said absently. "I don't suppose there's a piece lying around on top with two obtuse angles and a ragged bite out of the third side?"

"Gray? Corrugated? Black on white?"

"Red."

"Really?" she asked, excited. Redware was the most unusual of all the Anasazi pottery. It also came from the last period when they inhabited the northern reaches of their homeland. "Do you think we have enough shards to make a whole pot?"

Ten made a rumble that sounded suspiciously like Pounce at his most satisfied. He leaned over, pulled a large carton from beneath the table and folded back the flaps. With gentle care he lifted pieces of an ancient bowl onto the table. The background color of the pot was brick red. Designs in white and black covered the surface, careful geometrics that spoke of a painstaking artist working patiently over the pot.

A feeling of awe expanded through Diana as she saw the pot lying half-mended on the table. Ten had been as patient and painstaking as the original potter; the fine lines where he had glued shards together were almost invisible.

"You never did tell me why this kind of pot is so rare," Ten said, turning aside to the carton of unmatched shards.

"Polychrome pots are usually found south of here," Diana said absently. Her hands closed delicately around the base and a curving side of the red pot. "Either the potter was an immigrant or the pot was a piece of trade goods. But this pot, plus the surface and regular shape of the sandstone masonry in September Canyon, make it certain that the site is from the Pueblo III period of the Anasazi. Or nearly certain. Since we don't have a time machine, we'll never be one hundred percent positive that we have the true story."

"We know the most important thing."

Diana looked up from the fragment of the past held between her hands.

"They were people like us," Ten said simply.

"They built, laughed, wept, fought, raised children and died. Most of all, they knew fear."

"Actually," Diana said, frowning over the box of shards, "the most recent theory states that the Anasazi moved into their cliff houses for reasons other than fear."

Ten's left eyebrow arched skeptically. "They just liked the view halfway up the cliff, huh?"

"Um, no one said anything about that. The theory just states that we were premature in attributing a fortress mentality to the Anasazi. They could just have been preserving the top of the mesa for crops and didn't build on the canyon bottom because of floods. That left the cliffs themselves for housing."

Ten grunted. "What did the professorial types say about the signal towers on top of Mesa Verde? They were used to pass the news of births, right?"

Diana gave Ten a sideways look, but he appeared to be engrossed in the red potshards she was finding and carefully placing in front of him. Already he had found two to glue together and was positioning a third.

"The towers could have been used to welcome visitors," Diana said neutrally, "or to show the way up onto the mesa for people who were from other areas."

"People from other areas tend to be strangers and strangers tend to be unfriendly."

"Perhaps the Anasazi believed that strangers were simply friends they hadn't met yet."

"That would certainly explain how the Anasazi died out so fast," Ten said sardonically.

"In some academic circles, your point of view would be considered philosophically and politically retrograde," Diana said without heat. One of the most pleasurable things about her time with Ten was the discovery of his agile, wide-ranging mind. She had come to look forward to the hours spent sorting shards and talking about the Anasazi almost as much as she enjoyed working on the site itself. "Here's the shard that goes in the middle."

"Thanks," Ten said. "Hang on to it until the glue dries on these two. Whatever made the professors give up on good old common sense to explain the Anasazi cliff dwellings?"

"Such as?"

"Birds don't fly because they like the view up there. Birds fly because cats can't."

Diana smiled. "Don't tell Pounce."

"I don't have to. He figured that one out all by himself, which is more than I can say for whoever dreamed up that New Age fertilizer about cliff houses being invented for any reason other than self-defense. In a word, fear."

"Logical, but it doesn't explain why there was no increase in burials about the time the Anasazi abandoned the mesa tops and took up living in the cliffs."

"Burials?"

"Self-defense indicates war," Diana explained. "War indicates wounding and death. Death—"

"Leads to burials," Ten interrupted.

"Right. Even around the time the Anasazi disappeared altogether, there was no increase in burials. Therefore, the theory that hostile tribes forced the Anasazi into cliff houses has a big flaw. No extra deaths, no war. Simple."

"More like simpleminded. Those theorists ought to pull their heads out of their, er, books and have a reality check."

"What do you mean?"

"Only winners bury their dead."

The flatness in Ten's voice made a chill move over Diana's skin.

"You sound very certain," she said.

"I've been there. That's as certain as it gets."

"There?"

"On the losing side. It hasn't changed all that much over the centuries. I doubt that it ever will. Pain, fear, death and not enough people left to mourn or bury the dead. But there are always enough vultures."

Ten's narrowed eyes were like splinters of clear glass. Diana could not bear to look at them and think of what they had seen.

He turned and searched through the box of potshards. When he looked up again, his expression was once more relaxed.

"In any case," Ten continued, "anybody who's

read a little biology could tell your fancy theorists that building Stone Age apartment houses halfway up sheer cliffs took an immense amount of time and energy, which meant that the need driving the society also had to be immense. Survival is the most likely explanation, and the only animal that threatens man's survival is man himself.'' Ten smiled grimly. ''That hasn't changed, either.''

''Fear.''

''Don't knock it. No animal would survive without it, including man.'' Ten held a shard up to the light, shrugged and tried it anyway. It fit. ''Maybe the Anasazi were no longer actively involved in war. Maybe they just feared it to the point that they retreated to a hole in the cliffs and pulled the hole in after them.'' Ten looked up. ''You can understand that kind of fear, can't you? It's what drew you to the Anasazi in the first place. Like you, they built a shell around themselves to wall out the world. And then they began to shrink and die inside that shell.''

Diana concentrated on two shards that had no chance of fitting.

Ten waited a few moments, sighed and continued. ''When you retreat to a stone cliff that's accessible only by one or two eyelash trails that a nine-year-old with a sharp stick could defend, it's probably because you don't have much more than nine-year-olds left to defend the village.''

"But there's no hard evidence of repeated encounters with a warlike tribe," she said coolly.

"Isn't there? What does Anasazi mean?"

"It's a Navajo word meaning Ancient Ones, or Those Who Came Before."

Ten smiled thinly. "It also means Enemy Ancestor." He picked up an oddly shaped shard and stared at it without really seeing it. "I suspect that at the end of a long, hard period, during which they'd had to cope with war or drought or disease or all three, a kind of madness overtook the northern Anasazi."

The quality of Ten's voice, rippling with something unspoken, caught Diana's attention.

"What do you mean?"

"I think a dark kind of shaman cult overtook them, using up everything the society had and demanding even more. Maybe the fears the shaman cult played on had some basis in reality, or maybe they lived only in the Anasazi's own nightmares." Ten shook his head. "Either way, fear ruled the society. The people retreated to the most impossible places they could reach and walled themselves in with rooms and held ceremonies in buried kivas. When they ran out of space in the alcoves, they built bigger and bigger kivas along the base of the cliff."

Ten's voice shifted, becoming subtly different, more resonant yet softer.

"Their rituals became more and more elaborate," he continued quietly, "more demanding of the people's mental and physical resources. Darker. It's possible for a culture to exist like that, but not for long. It goes against the deepest grain of survival to huddle in a stone crypt.''

"Is that what you think happened? The Anasazi died in the city crypts they built for themselves?''

"Some did. Some escaped.''

The odd timbre of Ten's voice made the hair on Diana's scalp stir in primal response, the same stirring she had felt with Ten once before, when she had stood on a desolate mesa top and felt centuries like cards being shuffled, revealing glimpses of a time when reality had been very different, and so had she and Ten.

"How did they escape?'' Diana asked, her voice strange even to her own ears.

For a long time there was only silence punctuated by the sounds of the wind sweeping over the ancient land. Just when Diana had decided that Ten wasn't going to say any more, he began speaking again.

"Another shaman came down from the north, an outlaw shaman with a vision that swept through the Anasazi, a vision that spoke of light as well as darkness, life as well as death.'' Ten looked up suddenly, catching and holding Diana with eyes as clear as rain. "The Anasazi who believed the outlaw shaman climbed down out of their beautiful, dangerous, futile cliff cities and never went back again.''

10

Luke leaned toward little Logan, smiling, speaking in a deep, gentle voice to the baby who studied him so intently.

"Definitely your eyes, Carla," Luke said, running his fingertip over his wife's cheek.

"The mouth is yours, though," she said, smoothing her cheek over his hand.

"We're in trouble then. He'll have half the state mad at him as soon as he learns to talk."

Carla laughed softly, brushed her lips over Luke's palm and settled back against his chest. The nursing shawl slipped to one side, revealing the milk-swollen curve of her breast. With a slow caress Luke adjusted the shawl, then resumed the gentle back-and-forth motion of the big rocking chair he had made before Logan had been born.

Despite its size, the chair was still a snug fit for the three of them—Logan, Carla and Luke—but no one had any intention of giving it up for the couch. The quiet evenings when Carla nursed the baby while sitting in Luke's lap had become the highlight of the day for everyone involved.

"Hi," Carla said, looking up as Diana came from the kitchen into the living room. "Ten was asking about you a few minutes ago. Something about a box from 11-C?"

"More red shards. He hopes. He has this theory about where the rest of the red pot is. So far he has been right."

A night of broken sleep and restless dreams had convinced Diana that Ten had been right about more than the pot, but she didn't know how to reopen the subject with him, any more than she had known how to respond last night, when he had spoken about fear and the Anasazi and one Diana Saxton. Instead of speaking then, she had handed him another shard and the conversation had disintegrated into elliptical phrases describing pieces of broken pots.

"Is Ten in the bunkhouse?" Diana asked.

"He's in the barn checking on a lame horse."

Diana hid her feeling of disappointment. Whether in September Canyon or at the ranch headquarters, she looked forward to the evenings with Ten despite the tension that came from her increasing awareness of him as a man. She noticed him in ways that she had never noticed any man at all. The dense black of his eyelashes, the equally dense beard shadow that lay beneath his skin no matter how recently he had shaved, the springy thatch of hair that showed beneath his open collar, the endless flex and play of muscles beneath his skin, the easy stride of a man who was at home in and confident of his body.

But most of all, Diana noticed the frank masculinity of Ten, the male sensuality that was both subtle and pervasive. It compelled her senses in the same way that his intelligence compelled her mind.

"If you see Ten," Diana said to Carla, "tell him I've cleaned the calcium deposits from the 11-C shards, given them permanent labels, and they're ready for his magic touch."

"Sure. Want to stay for pie? We're having some as soon as we put our greedy son to bed."

"No thanks. Your cooking is straining the seams of my jeans as it is. It's getting indecent."

"Haven't heard any of the men complaining about the fit of your jeans," Luke drawled.

"Luke!" Carla said, laughing.

"Well, have you heard them complaining?" he asked innocently before switching his attention to Logan. "Hurry up, son. Your old man is ready for dessert."

Carla laughed and murmured something Diana couldn't hear. Silently she retreated from the living room doorway, heading for the kitchen. It wasn't that she felt unwelcome, for she knew that the opposite was the case. Carla and Luke loved to question Diana about the progress of the dig and the pots that Ten and she together had proven to be so adept at assembling from shards. It was just that she wasn't sure she could look at Luke and Carla and their baby without letting her own hunger show.

What a pity it takes a man to make a baby.

It wasn't the first time the thought had occurred to Diana, but the strength of her yearning for a baby was growing. Tonight it had shaken her, making it hard for her to think.

But then, that wasn't new, either. Diana hadn't been thinking too well around Ten lately. A look from him, a phrase, a slight lift of the corner of his mouth, and she would begin thinking all over again about how gentle he had been with the kitten, how patient he was with the fragile, brittle shards, how easy and yet how exciting he was to be with.

Stop it. Next thing you know you'll be asking him to kiss you.

A curious sensation prickled through Diana, making her shiver lightly. She wasn't sure what it was that had caused her reaction. She knew what it wasn't, however.

It wasn't fear.

Diana let herself out into the night. Overhead the Milky Way was a river of light flowing silently across the sky. There was no moon to pale the glitter of the stars, no clouds to blur the razor edges of MacKenzie Ridge's silhouette. Nothing moved but the wind. It infused the night, filling it with whispers that could have been her own thoughts or echoes of ancient Anasazi prayers chanted to unknown gods.

When Diana opened the door to the old ranch house, Pounce materialized from the nearby bushes and slipped into the house ahead of her. She closed the door, bent down and lifted the big tomcat into her arms.

"Hello, Pounce. How was mouse hunting tonight?"

The cat purred and began kneading Diana's chest.

"That good, hmm?" Diana murmured, rubbing the supple body and sleek fur. "Then I won't bother putting out that dry cat food Carla gave me yesterday."

Pounce purred his agreement.

"Yeah, that's what she said. You only eat the dry stuff when nothing else is available."

Sure enough, Pounce ignored the kibble that Diana prepared with one hand while she held on to the cat with the other. Even a saucer of milk didn't interest him. All he wanted was what he was getting—a chance to snuggle with his favorite human being.

Carrying Pounce, Diana walked through the workroom to her bedroom. The carefully made bed looked uninviting. It was too early to sleep. Even if the hour had been right, her frame of mind was not. She was too restless to sleep.

Unfortunately she was also too restless to work on the shards. She tried, but for once the lure of putting together an ancient puzzle couldn't hold her attention. After fitting a few pieces together, she turned off the big gooseneck lamp and sat at the work table with no more illumination than that provided by the lamp in the far corner of the room. The shadows cast by that lamp were soft and inviting, making velvet distinctions between light and dark.

Pounce leaped into Diana's lap and *yeowed* in soft demand. Absently she stroked the cat, drawing forth a ripple of purrs. For a long time there was no other sound. Then a knock came on the front door and Ten called out. Hearing Ten's deep voice sent another curious frisson through Diana.

"I'm in the workroom," she answered.

Her voice was unusually husky, but the words carried well enough. The door opened and closed and Ten walked into the room. With a gesture that had become familiar to her, he removed his hat and set it on the small table beneath the lamp.

"That old mouser must think he's died and gone to heaven," Ten said.

The corner of his mouth tugged up, sending another glimmer of heat through Diana.

"Did you mean what you said?" she asked before she could think of all the reasons to be silent.

"I always mean what I say. When it comes to you and that cat, I'm damned certain."

Diana took a deep breath. "Would you really trade places with Pounce?"

This time the curve at the corner of Ten's mouth expanded into a true smile. "Why? You have some mice that he's too lazy to catch?"

Her lips tried to smile but were trembling too hard. She could barely find the courage to force out her next question.

"Would you really like to be touched by me?" she asked. "I mean, do I…attract you?"

"Sure," Ten said offhandedly, reaching for the switch on the gooseneck lamp.

"Would you…kiss me?"

Ten's hand froze in midair. Amusement vanished from his expression. His eyes narrowed until there was little left but a silver glitter as he turned and looked at the woman who was only a few feet away.

"You're serious, aren't you," he said.

She nodded because her throat was too tight for words.

"What happened to all the No Trespassing signs?"

Diana opened her mouth. No words came from her constricted throat. She licked her lips. Ten watched the motion with a heavy-lidded, sensual intensity that would have frightened her once. Now it came as a relief. It gave her the courage to put into words the realization that had been growing in her mind for a long time.

"Watching Carla and Luke and their baby has made me understand that I'm missing something wonderful and—and vital." Diana's voice shifted, becoming even lower, more husky. She spoke swiftly, as though afraid of being interrupted and then not having the courage to continue. "But until I get over being afraid of men, I won't have a chance for the kind of life I want. Men want sex. I have to be able to give a man what he wants in order to get what I really want—a baby of my own."

Ten's left eyebrow rose in a wicked black arch. "Honey, you don't need a man to get a baby." His mouth tugged up at the corner in response to Diana's shocked look. "If you don't believe me, ask any veterinarian."

Silky hair flew as Diana shook her head vigorously. "No. That's not what I want. Too cold. I want my baby to be conceived in warmth, in a—a joining of two people. Not a doctor's office. That wouldn't—I just—no." She took a fast, harsh breath, trying to control her nervousness. "So I have to start somewhere. A kiss seems a logical beginning."

"Why me?"

Diana looked away, unable to bear the diamond clarity of Ten's eyes.

"Because I—I trust you," she said, her voice uneven. "I've seen you handle kittens and delicate pieces of pottery. You're as gentle as you are strong. When I was trapped in the kiva, I was helpless, completely at your mercy. You could have done anything, but what you did was pull me out, comfort me, take care of me. Never once did you so much as hint that

I owed you thanks, much less the use of my body for sex.''

Unwavering gray eyes watched Diana. "And now you want me to kiss you?''

Closing her eyes, she nodded.

"Despite your fear of men," Ten added.

Again, she nodded. Then, in a whispered rush, she said, "I like you, Ten. I know I could bear being kissed by you, but the thought of any other man makes me—cold.''

A visible shudder of fear and revulsion went through Diana. Ten saw it but said nothing.

"Anyway," she added with desperate calm, "if you know going in that all it's going to be is a kiss, you won't push for more, will you? If I'm honest?'' Diana opened her eyes and looked at Ten with unconscious pleading. "I'm not a tease. Truly. It's just that I can't bear being touched by men.''

"What happened?" Ten asked calmly. "Why do you have such a poor opinion of sex in general and men in particular? What makes you afraid that every man you kiss will demand sex?''

"Because it's true.''

"You don't believe that.''

"The hell I don't," she said, her voice low and flat.

Ten stared at Diana. All her softness and unconscious pleading was gone, all hope, all color; and what was left was a bleak acceptance that made her voice as flat as the line of her mouth.

"Look," Ten said reasonably, "no man worthy of the name is going to share a few kisses with a woman and then demand a turn in the sack."

Diana shrugged. The movement was tight, jerky, saying more than words about the tension within her, a tension that had been pulling her apart for too many years.

"Maybe you're right," she said. Then she made an angry, anguished sound. Years of bitterness burst out in a torrent of words. "But the only way to find out which men are decent is to try the kisses, all the while praying very hard that when the time comes he'll take no for an answer, because if he doesn't, he's bigger than you are, stronger, and you've been dating him for months and no one on earth will believe that he forced you."

"You're acting as though all men—"

"Not *all* men," she interrupted savagely. "But too damned many! If you don't believe me, ask the psychologist who did a study for UCLA. The statistics are illuminating. More than a third of all women have their first sexual experience as the result of rape."

"*What?*"

"Rape," Diana said savagely. "I'm not talking about being beaten senseless or having a knife at your throat until the rapist is finished, although God knows

I talked to too many girls who got initiated that way, in outright violence.''

Diana's breath came in harshly, but she gave Ten no chance to speak. ''I'm not even talking about incest. I'm talking about the dumb middle-class bunnies who believe that no means no, who believe that the boy they've been dating for three months won't use his strength against his girlfriend, won't keep pushing and pushing and pushing her for sex, taking off her clothes while she says no, putting his hand between her legs even when she tries to push it away, and each time they're alone he pushes harder and harder until finally he was holding me down, telling me all the while how it was okay, nice girls did it all the time, he'd still love me in the morning, in fact he'd love me more than ever—''

''Diana,'' Ten said, his voice low, shocked.

She didn't even hear him. ''—and I was too well brought up to claw and scream and kick, and above all *I couldn't believe Steve wouldn't stop*. Nice middle-class girls don't get raped by nice middle-class boys. He had stopped the times before. He would stop this time. He had to. He simply had to. God help me, I still didn't believe it when he was finished and I was bleeding and he was zipping up his pants suggesting we have a burger and some fries before we went to his apartment and did it some more.''

Diana blinked, shuddered again and made a broken sound. ''To this day Steve doesn't know why I broke our engagement. The last time I talked to him, he got mad and said if I didn't want sex, I shouldn't ask for it by wearing heels and sexy hairstyles and perfume and I shouldn't make out at all. I was a good middle-class girl, so I believed him. I believed it had been my fault.''

Diana's hands clenched until her nails dug into her palms, but her voice remained the same, flat and without warmth. ''When I could bring myself to date again—it took more than a year—I was very careful not to lead a man on. No makeup. No perfume. No skirts. A few kisses, that was all, and then only after several dates. It didn't matter. Two of my dates called me a tease. Some called me worse.''

Pounce made a soft sound of complaint and leaped to the floor, sensing the tension in Diana. She didn't notice the cat's absence.

Neither did Ten. He was still caught in the moment of shock and rage when he had realized why Diana feared men. He heard her words only at a distance. His hands clenched and unclenched reflexively as he tried to reason with himself, to drain off the useless rage that was consuming him. What had happened to Diana had taken place a long time ago. Years.

But for Ten, it had happened just a few seconds ago.

''Only one of the men came back for more than a few dates,'' Diana continued tonelessly, determined to tell Ten everything so that no more questions would have to be asked or answered. "Don never pushed me. Not once. Not in any way. Eight months later he asked me to marry him, and he told me about how perfect it would be, two virgins learning together the ultimate mystery of sex on their marriage night." She made a helpless gesture with her right hand. "He was a kind, decent man. I couldn't lie to him. So I told him."

When Ten spoke, his voice was as carefully controlled as the coiled strength of his body. "What happened?"

"He tried to believe it wasn't my fault, but when he found out I hadn't gone to the police..." The downward curve of Diana's mouth became more pronounced. "We saw each other a few more times after that, but it was over."

"Did you love him?"

Slowly Diana shook her head. "I didn't love Steve, either. I just wanted to believe it was possible for a man and a woman to share something beautiful, that a man can be decent and civilized with a woman who is weaker than himself."

"I take it your father wasn't."

"My father was a soldier. A commando."

Ten's eyes widened but he said nothing.

"Dad was short-tempered when he was sober. When he drank, he was violent. The older I got, the more he drank. He and Mom..." Diana's voice died.

"I never understood why she stayed with him. But she did."

"He's dead?"

"Yes." Diana looked up at Ten for the first time since she had begun talking about her past. "Steve was a jet jockey for the air force. I haven't had very good luck with soldiers. Any more questions?"

"Just one."

Diana braced herself. "Go on."

"Do you still want me to kiss you?"

Nervously Diana smoothed the soft folds of her oversize cotton sweater. She tried to speak, decided she didn't trust her voice, and nodded her head.

"You're sure?" Ten asked.

There was no emotion in his voice, no expression on his face, nothing to tell Diana what he was thinking. He was as dark and enigmatic as the windswept night, and like the stars, his eyes were a glittering silver.

"Yes," she whispered. "I'm sure."

Ten held out his hand. "Then come to me, Diana."

11

Diana trembled at the sound of Ten's voice, a gentle velvet rasp, like a cat's tongue stroking her. For an instant she didn't know if she would have the strength to walk. But even as the thought came she was standing up, walking, closing the small distance that separated her from Ten. She put her hand in his. The warmth of his hard palm was like a flame against fingers chilled by nervousness.

Ten held out his other hand. A moment later, small cool fingers nestled against the cupped heat of his palm. He lifted Diana's hands to his mouth and breathed warmth over her skin before kissing her palms gently. The unexpected caress made Diana's breath break. Before the sweet sensations had run their course through her body, Ten was lowering her hands, releasing her from his warmth.

Diana had asked to be kissed. He had kissed her.

She made a questioning sound that had more disappointment in it than she realized.

"Ten?"

"What?" he asked softly.

"Would you kiss me again?" she whispered.

Ten's smile made Diana want to curl up in his arms like a cat.

He held out his hands and once more felt her smooth, cool fingers come to rest within the curve of his palms.

"You're so warm," Diana said. She closed her eyes and let out her breath in a long sigh, openly savoring the simple touch of her skin against Ten's.

Diana's unguarded, sensual response sent a shock wave of heat through Ten. He hoped she had no idea how fiercely she aroused him with her unknowing sensuality and haunted eyes, her womanly curves badly concealed beneath a sweater big enough for him to wear, and her slender hands lying so trustingly within his.

Ten brought Diana's hands to his mouth and brushed a kiss into first one of her palms, then the other. The tiny sound she made at the touch of his lips was as much a reward as the warmth he could feel stealing softly beneath her skin. He lifted his head and looked at her. She was watching him with eyes that were luminous, approving. Then her dark lashes lowered and she returned the kisses he had given her, breathing a caress into the center of his palm.

"Thank you," Diana whispered.

"My pleasure."

She searched Ten's face with wide indigo eyes, hardly able to believe what her senses were telling her. He had enjoyed the undemanding caresses as much as she had.

"You mean that, don't you," she said finally.

Ten nodded.

"It's a relief to find a man who doesn't want... everything."

An odd smile haunted Ten's lips for a moment. "Don't fool yourself, Diana. I want everything, but I'll never *take* any more than you give me. And I mean give willingly, not because I push you so hard on so many fronts at once that you don't know where to fight first."

Diana smiled uncertainly. "Does that mean you'll kiss me again?"

"I'll kiss you as many times as you want me to."

"And you won't push for more?"

"No."

"Even if you get aroused?" The stark question shocked Diana when she heard her own words, but it was too late to call them back.

"Honey," Ten said, his voice rich with rueful laughter, "if you were standing about two inches closer to me, you'd have the answer to your question."

Confusion showed on Diana's face. Without thinking, she looked down Ten's body. The evidence of his arousal was unmistakable and frankly intimidating. She looked up again, her face suddenly pale.

"Don't worry, honey," Ten said matter-of-factly. "I've been that way every night we've sat around talking and sorting through pieces of the past, and more often than not during the days, too."

"You have?" she asked faintly. "I didn't know."

"I did my best to make sure of that," Ten said dryly. "I'm only pointing it out now so that you'll know you don't have to be afraid of me when I'm aroused."

"But I didn't mean to. Believe me, Ten. I didn't mean anything of the sort!"

"I know. I can't keep myself from responding to you, but I can make damn sure I don't act on it."

"But if I didn't mean to, why..." Her voice faded. "Has it been so long since you've had a woman?"

Ten looked at Diana's confusion and didn't know whether to laugh or swear. Very lightly he stroked his index finger over the inside of her wrist. The touch was gentle but hardly soothing. He felt her pulse rate accelerate, which made his own quicken in response.

"Diana, I could have had a woman five seconds before I walk into a room where you are and I'd still want you. I admire courage, intelligence and a sense of humor. It didn't take long for me to find out that you've got plenty of all three, as well as a fine body you do your best to hide."

Color crept up Diana's cheeks, but she made no move to separate her hands from Ten's while he continued talking in the velvet tones that made her weak.

"I've wanted you since the first day you were here, when you put your own uneasiness aside and helped me with that kitten."

Diana's eyes widened in surprise.

"I respect a woman's right to choose or refuse a man," Ten continued. "You made it clear that you were refusing. You're still making it clear. You're as safe as you want to be with me, no matter what kind of kissing or petting we do."

She barely heard what Ten was saying. She was still trying to absorb the realization that he was more aroused than Steve had ever been, yet Ten had made no move toward easing himself at her expense. Nor had he berated her for teasing him into such an uncomfortable state and then refusing to follow through.

Then the rest of what Ten was saying sank in: *You're as safe as you want to be with me, no matter what kind of kissing or petting we do.*

She didn't doubt it. Despite the provocation Baker had given—and the pothunters—Ten had never lost control over his own actions.

"Where did you learn such self-control?" Diana asked, watching Ten with dark, curious eyes.

"The same place I learned how to fight."

"That kind of training didn't do my father any good. Or Steve."

Ten banked the rage that came to him whenever he thought of a man hurting Diana. "They weren't men, honey. They were boys who never learned the most important part of a warrior's training—self-control. If a man doesn't control himself, someone else will. There are times and places where being out of control can cost a man his life. Your father was lucky. He was never in one of those places. As for Steve, if that fly-boy's luck holds, I'll never meet him."

Ten's voice was so caressing that for an instant the meaning of what he was saying didn't make any impact. When it did, Diana looked quickly at Ten's eyes. There was nothing of amusement or indulgence there, only the icy promise of retribution she had seen twice before in Ten's eyes—and each time a man had ended up flat on the ground with Ten towering over him.

"Now I've frightened you," Ten said, stepping back, releasing Diana. "I'd never hurt you, but after your experiences with the male of the species, I don't expect you to believe that." He turned toward the gooseneck lamp, reaching for the switch. "Let's take a look at those new red shards you got out of the carton." Ten hesitated, glancing at Diana over his shoulder. "Or would you feel more at ease if I left you to work alone?"

Diana's hand went to Ten's, covering his fingers, preventing him from turning on the harsh light. She tugged lightly. He let go of the switch, allowing her to control his hand. She lifted it to her face. Closing her eyes, she stroked his hard palm with her cheek.

"Diana?"

"It's all right."

"Is it? Your hands are trembling."

Helplessly she smiled. "I don't know why they are, but I know it's not fear."

"Are you sure, honey?"

"I know what being afraid of a man feels like. I'm not afraid of you, Ten."

He searched Diana's eyes for a long moment, then gave her a slow smile that did nothing to steady her heartbeat or her hands. Watching him, trying to smile in return even though her lips were trembling, she found Ten's other hand and brought it to her mouth for a quick brush of her lips. Then she turned her other cheek into his palm, framing her face in his warmth, holding his hands against her skin.

"Ten," Diana said huskily, closing her eyes, savoring the slow caress of his fingers, "will you share a few kisses with me until I ask you to stop? I know this isn't fair to you, but—"

"It's all right," he said, interrupting, his lips against Diana's, feeling them tremble against his own. "Life is never fair. You of all people should know that."

"But—"

"Shh," Ten said, sealing her lips with a tender stroking of his thumb. "It's all right, baby."

Diana's eyes opened. Indigo depths shimmered with the possibilities that were unfolding within her, possibilities that existed because of the powerful man who was holding her with such care.

"Kiss me," she whispered.

"How?" he asked in a velvet voice. "Hard or gentle? Deep or cool? Fast or so long that you can't remember a time when we weren't kissing? I've never had that kind of kiss, but looking at you, I believe it exists."

Diana's eyes widened and she shivered lightly at the thought of trying each and every way of kissing Ten.

"How do you want to kiss me?" she asked.

"Every way there is."

"Yes," she sighed.

Ten's breath came out in a husky rush that Diana felt an instant before his lips touched hers. His lips were smooth and incredibly soft, fitting over hers tenderly yet completely. He brushed against her mouth again and again, letting her become accustomed to his textures, enjoying hers in return, and what he enjoyed most of all was the way her lips began to follow his, silently asking for more.

Smiling, ignoring the heavy beat of his own blood, Ten gave Diana more of the undemanding caresses. Her mouth relaxed and softened and her breath sighed between her slightly parted lips. The tip of his tongue touched the sensitive peak of her upper lip, then withdrew, only to return and touch her again. She made a murmurous sound and tilted her face more fully up to his. Her reward was a warm, gliding caress that went from corner to corner of her smile. She made another low sound that became a tiny cry of surprise when his teeth closed tenderly on her lower lip, holding it captive. Instantly he released her and began the elusive, gliding kisses all over again.

"Ten," Diana said, the word more a sigh than his name.

"Too much?"

"No." Her teeth closed a little less than gently on Ten's lower lip. She heard his breath break and released him, whispering, "Not enough."

"Does that mean you won't run if I taste that beautiful mouth?"

"Yes."

"The way you were hanging on to my hands, I wasn't sure."

Belatedly, Diana realized that she was imprisoning Ten's hands against her face, holding him hard enough to leave marks on his tanned skin.

"I'm sorry," she said quickly, releasing his hands. "When you started kissing me I forgot everything else."

Ten bent and touched a corner of her mouth with his tongue. "That's all right, honey. I just thought you might be worried that I'd start straying out of bounds if you let go of my hands."

"What?"

"Don't you remember high school? Nothing below the collarbone in front or the waist in back."

Diana started to laugh, but the look in Ten's eyes took her breath away. His words were light, his voice was velvet, but his eyes were a smoldering gray that made her knees weak.

"I remember."

"That's the way it will be for us. If you want my hands anywhere else, you'll have to put them there."

"But then you would—you would expect more."

"I expect to spend this night like I've spent every night since I pulled you out of that kiva—hungry as hell. That's my problem, not yours. You've done nothing to encourage me."

"Nothing? What about right now?"

"This isn't encouraging." Ten lowered his mouth another fraction of an inch. His teeth closed tenderly on Diana's lower lip. The tip of his tongue caressed her captive flesh until she made a small sound at the back of her throat. He released her, gave her a quick, biting kiss and looked at her flushed lips with hunger. "This is pleasure, honey, pure and simple."

"Steve always—he said it hurt him."

Ten's answer was another brush of his lips against Diana's, but this time there was no lifting, no gliding, no teasing. His fingers eased into her hair, rubbing her scalp, holding her with gentle care while he joined their mouths in a different kind of kiss. The caressing pressure of his lips increased, tilting her head back, yet still she felt no uneasiness.

Slender fingers threaded into the thick pelt of Ten's hair, holding him even closer, wanting the kiss not to end. When Diana murmured his name, he accepted the invitation of her parted lips. His tongue glided between her teeth, seeking the moist heat beyond, finding it in a slow, deep tasting that was like nothing she had ever known. He memorized the contours of her mouth with teasing, sliding touches, caressing her, enjoying her, cherishing her. Only when she whimpered and pressed even closer to his body did he complete the seduction of her mouth.

Diana had never realized just how sensitive her tongue was, how it could discriminate so vividly between the satin smoothness and intriguing serrations of Ten's teeth, the silken texture and beguiling heat of his mouth, the nubby velvet enticement of his tongue sliding against hers in a dance of penetration and retreat that made her forget who was stronger, who was weaker, who was frightened and who was not. Tender and sweet, hot and wild, the kiss shimmered with both restraint and the sensuous consummation of two mouths completely joined.

Diana was never certain who ended the kiss or if it had truly ended at all. Slowly she realized that her arms were around Ten's neck, his arms were around her, supporting her and arching her into his body at the same time, and he was looking at her mouth as though he had just discovered fire.

"Ten?"

The huskiness of Diana's voice made his whole body tighten. Her heavy-lidded, luminous eyes told him that she had been as deeply involved in the kiss as he had. When she looked at his mouth and her own lips parted in unconscious invitation, Ten made a sound that was part laugh, part groan and all male.

"Do you want to taste me again?" he asked.

The shiver of response that went through Diana was clearly felt by Ten.

"Then take me," he said huskily.

Indigo eyes widened for a startled moment, then her lashes swept down as she looked at Ten's mouth. Her breath rushed out in a sigh that he tasted in the instant before she took his mouth, relearning his textures in a sharing of tongues that had neither beginning nor end, simply the hushed intimacy of their quickened breaths intermingling with the night.

Diana's last thought before the kiss ended was wonder that she could tremble and yet know not the least bit of fear. She had never felt so safe in her life...or so sweetly threatened.

12

"Not a chance," Ten said flatly. "If you think I'm letting you excavate that kiva, you're crazy." He pulled Diana out of the truck and shut the door hard behind her. "You're not going anywhere near that hole."

Diana blinked and stared at the man who had suddenly become every inch the ramrod of the Rocking M rather than the restrained lover who last night had taught her the pleasure of being kissed. Just kissed. All through the long drive to September Canyon, memories had come at odd times, making her shiver; then she would look over at Ten and he would smile at her, knowing what she was thinking.

He wasn't smiling now. Neither his stance nor the taut power of his body suggested that there was a bit of gentleness in him.

"I want your promise on that, Diana."

She waited for the fear that had always come to

her in the past when a man had stood hard-shouldered in front of her, his very size a threat that didn't have to be spoken aloud.

"Or else?" she asked tightly.

"Or else we've had a long drive out here for nothing, because we're going back."

"And if I refuse to go back?"

"You'll go anyway."

Diana looked at Ten's gray eyes and wondered how she had ever thought of them as warm, much less hot enough to set fires.

"Ramrod. It does suit you."

He waited.

"I'll stay on this side of the canyon," Diana said angrily. "You have my word on it. Not that you need it. You could enforce your edict and you damn well know it."

"Could I?" Ten asked in a cool voice. "You're smart and quick. You could find a way to go exploring before I could stop you. But now that you've given your word, I won't wake up in a cold sweat, seeing you lying beneath stone, only this time you aren't moving, this time you don't get up and walk away."

Diana felt the blood leave her face. She made a small sound and reached for him.

"Ten?" she whispered, touching his face.

He closed his eyes for an instant. When they opened again, they were alive once more. He bent and kissed Diana's upturned mouth quickly, then more slowly. When he lifted his mouth he whispered, "I'm glad you weren't afraid of me just now."

"I wasn't?"

Ten framed Diana's face between his large hands. "You dug in and gave as good as you got. Then you decided that it wasn't worth a long drive back to the ranch, so you agreed. That's not fear, honey. That's common sense. Me, now. I was scared."

Diana laughed in his face.

"It's true," he said. "I was afraid you'd be frightened of me and then you wouldn't let me kiss you again."

Memories of the previous night rose up in Diana, sending heat glittering from her breasts to her knees.

"What sweet sounds you make," Ten murmured, listening to the soft breaking of her breath. "Will you panic if I put my arms around you and give you the kind of kiss I wanted to give you this morning?"

Her breath came out in a long rush. "I've been hoping you would. I know it sounds crazy, but I feel like it's been forever since I kissed you. I miss your taste, Ten. I miss it until I ache."

"Open your mouth for me, honey," he whispered. "I missed you the same way, aching with it."

The heat and sweetness of Ten's mouth locked with Diana's. His taste swept through her, stealing her breath, her thoughts. Her arms tightened around his neck as she sought to get closer to him, then closer still. Soft sounds came from her throat as she gave in to a sweeping need to hold him so fiercely that he couldn't let go of her until his kiss had soothed the aching that had made sleep elude her through the long hours of the night.

Gravity slipped, then vanished, leaving Diana suspended within the hard warmth of Ten's arms. With catlike pleasure she kneaded the flexed muscles of his arms and shoulders, urging him to hold her more tightly, not caring if she could breathe. She felt no fear at the blunt reality of Ten's strength closing around her in a hot, sensual vise, for that was what she wanted, what she had ached for without knowing why or how.

Not until Diana was dizzy from lack of air did she permit the kiss to end, and even then she clung to Ten, her face against the sultry skin of his neck, her body shaking with each breath.

"Oh, baby," Ten said, shuddering with the force of his violent self-restraint. "There's a fire in you that could make stone burn. If you ever want more than kissing from a man, come to me."

Diana made an inarticulate sound and pressed her mouth against the corded tension of Ten's neck. The touch of her tongue on his skin went through him like lightning.

"You taste good," she said slowly, touching him again with her tongue. "Salty. Does your skin taste like that everywhere, or just on your neck?"

Desire ripped through Ten as he thought of his whole body being tasted by Diana's innocent, incendiary tongue. Very carefully he lowered her until she could stand on her own feet. He forced himself not to look at her reddened lips and cheeks flushed by desire. He wanted her until he was shaking with it. He had never wanted a woman like that. And that, too, shook him.

"Ten?"

"If you want to get any sketching done, we'd better unload the truck. You'll lose the best light."

"Sweet light."

Ten lifted a single dark eyebrow.

"That's what photographers call late-afternoon light," Diana explained. "Sweet light."

An image came to Ten of Diana wearing only slanting gold light, the womanly curves of her body glowing and her husky voice asking him to touch her. With an effort he banished the image, forcing himself to concentrate on what must be done.

"Where do you want to sketch first?" he asked. His voice was too thick, but he could do nothing about that for a few minutes, any more than he could quickly banish the hard proof of his hunger for her.

"I've done all the close-ups of the ruins I can do until the grads clear out more rubble and excavate to a new level," Diana said. "I need to do some perspective sketches, showing the ruins in relation to their natural environment, but to do that, I've got to be on the opposite side of the canyon.''

Shrugging, Diana said nothing more. She had agreed not to cross over to the other side of the canyon, which meant that she had no sketches to do at the moment.

Silently Ten swore, knowing his reluctance to let her near the kiva was irrational.

''Get your sketching gear together. I'll go over the area myself. If nothing else gives way, you can sketch anywhere you like. Just make sure I'm within calling distance. And don't go near that damned kiva.''

Fifteen minutes later Ten and Diana had unloaded the truck and were ready to go. He set out for the ruins at a pace that made her work hard to keep up. She didn't complain. One look at the line of Ten's jaw told her that he wasn't pleased to be leading her back toward the kiva.

Within a few minutes Diana was tasting the same kind of dread that had haunted Ten. Watching him quarter the area at the bottom of the cliff where she had fallen through, waiting for him to stumble into an ancient trap, standing with breath held until she ached; it was all Diana could do not to call Ten back even though she knew that the chance of his finding another intact kiva was so small as to be insignificant.

The chance had been equally small for her, and she had stepped through the roof of a kiva anyway.

Half an hour passed before Ten was satisfied that

the terrain concealed no more traps. If there were any other kivas, they had been filled in by dirt long ago or their ceilings were still strong enough to carry his one hundred and eighty pounds. Either way, Diana should be safe. The kiva she had fallen into on her first day was a hundred feet distant, clearly marked by stakes.

Ten signaled for Diana to join him. She scrambled up the rugged slope with the offhanded grace of a deer. Very quickly she was standing close enough for Ten to sense the heat of her body.

"Find anything?" she asked breathlessly.

"Potshards, masonry rubble and that."

Diana followed the direction of Ten's thumb. It took her a moment to realize what she was seeing. Sometime in the past five to eight hundred years, a piece of the cliff had fallen, all but filling the alcove below. Once the opening had held rooms. Now it held only an immense mound of cracked, broken sandstone. Water seeped in tiny rivulets from beneath the stone, telling of a spring hidden beneath. Her trained eye quickly picked out the angular stones and random potshards that marked an Anasazi site.

"I hope they were already gone when the cliff came down," Diana said in a low voice, remembering what Ten had said.

...lying beneath stone, only this time you aren't moving, this time you don't get up and walk away.

Ten's big hand stroked her head from crown to

neck. "Somehow," he said slowly, "I don't think they were. In fact, I'm...certain." He caressed her sensitive nape with the ball of his thumb before he lifted his hand and stepped away. "Better get sketching, honey. Even stone doesn't last forever."

Intent and relaxed at the same time, Diana sketched quickly, not wanting to lose the effect of slanting afternoon light on the ruins across the canyon. At her urging, Ten had crossed the small creek again and stood looking toward the ruins, giving scale to the cliff and the ragged lines of once whole rooms.

"Just a few more minutes," she called.

Ten waved his understanding. Diana's pencil flew over the paper as she added texture and definition to cliffs and canyon bottom, cottonwood and brush. The heightened contrast gave an almost eerie depth to the sketch.

The drawings she had made before had been accurate representations of the ruins as they were today. The drawing she was working on now was a recreation of the ruins as they had looked long ago, when the sound of barking dogs, domesticated turkeys and children's laughter had echoed through the canyon, a time when women ground corn in stone metates or painted intricate designs on pottery while their men discussed the weather or the gods or the latest rumor of raids from the north. The narrow canyon would have been alive with voices then, especially on a day like today, when the sun was hot and vital, pouring light and life over the land.

Yet today, despite Diana's usual custom, she wasn't sketching people among the buildings. Nor was she sketching the burning blue radiance of the sky. There were heavy clouds surrounding the sole figure in her drawing, a man standing on the margin of the creek. The man was both dark and compelling, black hair lifting on a storm wind, an outlaw shaman calling to his brother the storm.

The power of the man was revealed in the taut male lines of shoulder and waist, buttocks and legs, a strength that was rooted in the center of the earth and in a past when the lives of humans and spirits had been intertwined. Standing with his back to the collapsed alcove, the shaman was a still center in the swirling violence of the wind. His brother the storm had answered the shaman's call.

The shaman turned around and looked at Diana with eyes the color of rain, eyes that saw past the surface of reality to the soul beneath.

Diana shivered, blinked, and realized that she had been staring at the finished drawing so intently that her body was cramped in protest. Automatically she flipped the sketch tablet closed, both protecting and concealing the drawing. She slipped the tablet into its carrying case and stood up. Moments later she was hurrying down the slope toward Ten.

He turned at the sound of her approach, watching her with eyes the color of rain.

"Finished already?" Ten asked, holding out his hand to take Diana's pack.

She gave him her hand instead. Slowly he laced their fingers together until their hands were palm to palm. The sensitive inner skin of her fingers felt the hard pressure of him everywhere. The slow, complete interlocking was as intimate as a kiss. His palm was warm and hardened by work, making her wonder how it would feel on her skin if he were given the freedom of her body.

The thought haunted Diana while she and Ten went through their normal end-of-the-day chores—a basin bath behind the screen, then preparing dinner and cleaning up the campsite. Although the sun had vanished behind stone cliffs, true sunset was still an hour away. Shadows flowing out from the rocks had taken the edge off the unusual heat of the day, but the canyon walls still radiated the captured warmth of the sun.

Diana felt no need to pull her customary loose sweater over the sleeveless cotton blouse she was wearing. In fact, after her camp bath she had substituted sandals and shorts for hiking boots and jeans. Ten was feeling the heat, too. After his bath he hadn't bothered to put on a shirt or socks and boots. At the moment he was stretched out on his bedroll, which he had moved to the edge of the overhang, hoping to catch a vagrant breeze.

"Too bad we're not camping at Black Springs," Ten said, stretching slowly, fully. "There are pools big enough to cool off in."

"Sounds like heaven. Not that I'm complaining," Diana added, frowning over a handful of shards. "I've been at sites where the only water we had was strictly for drinking."

She turned away from the shards she had been sorting, saw Ten sprawled with feline ease across his bedroll and felt an increasingly familiar glittering sensation from her breasts to her knees. Without stopping to think, she walked over and sat next to him.

"Ten?"

His eyes opened. They were a burning silver.

Diana's thoughts scattered, and with them her ability to speak coherently. "Can I—that is, would you—could we—?"

"I thought you'd never ask."

Large hands closed around Diana's face, bringing her closer. Their mouths fitted together smoothly, seamlessly, and at the first taste of each other they both made low sounds of pleasure. Ten's hands shifted, lifting Diana, easing her across his chest until most of her weight was pressed against him. The shiver that went through her was as clear as lightning at midnight. He groaned and released her.

"Dammit, honey," Ten said heavily. "I didn't

mean to frighten you. I didn't think how you would feel being on a man's bed again, and me half-naked at that.''

Diana shook her head. "It wasn't in a bed. It was the front seat of a car. That's why I always sit so far away in the truck. And he never—never completely took off his clothes. Or mine.''

Ten closed his eyes so that she wouldn't see the rage tugging against his control. He held her gently against his chest, stroking her head and back, kissing her hair, wishing that he could change the past.

But he could not. He could only hold Diana and want her until it was a kind of agony.

The slow stroking of Ten's hand sent currents of pleasure through Diana, making her breath sigh out. She smoothed her cheek against his chest, encountered a resilient cushion of hair instead of cloth, and made a murmurous sound of discovery. Ten's hand hesitated, then continued its languid journey from the silky hair of her head to the intriguing line of her back. Though the pressure was unchanged, the caress was different, sensual rather than soothing, enticing rather than calming. He felt the heat of her breath on his breastbone as she kissed him lingeringly. Then he felt her lips open. She hesitated.

"Go ahead," Ten said. "Find out if I taste the same there as I did on my neck."

Diana lifted her head until she could see his eyes. "You won't mind?''

His smile was slow, hot, infinitely male. "Baby, you can put that sweet mouth anywhere on me that you want."

Deep blue eyes widened in shock and...curiosity. The shock he had expected. The curiosity made him want to pull her hard against his body and show her just how much he wouldn't mind any damn thing she wanted to do to him.

The first, exploring touch of Diana's tongue made Ten's breath stick in his throat. He had expected a darting taste followed by a smart comment about the limitations of camp baths. He hadn't expected a sleek, hot foray through the thicket of his chest hair. He hadn't expected her purring sounds of pleasure as she tasted him. Most of all, he hadn't expected her nipples to harden against him when she found and caressed his own nipple to a tiny, aching point.

Ten lay rigidly, fighting his own arousal and the sudden, violent need to touch Diana, to hold the sweet weight of her breasts in his hands, to taste and suckle and tease her until she writhed in an agony of pleasure. But all he permitted himself to do was slide the fingers of his left hand deeply into Diana's hair, holding her mouth against him while his right hand kneaded her back from nape to waist, pressing her even closer to the growing heat of his body. When he could bear no more he eased her mouth back up his chest until he could slide his tongue between her teeth, kissing her deeply, drinking her, mating with her in the only way she would allow.

By the time Ten released Diana's mouth she could barely think, much less speak. Her lips felt flushed, full, sated, but the rest of her body ached.

"I want—more than kissing," she said. "But I don't know how much more."

"It's all right," Ten said, kissing Diana's lips gently. "We'll take it slow and easy. The only rule will be the oldest and best one of all. Anytime I do something you don't want, tell me. I'll stop."

"That isn't fair to you. Yes, I know," she said quickly, before Ten could speak. "Life isn't fair. But I don't want to make it any harder on you."

The left corner of Ten's mouth tugged up. "Honey, it can't get any harder than it already is." He brushed another kiss over Diana's mouth, scattering her objections. Moving slowly, he lifted her from his body and stretched her out on her side with her back to him. "You'll feel safer this way, nothing in front of you, nothing holding you down, nothing trapping you. Just me behind you, and you know I'd never take you by surprise, don't you?"

"Y-yes," Diana said. It was the truth. If she hadn't trusted Ten at an instinctive level, she wouldn't even be in September Canyon with him, much less still shivering from his kisses. She let out a long breath that she hadn't been aware of holding and realized that Ten had been right about another thing. She did feel safer lying on her side with nothing in front of her but the view of a canyon slowly succumbing to the embrace of twilight. The setting couldn't have been farther from her memories of being wedged between cold machinery and Steve's relentless body.

"Ten?"

"Hmm?"

"You're right. I feel safer this way."

"Good," Ten murmured, glad that Diana's back was to him, for it gave him the freedom to look at the line of her waist flaring into her rounded hips and then tapering slowly to her ankles. If she had seen the hunger and male approval in his eyes as he looked at her, she might have felt less relaxed with her back to him.

Ten's long index finger traced the line of Diana's body from the crown of her head, over her right ear, down her neck, over her right shoulder, down her ribs to her waist, up the rise of her hips, then down every bit of her right leg to her ankle. The primal ripple of her response followed his caress, telling Ten that her whole body had become sensitized to passion.

"That," he said, kissing the nape of Diana's neck, "broke every one of the high school rules about collarbones and waist. Feel like bolting yet?"

13

Diana laughed shakily, wondering at the curious weakness that had followed Ten's caress. He had broken the rules, but in such a way as not to touch any of the forbidden areas.

"Does that little laugh mean I can do it again?" Ten asked.

The subdued humor in Ten's voice was another kind of reassurance to Diana. Steve had been deadly serious whenever they had been alone, intent on getting as much from her sexually as he could, as quickly as he could.

"Yes," Diana whispered.

A shiver of response followed the seductive movement of Ten's fingertip from Diana's head to her heels. This time he slid beneath her arm, as well, caressing the sensitive skin.

"You're a pleasure to touch," Ten said, kissing Diana's nape again. "Soft, resilient, alive." His

tongue traced the line of her scalp to her ear. He
smiled to hear the sudden intake of her breath. "You
have the sweetest curves. Here," he said, biting her
ear gently. "And here." His fingers curled around her
arm caressingly. When his fingers moved on, his
mouth lingered. He kissed the bare skin of her arm,
biting softly, drawing tiny sounds from her. "And
here."

Ten's hand shaped the tightly drawn line of her
waist, kneading lightly, then more firmly. Slowly, inevitably, his palm moved over the full curve of Diana's hip. "And here." His fingers fanned out, shap-
ing her. As his teeth closed over her nape, his hand
flexed into her resilient flesh, luxuriating in the feel
of her.

The unexpected caress drew a ragged sound from
Diana. Currents of sensation rippled through her,
making her want to shift restlessly. She stirred, and
her movements acted to increase the pressure of Ten's
hand. When his palm smoothed down her bare thigh,
she forgot to be worried that he would slide his fingers between her legs. Only when his hand had
stroked over her calves to her ankles did she realize
that the danger zone had been bypassed once more.

Ten continued the slow, undemanding sweeps of
his hand up and down Diana's body. The long caresses were punctuated by his teeth biting gently at
her nape, her shoulder, the elegant line of her back;
and each time his hand traveled back up her body, he

skimmed closer to the shadowed secrets between her thighs and the fullness of her breasts. He explored the smooth curve of her belly with slow pressures that eased her hips back into the muscular cradle of his legs. The pressure of her against his fiercely aroused flesh was a sweet fire that made his hands shake.

Breath held against a groan, Ten waited for Diana to retreat. When she didn't, he pressed her even closer, savoring the pleasure-pain of his own need for a moment before he released her, not wanting to frighten her. His hand shifted, stroking slowly up the center line of her body, giving her every chance to refuse the growing intimacy of his touch.

Buttons caught and tugged against Ten's hand. He made no move to undo them despite his aching desire to touch Diana without the barrier of cloth. He simply caressed her from navel to breastbone to neck and back again, following the center of her body, knowing only a hint of the womanly curves that were calling to him.

"Wait," she said huskily.

Immediately Ten's hand stopped, then withdrew. Before he could retreat farther, slender fingers covered his, holding his hand against her belly. Her shoulders moved, her fingers urged his—and suddenly Ten found his hand inside Diana's blouse, cupping the lush weight of her breast. A groan was pulled from his throat, a low sound of desire that mingled with the one she made as her nipple peaked in a rush of sensation that left her weak.

Diana's breath unraveled into broken sighs as Ten's hand moved slowly from one breast to the other, caressing her, cherishing her. When his finger slid beneath the thin fabric of her bra and circled the tip of one breast, she gasped at the unexpected pleasure. He teased her nipple again, then withdrew, leaving her aching for more.

"Ten?"

He made a sound that could have been "More?"

"Yes," she sighed.

A long finger skimmed over Diana's nipple again, but the sensation was much less acute, because there was cloth between them this time. Without stopping to think, she released the front fastening of her bra, baring herself to Ten's touch.

A hammer blow of desire went through Ten, making his hands shake. He eased one long arm beneath Diana's head, cradling her and at the same time giving both hands the freedom to caress her. He caught her nipples between his fingers and squeezed gently, smiling at the rippling cry of pleasure he drew from her lips. The sight of her rose-tipped, creamy curves nestled in his darker hands made fire pool urgently in his body, swelling him against his jeans until he could count each heartbeat as a separate surge of blood. He caressed her hard nipples again, wishing he could take the responsive flesh into his mouth.

Diana's breath fragmented into a low cry as Ten tugged rhythmically on her breasts, soothing and teasing her in the same skilled motions. He squeezed again, harder, knowing that she was now too aroused to feel a lighter touch. Her back arched in a passionate reflex that pressed her breasts against his hands. He rubbed slowly in return and was rewarded by a shivering cry of pleasure.

Deliberately Ten's hands retreated from Diana's breasts to her ribs, dragging slowly across her body, peeling away her bra and blouse. She made no objection, simply moved her shoulders sinuously, helping him. Her reward was the return of his hands to her breasts in a slow loving that drew ragged sighs from her lips; and then she felt the heat of his mouth going down her spine in a sensual glide that made her shiver repeatedly. Each restrained bite was a separate burst of pleasure sending glittering needles of sensation throughout her body. When his tongue traced her spine all the way up to her nape, she called out his name in a throaty voice she didn't recognize as her own.

"I'm right here, baby," Ten said, biting Diana's nape with enough force to leave small marks, tugging at the full breasts that lay within his cupped hands. "And so are you."

Slowly Ten released one breast and sent his hand down the front of her body again. "There is so much of you to enjoy," he said in a low voice. This time he didn't turn aside from the soft mound at the apex of her thighs. Nor did he linger. "Not just the obvious places, the battlegrounds of school kids," Ten continued, smoothing his hand over Diana's hip to the small of her back. "I like touching the rest of you, too." He traced the swell of her hip down to the back of her thighs, and from there to her firm calves and delicate ankles. "Smooth, firm…"

Ten's hand caressed higher, finding and stroking the inside of Diana's thighs as far as he could without seeming to pressure her for more than she was willing to give. His caress went from the back of her knee to the small of her back. He stroked first one hip, then the other, cupping and squeezing, drawing a surprised gasp of pleasure from her. She shifted almost restlessly, giving Ten's hand greater freedom. He moved his hand farther down, curling around her, holding her intimately. Heat burst through her, changing her gasp to a moan.

"Would you like lying just as you are now, but with no clothes to dull your pleasure?" Ten asked softly, kissing Diana's nape, her shoulder, her vulnerable spine. His hand tightened against her, subtly caressing her. "It's your choice, honey. You're as safe as you want to be."

"That's not…fair." The last word came out in a rippling sigh as Ten's hand flexed once more against her softness and heat.

"I thought you liked being teased," Ten said, smiling against Diana's spine despite the sudden, savage clenching of his own need.

"You're not teasing me," she whispered.

"I'm not?" Ten's hand flexed again and he groaned quietly at Diana's helpless response to his touch. "Baby, I'm sure as hell teasing one of us."

He felt her hand moving, heard the soft slide of a zipper and sensed the sudden looseness of her shorts. His hand bunched, catching cloth between his fingers, pulling it away from the hot secrets he longed to explore.

When Diana felt her remaining clothes being tugged down her legs, felt the powerful, cloth-covered male legs rubbing against hers, a shaft of panic went through her, memories of another time, another place, pain. Her legs clamped together and her body jack-knifed in an instinctive effort to protect herself.

Instantly Ten let go, leaving Diana's shorts and panties around her knees. Grateful that she couldn't see the tension in his body, Ten brushed a butterfly kiss on her shoulder.

"It's all right, Diana. It stops right here."

Gently Ten began to ease his left arm from beneath Diana's head. She grabbed his left hand and held it against her breast once more.

"Don't leave," she said raggedly. "I didn't mean to react like that. It was just when I felt the zipper scrape down my leg and felt your legs and you were still dressed—but it's all right now. I know where I am, who I'm with.''

Ten kissed Diana's shoulder again but made no move to reclaim the soft curves he had already made his own, much less the shadowed heat that lay newly revealed to his touch.

"Would it make you feel better if I weren't wearing my jeans?" Ten asked.

She laughed a little wildly. "Yes. I know it sounds crazy but—yes."

With a silent prayer that his self-control was as good as he thought it was, Ten rolled over, removed his clothes and returned to his former spoon position with Diana. The feel of her bare bottom nestled deeply into his lap made him clench against a savage thrust of need.

Diana and I could be dead naked together and she could still say no and that would be that. So cool off, cowboy. This one is for Diana, not me. As much as she wants, when she wants it, however she wants it. That's what I promised.

I must have been out of my mind.

The sweet heat and feminine curves of Diana's body called out to Ten in a siren song as old as man and woman and desire, making Ten want to curse his stupidity for promising not to coax or beg or demand from Diana what he had never needed so much before in his life.

He lay motionless, his left arm pillowing Diana's

head, his right hand clenched into a fist that rested on his equally clenched thigh.

"Ten," Diana whispered. "Please touch me again. It's all right. I trust you. I won't panic again. And I like—I like the feel of you without your jeans."

Slowly Ten's right hand loosened. He took a deep, secret breath, then another, relaxing himself in a ritual that was almost as old as desire itself.

"Are you sure?" he asked, not knowing of whom he asked the question.

Diana answered it for both of them. Without warning she took both of Ten's hands and rubbed her breasts against his palms, letting him feel the hardness of her nipples and at the same time easing some of the wild ache in her body. His strong fingers closed around her, plucking at the tight velvet peaks, coaxing a ripple of sound from her. After a moment the smooth heat of his right hand caressed her belly, her waist, the small of her back; then a single finger traced the shadow cleft between her hips.

If Diana had thought to conceal herself by locking her knees together and jackknifing her body, she had failed. Ten found her softness unshielded, defenseless, and he traced it lovingly. A sudden shudder took her whole body, surprising her. Her husky cry was matched by Ten's groan of discovery as her heat and pleasure spilled over him.

"Ten," Diana cried, feeling another of the strange, tiny convulsions building in her. "I—"

The word became a gasp and another shudder and then another as she felt his touch glide into her body, retreat, return, only to retreat once more, leaving her dazed and empty, aching. He skimmed the edges of her softness, probing sweetly, discovering the aching nub hidden between sleek, silken folds, rubbing it slowly, hotly, stripping away her breath, her thoughts, her restraint.

Diana twisted sinuously, trying to know more of the pleasure that was greater than any she had ever felt but still not enough; it was driving her mad. *Ten* was driving her mad, stealing into her so gently, retreating, always retreating when what she wanted, what she must have, was his own flesh filling the emptiness she had never known existed within her own body.

. "So soft," Ten said, his deep voice a rumbling purr. He teased Diana slowly, loving the wild tremors of her response when he slid unerringly into her softness, groaning as he touched as much of her as he could. "So damned hot."

Ten's name broke on Diana's lips, a strained sound that could have been either fear or passion. Slowly, reluctantly, he began withdrawing from her body. Her hand locked over his, holding him in place.

"Are you sure you want this?" Ten said hoarsely, rubbing his cheek along her bare hip.

"Yes."

"And this? Do you want this, too?"

His hand shifted. The sensuous pressure within Diana increased. The glittering sensation that had haunted her body condensed into a network of wild lightning. The sound she made was as involuntary as the tightening of her body around him. Afraid that he had hurt her, Ten withdrew before she could stop him.

"Baby? Was that pleasure or pain? You're so tight…"

Diana looked over her shoulder at Ten with sapphire eyes that burned in the aftermath of sensual lightning. Slowly she turned her whole body until she was facing him. When she spoke, her voice was low, smoky, as helplessly sensual as her response to him. She guided his hand from her shoulder to the dark triangle at the base of her torso. When he accepted her wordless invitation and returned to her body, a shaft of pleasure made her gasp and tremble even as she instinctively sought more of Ten's touch. His hand shifted and she felt herself gently stretched. Sensual lightning came again, as unexpected and ravishing as it had been the first time.

"You were right," Diana said when she could speak.

"About what?"

"This. It's as much pleasure as your senses can stand."

Ten laughed softly, then groaned as Diana's mouth caressed his bare chest. "We've just skimmed the surface," he said, bringing her mouth up to his. "But I'm glad you're enjoying it."

She smiled hesitantly. "Are you enjoying it, too?"

"Baby, I'd have to be dead and buried not to enjoy touching you."

Ten felt Diana's slender fingers searching restlessly over his chest, pausing to tease the flat male nipples, then moving on to his back. She probed the line of his spine between ridges of muscle, stroking him, learning what it felt like to hold a man in her arms. Closing her eyes, sighing, half-smiling, she kneaded the long, heavy muscles of Ten's back, openly savoring the heat and power of his body.

Seeing Diana's enjoyment at touching him was as arousing as anything a woman had ever done to Ten. The tips of Diana's breasts were like tight pink rosebuds pressing against him with each movement of her hands. When he could no longer bear looking at her breasts without caressing them, he bent his head to her. A startled gasp became a moan as he circled one bud with his tongue, then took her deeply into his mouth, tasting her, tugging softly on her, making her shudder with each soft stab of his tongue, each exquisitely restrained caress of his teeth, each movement of his fingers within the clinging heat of her body.

Sounds rippled from Diana, the elemental huskiness of passion combined with rising notes of feminine surprise. The hot movements of Ten's mouth and hands increased, deepened, quickened, and she called his name with every rapid breath she took, every stroke of sweet lightning scoring her, shaking her, until finally she shimmered and burned in his arms, her body consumed by the pleasure he had given to her.

Ten held Diana as close as he dared, stroking her trembling body with hands that also trembled, kissing her flushed cheeks, her eyelids, her reddened lips, until finally her breath came more evenly. Her lashes stirred and lifted, revealing eyes more blue than any gems Ten had ever seen.

"How can I...what do I say?" Diana whispered.

"Whatever you want."

"I love you, Ten."

The line of Ten's lips shifted into a bittersweet smile. Before she could say any more, he kissed her gently. "I'm glad you enjoyed it, baby. Damned glad."

Diana opened her mouth to object that what she felt was more than the aftermath of physical pleasure, but Ten's tongue slid between her lips. Without thinking she closed her teeth, lightly raking his tongue, then soothing it with slow motions of her own in a pattern he had taught her. The tightening of his body in response and the sweet friction of his own tongue made her nerve endings shimmer again, echoes of lightning from her breasts to her knees. Her breath caught, broke, caught again.

"Ten?"

He closed his eyes, trying to ignore both the soft heat of Diana's body and the hard heat of his own.

"I want more of you," Diana said huskily, sweeping her hands from his shoulders to his waist. "I want all of you. If you—do you want me, too?"

"Move your hands down a little more and tell me what you think," Ten said hoarsely.

She had moved her hands barely at all when she discovered precisely what he meant. The sound he made while she measured his arousal with a slow pressure of her palm could have been pain, but she was looking at his eyes and she knew it wasn't. She repeated the caress again, drawing another hoarse, low sound.

"Baby, you'll..."

Ten's breath hissed between his clenched teeth. His hand slid from Diana's knee to the apex of her thighs as he sought the secret well of her femininity. It was even hotter and softer than his memories. She whimpered and moved with his touch. Her response and her hands searching over his hard, eager flesh nearly undid him.

Very carefully Ten eased Diana's hands up his body, kissed her fingertips and palms and held them hard against his chest while he caught his breath.

"Ten? What's wrong?"

"Hush, baby. Nothing's wrong."

Ten turned away and took a packet from his jeans pocket. With the swift, sure motions of a man performing an accustomed task, he opened the packet. When he turned back to Diana he wasn't completely naked. He saw her rather startled, somewhat dismayed look. With a calm that was exactly opposite to what he was feeling, he put his finger under her chin and tilted her face up to his own.

"Want to change your mind?" Ten asked.

Rather tentatively, Diana ran her fingertips over Ten's tightly sheathed flesh. "It felt better...without."

He clenched his teeth against agreeing with her. It had felt one hell of a lot better to be completely naked. Just as she, now, felt exquisite to his bare fingers as he once more slid into her, testing her readiness to receive him and simultaneously drawing a low sound of pleasure from her as she melted at his touch.

"Sex is temporary," Ten said tightly. "Children aren't. It's a small price to pay for a big amount of protection."

Diana's head snapped up, surprise clear on her face. At that moment Ten realized she hadn't even considered the fact that she might become pregnant. He wanted to swear and laugh and then swear some more at her trust, but most of all he wanted to plumb the depths of her heat with the very flesh that she was once again caressing tentatively. Though her touch was muffled by the price of protecting himself against the lifetime complications of fatherhood, the feel of her hand was nonetheless driving him to the edge of his control.

"Baby?" Ten said.

The aching restraint in his voice made Diana's heart turn over. "Yes," she whispered. "Whatever you want, just show me."

"The first time, it would be easier if…will it bother you to be beneath me?"

"No."

"Are you sure?"

Holding Ten's eyes with her own, Diana lay back and opened herself to him. Her complete trust pierced Ten, making him tremble with an emotion that was deeper and more devastating than desire. Slowly he settled between her legs, watching her for any sign of fear or pain. He saw only blue eyes that widened slightly at the gently probing pressure between her legs, then her eyes closed and she unraveled in a long, shivering acceptance of him within her body.

The ease with which Ten became a part of Diana was another instant of piercing emotion deep within him…and then he was moving and she was clinging to him, measuring him in a new way, moving with him, loving him as she had never loved another man.

Fire swept through Ten's restraint, burning him, burning her, each wanting more and yet more. Instinctively Diana's legs shifted, wrapping around his lean hips, luring and demanding with the same motions. He answered with hard, sweeping movements, driving into her, filling her, drinking from her sweet mouth until he felt his self-control slipping away. He fought against ecstasy, not wanting it to come to him so soon, not wanting to end the burning arousal that was in itself a savage pleasure; then it was too late, the pleasure was too piercing, too overwhelming.

Ten took her one final time, all of her, and held himself there while ecstasy stripped everything away but Diana and the deep, endless pulses of his own release.

14

Ten sat in the rocking chair, moving it with a gentle rhythm, looking down into Logan's turquoise eyes. The baby stared with absolute seriousness back into Ten's eyes.

"I know, old man," Ten said, smiling. "I don't look like your momma. What's worse, I'm not built like her and you're getting too hungry to be pacified by a rocking chair and a soothing voice much longer. But I'm afraid you'll just have to lump it for a while. Luke has been trying to show Carla that new colt all day, and this is the first chance they've had. You don't begrudge your parents a few minutes alone together, do you?"

Ten smiled to himself as he spoke. He suspected the new colt wasn't all that was keeping Luke and Carla away from the house. The men were scattered all over the ranch, Diana was working on sketches at the old house, Ten had promised to watch Logan, and the barn was empty of all but a few horses. Ten wouldn't have blamed Luke for taking advantage of the opportunity to steal a few kisses or even the whole woman.

The thought of enjoying a similar opportunity to have Diana alone within the twilight silence of the barn had a rapid and very pronounced effect on Ten's body.

"Damn," he muttered softly. "It's not like I've been exactly deprived in that department, except for the weekends."

When they were away from September Canyon, Ten was careful not to show any difference in his treatment of Diana. Some women could have laughed off or ignored the cowhands' brand of humor with regard to "unwed marriage" or "riding double" or the like, but Ten didn't think Diana was one of them. When the hands discovered, as they quickly would, that no marriage was planned, the humor would degenerate into sidelong looks and blunt male speculations. Diana's trust and uninhibited sensuality deserved better than that. She was very different from the kind of women the cowboys associated with summer flings.

The only time Ten allowed himself to be alone with Diana was in the old house, in the workroom, sorting shards after dinner, the curtains open and both people plainly in view to anyone who cared enough to glance in. Outwardly, as long as anyone was around, nothing had changed since Diana had become his lover.

As much as Ten was tempted by proximity, he didn't so much as kiss Diana when they were at the ranch house. He didn't trust himself to stop with a kiss or two. On Friday, the drive back from September Canyon had taken so long that dinner was over hours before Ten and Diana made it to the ranch house. Part of the trouble had been a rain-slicked road. The other part had been Diana; Ten hadn't been able to keep his hands off her. What had started as a quick kiss had ended with both of them breathing too hard, too fast, their breath as steamy as their bodies had become.

All that had prevented Ten from taking Diana right there was the fact that her first, unhappy experience with sex had been in the front seat of a vehicle. So he had put the truck back in gear and driven to the ranch with the weekend stretching like eternity in front of him. But it had been a near thing. He had never been like that with a woman, riding the eroding edge of his own self-control until he wanted to put his fist through a window in sheer frustration.

Two nights in the bunkhouse did nothing to make him feel better. No matter how hard Ten tried not to, he kept seeing Diana holding out her arms, opening herself to him. The memory made heat and heaviness pool thickly between his thighs, a reaction that had become uncomfortably familiar since he had first seen Diana.

Becoming her lover had meant only a temporary improvement in the condition, followed all too soon by an even more pronounced return of the problem. Knowing the passion that lay behind Diana's smile didn't help to cool Ten's response. He wanted to make love to her after an evening of conversation and laughter, and then again in the middle of the night, and then he wanted to kiss her slowly awake in the morning, bringing her from dreams to passion, watching the pleasure in her eyes when she woke up and found him inside her. But he couldn't do that on the weekends, when they returned to the ranch house.

Logan bunched up his little fists and cried.

Ten sighed. "I know how you feel, nubbin. I know how you feel."

He shifted the baby and stroked the tiny cheek with his fingertip. Logan's hands flailed with excitement until more by chance than anything else he connected with Ten's left index finger, bringing it to his mouth. Instantly the baby began sucking on Ten's callused fingertip.

"Uh, old man, I don't know how to break this to you, but…oh, the hell with it. You'll figure it out for yourself soon enough."

The controlled, throaty rumble of a powerful car engine distracted Ten. He looked out through the window into the last light of evening. The paint job on the car was a dirt-streaked, sun-faded black, but everything that affected the car's function was in top shape. The tires were new, the lights were bright and hard, and the engine purred like a well-fed cougar.

Even before the driver got out and stretched, Ten knew that Nevada Blackthorn had come back to the Rocking M.

Smiling with anticipation, Ten watched his younger brother climb the front steps with the lithe, coordinated motions of an athlete or a highly trained warrior. The knock on the door was distinct, staccato without being impatient. Ten's smile widened. There had been a time when his brother would have driven up in a cloud of dust and knocked on the door hard enough to rattle the hinges.

"Come on in, Nevada."

The door opened and shut without noise. Nevada crossed the room the same way. Without noise. Tall, wide-shouldered, his thick black hair two inches long and his dense beard half that length, Nevada looked as hard as he was. Even as his pale, ice-green eyes took in the room with its multiple doorways, his unnaturally acute hearing noted the near-silent approach of someone coming toward the living room through the kitchen.

Knowing that Ten was baby-sitting Logan, Diana had been all but tiptoeing across the kitchen as she headed for the living room. She didn't get that far. Two steps from the doorway she froze at the sight of the lean, long-boned, broad-shouldered stranger who moved like Ten when he was fighting.

Ten held Logan and watched Nevada cross the floor toward the rocking chair. Rain-colored eyes measured the changes in Nevada—the brackets of anger or pain around his flat, unsmiling mouth, the razor-fine physical edge, his muscular weight always poised on the balls of his feet because he had to be ready to throw himself into flight or battle at every instant. For Ten, looking at Nevada was like going back in time, seeing himself years ago, youthful dreams and emotions burned out by the timeless cruelty of war.

Silently Nevada stood in front of the rocking chair, staring down at his brother and the baby.

"I will be damned. Yours?"

Ten shook his head. "Not a chance. I know what kind of husband I make. I'm definitely a short-term man. Marriage should be a long-term affair."

Nevada grunted. "The bitch you married didn't make much of a wife, long or short."

The corner of Ten's mouth curled sardonically. "It wasn't all her fault. Women aren't interested in me for more than a few weeks."

"The way I remember it, you weren't real interested yourself after a few weeks. Two months was your limit. Then you were tugging at the bit, looking for new worlds to conquer."

"The curse of the Blackthorns," Ten agreed, his voice casual. "Warriors, not husbands."

Diana stood motionless, her throat clenched around a cry of protest and pain, realizing that she had lost a gamble she hadn't even understood she was taking. She had understood the risk of physical injury she took in trusting Ten, and she had been lucky; Ten had given her extraordinary physical pleasure and no pain at all.

But she hadn't understood that she was risking her emotions and unborn dreams. Now she felt as she had the instant the kiva ceiling had given way beneath her feet.

No wonder Ten has been so careful not to touch me when other people are around. He doesn't want them to know we're lovers. They might assume something more, something that has to do with shared lives, shared promises, shared love. But he doesn't see us that way.

I didn't know I saw us that way until now, just now, when a dream I didn't even know I had burst and I fell through to reality.

God, I hope the landing is easier than the fall.

Diana clenched her teeth and forced herself to let out the breath she had instinctively held at the first instant of tearing pain. Silently, gradually, she took in air and let it out again, bringing strength back to her body. After a few aching breaths, her ears stopped ringing. The words from the other room began to have meaning again, Nevada speaking in tones that were like Ten's but without the emotion.

"Heard anything from Utah?"

"He's tired of jungles," Ten said.

Nevada grunted. "Anytime he wants to swap sea-level tropics for Afghanistan's high passes, he can have at it."

"Thought the country calmed down after the Russians left." Ten gave Nevada a measuring, gray-eyed glance. "Thought that was why you decided to come home."

"The Afghani tribesmen have been killing each other for a thousand years. They'll be killing each other a thousand years from now. They're fighting men. They'd take on Satan for the pure hell of it."

"So would you."

Nevada's pale green eyes locked with Ten's. "I did. I lost."

Ten held out his right hand. "I don't know of any man who ever won. Welcome back, brother. You've been a long time coming home."

The deep affection in Ten's voice went through Diana, shaking her all over again, telling her that she was jealous of Ten's brother. The realization appalled her, and the pain.

All the old wives' tales are true: the landing is worse than the fall.

Diana looked around almost wildly. She had to leave, and leave quickly, before she was discovered.

She couldn't face Ten with jealousy and despair and pain shaking her.

"Never thought I'd say it," Nevada said quietly, "but it's good to see your ugly face again. Now maybe you'll introduce me to the lady standing behind me."

Ten leaned sideways, looking around his brother's body toward the front door.

"Kitchen door," Nevada said, stepping aside.

Diana heard the words but took another step backward anyway, wondering bitterly how Nevada had known she was behind him. She hadn't made a sound. In fact, she had barely breathed, especially after hearing Ten's matter-of-fact summation of his lack of enduring appeal to women.

And theirs to him.

"Diana? Is that you? Come on in, honey. I want you to meet my brother Nevada. Nevada, this is Diana Saxton."

Nevada turned around and Diana knew she couldn't flee. The pale green eyes that were examining her were as passionless as Nevada's voice. She had an unnerving sense of looking into the eyes of a wolf or a cougar.

"How did you know I was here?" Diana asked almost angrily.

"Your scent."

Nevada's neutral tone did nothing to calm Diana. The man's unsmiling, measuring aloofness overwhelmed all other impressions she had of him, even the obvious one of his dark, hard, male appeal.

Nevada looked from Diana to the baby sucking industriously on Ten's finger. "Yours?"

"No," she said in a strained voice. "That's Logan MacKenzie."

"Luke's baby?" Nevada asked, looking at Ten.

Ten nodded.

"You mean that long-legged little girl you told me about finally ran him to ground?"

"She sure did. Then she let him go. He decided he didn't want to go anywhere without her."

Nevada shrugged. "To each his own. For the Blackthorns, that means single harness, not double."

Ten looked at Diana's tight, pale face and at his brother, who was a younger, harder reflection of himself. Ten looked down for a long moment at the baby in his lap, then he met again the unsmiling eyes of a warrior who had fought too long.

"Hope you haven't lost your taste for sleeping out," Ten said. "Jervis is getting damned tired of weekends in September Canyon."

"I don't sleep much, so it doesn't matter where I lie down."

Ten's eyes narrowed as he remembered the years he had spent relearning how to sleep like a civilized man instead of a wild animal, coming alert with every unusual noise, waking up in a single rush with a knife in one hand and a man's throat in the other.

"It will pass," Ten said quietly.

Nevada said nothing.

Logan began to fret, no longer pacified by Ten's unyielding fingertip.

Nevada watched the baby for a moment, then said, "Company coming from the barn. Man and a woman."

Ten shook his head at the acuity of Nevada's senses. "I'm glad I don't have to live like that anymore, every sense peeled to maximum alertness."

"Beats dying."

The very faint sound of a woman's laughter floated into the living room. Logan's fretfulness increased in volume.

"Honey," Ten said to Diana without looking away from the baby, "go tell Carla to get a move on it. Logan is getting set to cloud up and rain all over me."

There was no answer. Ten glanced up from Logan's rapidly reddening face. Diana was gone.

"How long was she standing there?" Ten said, his voice as hard as Nevada's.

"Long enough to know you're not interested in marrying her."

Ten closed his eyes and hissed a single, savage word. It would be a long drive to September Canyon tomorrow, and all the way Diana would be tight, angry, thinking of a thousand reasons why she shouldn't melt and run like hot, wild honey at his touch.

Logan began to cry in earnest, gulping in air and letting it out in jerky squalls.

"That's a strong baby you have there," Nevada said. He bent down. A long, scarred finger traced Logan's hairline with surprising delicacy. "It's good to hear a baby cry and know its distress is only temporary, that food and love are on the way."

"Less volume would be nice."

Nevada shook his head and said in a low voice, "The ones who are too weak to cry are the hardest to take."

Ten looked up quickly. His brother's eyes were hooded, unreadable. The front door opened and Carla rushed in.

"I'm sorry, I thought Logan would be all right for a few more minutes." She saw Nevada, noted the similarity to Ten in build and stance and smiled. "Nevada Blackthorn, right?" she asked, reaching past the bearded man for her hollering baby. "I'm Carla. Welcome to the Rocking M. We've never met but I've heard a lot about you." As she hurried from the room with Logan in her arms, she called over her shoulder, "Luke, look who finally got here. Now Jervis can go back to chasing cows."

Soon after Carla disappeared into the next room, the sound of the baby's crying ended abruptly, telling the men that Logan had found something more satisfactory to suckle than a man's callused fingertip.

Luke shut the door and walked across the living

room. For a few seconds there was silence while Nevada and Luke measured each other. Then Luke nodded and held out his hand.

"Welcome back, Nevada. The Rocking M is your home for as long as you want it."

After a moment Nevada took the hand that was offered. "Thanks, MacKenzie. You won't regret it."

Luke turned to Ten, measured the expression on his face and asked rather warily, "Something wrong, ramrod?"

"Not one damn thing." Ten stood and crossed the room in long strides. "Come on, Nevada. I'll show you where you'll be sleeping."

The front door closed behind Ten.

Luke looked questioningly at Nevada.

"Woman trouble," Nevada said succinctly.

"What?"

"Five foot three, blue eyes, a fine body she tries to hide underneath a man's sweater."

"Diana?"

Nevada nodded.

"Did you say Ten's *woman?*"

Nevada shrugged. "She will be until she tries to put a permanent brand on him. Then she'll be looking for another stud to ride. Blackthorns don't brand worth a damn."

15

Ten was right about the length of the drive to September Canyon. And the silence. Diana slept most of the way despite the roughness of the road, telling Ten two things. The first was that she trusted his driving skills, but he already knew that. The second was that she must have slept damned little the night before to be able to sleep so soundly now in the rolling front seat of the pickup truck.

When Ten could take it no longer, he said, "Diana."

Her eyes opened. They were dark, clear, and their color was an indigo as bottomless as twilight.

"Pounce's purring must have kept you up all night," Ten said, watching the road. One look at Diana's eyes had been enough.

"Pounce hunts at night." The thought of the cat gliding through darkness in search of prey reminded Diana of Nevada. "Like Nevada."

"He lived as a warrior too long. Like me. And like me, Nevada will heal," Ten said matter-of-factly. "It just takes time."

Diana made a sound that could have meant anything.

Ten waited.

No more sounds came from the other side of the truck.

"I was glad to see that Nevada and Luke didn't have to sort things out the hard way," Ten continued. "They'll get along fine now that life has knocked some sense into both of their hard heads."

Diana said nothing.

With a hunger Ten wasn't aware of, he watched her for a few instants before the road claimed his attention again. Telling himself to be patient, he waited for her to speak. And he waited.

And waited.

Ten was still waiting when they forded Picture Wash and bumped up September Canyon to the overhang. It wasn't the first time he and Diana had gone for hours without conversation, but it was the first time the silence hadn't been comfortable. Getting out of the truck didn't increase Diana's desire to talk. They unloaded supplies with a minimum of words, each doing his or her accustomed part around the camp.

Without a word Ten carried the two bedrolls to the edge of the overhang, dragged two camp mattresses over and began making up the single, oversize bedroll he and Diana would share. He sensed her watching him, but she said nothing. When he straightened and looked around, he saw Diana shrugging into her backpack, clearly preparing to go out and sketch in the rapidly failing light. His arm shot out and his fingers curled hard around her wrist.

"Dammit!" Ten said. "You were the one who came to me! I never promised you anything!"

Diana's eyes were wide and dark against her pale face. For a long, stretching moment she looked at Ten, letting the truth echo around her like thunder while painful lightning searched through her body and soul.

"Yes," she said huskily. "I know."

Ten's hands tightened. Her agreement should have made him feel better, but it didn't. He kept remembering the moment when she had looked at him with eyes still dazed by her first taste of sexual pleasure and whispered that she loved him.

Now her eyes were filled with pain. He had never felt another person's pain so clearly, as clearly as his own.

"Listen to me," Ten said roughly. "The pleasure you feel when we have sex—that isn't love. It will wear off. It always does. But until it does, there's no reason you shouldn't enjoy it to the fullest."

The slight flinching of Diana's eyelids was the only

betrayal of her emotions. "That's very kind of you, Tennessee."

Her soft, even voice scored Ten like a whip.

"*Kind?* I'm not some damn charity worker. I'm a man and I enjoy sex with you a hell of a lot more than I've ever enjoyed it with any woman. What we have in bed is damned rare and I know it even if you don't!"

Diana looked up into the blazing clarity of Ten's eyes. She didn't doubt that he meant exactly what he had said. She drew a deep breath, drinking his complex truth to the last bittersweet drop. Pleasure, not love. But a rare pleasure, one he valued.

"I'm glad," she said finally.

And that, too, was a complex, bittersweet truth.

Ten should have been relieved at Diana's acknowledgment that what they shared in bed wasn't love. But he wasn't relieved. She understood, she agreed—and somehow she had never been farther away from him, even the first day when she had turned and run from him.

Swearing beneath his breath, Ten stood with his fingers locked around Diana's wrist and wondered savagely how he and she could be so painfully honest with each other and yet somehow allow an important truth to slide through their fingers like rain through sand, sinking down and down and down, farther out of reach with every second.

"To hell with talking," he said savagely.

Ten bent his arm, bringing Diana hard against his body. His tongue searched the surprised softness of her mouth with urgent movements. The hunger that had been just beneath his surface blazed up, shortening his breath, making his blood run heavily, hardening his body in a rushing instant that he felt all the way to his heels; but Diana was stiff in his arms, vibrating with emotions that had little to do with desire.

"Don't fight me, baby," Ten said heavily against Diana's mouth, his voice as dark and hot as his kiss had been. "What we have is too rare and too good to waste on anger."

Ten probed the center of Diana's ear with the hot tip of his tongue, feeling her shiver helplessly in response. He probed again and was rewarded by another sensuous shiver. With a low sound of triumph, he caught the rim of her ear between his teeth and bit delicately, repeatedly, demanding and also pleading for her response.

The intensity and need within Ten reached past Diana's pain to the love beneath. She tried to speak, didn't trust her uncertain hold on her emotions and slid her arms around Ten's lean waist instead. His breath came out in a barely audible sigh of relief when he felt her soften against him.

"Diana," Ten whispered, hugging her in return, "baby, I don't want to hurt you. When you gave yourself to me that first time, looking right at me, knowing to the last quarter inch how much I wanted you..." Memory lanced through Ten, making him shudder. "Yet you held out your arms to me. No one has ever trusted me like that. I was so afraid of hurting you I almost didn't go through with it."

She looked at him with startled blue eyes.

"It's true," Ten said, easing his fingers into Diana's cool, soft hair. "I was arguing with myself all the way down into your arms. Then you took me so perfectly and I knew I wouldn't hurt you. Your body was made for mine. And somehow you knew it, too, didn't you? That's why you watched me with such curiosity and hunger, day after day, until I thought I would go crazy. Then you asked me to kiss you and I was sure I would go crazy. You fit my hands perfectly, my arms, my mouth, my body. I knew it was going to be so damned *good*. I was right. It was good then and it's even better now, each time better than the last."

The words caressed Diana even more than the heat of Ten's body or the pressure of his fingers rubbing slowly down her spine.

"Is it that way for you, too?" Ten asked. "Tell me it's that way for you, too."

He bent to kiss Diana's neck with barely restrained force, arching her against his body, letting her feel his strength and what she had done to him.

"Baby?"

"Yes," she said as she gave herself to his power. "You must know it is, Ten. Don't you know?"

"I do now," he whispered against her hair, and then he whispered it again.

Slowly Ten straightened. He held Diana gently against his chest, just held her, as though he were afraid to ask for any more than she had already given.

And he was.

"Go ahead and sketch while you still have light," Ten said finally, kissing Diana's eyelids, brushing his lips gently across her mouth, caresses without demand. "I'll open the new box of shards and see what the grads found over the weekend."

Shaking, feeling like crying in protest when Ten turned away, hungry for him in a way that eclipsed anything she had ever felt before, Diana looked blindly out over September Canyon. She couldn't force herself to walk away from the overhang and the man she loved more with every day.

And with every day she was closer to losing him.

The pleasure you feel when we have sex—that isn't love. It will wear off. It always does.

But it wouldn't for her. Diana knew that as surely as she had known she could trust Ten not to force anything more from her than she wanted to give. She had been right. He had taken nothing from her that she hadn't given willingly.

It wasn't Ten's fault that he didn't want everything she had to give to a man.

Though Diana knew sketching would be impossible, she took off her backpack, brought out her pad, opened it and sat down on the bedroll she would share that night with Ten. Adrift on the cool wind flowing down from the mesa top, she looked out over the canyon she loved. She saw neither trees nor cliffs nor even the wild beauty of the setting sun, only the image of the man she had come to love even more than the land.

In her mind she saw Ten's face with eerie precision, each line that sun and wind had etched around his eyes, eyes whose probing clarity had first unnerved, then fascinated her. The same was true of Ten's powerful, unmistakably male body; first it had frightened and then finally it had fascinated her.

Now, in the clear light of pain, Diana acknowledged what she had previously been too caught up within her own fears and needs to see—the shadows that lay beneath the clarity of Ten's eyes, the reserve that lay beneath his passion, the internal walls he had built as carefully as an Anasazi cliff fortress, walls keeping her out, his own words describing solitude.

He lived as a warrior too long. Like me. And like me, Nevada will heal. It just takes time.

But Ten hadn't healed. Not wholly.

She wanted to heal him. She needed to. But there were so few weeks left to remove scars that were years deep, a wounding so old, so accustomed a part of the man she loved, that Ten himself didn't even realize that he hadn't healed. He had scarred over, which wasn't the same thing at all.

"Such a pensive look," Ten said. Sitting down next to Diana, he glanced at the drawing in her lap. It was a close-up of September Canyon's ruins, detailing the precarious eyelash of a trail that led from the cliff dwellings up the face of the cliff to the mesa above. "Are you thinking about the Anasazi again, trapped within their own creation?"

"And time," Diana said, her voice husky, aching as she flipped slowly through the sketchbook. "Time is another kind of trap."

"Why? Are you getting behind in your sketching?"

"No. I'll be finished well within the deadline."

"Deadline?"

"The middle of August. That's when my contract with the Rocking M ends."

Ten looked deeply into Diana's eyes, wanting to protest what lay beneath her quiet words: when the contract ended, she would leave the Rocking M and Tennessee Blackthorn.

Diana looked only at the sketch in her lap, praying that Ten would reach past the wall he had built and ask her to stay without the pretense of archaeological work between them.

Ask me to stay, Ten. Ask me as a man asks a woman he wants and needs and might someday love. Please, love, ask me.

Silently, Ten's fingertips traced the line of Diana's chin, tilting her face up to his lips. He kissed her slowly, seducing her mouth for long moments before accepting the invitation of her parted lips and warm tongue. With controlled urgency he began undressing her, only to discover that he was being undressed, as well. Relief coursed through him almost as violently as desire. He kissed her again, drinking deeply, urgently, from the woman who haunted his sleep even when she was lying by his side.

By the time the kiss ended, their breathing was ragged and their clothes were scattered randomly around the bedroll. Ten's hand slid from Diana's ankle to the apex of her thighs. The deep, sultry welcome of her body made blood hammer in his veins until he could hardly breathe.

"It's a little soon to be mentally packing your gear, isn't it?" Ten asked in a low, rough voice as he caressed Diana, calling forth a husky moan and a tiny, searing melting. "A lot could happen in the next few weeks."

"Could it?" Diana asked, hope leaping even more hotly than desire within her body.

"Sure. The Rocking M is going to need some expert advice on excavating the kiva you discovered. Who better than you to give it?"

Before Diana could speak, Ten took her mouth. The slowly building pressure of his kiss arched her across his hard forearm. She gave herself to the kiss and to the man, feeling desire and regret, caring and hunger, passion and restraint in Ten's embrace, every emotion except the love that filled her until she ached.

When the long kiss ended, Ten lifted his mouth with tangible reluctance.

"There's no reason not to extend your contract."

"Luke might see it differently."

"September Canyon is my land. The dig is being underwritten by my money. If I want it to go beyond the middle of August, it will."

Diana shuddered from desire and grief mixed together, feeling as though she had been turned inside out until everything she was and could be lay exposed to the cool sunset light. Bittersweet understanding of the difference between her own needs and Ten's knifed through her, and in its wake an anguished acceptance.

She wanted his laughter, his grief, his victories, his defeats, his silence, his conversations. She wanted his body, his mind, his children and a lifetime of tomorrows. He wanted the passion that ran like invisible lightning between them, and he wanted every bit of it for as long as it lasted.

She loved him. He did not love her. But she could take from him one of the things she wanted and give him the only thing he wanted in return.

Diana rolled onto her side and began running her hands down Ten's muscular torso, caressing and inciting him with the same motions.

"No, there's no reason at all not to extend the contract," Diana said, finding and teasing a flat male nipple with her teeth, "except common sense."

"What does that mean?"

"Simple. As simple as this."

Her hands closed around the thick evidence of Ten's desire and he groaned with leaping need. She continued talking as she caressed the length of his body, scattering his thoughts, taking away everything but the heat of her mouth.

"The Rocking M—" Diana's tongue probed Ten's navel "—can't afford to pay me." She closed her teeth on the tightly flexed muscles that joined neck and shoulder. A shudder moved the length of his body. "Not as much as I earn being an assistant professor at the university."

"We could—work something out. Weekends. Vacations." Ten's breath came in with a hissing sound as Diana nuzzled his ear, teasing, biting. "Part-time work. Something."

Diana's eyes closed against a wave of pain, but her mouth and hands remained gentle, loving Ten, sharing with and returning to him the gift of passion he had given so generously to her. After a few moments she could trust herself to speak again.

"You don't have to pay me to come to the Rocking M." She bit the hard muscle of Ten's biceps in a sensual punishment that was just short of pain. "All you have to do is ask. Or you can come to Boulder when you feel like it.''

"Diana…"

She waited, hope penned within her acceptance like a wild animal.

Ten made a half-angry, half-helpless sound.

She let out her breath in a long, soundless sigh, knowing acceptance had been right and hope had been wrong.

"I agree," Diana said softly. "It's better to keep it just a summer affair."

"That's not what I said."

"No. It's what you meant."

"Dammit," Ten said roughly, "I learned long ago that I'm piss-poor husband material."

"Did you?" Diana asked, lifting her head, looking into Ten's narrowed eyes. "Or did you just decide sex isn't worth all the inconvenience of marriage?"

Bleak gray eyes searched Diana's face.

Smiling sadly, she turned away and let her mouth slide down the warm, muscular tension of his abdomen. "It's all right, Tennessee. I learned something long ago, too. Then you came along and taught me that I hadn't learned everything."

Diana's cheek rested for a moment on a dense cushion of black, curly hair. Her lips brushed flesh that was hot, smooth, hard, pulsing with the swift beat of Ten's life. When she moved her head to test the resilience of his thigh with her teeth, Ten made a deep sound. When her head turned again and the tip of her tongue touched him curiously, his breath came out in a low groan that was also her name.

"If I made you a promise," Diana said, biting Ten lightly once more, stroking the thick muscles of his thighs, skimming over without ever really touching the hard, violently sensitive flesh that she had aroused, "would you trust me to keep it? Would you trust me not to ask you for anything more, ever?"

Blindly Ten reached for his jeans, his fingers seeking the familiar packet, finding it.

"Tennessee," Diana whispered, brushing her lips over the musky cushion of hair, touching his hot flesh with the tip of her tongue. "Do you trust my promise?"

He groaned as a fine sheen of passion broke over his skin. His right hand clenched, crumpling the packet. "Baby, it's damned hard to think when you're doing that."

"Then don't think. Just answer from the instinctive part of you. Do you trust me to keep my promise about never asking for one more thing from you?"

"Yes," Ten said hoarsely, knowing as he spoke that it was true. He could trust Diana's word. "What do you—want?"

"This."

The sound Ten made was a combination of surprise and searing pleasure as Diana's mouth tasted him with lingering sensual curiosity.

"When I first asked you to kiss me," she whispered against his hot skin, "it was because I wanted to be able to lead a normal life, and that meant responding to men the way other women did. And it worked, up to a point. But then I began trying to imagine other men touching me the way you had, and I knew I wouldn't be able to go through with it."

"Fear?" Ten asked, the only word he could force past the passionate constriction in his throat.

Diana shook her head. Tendrils of silky hair brushed over Ten's skin in the instant before her mouth circled him in a caress that took what little breath he had remaining, tasting him, loving him as she never had before. When the caress deepened, Ten's whole body flushed with wild heat. She held him for long moments, savoring him, loving the wildness coursing through him at her caress. Slowly, reluctantly, she released him from tender captivity.

She lifted her head and met the smoldering brilliance of Ten's eyes. The look in them made her body melt. He felt it, knew that she wanted him as wildly as he wanted her, and had to close his eyes against the force of the need twisting through his body.

"It's not fear that will keep me away from other men," Diana said finally, biting Ten with great gentleness, feeling the wave of desire that swept through him almost as clearly as he did. "It's the fact that I don't want them. Other men wouldn't have rain-colored eyes that blaze with desire. Other men wouldn't have a scar below their jawline or one on their shoulder, their hip, the inside of their left thigh. Other men wouldn't be able to handle a brute and a kitten with the same ease. Other men wouldn't look like you, feel like you...taste like you.''

Ten made a hoarse sound of intense pleasure as the moist heat of Diana's mouth caressed him again. He called her name roughly, feeling the world being stripped away with each silky movement of her tongue.

''Make love without barriers for the weeks I have left on the Rocking M,'' she said. ''Be completely naked inside me. No matter what happens afterward, there won't be any demands, any regrets.'' Slowly Diana slid up Ten's body until the thick length of his arousal skimmed her softness, making her breath break. ''Ten?''

His own breath came in with a harsh, ripping sound as she melted over him. ''I'm not sure I can hold back with you, baby,'' he said roughly. ''You could get pregnant. Have you thought of that?''

''Yes,'' Diana said, shivering, melting, searing him with her need. ''Many times.''

Ten's right hand opened with a savage movement, sending the small packet tumbling onto the ground. He lay still but for the elemental tremors of desire coursing through his hard body.

''Last chance,'' he said thickly.

Her hips moved. Sultry fire licked over Ten. Shaking with a hunger he had never felt before, Ten knew he was going to take what he must have, what she was asking him for, what they both wanted until it was agony not to have it; but he had never taken a woman like this before, no barriers, nothing except violently sensitive skin and a need so great it kept him on the breaking edge of self-control.

When Ten's aroused flesh found the incredible softness and heat waiting for him, the sensation was so intense he couldn't breathe. He felt each separate pulse of Diana's response as he parted the soft flesh, sheathing himself within her slowly, deliberately, deeply, sharing her body and his own in an exquisite intimacy that was just short of anguish.

"I've never—been like this—before," Ten said thickly, his breath breaking. "Naked. Nothing held back. It's—I can't—"

He went utterly still, fighting desperately not to lose control.

"Tennessee," Diana whispered, looking into the silver blaze of his eyes, feeling the first waves of pleasure ravish her. "Give me your baby, Tennessee."

A sound of hunger and ecstasy was torn from Ten's throat, and then ecstasy alone, Diana's name repeated in shattered syllables as he gave himself again and again to the sweet violence of a union unlike any he had ever known.

16

Thunder cracked with a noise like rock shearing away from tall cliff faces, a naked violence of sound that made September Canyon tremble in the night.

Ten eased out of the blankets he shared with Diana and went to stand at the edge of the overhang. The chilly air took the heat from his body, but he barely noticed the temperature. The smell, taste and sound of the wind told him all that he needed to know. He and Diana would have to pack up and cross Picture Wash before dawn.

And Ten had counted on spending the hour before dawn quite differently.

"Damn."

"What's wrong?" Diana asked sleepily.

"Storm coming on. A big one."

By memory alone Ten went to the camp table, struck a match and lit the Coleman stove. The golden glow of naked flame danced in graceful reflections over the pale sandstone. He made coffee with the swift, economical motions of a man very familiar with the task. Then he walked to the warm blankets where Diana lay, grabbed his clothes and began dressing.

"Ten...?"

It was only a single word, but he understood all that she wasn't saying. Reluctantly he shook his head.

"Sorry, honey," Ten said, his voice gritty with hunger and regret. "We've got a lot of packing to do and not much time to do it."

Diana bit back her protest even as it formed. The storm didn't care if it were cutting short her last hours with Ten in September Canyon.

Silently she kicked off the blankets and began pulling on clothes, shivering as the cold wind washed over her body. Working by the light of a gas lantern, she packed quickly, forcing herself not to think how this day was different from any day that had come before or would come after.

As soon as Diana's personal gear was packed, she began working on the artifacts that were to be taken back to the ranch. She packed slowly, carefully, saying goodbye with her fingertips to the ancient pots and stone axes, fiber sandals and bone implements that she had come to know as well as she knew the less textured camping equipment of her own time and culture.

When each box was ready, she set it aside for Ten to carry to the truck. Periodic lightning shattered the black sky. Thunder rang repeatedly, a barrage that deafened. She ignored it, working steadily, thinking only of the task at hand. As she reached for another empty box, she found Ten's hand instead. Startled, she looked up.

"Leave it for the grads," he said in a clipped voice. "We have to cross while we can. It's raining like hell up on September Mesa."

She looked out into the encompassing blackness and saw nothing at all. "How can you tell?"

"Listen."

At first Diana thought what she heard was the wind, a low, muttering kind of sound. Then she realized that she was hearing water. September Wash was filling.

"Is it still safe to cross?" she asked, unable to suppress the hope in her voice. If the wash weren't safe, they would be forced to stay on this side until the water went down.

As though Diana had spoken her hope aloud, Ten shook his head. "This is a big storm. Carla will fret and then Luke will send men out in hell's own rain to look for us. I don't want anyone getting hurt looking for people who could have and should have gotten back."

The sky exploded into twisting, wildly writhing forks of lightning. Barely four seconds later, thunder hammered down.

"Time to go, honey."

Diana closed her eyes against the pain that was

lancing through her as surely as lightning lanced through the clouds.

Thunder filled September Canyon, followed by a gust of rain-scented wind that made piñons moan. No rain was falling, but there was no doubt that it would. Soon.

Ten opened the passenger door for Diana and helped her up into the cab. Her breast pressed against the lean male hand that was wrapped around her upper arm. Though the contact was accidental, it made every one of Diana's nerve endings shimmer. When she tried to fasten her seat belt, her hands were clumsy with the sudden rush of her blood.

Ten climbed in, saw Diana's difficulty and said, "Let me. That belt mechanism is getting kind of cranky. First you have to slack off and let it retract all the way. Like this."

He took the metal tongue from Diana's fingers, then followed the retreat of the harness across her lap. The sound of her indrawn breath was as much an inadvertent caress as his hand skimming across her body in the wake of the buckle's metal tongue. When he pulled the harness across her lap once more, his hand skimmed, hesitated for a breathless instant, then moved on. He inserted the metal tongue slowly into the locking mechanism. A subdued *click* broke the taut silence.

"See? Perfect fit." Ten's voice was low, gritty.

He touched Diana's mouth with his thumb and

swore softly, wanting her. And she wanted him. It was in her eyes, in the tightness of her body, in the huskiness of the few words she had spoken. He gave her a quick, hard kiss and forced himself to concentrate on other things.

Ten drove to the wash, studied the roiling water carefully and bit off a vicious curse. There was no doubt about it, no ignoring it. The wash was definitely still safe to cross.

He put the truck in gear and drove into the water. As soon as he reached the other side he spoke without looking at Diana.

"Hang on. I'm going to drive hard to get ahead of the storm."

The road was dry and familiar, its occasional vagaries and hazards well-known to Ten. He held the big truck to a punishing pace, boring through the predawn darkness, outrunning the storm outside the truck, ignoring the one within as long as he could.

Finally the truck climbed up for the long run across Wind Mesa. For a time the road snaked along the very edge of the highland, giving a breathtaking vista of predawn light locked in luminous embrace with a high, slowly seething lid of clouds. The tenuous light was eerie, astonishing, flawless, utterly without color.

Ten stopped the truck at a point where the road gave an uninterrupted view of the dark land below.

"We're at least an hour ahead of the rain," Ten said, releasing his seat belt. "Want some coffee?"

Diana made a murmurous sound of approval that could have meant the view, the idea of coffee or both.

By the dim illumination of the dashboard lights, Ten opened a thermos and poured coffee. A clean, rich fragrance filled the cab. He handed the half-full cup to Diana, who refused it with a shake of her head.

"You first," he insisted.

"Afraid of poison?" Diana asked huskily. She forced herself to smile, concealing the sadness that had grown greater with each mile flying beneath the truck's broad tires.

Ten's own smile flashed briefly. "No, but I've discovered that coffee tastes sweeter if you drink out of my cup before I do."

Diana said his name softly, then bent her head and sipped the hot liquid. Ten flicked off the lights, killed the engine and rolled down his window. Cool air breathed across the cab, air redolent of distance and unfettered land. In silence they passed the cup of coffee between them while spectral light slowly filled the space between clouds and earth, transforming everything, infusing the very air with radiance.

"Spirit light," Ten said finally.

Diana looked up at him questioningly.

"That's what Bends-Like-the-Willow, my grandmother, called it. The kind of light that enables you to see right through to the soul of everything."

"She was Indian?" Diana asked.

Ten's smile was a thin, hard slice of white in the

truck's interior twilight. "Honey, there aren't many families that were in America before the Civil War that don't have Indian blood in them. The first Blackthorns came over from Scotland more than two hundred years ago."

"Did they marry Indians?"

"Sometimes. Sometimes they just slept with them. Sometimes they fought with them. Sometimes Blackthorn women or children were taken in raids." Ten shrugged. "There has been a lot of mixing and matching of bloodlines, one way or another. If children were the result of a town marriage, they were raised white. If children were the result of no marriage, they were raised Indian."

Ten sipped coffee from the shared cup before he resumed talking about the past, because anything was better than talking about the unshed tears in Diana's eyes and the turmoil in his own mind.

"By now there's no way to tell who got which genes, native or white or everything in between. Nevada and I have black hair and a copper tone to our skin. Utah has skin like ours, but he has blond hair and black eyes." Ten shrugged. "In the end, it's the quality of the person that matters, not the rest. That's what Bends-Like-the-Willow had. Quality."

"Was it a 'town marriage'?"

He shook his head and smiled oddly. "The Blackthorns were warriors. They leaned toward informal marriages. Up until the last generation, we were raised mostly in Indian ways. Bends-Like-the-Willow was quite a woman. Her father was a MacKenzie.''

"As in the Rocking M MacKenzies?"

Thunder belled again, filling the canyon.

"Probably," Ten said. "Her mother was Ute. Her father was a wild young white who rode out one night and never came back. Luke has a few like that in his family tree. One of them disappeared at about the right time and place."

"Is that how you came to own part of the Rocking M?"

Smiling sardonically, Ten shook his head. "Honey, a hundred years back, nobody gave a damn about part-Indian kids born on the wrong side of the blanket. It's only in the last generation people have started to get all puffed up and sentimental over Indian ancestors whose skeletons have been rattling in white closets for a long, long time."

"Then how did you end up here?"

"When I got out of the warrior business, I was like Nevada. Hurting and not knowing what to do about it. Needing a home and not knowing how to get one. Luke's father was selling off chunks of the Rocking M to pay for his drinking. I bought in. The ranch has been my home ever since."

Diana waited, but Ten said no more. She followed his glance out the windshield. The land lay beneath the storm like a woman waiting for a lover. Though no rain had fallen, the storm had brought an eerie glow to the air, a timeless gloaming that made all distances equal. There were no shadows to define near and far, no sun's passage to mark hours across the sky, no waxing or waning moon to measure weeks, nothing but the eye and mind of man to draw distinctions.

"Spirit light," Ten said, his voice harsh. "When you see everything too damn clearly."

He looked at Diana and saw too much, his own hunger clawing at him, telling him that he would remember her too long, too well.

Diana looked away from the eerie clarity of the land and saw Ten watching her with silver eyes that burned.

"What are you thinking?" she asked before she could stop herself.

"I'm remembering."

"What?"

"How you look when your skin is flushed with heat and you're as hungry for me as I am for you."

Knowing he shouldn't, unable to stop himself, Ten slid partway across the big seat, took the coffee cup from Diana and set it on the dashboard. Her dark blue glance went from his eyes to the clean, distinct line of his mouth. Even as she leaned toward him, he pulled her close, lifting her, turning her so that she was half-lying across his lap. His mouth came down over her parted lips, filling her with his taste and his hunger, wordlessly telling her about the need that would make the coming days restless and the nights endless.

Diana gave back the kiss without restraint, loving the taste of Ten, coffee and man and passion. The kiss deepened even more, becoming an urgent mating of mouths. When she felt the hard warmth of his palms sliding beneath her sweater, she twisted sinuously, bringing her breasts into his hands. His fingers stroked, caressed, teased until exquisite sensations radiated from her breasts to the secret core of her, melting her in a few shuddering moments.

With a soft whimper Diana began to move against Ten's body. She felt rather than heard the rasping groan he gave when his hands released the catch on her bra, allowing him the freedom of her breasts. He pushed up her loose sweater and bra and looked at her. Flushed by passion, soft, creamy, resilient, tipped with tight pink buds of desire, her breasts begged for his mouth.

"Baby?"

"Yes," Diana whispered huskily, raising her arms and arching her back as she reached to remove her sweater.

Ten didn't wait for her to finish. He kissed one peak, licked it with catlike delicacy, then gave in to the need driving him. His mouth opened over her in a caress that sent sensual lightning glittering through her. With a ragged cry she threw off the sweater and held his head against her breast, asking for and receiving a different, harder caress.

Even as Ten's mouth sent forerunners of ecstasy shimmering through Diana, his hands closed on her hips, shifting her until she was sitting astride his lap. One hard palm slid between her legs, cupping her, stroking her, making her burn. Sweet cries rippled from her, cries like fire consuming Ten, cries that made him wild with need. He unfastened the front of Diana's jeans and pushed his hand into the scant space between denim and her body. Hungrily he forced aside cloth until he could search through the warm nest to find the sultry woman-heat he needed to touch more than he needed air to breathe.

And then Ten found what he sought. He took as much as he could of Diana's softness and wanted more, much more, his body straining and his breath a groan.

The hoarse sound Diana made and the feel of her struggling against his hand brought Ten to his senses. He closed his eyes and took a tearing breath, afraid to look at her, afraid to see the fear and horror in her eyes as she remembered another out-of-control man, the front seat of another vehicle.

"God, baby, I'm sorry," Ten said hoarsely. "I've never lost control like that."

He heard Diana take a broken breath, then another, and felt her incredible softness pressing intimately against the hand that was still tangled in her jeans.

Very carefully he dragged his hand free. Another broken sound from her scored him.

"Baby, I'm sorry," Ten whispered, looking at Diana's wide eyes, wanting to cradle her and yet afraid to touch her. "I didn't mean to frighten you."

"You—didn't."

The words were like Diana's breathing—ragged. Ten shook his head slowly, not believing her.

"I heard you," he said flatly.

"I wanted you—so much—it hurt. I didn't know—it could be like that."

The last word was spoken against Ten's lips just before he brought Diana's mouth over his own. The kiss was deep, searching, wild. She returned it with a hunger that made both of them shake.

"If you kiss me like that again," Ten said finally, breathing hard, "I'm going to start taking off those boots you're wearing."

"My boots?"

"And then your jeans," Ten said, sliding his hand inside denim once more, searching for Diana's softness, finding it, drawing liquid fire and a ripping sound of pleasure from her. "I want you. Right here. Right now. Do you want me like that?"

With fingers that trembled, Diana reached blindly for her bootlaces. Ten made a low sound as his hand slid more deeply into her jeans. He smiled almost savagely, savoring her heat and the ragged breaking of her breath. Each movement she made as she worked over her laces increased the effect of his hidden caress. Ten made no move to help with the boots, for his other hand was too busy stroking the firm curves of her breasts to be bothered with such unrewarding objects as boots and socks.

One boot, then the other, fell to the floor of the truck, followed by the rustling whisper of socks. Slowly Diana shifted her body to the side, not wanting to end the wild, secret seduction of Ten's hand, but at the same time wanting to be free of the confinement of her jeans.

This time Ten helped, lifting Diana and peeling the rest of her clothes away, letting them fall to the floor. She shivered with heat rather than cold as she sat astride Ten once more. He looked down at his lap and the woman whose body was flushed with the passion he had aroused.

Slender hands reached for Ten's belt buckle.

"Baby, if you start there, that's where you'll finish. I want you like hell burning."

Diana looked into the hot silver of Ten's eyes and knew if she didn't take his boots off first, they wouldn't get taken off at all. His hand slid up her thigh, touched, tested deeply, knew the scalding need of her body.

"Yes," she whispered. "Like hell burning."

Watching Ten's face, Diana opened the buckle. Leather pulled free of the loops with a sliding, whispering noise. Metal buttons gave way in a muted rush of sound. She reached down only to find that he was there before her, his hard flesh parting her as he watched her take him, and he was filling her even as she watched. Her breath unraveled into a low moan as she was hurled into ecstasy. He drove into her again, burying himself in the clinging, generous heat that had haunted his dreams, and then ecstasy convulsed him and he held her hard, deep inside her, his mouth against her hot skin and her cries washing over him, echoing the sweet lightning of his own release.

Locked within ecstasy, surrounded by the cruel clarity of spirit light, Ten knew this was the way he would always remember Diana, and the realization was a knife turning, teaching him more about pain than he wanted to know.

17

The knock on the door was both unexpected and the answer to Diana's secret hopes. Even as her heartbeat doubled, she told herself that she was being foolish.

It isn't Ten. He hasn't so much as telephoned in the weeks since I left the Rocking M, so what makes me think that he would waste a Friday driving all the way to Boulder to see me?

The cold, rational thoughts didn't diminish the fierce, hopeful beat of Diana's heart. She pushed away from her drawing table, took a deep, steadying breath and walked the few steps to her studio apartment's front door.

"Who is it?" she asked.

"Cash McQueen. Carla MacKenzie's brother."

With hands that weren't quite steady, Diana unlocked the door and opened it. Once she would have been unnerved at the sight of the big man who almost filled her doorway. Now the only emotion she felt was a disappointment so numbing that it was all she could do to speak. She forced her lips into the semblance of a smile.

"Hi. I thought you were in...South America, wasn't that it?"

"It was. I got back last week."

"Oh. Did you find what you were looking for?"

Cash smiled slowly, transforming his face from austere to handsome. His eyes lit with a rueful inner laughter. "No, but not many of us do."

Diana felt a flash of kinship with the big man. "No, not many of us do."

"May I come in?"

"Of course," she said, automatically backing away from the door, allowing Cash to enter. "Would you like some coffee? Or perhaps a beer? I think one of the grads left some here last night."

"Thanks, but I'll have coffee. Party last night?" he asked, looking around with veiled curiosity.

Diana's mouth curved in something less than a smile. "Depends on your definition of party. If it includes chasing elusive potshards through mismarked cartons, we had one hell of a party here last night."

"I thought all the September Canyon stuff was staying at the Rocking M."

"It is. This is from a different site. Still Anasazi, though, as you can see. They're my first love."

While Diana disappeared into the kitchen, Cash walked carefully around the apartment. It was in a state of casual disarray that resembled an academic office more than living quarters. Scholarly periodicals, books and photos covered most flat surfaces, except for a worktable. There, potshards and partially reconstructed pots reigned supreme. Photos and sketches were tacked to the walls. A bin full of sketches stored in protective transparent sleeves stood in a corner.

"Cream or sugar?" Diana called from the kitchen alcove.

"Black."

Cash walked over to the bin and began flipping slowly through the contents, studying various drawings. When Diana returned, he looked up.

"These are very good."

"Thank you." Diana set a mug of coffee on a table near Cash and cleared periodicals from a chair. "But photos are preferred by most scholars, unless they're trying to illustrate a point from their pet theory. Then they're delighted to have me draw what no one has yet had the good sense to discover in situ."

Male laughter filled the small room. Diana looked startled, then smiled self-consciously.

"I didn't mean that quite as peevishly as it came out," she said, clearing away a second stack of periodicals and sitting down. With a casualness that cost a great deal, she asked, "How's everything on the Rocking M?"

"That's why I'm here."

Diana's head turned quickly toward Cash. "Is something wrong?"

"You took the words right out of my mouth."

"I don't understand."

"Neither does Carla."

"Mr. McQueen," began Diana.

"Cash."

"Cash," she said distractedly. "You came here for a reason. What is it?"

With a characteristic gesture of unease, Cash jammed his hands in the back pockets of his jeans, palms out. He looked at the small woman with the haunted indigo eyes and lines of strain around her full mouth. Cash didn't know what was wrong, but he was certain that something was.

Carla, what the hell have you gotten me into this time? You know better than to try and set me up with another female in a jam.

Cash looked closely at Diana. Despite her abundant femininity, she wasn't sending out the signals that an available woman did. She had smiled at the sound of his laughter, but then, a lot of people did. They hadn't learned that laughter was a perfect camouflage for his view of people in general and women in particular. One woman, however, was exempt from Cash's distrust—Carla.

"My sister would like to see you again," Cash said, "but apparently you're angry with her."

Diana started to speak. No words came out. All she could do was shake her head.

"Does that mean Carla has it all wrong and you'd be glad to come out to the Rocking M next weekend?" Cash asked smoothly.

"No." The stark refusal was out before Diana could prevent it.

Not that it mattered. She wasn't going back to the Rocking M. Not this weekend. Not the weekend after. Not ever. She couldn't bear seeing Ten again and pretending that nothing had ever happened between them in September Canyon. Nor could she pretend that his baby wasn't growing day by day within the loving warmth of her womb.

"Carla's right," Cash said. "You're angry with her."

"No."

"With Luke?"

"No," Diana said quickly. "It's nothing personal." She licked her lips with a tongue that was dry. "I'm—I'm very busy. The school year is just getting rolling. There are a lot of things I have to do."

Cash's eyes narrowed to brilliant blue slits. "I see." And he did. He saw that Diana lied very badly. "Surely you'll have everything under control by, say, November?"

"I don't know."

"Probably?"

She gave him a dark look. "I don't know!"

"Well, I know that Carla will have a strip off my hide if you don't turn up for Thanksgiving. Now I can probably finesse my little sister, but I'd hate like hell to try finessing the Rocking M's ramrod with anything less than a bulldozer."

Color drained from Diana's face, silently telling Cash that Carla's guess had been correct: it was Tennessee Blackthorn who was keeping Diana away from the ranch.

"I can't see that the..." Diana's voice dried up. She swallowed painfully and continued. "What does Ten have to do with this?"

"You tell me."

"Nothing."

"Whatever you say," Cash muttered, not believing Diana and not bothering to disguise it. "Ten has developed a passion for all things Anasazi. If the recent past is any example, he's going to be a miserable son to live with until that kiva gets excavated."

Diana's eyelids flinched, but her voice was under control when she spoke. "Then by all means he should have the kiva excavated as soon as possible."

"Amen. How long will it take you to pack?"

"I'm not going anywhere."

"You're not making any sense, either."

"Mr. McQueen—"

"Cash."

"—the kiva can be excavated by any number of

qualified archaeologists. I'm sure Ten knows it. If not, he'll know it as soon as you go back and tell him."

"I already have. He almost tore off my head. Either you excavate that kiva or it doesn't get done."

"Then it doesn't get done."

"Why?"

"Would you like more coffee before you leave?"

"None of my business, is that it?"

"That's it."

"Would it make any difference if Carla dragged the baby all the way out here to talk to you?"

"I'd love to see Carla and Logan, but they would be going home alone."

"What if Ten asked you to excavate his damned kiva?"

Diana's eyes darkened and her tone became as bittersweet as the line of her mouth. "He already did."

For the first time Cash showed surprise. "You refused?"

"Yes."

"Why?"

"Ask Ten."

"No thanks. I like my head just where it is. Lately that boy has a fuse that's permanently lit. The only one willing to take him on is Nevada. They had hell's own brawl a week ago. Never seen anything quite like it. A miracle no one was killed."

Diana remembered Nevada's dark, cold power. She closed her eyes and fought against showing her fear and love and despair. It was useless. When she opened her eyes she saw that Cash knew exactly how she felt.

"Is he all right?" Diana asked tightly.

"Nevada's a little chewed up, but otherwise fine."

"Ten," she said urgently. "Is Ten all right?"

Cash shrugged. "Same as Nevada."

Diana hesitated for a moment, then went to the bin and withdrew a two-by-three-foot folder. She opened it and silently looked at the drawing. Within the borders of the paper, September Canyon lived as it had once in the past, stone walls intact, houses and kivas filling the alcove. But the people were no longer walled off within their beautifully wrought prisons. They were responding to the call of an outlaw shaman who had seen a vision filled with light.

Women, children, warriors, every Anasazi was pouring out of the cliff dwelling, walking out of the alcove's eternal twilight and into a dawn that blazed with promise. Their path took them past the shaman, who stood in the foreground within the shadow of the cliff, watching with haunted eyes, his outstretched arm pointing the way for the stragglers as they filed past below. Something in the shaman's position, his eyes holding both light and darkness, his body removed from the other Anasazi, stated that he was not walking out of darkness with his people.

The face, the lithe and muscular body, the stance,

the haunted crystalline eyes were those of Tennessee Blackthorn.

"I sketched this for the owner of September Canyon," Diana said, closing the folder and holding it out to Cash. "It's a bit awkward to mail. Would you take it to the Rocking M for me?"

"Sure." Cash looked at the folder and then at Diana. "You do know that Ten owns September Canyon, don't you?"

"Thank you for taking the sketch." Diana went to the front door and opened it. "Say hello to Carla and Luke for me."

"Should I say hello to Ten, too?" asked Cash on his way out.

Diana's only answer was silence followed by the door shutting firmly behind Cash. He raised his fist to knock on the door again but thought better of it when he heard the broken, unmistakable sounds of someone who was trying not to cry. Swearing silently about the futility of trying to talk rationally to a woman, he turned away and went toward his beat-up Jeep with long, loping strides. If he hurried, he would be at the ranch house before the afternoon thunderstorms turned the road to gumbo.

The next night, barely fifteen minutes after the last grad student left, Diana spotted the scruffy knapsack slumped in a corner. Bill usually remembered halfway home, turned around and came back. It had become a ritual—the knock on the door, the knapsack extended through the half-open door and the embarrassed apologies. Tonight, however, she wondered whether the knapsack would be an overnight resident. Bill had left with Melanie, and the look in his eyes had nothing to do with unimportant details such as knapsacks.

Diana glanced at the clock. Midnight—if Bill were going to retrieve his property, he would be back soon. With a shrug, she sat down at the table full of shards and picked up two. The edges didn't match, but that didn't matter. Diana wasn't seeing them. She was seeing other shards, other shapes and a matching that had been superb.

At least for her.

I've got to stop thinking about it. I've got to stop asking where I went wrong and why I wasn't the woman for Ten when he was the man for me. I've got to stop thinking about the past and start planning for the future. He trusted me enough to give me his baby. That has to be enough.

The sound of knuckles meeting the apartment door was a welcome break from Diana's bleak thoughts.

"Hang on. I'm coming," Diana called out.

She snagged the knapsack by its strap, opened the front door without looking, held out the knapsack at arm's length and waited for Bill to take it.

The door opened fully, pushing Diana back into the living room. The knapsack hit the floor with a soft thump, falling from her nerveless fingers.

Ten walked into the room and shut the door behind himself, watching Diana with hooded eyes that missed none of the subtle signs of stress—the brackets at the side of her mouth, the circles beneath her eyes, the body that was too thin. And most of all the eyes, too bleak, too dark.

Ten didn't know what he had expected Diana to do when he walked back into her life, but shutting down like a flower at sunset wasn't one of the things he had imagined. He kept remembering the moment when she had looked at him with eyes still dazed by pleasure and whispered that she loved him. She must have accepted his explanation that what she felt was temporary rather than lasting, for she had never mentioned love again. Yet the moment and the words had haunted him at odd moments ever since, tearing at his emotions without warning, making it painful to breathe.

But nothing had prepared him for the cruel talons sinking into him when he had opened the folder and seen himself standing alone, watching life pass by in a shimmering parade while he stood lost in shadow.

"You look tired," Diana said tonelessly. "Is the ranch still shorthanded?"

Ten made a dismissing motion. "I didn't come here to talk about the Rocking M's personnel problems."

Diana waited, asking in silence what she didn't trust herself to put into words. *Why are you here?*

"I came here to find out why you won't come back and excavate the kiva," Ten said bluntly.

"I have enough work to do in Boulder," she said, lacing her fingers together, trying to conceal their fine tremors.

"Bull."

Her hands clenched. "Why do you want me to excavate the kiva? Why not some other archaeologist?"

"You know why."

"Yes." Her lips curved down. "Sex."

Ten flinched but said nothing.

Diana turned away, knowing that she couldn't conceal her feelings any longer if she kept looking at him. When she spoke, her voice was desperately reasonable. "Don't you think that's rather a long drive just to get laid?"

Ten hissed a vicious word. "That's not what I meant and you know it!"

"Then what did you mean?"

"Are you pregnant?"

The bald question seemed to hang in the stillness like a wire being pulled tighter and tighter until it hummed just above the threshold of hearing.

"Don't worry, Tennessee," Diana said. "I keep my promises and I know you made none. Whether or not I'm pregnant, you're free."

"Dammit, Diana, *are you pregnant?*"

She let out a long, soundless breath. "You aren't listening. If I'm pregnant, I continue teaching. If I'm not pregnant, I continue teaching. Either way, I'm not going to excavate that kiva, so it makes no difference to you."

"No difference? What do you take me for!"

"A man who prefers living alone."

In the silence, the sound of Ten's sudden intake of breath was appallingly clear. Anger and the cold fear that had driven Ten since he had looked at the sketch exploded soundlessly inside him.

"You said you loved me."

More accusation than anything else, the words scored Diana. "And you told me I didn't know what love was. You told me what we had was sex. Sex doesn't last."

The bleakness of his own words coming back to him cut into Ten more deeply than any intentional insult could have. Like the sketch, the words were a wounding that sliced through old scars to the living flesh beneath.

"My God, how you must hate me," he whispered. "That's why you sketched me as an outlaw too cruel to be part of his people's freedom."

The pain beneath Ten's words shattered the last of Diana's control. She spun around, her face white. "That's not what I sketched!"

Ten's breath came in hard when he saw the tears glittering on Diana's pale cheeks. He started to speak but she was already talking, words tumbling out, her voice shaking with her need to make him understand.

"I saw a man who turned away from the possibility of love even as he freed me to love for the first time in my life, a love that you didn't believe in. But that's not the point. The point is that you gave me a great deal that is of lasting value and took as much as you wanted from me in return, and what you wanted wasn't lasting. It was a very beautiful, very passionate, very brief affair. I don't hate you. End of story."

Long, lean hands framed Diana's face. Ten bent and kissed away her tears as delicately, as thoroughly, as he had once kissed away her fear of him.

"Ten," she whispered, "don't. Please don't."

"Why? If our affair was that good," he asked in a dark velvet voice, "why can't it go on?"

"What if I—" Diana's voice broke. "Oh, Ten, don't you see? What would happen if there were a child?"

Ten bent again, taking her mouth, making it impossible for her to do anything but kiss him in return. Diana made an odd, broken sound and held on to him, taking and giving and trembling. By the time the kiss ended, she was crying wildly.

"Shh, don't cry," he said repeatedly, trying to kiss away the tears again, but there were too many this time. "Don't cry, baby. It tears me apart. I never wanted to hurt you like this. Everything is all right, baby. Don't cry."

Diana thought of the child growing inside her and felt a dizzying combination of love and despair. Ten was back, but only for a night or two. A week. Maybe even a few months.

And then he would leave again. *What we have isn't love. It passes.*

"I'm sorry—I can't stop crying and I—I can't—I can't continue our affair."

Ten made a hoarse sound that could have been Diana's name and tried without success to stem the hot silver flood with his thumbs. He kissed her gently, then kissed her again and again, breathing his words over her lips as though wanting to be certain that she absorbed his words physically as well as mentally, that she believed him all the way to her soul.

"Listen to me, Diana. You're the only woman I've ever been completely naked with." His lips brushed hers slowly. "You're the only woman I've ever trusted enough to have my child." His tongue traced her lips. "You're the only woman I've ever wanted so much it haunted me to the point that I couldn't sleep. Not just your beautiful body, but your quicksilver mind and your laughter and your quiet times and even the anger that makes your eyes almost black. I want all of you. Don't turn away from me. Please. I can't bear losing you. Tell me I haven't lost you. Tell me that you still love me."

The dark, ragged velvet of Ten's voice wrapped around Diana, stripping away her defenses, leaving only the truth of her love.

"I'll always love you," Diana said, her voice

breaking. "That won't change. But other—other things will. You—I—"

Ten's mouth closed over hers in a kiss that was a promise as well as a caress, a yearning hope as well as a burning hunger, a need and a sharing as complex as love itself. When he finally lifted his mouth he was trembling with more than desire.

"I love you, Diana. It's the last damn thing in the world I expected to happen. But it did and I'm not going to fight it any longer. Don't cry, love," Ten whispered, rocking Diana against his chest. "Don't cry. Just hold on to me and let me hold on to you. I've never been in love before. I've never wanted to live with a woman, to have children with her, to build a life around something other than silence." He looked down at Diana with hungry silver eyes. "Will you marry me? Will you have my children?"

Diana tried to speak but couldn't. She took Ten's hand in hers, kissed his hard palm and silently put it over the soft curve of her body where his baby was growing. She watched his eyes widen, felt his hand probe gently, heard the sudden raggedness of his breathing.

"Diana?"

"Yes," she said, laughing and crying at once. "Oh, yes!"

Ten's arms closed around the woman he loved and he lifted her off the floor in a huge hug, laughing with a joy he had never thought to feel—an outlaw walking out of the shadowed past into a future filled with light.

**A beautiful thief… A lost legacy…
A reckless passion**

CANDACE CAMP

PROMISE ME TOMORROW

Marianne Cotterwood can't remember her life before
ending up in an orphanage and then being taken in by a
warmly eccentric family of pickpockets and thieves. But she
is a natural thief—and very successful. Until Lord Lambeth
catches her in the act.

The desire Lord Lambeth feels for Marianne is as powerful
as his need to unravel her mystery. And now that a
dangerous shadow from her past is closing in, Marianne
finds she has no choice but to place her trust in the one man
she fears may be as reckless as she....

"A smart, fun-filled romp."

—Publishers Weekly on *Impetuous*

On sale mid August 2000 wherever paperbacks are sold!

MIRA®

Through the darkness,
love illuminates the way home....

GINNA GRAY

THE
PRODIGAL
Daughter

Seven years ago
Maggie Malone lost
everything one hellish night
and left Ruby Falls, Texas, in
disgrace. Now Maggie has
come home.

Her father is dying
and so is their proud
family business. Maggie had once dreamed of
running the empire—and old dreams die hard. But
to claim them, she'll have to confront the father
who denies her, the family who resents her, the
secrets that surround her, the man who wants
her...and the treachery closing in on them all.

Ginna Gray "is one of the most consistently
excellent writers in the genre today."
—*Romantic Times*

*On sale September 2000
wherever paperbacks are sold!*

MIRA®

Visit us at www.mirabooks.com

MGG603